With more than 75 maps and 200 photographs
Timelines, glossary and bibliography

THE START OF A NEW MILLENNIUM is an opportune vantage point from which to survey the history of humankind. This atlas, with its superbly detailed and meticulously researched maps, graphically presents the story of human evolution and the development of societies and civilizations in all parts of the globe as revealed by archaeology.

The atlas is in three parts. The first starts with the emergence of the earliest hominids in Africa four million years ago and traces the evolution and spread of modern humans into almost every part of the world before the end of the last Ice Age. The second presents global coverage of the major advances achieved by humankind in the succeeding ten thousand years. The third divides the world into five broad geographical regions to take a closer look at these advances and to examine significant changes in the story of human development in each, from hunter–gatherers and early farmers to the rise of organized states and empires.

As Paul Bahn comments in his introduction, archaeologists in the field have two principal means of obtaining information about a site: survey and excavation. The first involves looking at and recording the vestiges of the past that are visible on the surface. The second goes beneath the soil: vertically, to expose the sequence of layers built up over time, and horizontally, to explore a particular level over a wider area to see what was happening in a specific period. The atlas epitomizes both these approaches by telling the human story at global and regional levels, explaining what occurred over time, and also by taking a close look at certain places at certain times to give some idea of how things changed. The maps bring together a wide range of information that is not normally presented in this form.

Lavishly illustrated, stunningly presented and accessibly written by an international team of archaeologists, the book is a lively and informative summary of current archaeological knowledge that will enhance the pleasure of finding out about the human past.

THE ATLAS OF

World
Archaeology

THE ATLAS OF
World
Archaeology

EDITED BY PAUL G. BAHN

Checkmark Books™
An imprint of Facts On File, Inc.

Project Director Susan Kennedy
Cartographic Director Richard Watts
Art Editor & Designer Frankie Wood

Editors Susan Kennedy, Peter Lewis
Cartographic Editor Tim Williams
Designer Martin Anderson
Design Concept Ayala Kingsley
Picture Researchers Deborah Pownall,
   David Pratt
Picture Manager Claire Turner
Index Ann Barrett

Planned and produced by ANDROMEDA OXFORD LIMITED
11–13 The Vineyard, Abingdon, Oxfordshire, OX14 3PX, UK
www.andromeda.co.uk

Checkmark Books, an imprint of Facts On File, Inc. 11 Penn Plaza, New York, NY 10001

Checkmark Books are available at special discounts when purchased in bulk quantities
for businesses, associations, institutions or sales promotions. Please call our Special
Sales Department in New York at (212) 967-8800 or (800) 322-8755

You can find Facts On File on the World Wide Web at http://www.factsonfile.com

Library of Congress Cataloging-in-Publication Data
The atlas of world archaeology / edited by Paul Bahn ; foreword by Barry Cunliffe.
   p. cm.
   Includes index.
   ISBN 0-8160-4051-6 (acid-free paper)
   1. Archaeology. 2. Civilization, Ancient. 3. Civilization, Ancient--Maps.
4. Excavations (Archaeology) 5. Antiquities. I. Bahn, Paul G.

CC165 .A85 2000
930.1'09--dc21   00-025225

Production Director for Andromeda: Clive Sparling
Originated and printed in Hong Kong

10 9 8 7 6 5 4 3 2 1

This book is printed on acid-free paper

CONTENTS

HALF TITLE Bronze ornament in the shape of a snake, Late Bronze Age, from Jutland, Denmark.

TITLE Terracotta camel head belonging to the Indus valley civilization.

CONTENTS Bangle from Nong Nor, Thailand, Bronze Age (top left); Marble figurine of the Cycladic culture, southern Aegean, c.2800 BCE (bottom right).

THIS PAGE Ivory plaque with figure and lotus flower; Phoenician work of the 8th century BCE, from the palace at Nimrud (right); Clay votive object in the shape of a chariot with swans, Bronze Age, from Serbia (bottom right).

PREFACE

BY BARRY CUNLIFFE   *Professor of European Archaeology, University of Oxford*

Over the last century our knowledge of the past has changed in a most spectacular way. Think back a hundred years to what we knew, or did not know, then. In Europe, the great palaces of Crete lay deep beneath the soil and the Minoan civilization had yet to be discovered. In Africa, the majestic ruins of Great Zimbabwe, though admired, were entirely misunderstood, depriving Sub-Saharan Africa of recognition of one of its most innovative indigenous developments. In spite of China's rich historical record, the complex roots of Chinese civilization were entirely undreamed of. True, a great deal was written of the Greeks and Romans, Aztecs and Incas were beginning to grip the imagination, and fascination for things Egyptian had become almost an obsession. Excavations in the valleys of the Tigris and Euphrates were beginning to supply the museums of western Europe with exotic artifacts from the cradle of world civilization. It was a heady time of excitement and surprise when at least a few of the peaks of the archaeological record were beginning to emerge above the clouds of obscurity.

But so much remained unknown. There was no real sense of the time depth of the human story. To suggest then that human evolution was well under way four million years ago would have been regarded as eccentric in the extreme. For most of the world, little could be glimpsed before the ethnographic present, which began at the time of the first European contact. The last hundred years of archaeological activity have changed all this. Hitherto blank areas of the world are now fast being peopled and previously unknown communities being given histories. It is now possible to see the world and its human saga as a whole and to put the better known pinnacles of achievement into their proper perspectives.

The most significant advance for world prehistory has been the development of scientific dating methods since the early 1950s. The impact of this, difficult for some to accept at first, has been colossal, making it possible for the first time to sort unrelated sites and sequences throughout the world into their relative time slots. The surprises are far from over. Unexpectedly early scientific dates for the first humans in South America and Australia are requiring much new rethinking and the possibility of still earlier discoveries is ever present: in this area the last word can by no means be written.

Our much improved chronological perspectives make it possible to explore more fully the intricate relationships between different peoples. As communities became sedentary and more complex in their social structures, so their elites demanded more luxury goods to demonstrate their status. Inevitably, "trade" routes developed along which rare commodities could be transported in cycles of exchange embedded in delicate systems of social interaction. In this way, communities spread over huge geographical areas would be brought into contact and through these networks ideas and knowledge would rapidly pass. One has only to look at maps like that representing the 3rd and 2nd millennia BCE in western Asia on page 71 to appreciate something of the complexity of the links that bound the east Mediterranean to the Indus valley, or the map on page 75 to see how the communities of Europe, from the Black Sea to Ireland, were inextricably interlinked.

In complex systems like this some regions became intensively innovative. In the language of World Systems, they became the "cores" around which "peripheral" regions developed to help meet the demands of their fast-growing neighbor. Relationships of this kind were by no means one-way and frequently peripheral communities grew to become important centers of development in their own right. It is the richness of the archaeological record that is at last enabling these fascinating dynamics to be mapped and explored.

One issue that is unresolved is the degree to which people physically migrated. It has become unfashionable to talk of large-scale folk movements in prehistory — yet some movements, if only on a small and incremental scale, must have taken place. Until quite recently there has been no objective way to approach these problems, but the development of the study of mitochondrial DNA from human tissues has opened up vast new possibilities. In the next few decades, these will have a major impact on our understanding.

In archaeology nothing is static – the subject bounds on. This atlas is a timely celebration of a century or more of arduous archaeological endeavor. It presents, in a most accessible way, a finely balanced summary of what we know and at the same time introduces us to the sense of anticipation for the new discoveries that are surely soon to be made ◆

INTRODUCTION

BY PAUL G. BAHN

People have always known that others came long before them: indeed, what the 16th-century English antiquary William Camden called our "back-looking curiositie" seems to be one of the features that characterize humankind and separate us from other animals. But before the advent of archaeology, the only knowledge of these past times came from written records, oral histories, religious beliefs, legends and superstition. During the 17th and 18th centuries, primarily in Europe, the first steps were taken towards developing a formal study of the past. Early pioneers were mostly clerics, lawyers, medics and the like who, as antiquaries, took a close interest in studying surviving ancient monuments such as barrows and menhirs and gradually realized that history could be pieced together from traces left behind in the ground and in the landscape. At the same time, discoveries of Greek and Roman sculpture helped inspire a tremendous interest in all aspects of the Classical world, while the Napoleonic invasion of Egypt sparked off an enthusiasm for the antiquities of the Nile, and the Near East attracted those eager to explore the lands and places mentioned in the Bible. Amateur archaeologists, especially in Britain, France and Scandinavia, indulged in a great deal of digging of ancient burial mounds. With time, such excavations became attempts to understand the past rather than simply recover buried treasure.

Scientific advances

During the early 19th century, as the study and understanding of stratigraphy advanced, the Earth's geological history became better understood. Discoveries of human fossil bones in ancient strata made it increasingly clear that humankind was of enormous antiquity, but this realization conflicted with conventional religious accounts of the Creation and people were often reluctant to publish their views. A major turning point came in the mid-19th century when Jacques Boucher de Perthes (1788–1868) discovered stone tools in the same gravel layer as the bones of extinct mammoth and wooly rhinoceros at St Acheul, near Amiens, France, only a few years before Charles Darwin (1809–82) set out the scientific basis of human evolution in his seminal work *Origin of Species* (1859). After this, investigation of the remote past became less of a pastime for amateurs, and more of a science with specialist practitioners and established procedures and terminology. In the second half of the century, major archaeological museums were established throughout Europe, and many of the "top nations" founded official "schools of archaeology" in foreign lands, which were the bases for future excavations. Similarly, Harvard University's Peabody Museum sponsored archaeological research in Latin America.

By this time, there was an ever-increasing appreciation of context as important archaeological information. More rigorous standards of excavation were set, with an emphasis on stratigraphy and the careful recording of the context and association of finds, and on the establishment of a reliable chronological framework. Relative chronologies were developed through "typologies" – the arrangement of similar artifacts into sequences spanning space and time.

Towards a world archaeology

As the 20th century progressed, every part of the world began to make a contribution to piecing together our image of the past, and innumerable major discoveries of every kind were made – tombs, treasures, cities, even whole civilizations. But of even greater overall importance to archaeology were advances in other fields. Aerial photography – at first from balloons and then from planes – brought together two infant technologies to provide archaeology with a potent new tool for identifying and surveying countless different sites. Low surface features such as buried banks and ditches, undetectable at ground level, can be seen from the air as shadows in low light, or as changes in soil type or coloration, or as variations in the height of crops growing in open fields (crop-marks). Aerial photographs added a new perspective to the understanding of complex sites, such as Stonehenge. They were instrumental in revealing the presence of the Nasca lines in the Peruvian desert in the 1940s.

By mid-century, environmental studies were coming to play an increasingly important part in archaeological investigation. The key that first unlocked ancient environments was pollen analysis. By studying the dispersal of pollen grains preserved in lake and bog sediments, specialists were able to read the record of past vegetation and identify both natural and human-induced changes. Inevitably, this had a major effect on studies of early agriculture. Environmental studies as a whole, including the recovery and more detailed analysis of plant and animal remains, gave archaeology a more rounded view of the past, which until then had been largely devoted to pigeon-holing artifacts and using them to produce typologies and sequences.

A major step forward came with the development of dendrochronology, or tree-ring dating, based on the simple principle that a tree adds a ring to its growth every year, the size and composition of which is determined by that year's climate. Since climate changes

RIGHT A color plate from Johann Georg Ramsauer's pioneering record of his excavations of an Early Iron Cemetery at Hallstatt (Austria) in the 1850s. Each grave (more than a thousand were excavated) was meticulously illustrated and described in writing.

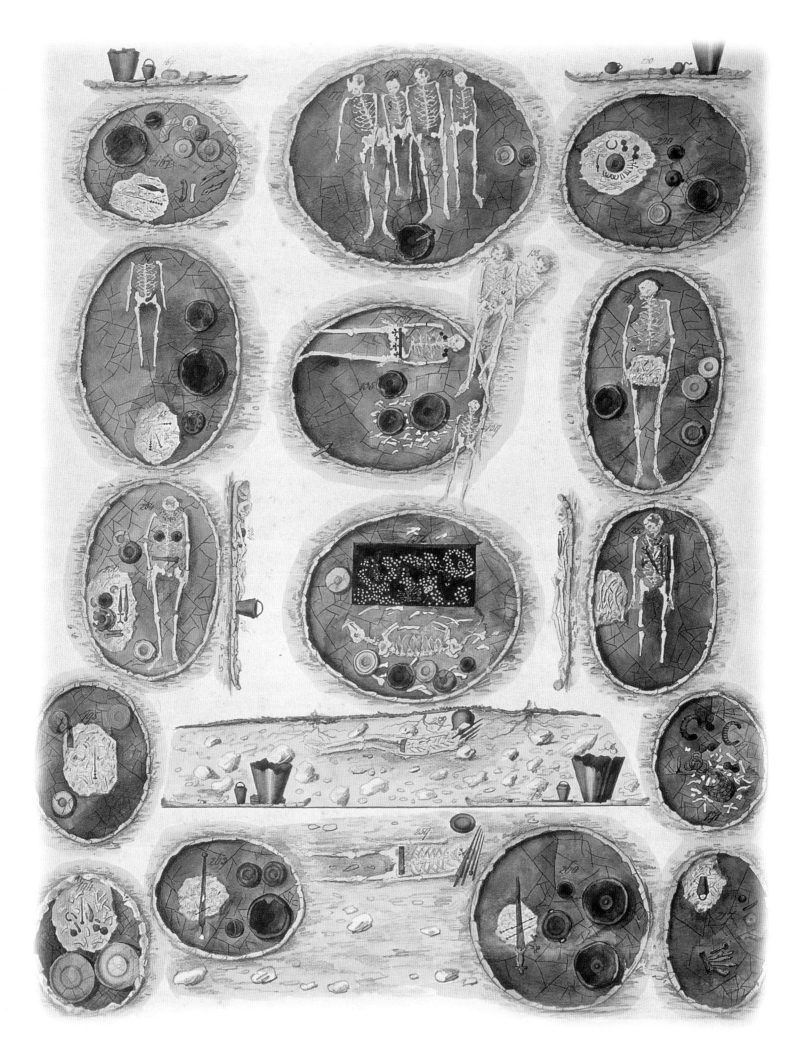

9

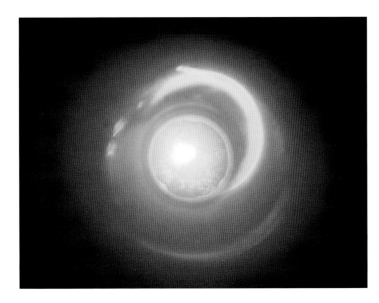

ABOVE A tiny sample of bone is combusted in oxygen. Once the carbon in the bone is converted to carbon dioxide gas, the ratio between the radioactive Carbon 14 isotope and the stable Carbon12 isotope can be measured to quantify how long ago death occurred.

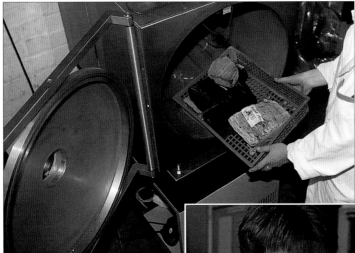

ABOVE New laboratory techniques are making it possible to preserve greater amounts of organic material than ever before. Here a sample of wet timber recovered from an excavation is being placed within a freeze dryer to halt the processes of decay.

RIGHT An archaeologist in Germany uses a microscope and suction device to examine and clean a vessel found in an Iron Age grave at Glauberg, near Frankfurt. A great deal of archaeological activity now takes place away from the excavation site.

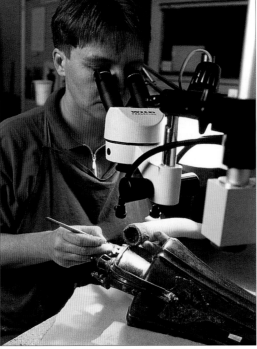

slightly from year to year, a tree accumulates a series of rings of different sizes, and by overlapping samples from trees of different ages within a controlled area, it is possible to build up a master sequence stretching back from the present into the past. The rings of any ancient timbers can then be compared with this, and their age pinpointed. The longest known sequence, based on the Bristlecone Pine for western America, extends back 9,000 years. Although dendrochronology can provide a reliable method of dating, its use is limited to areas where timber was much used and/or where it has been preserved by dry or damp conditions. It has had its most impressive results in the American Southwest and Scandinavia.

The development of radiocarbon dating, first proposed in 1947 by W. F. Libby (1908–80), had a revolutionary impact in the post World War II era. Its method of absolute dating is achieved by measuring how much of the radioactive isotope Carbon 14, which decays at a known rate after death, is contained in any sample of organic material (wood and plant remains, bone, peat, shell), and can yield reliable dates as far back as 50,000 to 75,000 years ago. At first there was some resistance to the technique by traditionalists, especially in central and eastern Europe, who clung to a chronology built on historically documented dates, but once the initial imperfections in the dating method had been eliminated and more consistent results had been obtained, it became a cornerstone of modern archaeological research.

By the 1960s, archaeology had become a strong and thriving discipline spanning the globe, with an ever-expanding body of material to study and a burgeoning array of new techniques at its command. Up until now, European or American archaeologists had carried out virtually all research anywhere in the world – their governments and academic institutions alone had the means to fund excavations and train practitioners – but gradually more and more countries began producing their own specialists. Today, in consequence, although the Western nations still maintain their foreign "schools" and carry out archaeological projects on a worldwide basis, most overseas work is done in partnership or collaboration with nationals, and every country has its own archaeological establishment.

New challenges

In the past few decades a number of major transformations have burst upon the archaeological scene. Naturally, further advances in the sciences have yielded new approaches and new sources of data – not just a whole battery of different dating methods that can be applied to a variety of materials and cover a wide range of timespans, but also a variety of new techniques including satellite imagery and geophysical survey methods for locating, mapping and exploring sites, scuba gear

LEFT Archaeologists use a string grid to record the position of petroglyphs, images pecked into the face of a rock in the Petrified Forest National Park, Arizona. In the past, such images were recorded by rubbing, taking molds or, even worse, being chalked or painted. Today, however, they are studied by photography and by tracings made without direct contact with the rock face. Archaeologists can discover a great deal from rock art by careful study of its location, content, techniques, and changes through time. However, attempts at interpretation of the images still fall prey all too often to speculation or wishful thinking.

and submarines for underwater archaeology, various computer techniques for processing, imaging and analyzing data, scanning electron microscopy with a wide application of uses, bone chemistry, genetics, mitochondrial DNA – the list is endless. Archaeological investigation is now so wide-ranging that it requires a myriad of specialists in different fields of expertise to produce the fullest possible picture of the past.

This has had a number of consequences. In stark contrast to the early pioneering days, when sites were dug quickly with pickaxes or even explosives, usually by unskilled workmen, and simply in order to extract collectable or interesting objects, the pendulum has swung to the other extreme. Excavation is now an extremely slow, painstaking process, with frequent stops to brush aside and carefully sieve the soil, and to record the exact three-dimensional position of every find. Since excavation is also destruction, it is the duty of the excavator to keep a record of every conceivable scrap of information about what was done and what was found. Large excavations have consequently become huge multidisciplinary enterprises that are extremely costly in time and money. This is one reason why more and more archaeologists are turning to less expensive approaches to the past such as survey, or to museum and archival work.

A principal aim of archaeology has always been the preservation of the material past. But another problem for today's archaeologists is the sheer quantity of material there is to keep. Early excavators used to preserve only the "best" or "most important" finds and saved very little of their more mundane material such as animal bones or plain potsherds. Now that it is thought necessary to retrieve and store everything, most museums are bursting at the seams and cannot accept any more finds. There is not only an enormous backlog of unstudied material but an ever-growing headache as regards conservation and preservation of all that we already have. The problem is so acute in some areas that excavators have reburied their finds for future generations to "rediscover".

The threats posed to the world's archaeological sites are many and various, and include weathering, decay, tourism, vandalism and warfare. But by far the worst – and it grows worse every year – is the damage done by looters to obtain objects of artistic or monetary value for private collectors. The antiquities trade is a pernicious one, which feeds and is fed by the wholesale plundering of what is a very finite resource that belongs to the whole of humankind – the material remains of the human past. Ripping the stuff out of the ground causes destruction not only of its archaeological context – the source of much information – but also of associated material that has no "value" for the collector but would be priceless in terms of information if excavated properly. This applies not only to those who rob Etruscan graves of their art objects or strip the sculptures from Cambodian temples to supply the international market, but also to weekend "treasure hunters" armed with metal detectors.

Present and future concerns

Archaeology today has "lost its innocence". Partly this has come about through its practitioners themselves realizing that they needed to tighten up their reasoning and make explicit their assumptions and prejudices, and partly through minorities, both within and outside the subject, making their demands and opinions known. Both constituted a rude awakening for a discipline that had become somewhat complacent after more than a century of developing its techniques and approaches. It has been forced to carry out a critical examination of its practices, not only in terms of theoretical underpinnings but also with regard to its treatment of women in the profession and in its picture of the past. Most especially, it has had to rethink its attitude towards indigenous peoples and the use it makes

ABOVE Mummy bundles, placed on a high Andean rock ledge 500 years ago, have been ripped open and discarded by looters looking for treasure.

of skeletal material. After going unmentioned for a century, ethics has reared its head, and today no archaeologist would dream of carrying out fieldwork, let alone excavation, and certainly not disturbance of the dead, without full consultation with the local authorities, indigenous peoples or traditional owners of a site. The ways in which the past is presented to the public in the press, books, or museums have also come under scrutiny, and far more thought is now put into the messages that are being conveyed in these media.

Thanks in part to the media, archaeology has become a victim of its own success. As more and more people choose to study the subject at university, the numbers of graduates with degrees – or even highly specialized doctorates – in archaeology are increasing yearly, but the opportunities to exercise the basics of their craft – survey, excavation, analysis and interpretation – are limited: few institutions or governments have ready resources to fund large-scale excavations. Outside the academic discipline of the universities, modern archaeology is now predominantly a business, a high-tech enterprise. In the United States, for example, "Cultural Resource Management" (CRM) – the assessment, monitoring and salvaging of sites ahead of construction projects or roadbuilding – accounts for more than 90 percent of all archaeological work, and is largely funded by the private sector. In Europe and other parts of the world there is also a constant demand for more time and greater effort to be devoted to conservation, heritage studies, museology, the requirements of tourism, and combating looting and vandalism.

This means that the archaeologists of the future will not only have to equip themselves with the basics of fieldwork, but will also need to become proficient in conservation and museum studies, in cultural resource and business management, in heritage and antiquities law, and in dealing with the public and negotiating with developers. The number of purely research excavations will undoubtedly continue to fall, but we already know of far more archaeological sites and have unearthed far more material than could possibly be studied by all existing archaeologists in several lifetimes. It would perhaps be no bad thing if most of the untouched sites were left for future generations to investigate with better techniques than our own, and if archaeology adapted to the pragmatic requirements of the modern world. But of course, new discoveries about the past will continue to be made and amaze us.

The Atlas

For those archaeologists who carry out fieldwork, there are two principal means of obtaining fresh information: survey and excavation. Survey involves looking for and recording (or collecting) those vestiges of the past that occur on the surface – either to assess the extent and layout of a site, or to study settlement patterns, the distribution of sites of different kinds and periods across the landscape. Excavation, on the other hand, requires searching beneath the soil, exposing the actual relics of the past. It usually involves a mixture of "vertical" and "horizontal digging" – vertical to expose the sequence of layers, one above the next, as the site built up over time; and horizontal to explore a particular level over a wider area, to see what was happening in a specific period.

This Atlas endeavors to epitomize these two aspects of archaeology – the vertical and the horizontal – by attempting to present information in both senses: it tells the human story at the global and regional levels, explaining what happened over time, but also makes use of the maps to take a close look at certain places in certain periods. The maps also try to give some idea of how things changed over time, and bring together a wide range of information that is not usually presented in this form.

It is, of course, difficult to make a simple map convey a whole range of information without making it too complex to be useful, but nevertheless the intention has been to produce far more than a basic set of distribution maps, which tell one little about the real past. The problem with all archaeological distribution maps is that they probably bear little relation to reality: they are based on information of varying quality and reliability, accumulated over a century or more of work by a range of scholars of varying abilities and interests. Such maps tend to show where the most work has been done, rather than where most of the sites were originally located. There can be many factors that affect where archaeologists choose to carry out their investigations – politics, climate, warfare, social life, and so forth. Moreover, different scholars have looked for different things, and it is a fundamental truism of archaeology that one tends to find primarily what one is looking for – other things are ignored or missed until they, too, are looked for.

Maps illustrate the basic distortions that affects all of archaeology: they display what has actually been found, which is usually only a small fraction of what has survived, which in turn is a tiny fraction of what originally existed. For most periods of the past, our techniques for dating sites and material are not precise enough to guarantee that any two sites were occupied contemporaneously. In consequence, it is difficult to assess how many "dots" on any map were truly in use or occupied at the same time. With these warnings in mind, we have sought to make the maps in this Atlas the best that are currently available. Based on the most up-to-date evidence, they offer a view of the way communities and societies have evolved and interacted with each other over time. But it goes without saying that they should in no way be regarded as definitive. In five or ten

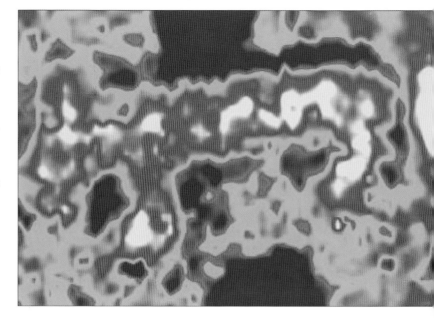

ABOVE An image map of Little Bear Mound, Iowa, using magnetic data. Geophysical surveys using methods such as magnetometry and ground penetrating radar to investigate subsurface features non-invasively are now an integral part of archaeological research.

years they will need to be updated; in a hundred years from now, our knowledge of the human past will probably have been transformed by new discoveries and hitherto unimagined techniques .

The Atlas is in three parts. The first looks at human origins from the earliest hominids to the end of the last Ice Age. The second presents global coverage of the major advances achieved by humankind in the succeeding 10,000 years. The third divides the world into five broad geographical regions to take a closer look at these advances. One mundane problem has afflicted the Atlas – sheer lack of space. Inevitably, hard decisions had to be made, not only in terms of subject matter covered, but also as regards the cut-off point to be adopted in each part of the world. As the names we assign to cultures and periods are all quite artificial, and as such slices of time are of widely varying duration, it made little sense to adopt the same cut-off date for every part of the globe. Hence, in the Old World (Europe and Asia), coverage ends in early modern times (c. 500 CE); in Africa, the Americas, Australia and the southern Pacific, it extends to the arrival of Europeans, sometimes no more than two or three centuries ago ◆

NOTES ON USING THIS ATLAS

Bold type is used on the maps to indicate a site that is mentioned in the accompanying text.

Dates are usually given as BCE (Before Common Era) and CE (Common Era) but appear as m.y.a. (million years ago) and y.a. (years ago) on the timelines and before 8,000 BCE.

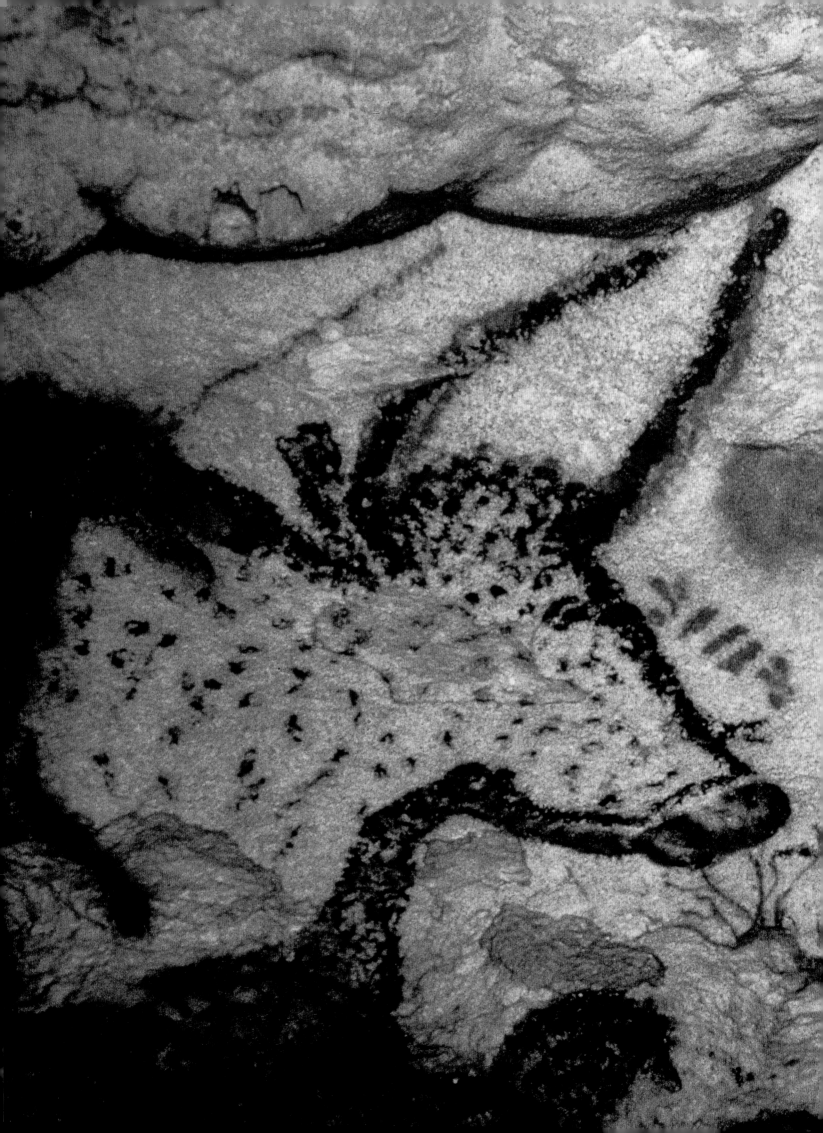

Part One

THE FIRST HUMANS

*Painted aurochs, horses and deer
from the "Hall of the Bulls", Lascaux, France*

The Earliest Hominids

Hominids are members of a mammalian group or family that includes upright-walking creatures with comparatively large brains; humans are the sole living representatives. Fossil bones and genetic studies indicate that the hominids shared an ancestor with the African great apes, from which they split between about 8–6 million years ago. Although great apes and humans differ considerably in appearance, African great apes are genetically the closest living relatives of modern humans: chimpanzees and humans share 98.4 % of their genetic material, while gorillas differ from humans in only 2.3 % of their genetic composition. This degree of similarity suggests that the last ancestor shared by the great ape and human lines was probably a chimpanzee-like creature, and that changes in genetic regulatory mechanisms played a role in the evolution of a divergent lineage that set out on the road to humanity. The process of hominization apparently began in Africa, the only continent on which fossils of the earliest known hominids are found. Recognition of an early hominid skull was made in 1924 by Raymond Dart, who later gave it the scientific name *Australopithecus africanus* ("southern ape of Africa"). The name "australopithecine" is commonly used today as the descriptive term for one of the earliest hominids. Dart's claim that the skull (popularly known as the "Taung child") was an intermediate stage between apes and humans sparked fierce public and scientific debate at the time, and won general acceptance only decades later. Large numbers of australopithecine bones have subsequently been discovered at other sites in South Africa, but the majority of early hominid fossils have been found in the Rift Valley of East Africa. There have been findings at a single site, Bahr el Ghazal, in Chad.

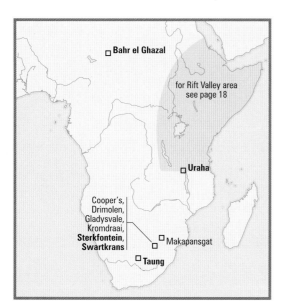

The Rift Valley is a natural fault made up of a series of splits, or fissures, in the Earth's crust that runs for nearly 1,800 mi/3,000 km north–south in East Africa. It is a rich source of information about human origins because the volcanic deposits that have preserved an abundance of early hominid remains contain radioactive materials easily dated by various laboratory techniques. In 1959 Mary Leakey found a robustly built australopithecine at Olduvai Gorge, a deep cleft in the Rift Valley. The discovery of this 1.8 million-year-old fossil, which was initially given the scientific name *Zinjanthropus boisei* (today it is known as *Australopithecus* or *Paranthropus boisei*) intensified early hominid research in East Africa and stimulated the growth of paleoanthropology, a multi-disciplined approach to the study of human origins. Among the many treasures unearthed during the fossil hunt that followed was "Lucy", the 3.18 million-year-old partial skeleton of a small upright-walking female that was discovered at Hadar in Ethiopia in 1974 and subsequently given the scientific description of *A. afarensis* (see page 18).

The first hominids

The odds against the preservation and discovery of early hominid fossils are great. Until a few years ago, specimens older than 4 million years were particularly rare and represented by only a handful of bones, the earliest of which is a hominid upper jaw fragment from Lothagam in northern Kenya dating to between

ABOVE Olduvai Gorge, a canyon 25 mi/40 km long and up to 330 ft/100 m deep in the Great Rift Valley of East Africa, holds many clues to human evolution. Its geological history of volcanic eruption, uplift and erosion have created the ideal conditions for preserving fossils. When Louis and Mary Leakey made their discoveries there in the 1950s and 1960s, they were able to apply potassium-argon dating methods to the lava layers between which the hominid fossils were found, the first time these techniques (now replaced by argon-argon dating) had been employed. The discovery that hominids had been living beside a lake in the Gorge between 1.9 and 1.3 million years ago fundamentally and dramatically shattered the view then prevailing that humankind originated in Asia or Europe. Although much earlier hominid discoveries have been made in East and South Africa since the Leakeys' pioneering work, Olduvai remains crucially important to our understanding of human origins.

6 and 5 m.y.a. A wider window was opened on this distant period in human evolution when, in 1994–95, a team led by Tim White of the University of California announced the discovery of a collection of bones from a 4.4 million-year-old site at Aramis in the Middle Awash region of Ethiopia. They included a nearly complete skeleton of the most apelike and probably the earliest hominid yet known. Initially described as *A. ramidus*, after consideration the material was assigned to a new genus, *Ardipithecus*. Research is still being carried out to establish whether this ancient creature was indeed the earliest known hominid to walk on two legs.

In 1995, only a short time after Tim White's find at Aramis, Meave Leakey and colleagues discovered fossils dating from between 4.2 and 3.9 m.y.a. at two sites, Kanapoi and Allia Bay, near Lake Turkana in northern Kenya. With a similar but more primitive anatomy than *A. afarensis*, they were classified as a new species of australopithecine, *A. anamensis*, which is currently the oldest known.

The application of new laboratory techniques to fossil discoveries like these, and to the fossils already held in museum collections, allows researchers to extract ever more detailed information about early hominids. Such methods include the use of single crystal laser fusion to measure the ratio of radioactive isotopes present in fossil-bearing volcanic rocks so that evolutionary events can be pinpointed with greater accuracy (potassium-argon or argon-argon dating). The measurement of the ratios of calcium and strontium in bones can indicate whether the hominid had a herbivorous, carnivorous or omnivorous diet, while X-ray computed tomography (CAT scans) can even look inside bone and reveal internal anatomical structure.

Australopithecines aplenty

Meanwhile the quest to find more specimens to fill the many gaps in the picture continues. *A. afarensis* (4–3 m.y.a.), the lightly built (gracile) species to which Lucy belongs, is the best represented of the australopithecines. It is known from sites in Ethiopia, Kenya and Tanzania, including Laetoli where trails of hominid footprints made in damp volcanic ash nearly 3.7 million years ago indicate that australopithecines walked on two legs though not quite like modern humans. *A. garhi*, was identified in Ethiopa in 1999. Dating to 2.5 m.y.a., it is arguably descended from *A. afarensis*. A lightly built australopithecine, *A. africanus* (more than 2 m.y.a.), has been found at sites in South Africa. *A. bahrelghazali*, (3.5–3 m.y.a.) from northern Chad is similar to *A. afarensis*; it extends

the known range of australopithecines to 1,550 mi/ 2,500 km west of the Rift Valley.

Sites in South and East Africa have also yielded fossils of heavily built australopithecines, including *A.* or *Paranthropus robustus* (2–1 m.y.a.), *A.* or *P. aethiopicus* (2.7–1.9 m.y.a.) and *A.* or *P. boisei* (2.3–1.4 m.y.a.). Some researchers believe that the way of life of the heavily built australopithecines differed from that of their gracile counterparts, as their molar teeth have large grinding surfaces for processing tough, fibrous foods. They were probably not on the line leading to modern humans and became extinct about 1 m.y.a.

Small apes that walked

The australopithecines, and possibly also their precursors, the ardipithecines, probably lived over a wider area of Africa than the currently known distribution of their remains suggests. They belong to the human family because they walked on two legs, but differ from more recent humans in having relatively small brains. It was once commonly believed that the first members of the human family had large brains. But, with a few exceptions, australopithecine brains measure

AUSTRALOPITHECUS AFARENSIS

AUSTRALOPITHECUS AFRICANUS

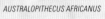

AUSTRALOPITHECUS AETHIOPICUS

AUSTRALOPITHECUS BOISEI

AUSTRALOPITHECUS ROBUSTUS

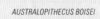

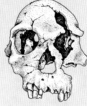

HOMO HABILIS

Hominid find

- Homo
- Robust australopithecines
- Australopithecines
- Ardipithecus

— East African Rift system

| 0 | 400 km |
| 0 | 300 mi |

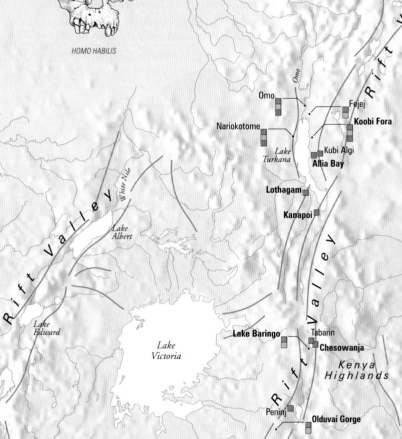

Hadar

Ethiopian Highlands

Aramis

Blue Nile

Awash

Belohdelie

Omo

Omo

Fejej

Koobi Fora

Nariokotome

Kubi Algi

Lake Turkana

Allia Bay

Lothagam

Kanapoi

White Nile

Rift Valley

Lake Albert

Lake Edward

Lake Victoria

Rift Valley

Lake Baringo   Tabarin

Chesowanja

Kenya Highlands

Peninj

Olduvai Gorge

Laetoli

Lake Tanganyika

Rift Valley

Lucy: a fossil celebrity

Lucy – whose partial skeleton of 47 bones was discovered by Donald Johanson at Hadar in Ethiopia in 1974 – is possibly the most famous of our human ancestors. She lived 3.18 m.y.a. and was probably in her late teens or early twenties when she died. Although fully grown, she only stood about 3 ft 7 in/1.1 m tall. She walked on two legs, but with slightly bent limbs. Curvature in her finger and toe bones suggests she may have climbed trees to collect fruits and nuts, or to escape from predators. Analysis of 3 million-year-old fossil pollen and animal bones indicates that her environment ranged from open grassland to woodland. Lucy was not deliberately buried and there is no evidence of an attack by a predator. She may have succumbed to illness or been drowned at the edge of a lake or delta stream, and her body then covered with sand or mud. The discovery of so many bones from a single skeleton is extremely rare, because any bones left lying in the African bush are generally quickly destroyed by scavengers or the processes of natural decay ◆

RIGHT *AUSTRALOPITHECUS AFARENSIS "LUCY".*

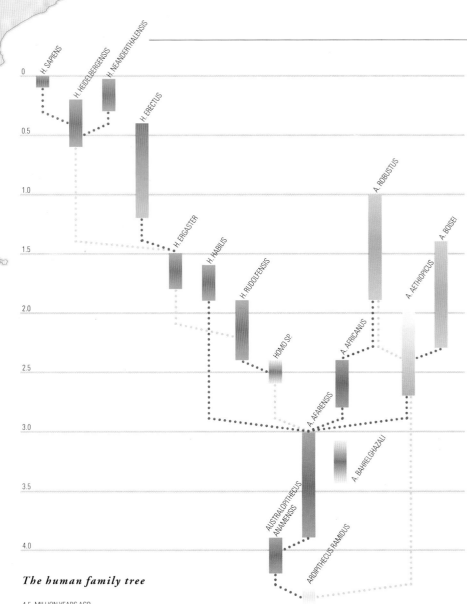

The human family tree

4.5 MILLION YEARS AGO

Labels on the tree (reading positions):
0, 0.5, 1.0, 1.5, 2.0, 2.5, 3.0, 3.5, 4.0

H. SAPIENS, H. HEIDELBERGENSIS, H. NEANDERTHALENSIS, H. ERECTUS, H. ERGASTER, H. HABILIS, H. RUDOLFENSIS, HOMO SP., A. ROBUSTUS, A. BOISEI, A. AETHIOPICUS, A. AFRICANUS, A. AFARENSIS, A. BAHRELGHAZALI, AUSTRALOPITHECUS ANAMENSIS, ARDIPITHECUS RAMIDUS

The First Humans

Until quite recently, *H. erectus* was considered the oldest known representative of the human genus *Homo*. The first known specimen was a half million-year-old partial skull found in Java, Southeast Asia, in 1891, and even after the discovery of the African australopithecines earlier this century, Asia was regarded as the place where true humans evolved. In 1959, two early *Homo* teeth, later dated to nearly 2 m.y.a., were found at Olduvai Gorge. Although they were the first African fossils to bridge the gap between the australopithecines and *H. erectus*, their discovery went almost unnoticed. Then, in 1964, a collection of bones, also from Olduvai, dating from 1.75 m.y.a., was identified as belonging to a previously unknown species of *Homo*. Because of a presumed link with tools, it was given the name of *H. habilis*, or "handy man".

Fierce debate followed the identification of *H. habilis*. Its brain volume of 680 cc was considerably larger than that of the ape-like australopithecines. However, some researchers preferred to include it within the australopithecines or to assign it to *H. erectus*. Others pointed out that australopithecines present in the same layers as the *H. habilis* fossils could have made the tools associated with it. Acceptance of this new hominid, and of an African origin for *Homo*, came only after the subsequent discovery of additional specimens from Olduvai Gorge, Koobi Fora in northern Kenya, and South Africa. One of these, a partial skeleton of *H. habilis*, 1.8 million years old, discovered by Tim White at Olduvai in 1986, has an apelike build with arms relatively long in proportion to the legs. *H. habilis* seemed to be a convenient straightforward evolutionary link between australopithecines and *H. erectus*, but it has become clear that the early stages of the development of *Homo* were more complex than previously considered and that several distinct species were probably present.

The oldest known toolmaker

Although *Homo* status has been claimed for several 2.5 million-year-old fossils, including a skull fragment from Lake Baringo (Kenya), a jaw from Uraha, (Malawi), and a partial skull from Sterkfontein, (South Africa), the question is still much debated. The oldest known *Homo* remains, securely dated to 2.3 m.y.a., are an upper jaw and teeth (catalogue number AL 666-1) from Hadar (Ethiopia). Until more is known about these very fragmentary fossils, they have provisionally been described as a species of *Homo*, *H. sp*. Some 20 simple basalt and chert stone flakes and cores were found with the remains, providing the earliest known evidence of stone tools in direct association with hominid fossils.

some 500 cc or less. Early *Homo* brains exceed 600 cc, and modern *Homo sapiens* are about 1,350 cc.

Australopithecines were probably dark-skinned and hairy. There were marked sexual differences: estimated male bodyweight was 88–110 lb/40–50 kg; female 60–77 lb/27–35 kg. Males stood approximately 4.2–5 ft/1.3–1.5 m tall; females a little over 3 ft/1 m. Studies of the behavior of great apes may suggest something of australopithecine behavior, but walking on two feet (bipedalism) probably resulted in unique ways of obtaining and processing food, territoriality, mating and social behavior. It seems likely that they ate a wide variety of foods, including meat scavenged from carnivore kills, small mammals, insects and plant foods. Some experts consider that australopithecines may have possessed the ability to make simple stone tools, as the oldest known tools date to some 0.3 million years before the oldest known *Homo* remains. There is no evidence that australopithecines used fire, built shelters, made art, or buried their dead, but vocal communication in various social settings may have had a role in the later development of language ◆

ABOVE This simplified human family tree (after Johanson and Edgar, 1996) depicts only one conjectural evolutionary route. The hominid fossil data are patchy and paleoanthropologists often disagree about the relationships between species, the assignation of specimens to particular species, and even whether specimens are australopithecines or the larger-brained early *Homo*. Some australopithecines overlap in time with early *Homo* fossils. The development of bipedalism in australopithecines did not lead in a single line to modern humans; several different kinds of bipedal creatures evolved, all of which were successful for a period of time. All, apart from *Homo sapiens*, are extinct.

A hominid treasure chest

Koobi Fora, a narrow spit of land on the eastern shore of Lake Turkana (formerly Lake Rudolf), is one of the richest repositories of early hominid fossils and associated stone tools anywhere in the world. Because the remains are found in lake and stream sediments sandwiched between layers of volcanic ash, radioactive isotope dating can establish fairly precise age limits for them. The collection of fossils from Koobi Fora includes several examples of australopithecines and at least two early *Homo* species. The first of these is a fairly complete cranium, KNM-ER 1470, discovered by Louis and Mary Leakey's son Richard in 1972. Its relatively large brain volume of about 775 cc fully justified its classification as *Homo*, but Richard Leakey chose to leave the species indeterminate because initial estimates of its age placed it at some 2.9 m.y.a., a million years older than the *H. habilis* fossils from Olduvai Gorge. This date was later shown to have been calculated from contaminated samples and a revised date of about 1.8 m.y.a. was proposed. Recent estimates suggest it is certainly younger than 3.31 m.y.a., probably younger than 2.5 m.y.a., but is definitely older than 1.9 m.y.a. In 1986 the species was given the name *H. rudolfensis*, thereby indicating that more than one early *Homo* species was present in Africa 2 million years ago.

The workman

Another early Homo species identified at Koobi Fora, *H. ergaster*, dating to between 1.8 and 1.5 m.y.a., is represented by several well-preserved fossils. The first recognized specimen, a jaw with small molar teeth, was found in the same layer as a collection of stone tools, which provided its species name (*ergaster* is Greek for "workman"). One of the best examples of *H. ergaster*, and the most complete skeleton of an early hominid ever found, is that of a boy excavated between 1984–88

from sediments laid down about 1.5 m.y.a. near the western shore of Lake Turkana. Originally assigned to *H. erectus*, the "Turkana boy" was equal in development to a modern 11-year-old. There are important differences with modern skeletons, but had he survived to adulthood, he would probably have had a brain size of around 900 cc, have stood 6 ft 1 in/ 1.82 m tall, and weighed 150 lb/68 kg. Early humans may have been much taller than previously believed.

Many pieces in the puzzle

Although fresh discoveries are constantly being made, our knowledge of the early evolution of our genus remains patchy and poorly understood. The task of fossil classification and relationships is fraught with puzzles and difficulties. It would be foolhardy to attempt to reach too many firm conclusions from the fragmentary information currently available, but of the early *Homo* species known to have been living in Africa between 2.3 and 1.5 million years ago, it seems probable that *H. rudolfensis* is the oldest, followed by *H. habilis* and then by *H. ergaster*. Of these species, *H. ergaster* seems to have been closest to later *Homo* species in terms of brain size, skeletal build and locomotion, and we are probably safe in regarding *H. ergaster* as in the same line as modern humans ◆

The First Toolmakers

Study of the evolution of technology has an important part to play in piecing together the early hominid story. The earliest known stone tools are described as Oldowan – a name derived from Olduvai Gorge, where Mary Leakey in the 1960s identified and described large collections of tools found in the lowest layers, dating to between about 1.9–1.5 m.y.a. Oldowan tools were manufactured by a simple flaking technique – a smooth, rounded stone was used as a hammer to knock off small, sharp-edged flakes from another rock or pebble. Experiments with modern copies of such flakes, typically quartz or basalt, show that the early hominid toolmakers could have used them to cut open animal carcasses and slice through sinew and bone with relative ease.

Evidence from a number of sites in East Africa suggests that stone tools of the Oldowan type were being made well before 2.3 m.y.a. At present, the earliest known stone tools are simple chopping, scraping and cutting implements from sites in the Gona drainage of the Hadar region of Ethiopia, which are 2.6–2.5 million years old. Quartz pebbles, flakes and chips dating to 2.4–2.3 m.y.a. have been found in the Shungura Formation at Omo in southern Ethiopia. Also from Hadar is the jawbone of an early *Homo* fossil, dated to some 2.3 m.y.a. It was found in association with a small collection of basalt and chert artifacts and provides the first known link between stone tools and early hominids. Traditionally, *H. habilis* has been regarded as the first toolmaker, but there are good reasons to believe that other species of early *Homo*, such as *H. rudolfensis*, could also have been responsible for them.

It is very likely that early *Homo* obtained meat not from deliberate hunting but from scavenging flesh from dead animals. Sharp-edged flakes would have been ideal for the task of cutting hide and severing bone and sinew. Some animal bones at Oldowan sites have cutmarks on them that appear to have been made with a sharp flake. Pebbles used as hammerstones for striking flakes have also been found in great numbers at these sites. Oldowan tools were in use for more than a million years before being replaced by more highly fashioned Acheulean hand axes about 1.4–1.3 m.y.a. (see page 25).

Use of fire

Mastery of fire was a key step in the development of human technology. Fire provides heat, light and protection from predators; it smokes and dries meat, and plays a role in social development. Eventually it allowed humans to extend their range to the coldest regions of the planet. There is considerable debate about the earliest use of fire. It has been claimed that small flecks and lumps of baked clay found together with animal bones and stone tools at Chesowanja (Kenya), dating to some 1.4 m.y.a., provide early evidence of the use of controlled fire, as a natural bush fire has been dismissed as an explanation. However, the clay could have been formed when a tree stump was consumed by fire, or even by lightning or volcanic heating. More compelling evidence of early use of fire comes from Swartkrans (see box) but is not conclusive. *H. erectus* is traditionally credited with being the first fire-maker on the basis of ash layers dated c.400,000 years ago from Zhoukoudian (China) but now thought questionable (see page 24). The earliest unequivocal evidence of hearths comes from European sites such as Vértesszöllös (Hungary) and Menez-Dregan (northwest France), which may be at least 350,000 years old. However, hearths do not become commonplace in the archaeological record until the last 100,000 years ◆

Swartkrans: evidence for early hominids

Swartkrans is one of several ancient cave fillings in the Bloubank River Valley in Gauteng Province, South Africa. At least 126 australopithecine fossils – more than at any other site – have been found here. It has been demonstrated that many of these hominids were killed by predators such as leopards and saber-toothed cats, who dragged their prey into trees growing at the cave's mouth to protect it from hyenas, from where the bones dropped into the cave below. Holes in a skull fragment of one young australopithecine found at Swartkrans appear to match exactly the canine teeth on a leopard skull found in the same layer. More controversial is the discovery of a collection of 279 burnt bones. They are at least 1 million years old, and it has been argued that they are the oldest evidence for the use of fire by hominids. Experimental studies, together with chemical and microscopic analyses, indicate that the bones had been subjected to temperatures consistent with being burnt in a camp fire rather than scorched in a natural bush fire. However, no fireplaces have been found, and it is impossible to tell whether the fire, if it was deliberate, was made by early hominids or gathered from a natural fire ignited by lightning. Its purpose – whether for cooking, warmth, or to discourage predators – is also unknown ◆

ABOVE RADIOMICROGRAPH OF A FRAGMENT OF BURNT BONE FROM SWARTKRANS, SOUTH AFRICA.

African Genesis

In the million years between about 1.8 and 0.8 m.y.a., hominids not identical to ourselves but recognizably like us from the neck down inhabited the African savanna. They still had heavily built skulls with big brow ridges, but their brains were more than twice the size of those of australopithecines and some three-quarters those of modern humans. It was long assumed that the first hominid to have extended its range beyond Africa was *H. erectus*, believed to have appeared in East Asia around one million years ago. However, African fossils previously labeled *H. erectus* are now being identified as *H. ergaster*, the probable direct ancestor of modern humans, while East Asian *H. erectus* is regarded by some as a specialized local development not on the modern human line.

It was once thought that the early African hominids were great hunters. Imaginative reconstructions often depict them driving herds of elephant, rhinoceros or buffalo into swamps where the animals could be easily butchered. Recent studies do not uphold this picture: animal bones found in association with stone tools are unlikely to have come from slaughtered beasts but from dead animals scavenged by early hominids or by other animals. Plant foods probably formed a large part of their diet. No ornaments or art have been found with *H. erectus* or with early African *Homo* species like *H. ergaster*, and there is no evidence that they buried their dead.

Double-sided tools

Apart from a few rare wooden tools, almost all the cultural remains that have survived from this time are stone implements belonging to what is known as the Acheulean industrial complex. The characteristic Acheulean tool is a bifacial, or double-sided, handax, worked into a pointed pear-shaped piece with a cutting edge around all or much of the circumference. Tools with a broad ax-like cutting edge, called cleavers, were also made. The oldest Acheulean tools yet found come from Konso-Gardula in Ethiopia, where they date to some 1.4 m.y.a. They continued to be made in Africa until perhaps 150,000 years ago, making this one of the longest-lasting technologies the world has known. The earliest bifaces were made by removing pieces from both sides of a stone or stone flake with a stone hammer. Later, thinner bifaces were made using a bone or wooden hammer. Sometimes a core was specially prepared for the removal of a flake of pre-determined size and shape.

Acheulean tools were almost certainly hand-held, but some are so large it is difficult to imagine how they could have been put to use. Microscopic examination of scratches and abrasions on the surface of the handaxes show they were used on a wide variety of materials, including plant foods, meat and wood. They may have been all-purpose tools. It has even been suggested that some were used as throwing stones, something like a discus.

The journey from Africa

Paleoanthropologists once held that the acquisition of Acheulean stone-making skills was a determinant factor in the migration of early hominids out of the African savannas into new environments. The earliest handaxes found outside Africa, from Ubeidiya (Israel), date to at least 1 m.y.a. Acheulean tools are found in the Near East, Arabia and parts of India, and spread into Europe about 500,000 years ago (the type-site from which they are named is St. Acheul in northern France). They have not, however, been found in East Asia. Here, jagged-edged choppers and small flakes rather like those of the Oldowan type are the norm.

More recently it has been suggested that a hominid more primitive than *H. erectus* may have been the first to arrive in East Asia. This could explain the lack of bifacial tools in this area. Supporting this view are some very early dates recently proposed for human fossil specimens from Indonesia (Sangiran) and China. Fossils from Longgupo Cave in southeast China have controversially been dated to between 1.96 and 1.78 m.y.a. and are considered to have similarities with with African early fossils of about 1.6 m.y.a. These findings, however, are still the subject of lively debate ◆

BELOW The skullcap of Trinil 2, or Java Man (7.2 in/18.5 cm). Discovered in the early 1890s by a Dutch doctor who named it *Pithecanthropus erectus*, it was later classified as *H. erectus*, along with other early fossils from Java and China, including Peking Man. Trinil 2 was long considered to be the oldest known hominid fossil in the world, giving rise to the view that humans originated in Asia. The discovery of earlier fossils in Africa in the 1960s changed all this.

Spread of Archaic Humans

Uncertainties about the timing of the initial outward expansion of early hominids from Africa obscure the reasons why it occurred. These seem likely to lie in the increased brain size of *H. ergaster* and the adoption of improved stone-working skills. By the beginning of the Last Interglacial (the warm period that preceded the last major glaciation of the Ice Age, beginning c.130,000 to 125,000 years ago) early humans had colonized much of the Old World. This first expansion lasted well over a million years. Paleoanthropologists sometimes refer to it as "Out of Africa 1" to distinguish it from the later, much more rapid dispersal of modern humans (see pages 28–29). Archaic humans were far more limited than modern humans in their ability to adapt their technology to new environments. There is little evidence that they had moved into the colder regions of northern Asia. The first African exodus resulted in biological diversification instead of leading to cultural diversification, as happened with modern humans. By about half a million years ago various forms of *Homo* had emerged in Eurasia. Paleoanthropologists traditionally lumped them all within the single classification of "archaic *H. sapiens*", but it is becoming increasingly apparent that distinct species should be recognized in Africa, Asia, and Europe.

While the dating of the earliest East Asian sites (which may be as much as 1.9 million years old) is controversial, finds such as the Ubeidiya handaxes provide clear evidence that archaic humans had spread outside Africa by between 1.5 and 1 m.y.a. Initially they colonized the southern regions of Eurasia, where the tropical and subtropical environments they encountered would have been broadly similar to those of their African homeland.

Conservative development

Examination of the human fossil record in Asia suggests that there was very slow change with respect to skeletal features over hundreds of millennia. Sites dating to between 500,000 and 200,000 years ago contain the remains of people who were still quite similar to the African *Homo* population of more than a million years earlier. For example, a skull from Dali in northern China dating to c.230,000–180,000 years ago exhibits very archaic features such as a massive brow ridge and low cranial vault; *Homo* fossils of extreme archaic appearance from Ngangdong in Indonesia may even be as late as 100,000 years ago. There is, however, evidence of increased brain size in the fossils from some of these younger sites. Most of the Asian fossils that antedate the appearance of modern humans are classified as *H. erectus*.

Little is known of the diet and lifestyle of these early humans. Their tool collection remained limited

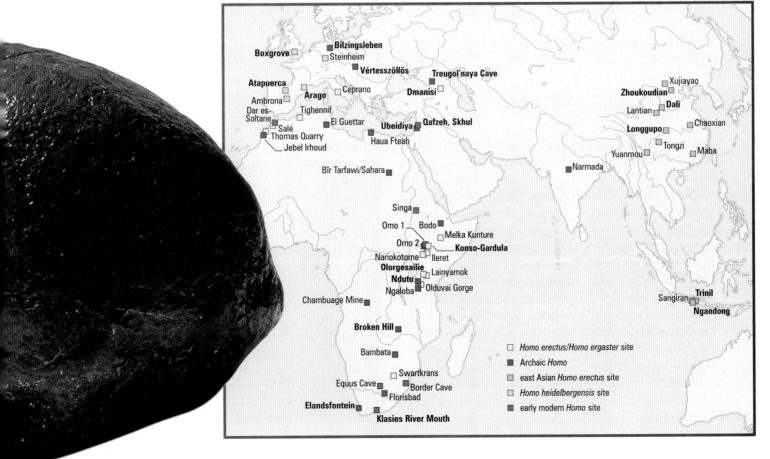

- □ *Homo erectus/Homo ergaster* site
- ■ Archaic *Homo*
- ■ east Asian *Homo erectus* site
- □ *Homo heidelbergensis* site
- ■ early modern *Homo* site

to simple choppers and flake implements. Ash layers from an occupation floor dating to about 400,000 years ago in Zhoukoudian Cave (northern China) have been taken to indicate the controlled use of fire on the northern edge of *H. erectus'* range , but it is now uncertain whether the layers do in fact represent former hearths (see caption on right).

Northern Eurasia

For several hundreds of millennia after the initial movement out of Africa archaic humans do not appear to have migrated into northern Eurasia. There is very little evidence of occupation above 40° N (approximately the line of latitude that connects Madrid, Spain with Beijing, China) before about 750,000 years ago, though a jawbone from Dmanisi (Republic of Georgia) may be as much as one million

LEFT The Zhoukoudian Cave complex, 29 mi/46 km southwest of Beijing, China, contains one of the largest collections of archaic *Homo* fossils (classified as *H. erectus*) dated to roughly 400,000 years ago. The tools associated with these fossils lack the handaxes found in Africa and much of western Eurasia at this time, and are confined to simple flake implements and some crude choppers. Four layers of ash point to the early use of controlled fire at the site. They were long thought to be the earliest evidence of fire from anywhere in the world, but the findings from Swartkrans may put this in question (see page 21). Moreover, doubts have recently been expressed as to whether the Chinese cave's deposits contain true ash at all. The Zhoukoudian caves were occupied for more than 200,000 years. During this time there was considerable oscillation between cold and warm climate. Hyenas and other carnivores also used for caves for shelter and many of the thousands of animal bones found there undoubtedly represent their hunted or scavenged prey. However, a few bones appear to display stone tool butchery marks or indications of roasting.

years old. Settlement of these northern latitudes presented archaic *Homo* with previously unknown environmental challenges in the form of cooler temperatures and more pronounced seasonal fluctuations. Plant foods, which on the evidence of tooth wear appear to have been the primary form of diet, would have been less plentiful in many regions. Although the early colonization of Europe seems to have been confined to warmer periods, some later occupation sites are associated with colder periods.

The oldest known *Homo* fossils in Europe come from the Gran Dolina cave at Atapuerca in northern Spain, where some three dozen bones dating to c.800,000 years ago are believed to have belonged to four individuals, including a child and an adolescent. Skeletal remains and handaxes discovered at Boxgrove, England, dating to 500,000 years ago, are the earliest evidence of occupation above 50°N, while artifacts from Treugol'naya Cave (Russia) show the presence of archaic *Homo* in eastern Europe at about the same time. The extinction of several large carnivores in Europe c.500,000 years ago may have opened up new opportunities for human scavenging and/or hunting at this time.

The early Atapuerca fossils exhibit marked differences with their African contemporaries, and recent molecular studies suggest that the two branches of *Homo* may have diverged by half a million years ago. Paleoanthropologists give the species name *H. heidelbergensis* (named for the type specimen discovered at Mauer, Germany in 1907) to the early European archaic population, but the Atapuerca fossils may belong to an evolutionary predecessor.

Over thousands of years, archaic humans in Europe gradually developed characteristic Neandertal features, many of which reflect adaptation to cold climates (see pages 26–27). Transitional specimens

Atapuerca: the oldest burials?

The Sima de los Huesos (Pit of Bones), a 50 ft/15.25 m shaft at the end of a large limestone cavern at Atapuerca in northern Spain, has produced an enormous collection of archaic *Homo* bones since excavations began there in 1983. So far about 2,500 bones from at least 32 (perhaps as many as 50) individuals, dating to between 300,000 and 200,000 y.a., have been discovered. The people were robust and quite tall; their teeth were worn, probably from chewing plants. Three well-preserved skulls have large brow ridges and projecting faces. Equal numbers of males and females have been recovered, with ages ranging from 4 to 35 years, but most are adolescents aged between 13 and 22. The cave is an enigma. No animal bones or stone tools have been found, so it is unlikely to have been an occupation site; nor do the bones show signs of having been eaten or dragged there by carnivores. As the bones are indiscriminately mixed together, it has been suggested that for several generations the bodies of the dead were carried into the cave and tossed into the shaft in a form of funerary ritual that may point to some embryonic religious belief ◆

RIGHT SKULLS, JAWS AND LIMB BONES LIE IN A TUMBLED HEAP IN THE PIT OF BONES.

	Industry	Tools	Distribution	User
LOWER PALEOLITHIC	2.4–1.5 m.y.a Oldowan	Simple flaked choppers and scrapers	Africa	Early *Homo* spp.
	1.4–200,000 y.a. Acheulean	Pointed handaxes, picks and flat-edged cleavers	Africa, Near East and Europe	Archaic humans
MIDDLE PALEOLITHIC	200,000–40,000 y.a. Middle Stone Age	Scrapers and points	Sub-Saharan Africa, India	Archaic and early modern humans
	Mousterian	Scrapers, points and small bifaces	Europe, Near East	Neandertals and early modern humans
UPPER PALEOLITHIC	40,000–34,000 y.a. Chatelperronian	End-scrapers, points and burins	France, Spain	Neandertals
	40,000–28,000 y.a. Aurignacian	Bone points, blades, end-scrapers and burins	Europe, Near East	Modern humans
	28,000–22,000 y.a. Gravettian	End scrapers, burins and bone points, bone tools	Europe	
	21,000–19,000 y.a. Solutrean	Bifacial, leaf-shaped points	France, Spain	
	18,000–12,000 y.a. Magdalenian	Bone harpoons, burins and microliths	Europe	
	50,000–10,000 y.a. Late Stone Age	Scrapers and bone tools	Africa	

ABOVE AND RIGHT Archaeologists distinguish a number of paleolithic tool industries by the type of artifact and the methods by which the tools were made. Handaxes are the hallmark of the Acheulean industry, which lasted from 1.4 to 0.2 million years ago and is associated with several forms of *Homo* in Africa and Eurasia. Handaxes are rare in Central and Eastern Europe and East Asia, where heavy stone tools are represented by choppers and chopping tools. Their wide distribution, and study of microscopic wear on their edges, indicate that they were used in a variety of environments and for a multiplicity of functions – they have been described as the "Swiss Army knife" of the Paleolithic. Shown right is a Late Acheulean handax made c.250,000 years ago. After about 250,000 years ago the techniques of tool manufacture improved and tools became smaller and more standardized. Handaxes largely disappeared about this time. With the spread of modern humans c.50,000 years ago, stone tool-making became more diversified, and specialized implements were also made with bone, antler and mammoth ivory (see pages 28–29).

include a 400,000-year-old skull from Arago, France, which possesses some Neandertal traits, and a 350,000-year-old skull from Vértesszöllös, Hungary. The latter was found with deposits that contained concentrations of burned bone, thought to represent the earliest known hearth in Europe. The controlled use of fire was probably essential for the settlement of northern Eurasia; an occupation floor with an early hearth has also been excavated at Bilzingsleben, Germany (c.300,000 years ago). But by and large archaic humans were not technologically innovative. Their handaxes resemble those that were being made in Africa a million years before, although some improvement in production techniques took place after 250,000 years ago.

The inhabitants of these northern regions would probably have required a heavier meat diet because their caloric demands would have been higher; plant foods would also have been less readily available. Yet it is not clear if the initial expansion into northern Eurasia was accompanied by an increase in hunting. Large mammal bones from some sites show evidence of cut marks from stone tools, but they may have been caused by butchering scavenged carcasses. Tools and controlled fire were perhaps used to exploit frozen carcasses during the winter months, when they were less accessible to scavenging carnivores. Convincing evidence for widespread hunting of large mammals in northern Eurasia does not appear until after 250,000 years ago.

Changes in Africa

As in Europe, but unlike the archaic humans of the Asian tropics and subtropics, African species of the genus *Homo* experienced significant evolutionary change during this period. The most important development appears to have been a marked increase in brain size, evident in the large, steep-walled braincase seen in fossils from Elandsfontein (South Africa), Ndutu (Tanzania), and Broken Hill/Kabwe (Zambia) dating to between 500,000 and 200,000 years ago. While these skulls exhibit clear differences with those of contemporaneous hominid fossils in Eurasia, the stone handaxes and simple flake tools found in association with them do not indicate that any marked behavioral changes had taken place. However, it was almost certainly the African form of *Homo* that evolved into modern humans, *H. sapiens*, who begin to appear in the local fossil record after 200,000 years ago (see pages 28–29) ◆

The Neandertals

Named for the site in the Neander valley, northern Germany, where they were first identified in the 19th century, Neandertals were a form of archaic *Homo*. When modern humans spread from Africa into Eurasia about 100,000 years ago, Neandertals were living in Europe, central Asia, and the Near East. Recent genetic research suggests they were probably the descendants of an evolutionary branch of the genus *Homo*, divergent from our own, which gradually evolved into a specialized variant adapted to survival in northern environments.

Neandertals are known from hundreds of fossils found widely distributed across much of Europe in a band between Gibraltar in the south and Belgium in the north, extending as far east as southern Siberia and sometimes as far south as the Near East. They evolved gradually out of their archaic predecessors in Europe. The earliest fossils showing distinguishable Neandertal characteristics may perhaps be dated as early as c.300,000 years ago and they survived in the western part of their range until around 30,000 years ago.

The Neandertals' adaptation to cold temperatures is apparent in the shape of their bodies. They were not dissimilar in build to the modern indigenous peoples of the Arctic, possessing a stocky frame with shortened extremities and a large head. Typically, the face is projecting and the cheekbones receding, with exceptionally large front teeth. Though their brain was of comparable size to that of modern humans, it may have been organized differently. Their limb bones show evidence of powerful muscle attachments, implying they were used to carrying out tasks requiring great physical strength and endurance. A remarkably high number bear marks of injury and damage, a further indication that their lives were arduous and stressful. Few Neandertals lived beyond the age of 40.

Lack of technical skills

The Neandertals' reliance on biological adaptation to cope with the climatic challenges of their northern environments was not matched by corresponding technological advancement. For most of their period and across most of their range, Neandertals are found with Mousterian tools, which are also associated with early modern humans in the Near East, while the most recent Neandertals of western Europe are found with Chatelperronian tools. But while their stoneworking technology was comparable to that of modern humans, it generally reflected a less efficient use of raw material. Much more significant is the scarcity of non-stone technology, particularly when compared with the elaborate implements made by their successors. Without bone awls and needles, they would have been unable to sew animal furs and hides together to make clothing. It is noticeable that the front teeth of Neandertal skulls are frequently worn down to the roots. This amount of wear is unlikely to have come about simply from chewing tough foods, and it is reasonable to assume they used their teeth and jaws for grasping and stripping tasks.

Hunters or scavengers?

Throughout their range, Neandertals occupied caves and rockshelters, or camped in open-air settings, especially when the former were scarce. Their occupation sites are not as highly structured as those of modern humans, and traces of artificial shelters and insulated houses, even in the coldest regions, are rare or altogether absent. Their limited technology has led to speculation that the Neandertals were ineffective hunters, especially of larger, more dangerous mammals, and relied heavily on scavenging for meat and even on a diet high in plant foods. There is, however, mounting evidence to suggest that medium and large mammals were hunted on a regular basis. In view of their large bodies, cold environments, and lack of sewn clothing, their caloric requirements are likely to have been high, and would have been better met by a heavy meat diet.

La Ferra
Lez
Atapuerca
Douro
Lagar Velho
Tagus
Columbeira
Zafarraya
Gorham's
Cave

PRE-NEANDERTAL/
HOMO HEIDELBERGENSIS
(ARAGO)

NEANDERTAL
(LA FERRASSIE)

ANCESTRAL MODERN HUMAN/
HOMO SAPIENS
(BROKEN HILL)

EARLY MODERN HUMAN
(QAFZEH)

Denisova Cave ☐

Neander Valley

Biache
Spy Engis
Ochtendung
Houppeville Schulerloch Kulna Cave Šipka
du Rocher
Bockstein Predmosti
Ehringsdorf Sala Tata
r-Cure Velika Pecina Molodova
saire Krapina Ripiceni-Izvor
Moustier Ohaba-Ponor
La Chapelle-aux- Quinzano Staroselye Kiik-Koba
Saints Mezmaiskaya
uniquel La Masque Cave
Rigabe Dzhruchula
Bañolas Tsona Tsopi
Saccopastore Azykh Cave
Monte Circeo
Leuca Shanidar
Asprochaliko Bisitun

CARPATHIAN MTS

ALPS

CAUCASUS MTS

Black Sea

Caspian Sea

Aral Sea

Teshik Tash

Mediterranean Sea

Amrit
Yabrud
Tabun Amud
Kebara

Elbe Vistula Bug Don Syr Darya
Oder Dnieper Amu Darya
Rhine Danube Dniester
Po Sava Danube Volgograd
Tigris Euphrates

■ Neandertal burial site
☐ other site with Neandertal skeletal remains
■ site with tool assemblage or other evidence
☐ area of ice cap
☐ ancient coastline

0 _____ 800 km
0 _____ 600 mi

ABOVE Neandertals are found in a geographical range extending right across Europe to Siberia and into the Near East. The earliest fossils have all been identified in western Europe, where the climate, moderated by the influence of the Atlantic Ocean, would have been relatively mild: sites such as Atapuerca (Spain) and Biache (France) date to between 300,000 and 150,000 years ago. Traces of Neandertals in their eastern range, where conditions would have been colder and drier, probably date to the last 130,000 years. Isolated teeth from Denisova Cave represent the farthest known limit of the Neandertals' expansion into eastern Eurasia. They may have moved into the Near East as temperatures fell at the end of the Last Interglacial c.70,000 years ago, though it is possible they were already there.

Communication and behavior

We do not know how Neandertals communicated with each other, but examination of their anatomy throws doubt on their ability to express a full range of speech sounds. Moreover, it seems probable – given the scant evidence for art or ornamentation – that they did not make use of symbols, which is a critical element in the development of human language. Nevertheless, their lives do not appear to have been entirely devoid of ritual and belief. There is compelling evidence from many sites and regions that the Neandertals buried their dead. Less convincing, however, are reports that stone tools, bones and even (in the case of a site at Shanidar, Iraq) flowers were placed in burials as "grave goods": such objects could have been present accidentally.

The last Neandertals

As temperatures began to fall at the end of the Last Interglacial about 70,000 years ago, the Neandertals seem to have abandoned some of the coldest regions of central and eastern Europe. Neandertals did not disappear from western Europe until 30,000 years

ago, possibly later. By this time modern humans had spread throughout northern Eurasia, and may have been responsible for forcing them into extinction.

Some paleoanthropologists believe that the Neandertals contributed, at least to some degree, to the genetic heritage of the living peoples of western Eurasia. This view remains highly controversial. Although it was claimed that a 25,000-year-old male child skeleton (i.e. about 5,000 years after Neandertals are thought to have disappeared) found in a grave at Lagar Velho, Portugal in 1998, exhibited a mixture of Neandertal and modern human characteristics, not all paleoanthropologists believe this skeleton reflected interbreeding between the two forms. Mitochondrial DNA studies suggest that all living humans are part of a relatively homogeneous population that originated in Africa within the last few hundred thousand years. In 1997, genetic researchers extracted and decoded a mitochondrial DNA fragment for the original Neander valley specimen. Analysis revealed significant differences with the DNA from all living human populations, suggesting an ancient split between the two lineages, perhaps more than 500,000 years ago ◆

Spread of Modern Humans

Although it is now widely accepted that anatomically modern humans (*H. sapiens*) evolved in Africa and spread around the globe, the debate continues about the nature of that dispersal. Most paleoanthropologists believe that a spreading wave of modern humans replaced existing populations of archaic humans entirely. Some, however, argue that archaic and modern humans interbred, and that the genes of the former contribute to the genetic makeup of the living peoples of the earth. The process of dispersal was clearly complex, involving multiple movements of people and genes. A major behavioral transformation probably marked the birth of true language and other traits that distinguish modern humans from the rest of the animal kingdom.

Skulls from Omo (Ethiopia,) Laetoli (Tanzania), Border Cave and Klasies River Mouth (both South Africa), dating to between 150,000 and 100,000 y.a., are all those of recognizably modern humans (*H. sapiens*), albeit with some archaic traits. Recent studies in evolutionary genetics also support the view that Africa was the home of the original modern human population. Remains of modern humans similar to those from Africa have been discovered in caves at Qafzeh and Skhul (Israel). They have been dated to 100,000–90,000 y.a. and provide the earliest known evidence for the presence of modern humans outside Africa, but like the African fossils, they are associated with simple flake tools of the archaic stone tool traditions (see page 25).

A behavioral revolution

The wider dispersal of modern humans throughout Eurasia probably began about 60,000–50,000 y.a. This coincides with the period when fully developed linguistic and modern technological skills appear to have been developed – a behavioral revolution that, according to paleoanthropologists, represents the second phase in the development of modern humans, which was perhaps more critical than the first.

There is disagreement about when this happened. Some people believe the process began almost 100,000 years ago and took place gradually, while others argue for a later, more abrupt transformation. The earliest evidence is uncertain and open to doubt. Barbed bone spear points from Katanda (Republic of Congo), which may perhaps be dated to c.90,000 y.a., are suggestive of highly sophisticated technological skills. However, it is only after 50,000 y.a. that abundant examples of art and advanced technology begin to appear in the archaeological record.

Anatomical evidence for linguistic abilities in fossil humans remains ambiguous, and it is the appearance of ornaments, engravings, sculptures, and other forms of symbolism in the archaeological record that unmistakably confirms the presence of modern human language. It has been argued that grave goods may be present with the remains at Qafzeh and Skhul, but the oldest uncontested evidence of ritual behavior are ostrich eggshell beads dating to 46,000 y.a. from Enkapune ya Muto (Kenya).

ABOVE Klasies River Mouth cave, located on the coast of Western Cape Province in South Africa, contains skeletal remains of early modern humans (*Homo sapiens*) that date to more than 100,000 years ago. Associated artifacts reflect none of the behavioral changes that accompany the global spread of modern humans after 50,000 years ago.

RIGHT Although archaic humans, including Neandertals, sometimes buried their dead, they did so with little evidence of "grave goods" or other signs of ritual. By contrast, after 50,000 y.a. modern humans often sprinkled the grave with red ocher and placed personal ornaments on the body. Sometimes they also interred tools, weapons, or art objects with the deceased. This modern human burial in the Grimaldi Caves on the coast of northern Italy, contains red ocher and body ornaments of perforated shell and animal teeth.

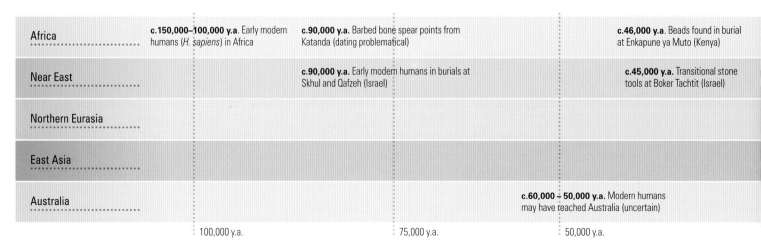

	100,000 y.a.	75,000 y.a.	50,000 y.a.
Africa	**c.150,000–100,000 y.a.** Early modern humans (*H. sapiens*) in Africa	**c.90,000 y.a.** Barbed bone spear points from Katanda (dating problematical)	**c.46,000 y.a.** Beads found in burial at Enkapune ya Muto (Kenya)
Near East		**c.90,000 y.a.** Early modern humans in burials at Skhul and Qafzeh (Israel)	**c.45,000 y.a.** Transitional stone tools at Boker Tachtit (Israel)
Northern Eurasia			
East Asia			
Australia			**c.60,000 – 50,000 y.a.** Modern humans may have reached Australia (uncertain)

Global colonization

The manipulation of symbols seems to be linked to fundamental improvements in technical abilities, and both undoubtedly played an important role in the global spread of modern humans after 50,000 y.a. They spread with remarkable speed, either wholly or largely replacing existing populations of archaic humans throughout most of Eurasia and entering Australia by at least 35,000 y.a. Their ability to invent new technology to cope with local environmental conditions was essential for successful global colonization. Only the extreme cold of northernmost Asia during the late Ice Age prevented their movement into North America (see pages 36–37).

The earliest known modern human sites in Southeast Asia are c.40,000 y.a. and sites are also widespread in Australia from this period. Evidence of human occupation as early as 60,000 y.a. has been claimed for some Australian sites (see pages 184–185). Recent research suggests that modern humans first entered southern Asia by way of the Horn of Africa over 50,000 y.a. To reach Australia (then a single landmass with New Guinea) they must have been capable of making short island-hopping sea voyages.

Modern humans did not move into northern Eurasia until roughly 40,000 y.a. Earliest occupation seems to have been in central and eastern Europe at sites such as Bacho Kiro (Bulgaria) and Kostenki (Russia). From here they apparently spread west displacing the local Neandertal population by about 30,000 y.a. – early modern human finds have been made at Willendorf (Austria), Vogelherd (Germany), Cro-Magnon (France) and Paviland (England). They had spread to southern Siberia by 40,000–35,000 y.a. Skeletal remains have physical features typical of populations derived from tropical regions, but evidence such as the manufacture of bone needles to sew clothing and the building of artificial shelters indicate that a number of survival techniques had been developed for living in colder regions. The earliest modern human sites in northern Eurasia also contain numerous examples of ritual burial and art ◆

40,000 y.a.	30,000 y.a.	25,000 y.a.	20,000 y.a.	15,000 y.a.
	c.27,500 y.a. Rock painting found at Apollo 11 Cave (Namibia)			
	c.30,000 y.a. Engraved art objects at Hayonim Caves (Israel)			
c.40,000–35,000 y.a. Modern humans present in Europe and southern Siberia	**c.30,000 y.a.** Cave art at Chauvet (France); portable art at Vogelherd (Germany)	**c.25,000 y.a.** Elaborate burials and art at Sungir' (Russia)		**c.15,000 y.a.** Cave paintings of animals and abstract signs from Altamira (Spain)
c.40,000 y.a. Modern human skull from Niah Cave (Borneo)	**c.29,000 y.a.** Modern human remains and tools at Badadomba lena Cave (Sri Lanka)			
c.40,000 y.a. Hafted ax found on Huon peninsula (New Guinea)		**c.26,000 y.a.** Ritual burial at Lake Mungo (New South Wales)		**c.13,000 y.a.** Largest known Ice Age cemetery at Kow Swamp (Victoria)

Specialized Hunters

Between approximately 30,000 and 10,000 years ago the Earth experienced the last major glacial period of the Ice Age. Modern humans occupied much of the Earth during this period, which is known as the Upper Paleolithic or Late Stone Age. Groups of nomadic hunter–gatherers inhabited a wide range of environments, from tropical forest, savanna, desert, and temperate woodland to frozen steppe. Unlike earlier forms of humankind, they adjusted to the particular demands of local environments primarily through cultural and technological modification, although limited physical adaptation eventually took place as well. The pattern of specialized hunting–gathering societies that is revealed in the paleoanthropological record created the basis for the linguistic, cultural, and racial diversity of the modern world.

FAR RIGHT The origins of modern humans in Africa c.150,000 y.a. and their dispersal throughout the Old World and into Australia c.50,000–35,000 y.a. probably caused the disappearance of archaic humans, including Neandertals. The dispersal of modern humans also led to the development of regional cultures after 35,000 y.a. Some 18,000 years ago, the Last Glacial was at its height, with maximum spread of ice sheets. Temperatures and sea level were at their lowest. These conditions were an added catalyst for the development of a diversity of specialized hunting techniques and survival strategies to cope with a diverse array of local environments, especially in northern Eurasia.

The last Ice Age reached its coldest maximum between 20,000 and 18,000 years ago. At this time glaciers covered the northern hemisphere as far as southern Britain. Throughout northern Eurasia, human populations developed strategies for survival in conditions of extreme cold that are without recent parallel. Limited plant resources and the high caloric demands of living at low temperatures encouraged the development of economies based heavily on the hunting of large mammals.

Conditions were harshest in the cold, dry, treeless plains of northern Eurasia (see box). Large grazing mammals such as mammoth, bison and horse were hunted for meat, and hare, arctic fox and other small mammals trapped for their pelts. Farther south, in the boreal forests of southern Siberia, there was abundant wood for building shelters and for fuel, and here the hunting economy was reliant on large herds of reindeer. Despite the remarkable success of their cold climate adaptations, humans were unable to survive in the most extreme Arctic environments. Occupation of much of Siberia probably ceased during the cold maximum and seems to have resumed after 18,000 years ago. Latitudes above 60°N may have been uninhabited until the climate began to warm after 14,000 y.a.

Environmental conditions were considerably milder in western Europe. All the same, mammals of the Arctic tundra such as reindeer ranged as far south as Spain and Italy. They were hunted for food, along with deer, ibex and horse.

New technologies

Considerable ingenuity was shown in the development of new technology to make specialized hunting weapons and implements. Petrological analysis of local toolkits shows that raw materials such as flint or obsidian were sometimes gathered across a very wide area. Tools such as harpoons, awls and needles for making skin clothing were also carved from antler, ivory and bone, often with intricate designs. Simple musical instruments were made by boring holes in hollow bird bones. The walls of cave-mouths and rockshelters, abundant in this part of Europe, were decorated with images of the animals that were so important in the lives of these Ice Age hunters (see pages 32–33).

Warm environments

Outside of the northern hemisphere the effects of glaciation were scarcely felt. Increased aridity and shrinkage of forests occurred in some parts of Africa and southern Asia, especially during the glacial maximum, but in other respects environmental conditions did not differ significantly from the present. Late Stone Age peoples were unable or unwilling to

---

Mezhirich: huts of mammoth bone

Mezhirich (Ukraine) provides a colorful example of how late Ice Age people adapted to one of the bleakest environments on Earth. About 15,000 years ago., when the maximum cold of the last major glacial period was only just receding and the area was a treeless steppe, hunters set up a campsite beside a tributary of the river Dnieper. They built at least four large houses ranging from 20–32 ft/6–10 m in diameter, constructed of several hundred mammoth bones and tusks arranged around a central hearth. It would have taken considerable effort to assemble so many bones, which were probably collected from local natural accumulations or "mammoth graveyards" at the mouths of streams and gullies. Around the houses, they dug large pits – probably down to the permafrost level – to provide cold storage for food and for mammal bones. These latter served as fuel in the absence of timber and had to be kept fresh to burn efficiently. Most of the remains of what they ate were probably consumed as fuel, but their diet is likely to have consisted mostly of hunted meat such as horse and bison. They almost certainly wore fur clothing similar to that of modern Arctic peoples. Despite their harsh life, the hunters of Mezhirich found time to create many ornaments, carvings, and other forms of art and adornment ◆

BELOW AN ARCHAEOLOGIST'S RECONSTRUCTION OF ONE OF THE MAMMOTH-BONE HOUSES.

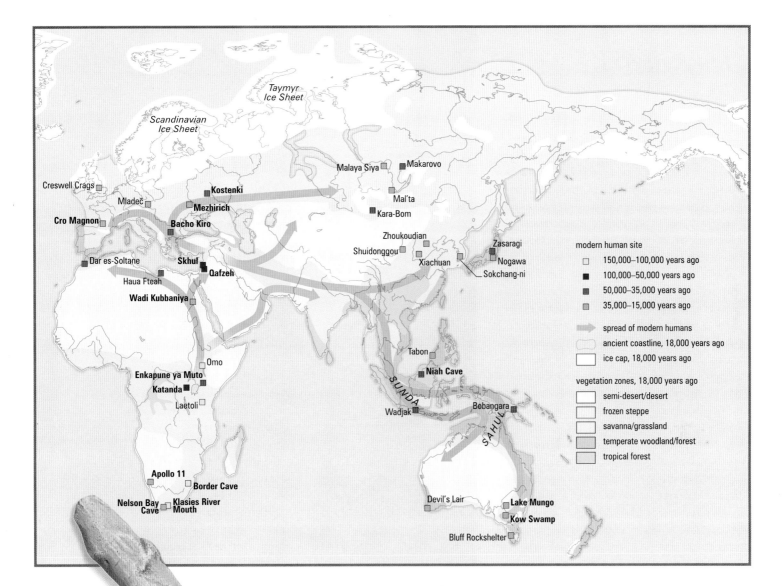

Taymyr Ice Sheet

Scandinavian Ice Sheet

Creswell Crags
Mladeč
Kostenki
Mezhirich
Cro Magnon
Bacho Kiro
Dar es-Soltane
Skhul
Qafzeh
Haua Fteah
Wadi Kubbaniya

Malaya Siya
Makarovo
Mal'ta
Kara-Bom
Zhoukoudian
Shuidonggou
Xiachuan
Zasaragi
Nogawa
Sokchang-ni

Omo
Enkapune ya Muto
Katanda
Laetoli

Tabon
Niah Cave
Bobangara
Wadjak

SUNDA
SAHUL

Apollo 11
Border Cave
Nelson Bay Cave
Klasies River Mouth

Devil's Lair
Lake Mungo
Kow Swamp

Bluff Rockshelter

modern human site
☐ 150,000–100,000 years ago
■ 100,000–50,000 years ago
▪ 50,000–35,000 years ago
▪ 35,000–15,000 years ago

➡ spread of modern humans
ancient coastline, 18,000 years ago
ice cap, 18,000 years ago

vegetation zones, 18,000 years ago
semi-desert/desert
frozen steppe
savanna/grassland
temperate woodland/forest
tropical forest

LEFT Bone and antler became increasingly common in tool and weapon manufacture during the Upper Paleolithic, probably in part because of the scarcity of hardwood during the Last Glacial. Carved implements often exhibit both functional and non-functional elements. These barbed points (6.7 in/ 17 cm and 5.5 in/14 cm in length) were probably used for harpooning river fish.

RIGHT An eyed bone needle, 2 in/5 cm long.

colonize extreme climatic areas like tropical rain forests and deserts, but many other environments contained more diversity of plant and animal life than today, offering wide opportunities for exploitation.

In the Near East and north Africa, hunter–gatherers were drawn to permanent water sources in valleys and oases. Archaeological investigation of a site at Wadi Kubbaniya on the river Nile has found evidence for intensive harvesting of wild plants, which were prepared for food on grinding stones. Freshwater fish were also a dietary staple of the Late Stone Age. In southern Africa, people living at coastal sites like Nelson Bay Cave exploited marine resources such as seal and shellfish. Similar hunting and gathering adaptations to local environments are evident from sites across southern Asia and Australia. For example, at Lake Mungo in southeastern Australia (see page 185), people hunted wallabies, wombats, and frogs and gathered large numbers of perch from the lake, probably with nets. Although expressions of art and symbolism are less common at this time than in northern latitudes, painted rock slabs dating to 27,500 years ago have been discovered in Namibia and rock art in Australia goes back to at least 20,000 years ago ◆

Ice Age Art

Objects that appear to have non-functional markings or shapes, and may therefore be termed art, are known from Neandertal times and even earlier, but it was during the period of the last Ice Age, from about 37,000–11,000 years ago, that art became fully developed. The modern humans of the Upper Paleolithic carved stone, bone and ivory and decorated their environment with marked designs. Their art is found in every continent, but the best studied and most abundant examples are from Eurasia.

To modern eyes, the most dramatic and attractive examples of Ice Age art are the powerful images of animals and humans that decorate caves across Europe from Gibraltar to the Urals, but are most numerous in northwestern Spain and southern France. The art first came to notice in the late 19th century, when one of the earliest, and most notable, discoveries of cave paintings was made at Altamira in northern Spain in 1879. Since then, a total of about 300 decorated caves and shelters have been discovered, and even today at least one new example turns up every year. Open-air engravings of similar Paleolithic style have also been found in Portugal, Spain and France. Much Ice Age art is in portable form – mostly carvings of stone, antler and ivory, and engravings on stone, bone and antler. Such items are found from North Africa to Siberia, but with particular concentrations in northwestern Spain, southwest France, and European Russia.

A variety of techniques

Most cave art is in the form of engraving or simple outline drawing; other techniques such as bichrome and polychrome painting, relief sculptures and clay modeling are rarer. Any sharp flint was used for engraving, while pigment was applied to the rock with fingers, pads, crayons or brushes. Sometimes stencils of hands or small animal figures were made by spitting or spraying pigment onto the rock. Some art was "public", on open view in cave mouths, but some was clearly private, hidden away in dark nooks and crannies.

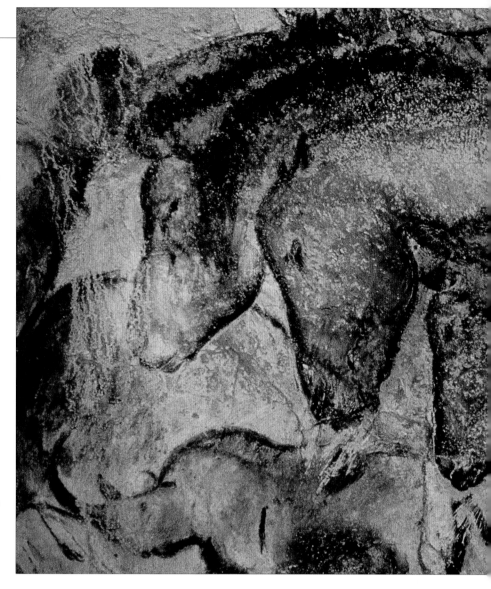

ABOVE Some of the paintings in France's Grotte Chauvet have produced radiocarbon dates of more than 30,000 years ago, but their enormous sophistication has caused some specialists to doubt the validity of these results and to assign the images to a later phase of the Ice Age.

RIGHT "Bison licking its flank", a carving in reindeer antler from La Madeleine, France, 4 in/10.5 cm long. Ice Age portable art comprises innumerable beautifully observed images of this kind, many of them dating, like this one, to the Magdalenian period (17,000–11,000 y.a.).

Excavation in a few caves such as Tito Bustillo (northern Spain) has found the actual pigments used to make the paintings, and experimental recreations of some panels suggest that much of the art was probably produced in a short time by extremely accomplished artists. Analyses of paint samples from the French Pyrenees suggest there were several distinct recipes for mixing pigments with mineral extenders. Iron oxide was the base for red paint, while recent work has shown that most black is charcoal (not manganese dioxide as once thought). The presence of charcoal has made it possible to obtain direct radiocarbon dates from images in twelve caves so far. Most have more or less confirmed the ages given for the paintings on the traditional basis of style. However, animal figures from Chauvet (France), whose age had been estimated at 20,000–15,000 years old on the basis of style, shading, animation and use of perspective, may be more than 30,000 years old. This finding, together with equally sophisticated ivory

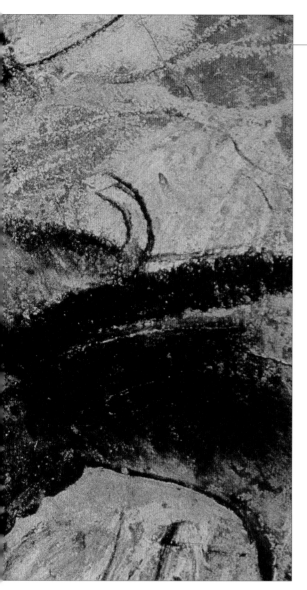

into the depictions in sophisticated ways. There is also a huge corpus of apparently non-figurative or abstract motifs, known as "signs". These range from simple and ubiquitous dots and lines to complex designs that are so highly localized in space and time they are thought to be ethnic markers.

There are distinct variations in quantity and technique – for example, some sites have only a few items of portable art or parietal (wall) figures, while others contain many hundreds. No examples of work in clay have yet been found outside the French Pyrenees, while bas-relief sculpture is limited to other parts of France such as the Périgord. And whereas clay figures are found (or have only survived) inside the dark depths of caves, sculptures are always in rock shelters or the front, illuminated parts of caves.

Moreover, studies of a number of caves have shown their "decorative program" – different areas were often selected for either engraving or painting, with some areas apparently being more important than others, or at least having a different value. The decoration is far from random. Sometimes the cave's acoustics seem to have been involved. Investigation in several caves has revealed a frequent correlation between the locations of decorations and the areas of best resonance for men's voices. In view of the obvious intelligence of the artists, it is clear that they not only took full advantage of the morphology of caves and of particular rock-shapes, probably manipulating lamp- and torch-flames to make images appear to move or to appear and disappear – they also used any acoustic peculiarities to the full.

What did the art mean?

It is impossible for us today to know much about the meaning of Ice Age art, and all explanations probably contain some degree of truth. It is important to realize that each interpretation reflects the spirit of the times in which it was made. At the beginning of the 20th century, simple ethnographic explanations concerning hunting and fertility magic were in favor; then came the binary sexual mythograms of French structuralism. With the Space Age came a focus on astronomical notation, with the Computer Age an emphasis on the cave as a coded repository of information, and with drugs and the New Age a return to simplistic notions of shamanism and hallucinatory experiences. But Ice Age art encompasses a vast array of techniques and forms, from beads to statuettes, from dots to polychrome animals, from cave depths to open-air rocks, and it endures over a huge timespan of at least 35,000 years (and probably far more). Self-evidently, no single explanation can suffice to explain its enormous ramifications. It is virtually certain, nevertheless, that the thought-processes behind much of Ice Age art were highly complex and sophisticated ◆

figurines from Vogelherd (southwest Germany), estimated to be more than 32,000 years old, indicates that Ice Age art did not, as many previously believed, simply progress steadily from crude, archaic fumblings to the masterpieces of Lascaux and Altamira, but had many beginnings and flourishings, and probably had far more ancient roots.

Themes and enigmas

Most of the art represents animals, though some depictions of human figures are known – particularly in engravings on stone slabs at La Marche (France), and in more than 100 figurines, primarily of women (the so-called "Venuses"), that are found from southwest France to Siberia. Horses and bovids (bison or wild cattle) are the most commonly displayed animals, followed by deer and ibex. Birds and fish are more common in portable art than in cave art and carnivores are generally rare – though large or dangerous animals such as big cats, bears, rhinos and mammoths, seem to be a feature of early art. At all periods, the animals – almost always adult – are shown in profile; there are few scenes, no background scenery or vegetation, and no groundlines. Bulges, cracks and reliefs in the cave wall are frequently incorporated

BELOW Engraved "bullroarer" with geometric motifs and covered with red ocher, from La Roche at Lalinde (Dordogne, France), 7 in/18 cm long and 1.5 in/4 cm wide. This type of instrument makes a loud humming noise when whirled around on a string. Ice Age people also had bone "flutes" at their disposal, as well as "lithophones", for which they struck stalactites in caves to produce sounds.

After the Ice

The retreat of the Scandinavian and North American ice sheets after c.18,000 years ago triggered many environmental changes, which in turn led to new opportunities for humans. As the periglacial tundra and permafrost withdrew from southern Europe, so did the migratory herds of reindeer that grazed these habitats. Small groups of hunters who had developed specialized economies based on the trapping, killing and utilization of these animals naturally moved with them as they followed the retreating tundra north and east into Siberia. Crossing by the wide Beringian land bridge, the first bands of hunter–gatherers entered Alaska to begin human settlement of the New World, the last great uninhabited land mass on Earth.

The retreating glaciers left long "tunnel valleys" across the landscapes of northern Europe, formed by the meltwater that ran under the ice. These acted as pathways along which the herds of reindeer traveled. Reindeer-hunting groups discovered that when the enormous numbers of migrating animals were funneled through these valleys, there were rich opportunities for hunting. At several Late Paleolithic sites in the Hamburg region of northern Germany, excavations have uncovered thick layers of reindeer bones, the result of large seasonal kills.

The nearby Baltic Sea was a freshwater lake at this time, while the southern part of the North Sea was a vast marshland connecting the southern half of Britain to the rest of Europe. People were able to move freely between the two. Recent dating of an antler point dredged up from the bed of the North Sea by the crew of the trawler *Colinda* in 1931 places it at nearly 12,000 years old.

Wooded habitats

As the land warmed, shrubs and trees such as dwarf birch began to colonize the boggy wastes left by the melting permafrost. Forest-dwelling deer and wild cattle replaced the reindeer herds. Temperatures did not rise steadily, however, and a few cold snaps resulted in the temporary re-establishment of periglacial conditions; but by about 10,000 years ago, the environment of northern Europe more closely resembled that of today than it did 5,000 years earlier.

Farther south, the warming of the climate was also felt. After about 18,000 years ago, people living along the Mediterranean coast and in the Near East began to use many different sorts of food resources instead of relying on a limited selection of game. In particular, foraging peoples in the Levant (Palestine and Syria) began to rely very heavily on harvesting wild wheat and barley (see page 56). They also hunted gazelle in great numbers, ambushing them along their migration routes in much the same way as the northern reindeer-hunters made their great kills.

The crossing of Beringia

Throughout the later Ice Age, as the climate warmed, groups of hunters moved steadily across the great treeless steppes of Siberia in pursuit of enormous herds of tundra-grazing musk ox and reindeer, and of groups of mammoths. Their journeys took them inexorably eastward. This was the first time that conditions had allowed humans to penetrate so deeply into northern Eurasia. From there, they reached Beringia, the great land bridge approximately 995 mi/1600 km wide (now submerged beneath the Chukchi and Bering Seas and the Bering Strait) that was an extension of the Eurasian steppe into Alaska before the melting of the ice sheets unlocked great quantities of water to raise sea levels and separate the continents.

The approximate date of the first crossing of Beringia and the earliest settlement of North America

RIGHT AND BELOW A stone bola, chopper and points from Monte Verde II in southern Chile, c.12,500 years old. As well as stone tools, this waterlogged site has yielded well-preserved artifacts of wood, fiber, bone and skin, together with the foundation timbers of several domestic structures. Monte Verde I, nearby, may be much older.

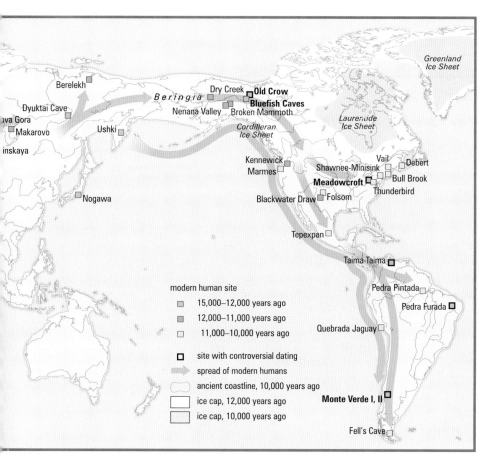

ABOVE The question of how and when the first humans entered North America is much debated. The most widely accepted view is that a passage was found through the ice sheets into the interior about 13,000 years ago, but an alternative, highly speculative account proposes that people traveled down the west coast of the continent in small watercraft prior to the melting of the continental ice sheets.

remains highly problematical. Early dates of 30,000–25,000 years ago ascribed to bone artifacts from a site at Old Crow in the Yukon Territory of northwest Canada do not now have general acceptance, and the best evidence currently available suggests that the earliest settlement sites at the North American end of the Beringian land bridge are the Bluefish Caves, also in Yukon Territory, dated to c.13,000 years ago.

At this time, most of Alaska and the Yukon valley of northwest Canada was unglaciated, but ice sheets

still covered almost all of Canada. In order for humans to travel farther south into the North American interior, it was necessary for them to find a passage free of glacial ice between the Cordilleran ice sheet in the west and the Laurentide in the east. It was traditionally supposed that the ice sheets did not begin to contract sufficiently for a corridor to open up between them until c.13,000 years ago. However, some sites south of the ice, like Meadowcroft Rockshelter in Pennsylvania (see box), have produced earlier settlement dates than the best-attested Yukon sites, possibly as early as 17,000 years ago. Dates of c.33,000 years ago have been claimed for open air sites at Pedra Furada (Brazil) and Monte Verde I (Chile). These findings make the timing of the initial colonization of the New World a matter of considerable debate, and until more gaps are filled in the archaeological record, the issue remains undecided.

The earliest Americans

There is little question, however, that as soon as they could do so, groups of hunters moved rapidly through the landscape and by c.11,500 years ago had spread to all parts of North and South America. They followed the large herd animals onto the Great Plains, where they found an environment rich in exploitable resources. Recent research indicates that the first Americans, far from being the big game hunters traditionally depicted, made use of a wide variety of animals and plant food resources. While it was formerly argued that Paleoindian groups played a major role in the extinction of large Ice Age mammals like mastodon and mammoth, it now seems more likely that these animals were already having difficulty adjusting to the warmer, more seasonal climate of the Holocene, and that human predation simply accelerated their demise ◆

Meadowcroft: an early occupation

Meadowcroft is a rockshelter located about 30 mi/48 km south of Pittsburgh, Pennsylvania. Its deep deposits contain 11 major layers, and radiocarbon dates indicated that the site was occupied intermittently from at least 14,000 (and perhaps even 17,000) years ago until about 250 years ago. The principal excavator of Meadowcroft, James M. Adovasio, has argued that the early dates from the lowest layers are evidence that colonization of the New World south of the northern ice sheets occurred earlier than many archaeologists

had thought. The suggestion by some critics that the charcoal samples used for dating were contaminated by older carbon is vigorously disputed by the excavators. Despite this controversy, Meadowcroft has provided important evidence on early stone tool manufacture and on changes in prehistoric vegetation, climate and diet. The stone tools, which consist largely of small blades, do not resemble the fluted blades commonly associated with the early big-game hunters of North America. On the basis of its animal bones and plant remains, Meadowcroft is interpreted as a seasonal shelter used by small groups of foragers who exploited the varied resources of the nearby valleys ◆

ABOVE MEADOWCROFT ROCKSHELTER HAS THE LONGEST HISTORY OF OCCUPATION IN THE NEW WORLD.

Part Two

POSTGLACIAL REVOLUTIONS

*A scene from the "Standard of Ur",
depicting sheep and cattle being led to a banquet*

The Beginnings of Agriculture

The great prehistorian V. Gordon Childe's description of the beginnings of agriculture as the "neolithic revolution" reflects its fundamental importance in human history. For hundreds of thousands of years, humans and their hominid ancestors had gathered edible wild plants, hunted wild animals (or scavenged the prey of other predators), and exploited marine resources. Foragers were generally nomadic, traveling from place to place to take advantage of the seasonal foods available in different areas. In most environments, a small forager group would need to utilize a large range to obtain sufficient resources to feed all its members, and population growth was restricted to levels that the land could sustain. Moreover, being mobile meant that property was limited to what could be carried. Crop cultivation tied people to their fields and to their stores of food, built up to tide them over the lean months and to provide grain for the next season's sowing. Permanent villages developed, and as people became settled they formed larger and denser communities; these settled groups amassed more possessions, including non-portable property. As farmers and herders increasingly manipulated the natural world to their advantage, the "neolithic revolution" transformed the relationship between human beings and the natural world.

The advantages of farming now seem obvious to us, but agricultural food production also has severe drawbacks. People in farming societies have to work far harder than those in a foraging economy: sowing, harvesting, winnowing and grinding cereals make heavy physical demands. Moreover, farmers are at the mercy of nature: if drought or flood destroys their crops they go short of food. Skeletal analysis shows that many early farmers had poorer diets than forager groups who could move elsewhere if food resources dried up.

Origins of food production

Such distinct disadvantages suggest that people did not simply begin to farm once they understood the principles of plant and animal reproduction. It is more likely that forager groups turned to growing their own food only when forced to do so. There is considerable debate and uncertainty among prehistorians about what circumstances brought about this transformation. Many theories turn on the idea that a combination of climate change and population growth forced foragers worldwide to start farming in order to maintain or expand their food supply. Plausible though this notion is, the circumstances, development, and outcomes of early cultivation around the world are so varied that no single nexus of causes seems universally applicable.

Farming began independently in several parts of the world at different stages of prehistory, as different collections of plants first came under cultivation and then became domesticated (genetically altered in ways that made them easier to harvest and increased their yield). Many early domesticates remain familiar and important foods in the modern world, while others are almost forgotten. A partial list of regions and species indicates the diversity of early food production: wheat, barley and legumes, along with sheep, pigs and cattle in the Near East; maize, beans and squash in Mexico; rice, millet

LEFT This Neolithic pottery statuette, found at a site in Hungary and dating from the 4th–3rd millennium BCE, hints at the central role that agriculture played in early communities. The male figure is thought to portray a deity, who carries over his right shoulder a sickle for harvesting grain. After emerging in the Near East in around 8500 BCE, farming first spread into eastern Europe during the 6th millennium BCE. By the time this idol was made, food production was established across much of the continent, with cereals such as oats and rye being widely grown.

Africa

Near East

c.13,000–10,500 y.a. Manipulation of wild wheat, barley and lentils produces domesticated varieties

Europe

Asia

Americas

c.10,000 y.a. Farm of squash in Mexic

11,000 y.a.

10,000 y.a.

permanent villages and by 8500 BCE some of these sedentary groups had become cultivators, keeping some grain back to sow for next year's harvest. The process of bringing about genetic change in these plants to produce domesticated strains took another two thousand years or so. Other wild plants like pulses (lentils, chickpeas and so on) underwent parallel transformations. The main impetus of domestication was to produce crops that could be easily harvested rather than to increase productivity.

In Mexico, farming developed very differently. Mobile foraging to take advantage of seasonal wild foods continued well beyond the end of the Ice Age and at this stage the wild ancestors of the plants that would later become important crops did not greatly figure in people's diets. However, about 7,000 years ago a few spontaneous genetic mutations seem to have occurred in one insignificant food plant, teosinte, to produce a primitive and very small form of maize (corn). This made it more attractive to local foragers, who began to incorporate it into the seasonal repertoire of wild plants. The earliest known corn cob in Mexico dates from 3600 BCE, but even after it had made its appearance as a cultivated crop, it still played only a subsidiary role in the human diet. Foragers were to maintain their strategy of seasonal mobility for many centuries more until farming became productive enough to persuade them to adopt a sedentary lifestyle and settle in villages.

It is most likely that each case of early domestication, wherever it occurred in the world, represented a historically unique combination of several important factors – climatic change, the availability and type of plant and animal species, the scheduling of seasonal foraging activities, and so forth – the precise nature of which depended on local circumstances. Yet for all its diversity of origin, the end result of food production was broadly similar wherever it occurred – a rise in population levels and the formation of permanent settlements. From these beginnings were to emerge all the subsequent social and political developments that have fashioned the world we know today ◆

ABOVE The domestication of animals probably began before the first systematic attempts at crop cultivation. After dogs were domesticated for hunting – as early as 10,000 BCE – livestock such as pigs, sheep, goats, and cattle were developed as early domesticates in India, the Near East, and north Africa between the 8th and the 2nd millennia BCE. This Saharan rock painting from Jabbaren, on the borders of present-day Libya and Algeria, possibly dates from this period. It indicates in remarkable detail a well-established culture of animal husbandry. Herders are depicted driving two different types of domesticated cattle.

and pigs in China; potato and quinoa along with llama, alpaca and guinea pigs in Peru; sorghum, tef, finger millet and yams in sub-Saharan Africa; yams and taro in New Guinea; sunflower, goosefoot and marsh-elder in North America.

Different routes to farming

There was no single common factor, or combination of factors, that led to the adoption of farming in all parts of the world. The course of events in the Near East, for example, differed fundamentally from that in Mexico. In the Near East, climatic changes at the end of the Ice Age produced moister conditions that encouraged the dense growth of wild cereals. Foraging groups gathered this natural harvest each year and learned to store the wild grain. They began to live in

	c.8,000 y.a. Cattle herding begins in Sahara		**c.6,500 y.a.** Farming of wheat and barley in Nile Valley	**c.5,500 y.a.** Cultivation of sorghum, millet and tef may have begun (well established by 3,500 y.a.)	
c.10,500–9,000 y.a. Management of wild sheep and pig herds leading to domestication		**c.7,000 y.a.** Canals used for irrigation in Mesopotamia			
c.9,000 y.a. Wheat, barley, cattle, sheep and pigs in Balkans		**c.7,000 y.a.** Farming spreads to central Europe	**c.6,300 y.a.** Farming reaches Britain		
c9,000 y.a. Millet farming in north China	**c.8,500 y.a.** Rice farming begins in south China	**c.8,000 y.a.** Farming and domestication of animals in Indus valley		**c.6.000 y.a.** Yams and taro cultivated in New Guinea (spreads to insular SE Asia by 4,500 y.a.)	
			c.5,600 y.a. Farming of maize and beans in Mexico	**c.5,000–4,500 y.a.** Quinoa and potatoes in Andes; sunflower, goosefoot and marsh-elder in North America	
9,000 y.a.	8,000 y.a.	7,000 y.a.	6,000 y.a.	5,000 y.a.	4,000 y.a.

Pyrotechnology: Kiln and Forge

The ability to build very hot fires was the springboard for two major technological advances in human prehistory – pottery making and metallurgy. The chipping of stone and the shaping of wood, bone and antler to make tools modifies the shape but does not alter the constituent nature of the raw material: stone is still stone, bone still bone. The application of intense heat to clay and metal ores causes chemical changes that permanently alter their structures: they cannot be returned to their original state. The use of heat in this way is known as "pyrotechnology".

Pyrotechnology had far-reaching consequences for humankind. The ability to make durable containers of fired clay, which would not be returned to earth again when dampened and which protected their contents from external moisture and vermin attack, permitted the long-term storage and transportation of liquids and grains. Metal ores, when subjected to heat, can be shaped and molded into artifacts, or alloyed with other metals to obtain new materials that do not exist in nature. Alloying copper (the first commonly used metal) with tin, for example, produces bronze, a much stronger material.

Beginnings of pottery

The deliberate heating of clay can be traced back almost 30,000 years. Pieces of fired clay, from sites in Moravia, Czech Republic, some of which appear to be figurines, are clearly not the accidental result of having been placed in or close to a fire. The first utilitarian use of fired clay are Jomon pottery vessels made in Japan and the East Asian mainland about 12,000 years ago. Over the next several millennia, ceramic skills developed independently in the Near East, Africa, Europe, and America, for storage containers and cooking pots. Since pottery is heavy and breaks easily, it is not very useful for mobile societies. Consequently, some degree of sedentism is usually

necessary for the manufacture of ceramic vessels.

The pliable nature of clay before it is fired, and the different techniques used in firing it, lend themselves readily to artistic expression. Numerous decorative methods emerged, ranging from incising and stamping to painting and burnishing, and vessel forms took on distinctive shapes. Different societies maintained their own methods of pottery manufacture and ornamentation, on the basis of which prehistorians identify distinct ceramic "cultures", though it is unlikely that the boundaries between style areas corresponded to actual group boundaries.

From copper to bronze

For metallurgy to develop, metals had first to be identified, either in their pure (or "native") state, or in ores. Native metals were the first to be worked in many areas, copper being the most common. But advancing to the next step, smelting metals from their ores, requires very high temperatures to be reached: the

RIGHT Ancient Egyptian goldsmiths are shown working on a variety of different artifacts in this wall painting (c.1300 BCE). The development of metallurgy created opportunities for elites to sponsor specialized workshops for the working of copper, bronze and gold. Craftsmen in these workshops produced objects that reflected the status and prestige of their patrons. Gold-working in Egypt reached high levels of accomplishment, as is shown by the wealth of spectacular objects discovered in tombs like that of Tutankhamun.

BELOW Some of the world's earliest examples of pottery come from the first settled farming communities of the Near East. This painted bowl was found at the site of Tell Abr in Syria, and is dated to around 4500 BCE.

Africa		c.9,500–8,500 y.a. Early pottery making in North Africa		
Near East		c.9,000–7,500 y.a. Pottery comes into use; earliest use of copper at Çatal Höyük (Anatolia)		
Europe		c.9,000–7,500 y.a. Pottery spreads to southeastern Europe	c.7,500– 6,500 y.a. Copper-working begins in the Balkans	
Asia	c.12,000 y.a. First pottery made by Jomon hunter–gatherers		c.8,000 y.a. Pottery at Mehrgarh (Pakistan)	
Americas			c.7,500–6,500 y.a. Ceramics present in the Amazon valley	
	10,000 y.a.	9,000 y.a.	8,000 y.a.	7,000 y.a.

melting point of copper is 1083°C. Smelting was thus a direct progression from the high-temperature kilns developed by skilled potters. In many parts of the Old World and in Andean South America, indigenous traditions of metal-working arose at different times once it became possible to heat kilns to the melting point of copper. Conversely, although the use of native copper was well developed around Lake Superior (North America) it never progressed further because the peoples in that region lacked pottery making expertise.

As copper is very soft, its most common early use was for ornaments, such as beads and pendants. Copper ores frequently contain impurities such as arsenic, and the smelting of such ore would have resulted in a stronger material than pure copper. The deliberate alloying of copper with another metal, most commonly tin, produces a yet harder material, bronze. Copper and tin ores do not occur together naturally, so bronze smelting was a major innovation, requiring knowledge of those metals' properties, as well as exchange networks to obtain supplies of each ore from separate locations.

BELOW As bronze is stronger and less brittle than copper it can be used for hard-wearing implements like swords, axes, spearheads and buckets. When melted, it flows more freely than copper, making it easier to cast in a variety of shapes, either in an open mold (as with this ax head from Thailand), or by the lost wax method. In this, a wax model is encased in clay and baked; the molten wax is then tipped away and liquid metal poured into the cavity.

Iron and gold

From earliest times, lumps of meteoric iron could be chipped and hammered into crude implements, but it was not until the 2nd millennium BCE that techniques for melting iron from ores were developed in Anatolia, thanks to the metal's high melting point. Iron soon proved itself superior to bronze for making everyday tools, although bronze was preferred for ornamental goods. Sub-Saharan Africa did not have a distinct period of bronze use before iron-working developed there in the 1st millennium BCE. Iron was unknown in Precolumbian America.

Gold, silver and lead were all important metals in antiquity, but gold has attracted most attention from archaeologists and has seized the imagination of the public because of its value today and its presence in spectacular tombs such as those of Tutankhamun, Mycenae, or Sipán (Peru). In northern Europe in later prehistory, gold was made into exquisite bracelets and neck-rings, many of which have been found in tombs and hoards. The Scythians of southern Russia were highly skilled at crafting gold and silver. In the New World, gold-working was most advanced in Central and northern South America, where techniques such as lost-wax casting were used ◆

			c.3,500 y.a. Bronze-working in Egypt	c.3,000–2,000 y.a. Iron in use in sub-Saharan Africa	
c.6,500 y.a. Complex metal casting in southern Levant	c.5,500 –4,500 y.a. Bronze comes into use		c.3,500 – 3,000 y.a. Iron-working emerges in Anatolia		
c.6,500–5,500 y.a. Ertebølle foragers (Denmark) adopt pottery	c.5,000 y.a. Gold in use at Varna (Bulgaria)	c.4,500–4,000 y.a. Bronze comes into use	c.3,000 –2,000 y.a. Iron is widely used		
	c.4,000 y.a. Bronze-working at Erlitou (China)	c.3,500 y.a. Bronze-working in Southeast Asia(Thailand)	c.2,500 y.a. Iron comes slowly into use in China		
c.6,500–5,500 y.a. Ceramics present in northern Colombia	c.5,500–4,000 y.a. Ceramics present on Ecuador coast and Panama	c.4,000–3,500 y.a. Ceramics in use in eastern North America and Mesoamerica	c.2,000–1,000 y.a. Copper and gold in Peru; copper in North America		
6,000 y.a.	5,000 y.a.	4,000 y.a.	3,000 y.a.	2,000 y.a.	1,000 y.a.

Further Advances in Farming

The domestication of animals represented a gradual major shift in perspective on the part of early agriculturalists. For hunting societies, animals were useful only when they were dead and could be exploited for their meat, hides, bones and antlers, and for several millennia after sheep, goats and cattle were first domesticated they continued to be kept for these uses alone. The realization that live animals were sources of valuable "secondary products" developed slowly, but the result of this transformation was to change the human economies in a dramatic way.

The placing of herds of domesticated herbivores under human control had the effect of ensuring that meat-providing animals could be bred for size and tameness and slaughtered at an optimal weight without the bother of hunting. This was a valuable resource, but while there were undoubted advantages to having supplies of docile animals close to hand, considerable effort had to be expended in tending domesticated herds and moving them to new pastures, and at this stage there was probably little to choose between hunting and herding in terms of output of energy. Sheep, goats and cattle had been domesticated for about two or three thousand years before agriculturalists came to realize their full potential, while alive, as sources of useful, renewable products, namely milk, wool, and motive power. These are commonly known as "secondary products" to differentiate them from the animals' "primary" function as sources of meat and hides.

Development of dairying

It is extremely difficult to establish with any certainty when animals first began to be exploited for products other than their meat, but it is currently believed that cow's milk was being processed by farming communities in central Europe at least as early as 5000 BCE. Archaeologists reached this conclusion after finding

ABOVE A Bronze Age petroglyph from Bohuslän province in southern Sweden depicts a plowman driving a team of oxen. The earliest representations of ox-drawn plows date from the 4th millennium BCE. These rudimentary implements could at first do little more than loosen the soil, but as technology improved over time with the invention of the wheel and the introduction of iron plowshares, so plowing grew in efficiency. Depending on the heaviness of the soil, early farmers yoked teams of two, four, or even eight oxen to their plows; the horse was not used for agricultural work until much later, in the medieval period. The use of animal traction for plowing increased crop yields and permitted the cultivation of soils which otherwise were not suitable for simple tillage.

a number of ceramic sieves, or perforated pottery vessels, that could not possibly have held liquid. The only plausible explanation of these artifacts was that they served as strainers for the separation of curds from whey in the manufacture of cheese. Until quite recently, similar ceramic sieves were used for this very purpose in many parts of the world .

Until this discovery, the general view among prehistorians was that the use of milk from livestock was a relatively late development. This view was premised on the fact that most human populations around the world are intolerant of the lactose in raw milk, which causes flatulence and diarrhea. Only over the last few millennia did the gene for lactose tolerance appear, and even then only in a limited number of populations. However, this interpretation ignored the possibility that early peoples might have used milk primarily for its by-products. Converting it into cheese mitigates the dietary problems associated with raw milk, and also yields a product that can be stored.

Once the idea of dairying in prehistoric times was established, it explained why early central European farmers apparently maintained such large herds of

	7,000 y.a.	6,000 y.a.	5,000 y.a.
Africa		**c. 5,800 y.a.** Donkeys used as pack animals in Nile region	
Near East		**c.6,000 y.a.** Onagers and donkeys used for traction and as pack animals	**c.5,000 y.a.** Dromedary camel used f traction in Arabia; horse-riding spread
Europe	**c.7,000 y.a.** Ceramic sieves suggest use of dairy products in central Europe	**c.6,200 y.a.** Use of cattle for pulling plows and wagons begins in central Europe	**c. 5,200 y.a.** Wool begins to replace plant fibers; horse-riding spreads
Asia		**c.6,000 y.a.** Horses domesticated on Eurasian steppes	**c. 5,000 y.a.** Chariots on steppes; oxe water buffalo as traction in South Asia
Americas		**c.5,600 y.a.** Llama and alpaca domesticated in Andes	

domestic cattle. Grazing cattle in forest clearings to the virtual exclusion of other livestock species would seem to have made little economic sense if they were only being kept for their meat.

Animal traction

A major use of animals is for their drawing power. Once again, it is hard to establish when this first generally occurred (there is evidence of reindeer being used to pull sleds in the far north of Europe before 5000 BCE), but archaeological records indicate that livestock were being harnessed to pull plows and wagons in much of temperate Europe shortly after 4000 BCE. The type of plow employed at this time, known as an "ard", was a simple device that broke the soil without turning it over. Archaeologists have discovered ard-marks, the scratches left by these implements, in soil surfaces preserved beneath funerary mounds in many parts of northern Europe. From a somewhat later period, many images of yoked oxen with plows appear on rock engravings in southern Scandinavia. Models of pairs of yoked oxen – for example, a famous draft team, made from copper, found at Bytyň (Poland) – also provide compelling evidence that animal traction was widely used.

The main advantage of plowing was that it enabled a farming household to increase the amount of land it had under cultivation without having to increase its labor force. Wagons, which are known from clay models such as the one from Budakalász (Hungary), would also have made farming more efficient. Wagons were not used for long-distance transport at this early date. Their primary use would have been within a short distance of the farmstead, to move crops, firewood, animal carcasses, and other bulky items. Later, in the 3rd millennium BCE, horses were used to pull chariots, which were invented on the Russian steppes and then spread to the Near East. Pack animals also came to be important as long-distance trade developed.

Clothing from wool

The existence of bone needles in the Pleistocene indicates that humans had long made garments by sewing animal fleeces or furs together. But the technology of spinning (drawing out and twisting together) fibers of wool taken from living sheep and goats and weaving the yarn thus produced into cloth appears comparatively late in the archaeological record. The disappearance of textile fragments of flax from Alpine lakeside sites during the 3rd millennium BCE coincides with the first appearance of wool cloth in the bogs of northern Europe, suggesting a widespread shift from plant to animal fibers across much of Europe at this period. Elsewhere in the Old World, the timing of this shift is uncertain, but by the 1st millennium BCE wool was in use throughout most of Eurasia.

Animals as wealth

This second phase in the domestication of herd animals, which gave them value while they were alive, must have had momentous impact on the organization of prehistoric society. Livestock would have come to be regarded as a form of capital, and a household with more animals would have been considerably wealthier than one with fewer. Given the reproductive rates of livestock and the potential of animal traction for increasing agricultural yields, the widespread use of secondary products would have resulted in the economic phenomenon of "increasing returns", whereby those who possess capital steadily accumulate more, thus widening the gap between themselves and the have-nots. Competition must always have existed among early farming households, but the ability to accumulate herds enabled some farmers to gain over their neighbors and even put them in their debt. In the natural balance of things, inequalities between households would have been short-lived. Having wealth in the form of animals permitted assets to be passed along to children, perpetuating inequalities across generations ◆

c.4,000 y.a. Chariots in use in Nile region; nomadic pastoralism in East Africa

c.2,200 y.a. Pastoralism reaches southern Africa; dromedary camel introduced to Sahara

c.4,200 y.a. Chariots in use

c.4,000 y.a. Chariots spread to eastern Europe

c.4,200 y.a. Horses introduced into South Asia; nomadic pastoralism develops on steppes

c.3,000 y.a. Nomadic pastoralism spreads to high plateaus of Central Asia

c.2,000 y.a. Water buffalo used for traction in Southeast Asia

c.3,800 y.a. Llamas used as pack animals in Andes; alpacas used for wool

4,000 y.a.

3,000 y.a.

2,000 y.a.

Early Cities and State Societies

Early cities are difficult to define in ways that apply uniformly around the world. The term "civilization" (which does not always find favor with archaeologists today) is sometimes used as a shorthand way of referring to the cultural milieu and social order of state societies. In this sense, cities are an integral part of complex, hierarchical societies in which certain institutions concentrate power. But just as the different early civilizations and state societies of the world varied widely in their organization and character, so too did the cities that went with them.

The simplest definition of a city is a place where relatively large numbers of people live in relatively high densities. But this raises immediate questions: how large, and relative to what? Archaeologists sometimes set a more or less arbitrary lower limit of 5,000 occupants for a settlement to be rated a city. But this crude way of reckoning means that many places that might on other criteria be classified as (large) villages or towns qualify as cities. Moreover, the application of an arbitrary definition point based on numbers alone might place many cities in one area but very few in another, although there may be sound intuitive reasons for concluding that both of them contained urban societies.

Another way of deciding whether or not a particular settlement is a city is to look at its relationship with other settlements within the wider landscape. A city may be held to be a place whose population cannot feed itself and so has to rely on supplies of food from villages in its hinterland. Cities are also places where economic factors are concentrated to such an extent that other settlements in the area must rely on them for access to many goods and services. In parallel with their economic density, cities also have a far greater concentration of religious and political activities than other neighboring population centers. In other words, the absolute size of a city is less important than its economic and political relationships with the settlements in the surrounding area: cities both dominate and depend on their hinterlands.

A third approach considers cities as centers of civilizations, places where social elites create and maintain "high culture" and sophisticated manners, the prime movers of the political life of states. In the end, though, most cities combine all three elements: large populations, economic and political centrality, and cultural dominance, but in ways and proportions that vary from civilization to civilization.

Different kinds of cities

In Sumer, in southern Mesopotamia, states and civilization were unthinkable apart from urban life. State and city arose together during the 4th millennium BCE and Warka (Uruk), the largest city of the region, held something like 80,000 people by 3000 BCE. Five hundred years later, around 80 percent of the regional population were city dwellers. Sumerian cities brought together the institutions and economic forces of state organization – palaces, temples, civic assemblies, scribal schools, artisans, and merchants – and acted quite literally as the containers of civilization, whose walls separated civilized people from barbarians. Broadly similar cities

BELOW An Egyptian papyrus manuscript from the Third Intermediate Period (c.1000 BCE) shows workers dragging a sled of building blocks under the supervision of an overseer. Many early states obliged their citizens to work directly for public institutions during part of the year (corvée labor), helping to maintain the irrigation works, roads and other improvements that supported communal life, as well as constructing the public monuments that still amaze us millennia later. Annual tax payments and compulsory military service might also be demanded, necessitating the creation of myriad layers of bureaucrats and accountants to keep track of these various contributions to public institutions.

	5,500 y.a.	5,000 y.a.	4,500 y.a.	4,000 y.a.
Africa	c.5,700 y.a. Towns developing in Egypt	c.5,000 y.a. State organization (Old Kingdom) in Egypt		
Near East	c.9,000 y.a. First villages and small towns appear	c.5,000 y.a. Cities and state institutions in southern Mesopotamia	c.4,300 y.a. Akkadian empire exerts influence over Near East – first imperial power	
Europe				c.4,000 y.a. Palace civilizations arise in the Aegean
Asia			c.4,600 y.a. Cities and state organization in Indus Valley	c.3,800 y.a. Cities and state organization in China
Americas				

ABOVE Teotihuacán, near the modern metropolis of Mexico City, was founded c.200 BCE. Massive monumental buildings and palaces were constructed, and the city expanded to cover some 8 sq mi/20 sq km. In its heyday, it was the main trading and cultural center of Mesoamerica.

enclosed vast areas of dispersed palaces and hovels, ditches and gardens. The great variety of city forms reflects the different cultural organizations of early states and civilizations around the world.

Urban societies

The emergence of cities created organizational and social problems that farming villages and small towns did not have to face. At the most basic level were questions of logistics: how was enough food to be moved from agricultural hinterlands to feed urban populations, and sufficient raw materials transported from source to satisfy the demand of urban craft workshops? Then there were problems of social cohesion. In villages, where everyone knows one another, a sense of communal responsibility and neighborliness can help to maintain the social balance and people can work together and iron out differences in customary ways. Larger towns erode this kind of solidarity. Without new rules of conduct and new organizations that bind people together, towns disintegrate all too easily into squabbling factions.

Early cities solved these problems through the presence of institutions that promoted economic integration and social harmony: temples and ritual specialists that reinforced communal identity or represented social hierarchy as part of the natural world-order, secular rulers backed by palace administrators, city and neighborhood assemblies, craft guilds and merchant associations, and so on. Such institutions are characteristic of all state societies, in which people belong to different economic classes and have different social status, pursue different occupations, and enjoy differing degrees of access to political or social power, but are still bound together by complicated webs of social and economic relations and of tradition and beliefs. Within the urban context, by linking families and wider interests together in various ways, sometimes by force of economic self-interest, at other times by bringing cultic or political authority to bear, they provided the economic channels and social glue that created and maintained cities ◆

appeared elsewhere in the world, as at Teotihuacán in Mexico. Here a huge urban population – as many as 200,000 inhabitants at the city's fullest height around 600 CE – lived in densely built residential districts around a well-defined ceremonial center.

Other early cities took different forms. The Maya of Central America, for instance, created very elaborate ritual political centers in a heavily built-up zone of dwellings for elite families, around which was a corona of less prestigious residences that extended for miles, interspersed with gardens and fields. Unlike Sumerian cities, Mayan cities had no formal boundaries, and incorporated agricultural land within the urban structure itself. The towns of early Egypt seem to have been a variation on this same theme. Hierakonpolis, a center of early state-formation in Egypt, was basically a cluster of village-sized settlements, some of which held seats of political authority, some concentrations of craft producers, and most communities of farmers. Chinese cities of the early Shang period (c.1700 BCE) represent still another approach to urban life, where massive walls

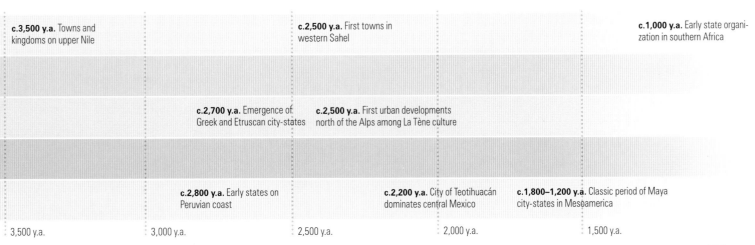

<table>
<tr><td>**c.3,500 y.a.** Towns and kingdoms on upper Nile</td><td></td><td>**c.2,500 y.a.** First towns in western Sahel</td><td></td><td>**c.1,000 y.a.** Early state organization in southern Africa</td></tr>
<tr><td></td><td>**c.2,700 y.a.** Emergence of Greek and Etruscan city-states</td><td>**c.2,500 y.a.** First urban developments north of the Alps among La Tène culture</td><td></td><td></td></tr>
<tr><td></td><td>**c.2,800 y.a.** Early states on Peruvian coast</td><td></td><td>**c.2,200 y.a.** City of Teotihuacán dominates central Mexico</td><td>**c.1,800–1,200 y.a.** Classic period of Maya city-states in Mesoamerica</td></tr>
<tr><td>3,500 y.a.</td><td>3,000 y.a.</td><td>2,500 y.a.</td><td>2,000 y.a.</td><td>1,500 y.a.</td></tr>
</table>

The Development of Writing

Human societies have used abstract symbols to represent meaning since the Upper Palaeolithic cave art of Europe. Signs scratched on pots and other artifacts are a common feature of many prehistoric cultures around the world. But while these marks may have conveyed specific facts about the maker, ownership or contents, they did not amount to a coherent system for recording meaning. Writing differs from such signs in its greater and more systematic scope, and especially in its ability to express complex meanings. The earliest writing systems are associated with complex societies in which the institutions of state government were beginning to take shape, such as Mesopotamia after 3500 BCE, or the Shang civilization of China around 1500 BCE. But the writing systems developed by early civilizations took very different forms and had their origins in quite different social contexts.

BELOW A clay tablet from Jemdet Nasr (Iraq), 4.3 in/ 11 cm high. It dates from around 3100 BCE and lists various commodities. The circular, crescent and D-shaped signs represent numbers. When the Sumerian pictographic system first developed, around 3300–3100 BCE, it employed more than 2,000 different symbols, often in complex combinations. Gradually the scribes developed the cuneiform system of writing by simplifying the signs so that they could be inscribed rapidly in wet clay using a reed stylus to make wedge-shaped marks (the Latin for wedge is *cuneus*, which gives the script its name). In developed cuneiform, word signs came to represent phonetic values, and the script was adapted successfully to other Near Eastern languages including Akkadian, Assyrian and Babylonian.

The earliest known examples of writing are found on clay tablets excavated at Warka (Uruk) in southern Mesopotamia dating to about 3300 BCE. The first institutions of state government were beginning to take shape among the agrarian-based cities of the region (see pages 60–61), and writing grew from a need to keep track of goods and to record official transactions. Earlier Neolithic societies of the Near East had long employed small clay objects (tokens) of different shapes and sizes – cones, disks, spheres, cylinders and so forth – as mnemonic devices to represent different quantities or commodities. These same communities also used carved stone stamp seals to impress clay tags with simple picture signs that probably denoted ownership. Around 3500 BCE, Mesopotamian accountants worked out a way of combining these two systems, by enclosing tokens in a hollow clay ball and marking the outside with impressions of both tokens and seals. These symbols thus combined a record of contents with proof of ownership. Soon, the tokens were eliminated and the ball flattened into a tablet, which was impressed with combinations of signs (for number) and pictographs to represent things (the head of a bull for cattle, an ear of barley for barley, a bowl for food) or action (a leg to mean to walk). It did not take long to create hundreds of symbols, and in order to organize them systematically, scribes created thematic lists (professions, place names, plants and animals, and so forth). With the addition of syllable signs, scribes were able to express the grammar of human speech, so that by 2500 BCE the Mesopotamian writing system was able to narrate stories and record affairs of state.

Ritual and politics

The early development of writing in Egypt is less well understood than in Mesopotamia, but it was clearly employed in contexts very different from record keeping. There is a view among archaeologists that Egyptian hieroglyphs may have developed from earlier symbols representing the identity of social

	5000 y.a.	4,500 y.a.	4,000 y.a.	3,500 y.a.
Africa	**c.5,300 y.a.** Hieroglyphic writing develops in Egypt			
Near East	**c.5,300–4,800 y.a.** Pictographic signs evolve into cuneiform script in Mesopotamia			**c.3,500 y.a.** Development of linear alphabetic scripts in Levant
Europe			**c. 3,900 y.a.** Development of Minoan scripts (Linear A and B)	
Asia		**c.4,600–4,000 y.a.** Indus script in use		**c.3,500 y.a.** Development of Chinese ideograms
Americas				

groups: the earliest hieroglyphics appear on small ivory tags found in princely graves dated to c.3300 BCE. Brief inscriptions that record the names of individuals or kinship groups are also found on ritual works of art such as palettes and mace heads, and on expensive craft products like stone jars.

During the Old Kingdom, hieroglyphs came to be associated with monumental art, and were painted on the walls of tombs or incorporated into carved reliefs as commentary and explanation of the depicted scenes.Over time, Egyptian scribes also developed a cursive version of the script for practical use, to record affairs of state and household accounts, but writing itself developed out of the ideological context of political power and authority.

Writing in China was also bound up with ritual and politics. From the 3rd millennium BCE, shamans interpreted cracks in burnt bones and tortoise shells as ancestral responses to questions put by the living. By around 1600 BCE, questions and answers were being recorded in writing on the oracle bones themselves, as well as on bronzes and other ritual objects. By late Shang times (around 1200 BCE), scribes were using some 3,000 signs, the foundation for the Chinese system of writing.

Some 3,000 years after the Egyptians, the Zapotecs of Mesoamerica also developed the use of pictorial writing (glyphs) on public art such as stone stele. The first glyphs are probably simple captions naming the people depicted on the stele. In the 3rd century CE, the Maya developed both the representational complexity of the subjects depicted on the stele, and the glyphs themselves, but retained the close link between pictures and words. Both art and writing concerned the dynastic histories of ruling families, especially their ritual relationships with the gods and the cyclical calendar of the cosmos.

Alphabets and literacy

The strong political associations of early writing systems and the complexity of their graphic systems meant that most people did not have access to them. Change came with the invention of the alphabet. Several forms of alphabetic writing developed along the eastern seaboard of the Mediterranean between 1500 and 1200 BCE. Over the next thousand years, scripts like Phoenician and Aramaic soon spread or inspired numerous imitations, including the Greek, Latin, Arabic and Indian alphabets. Containing only twenty or thirty individual signs, these systems were easier to learn and use than the more cumbersome syllabic scripts that preceded them. The spread of Judaism, Christianity and Islam, religions that based their authority on possession of a sacred book, was one result of this wider literacy ◆

ABOVE Egyptian hieroglyphs on a wall painting in the tomb of Queen Nefertari (19th Dynasty). As one expert has put it, hieroglyphic writing functioned as captions. The signs, highly pictorial in character, were an integral part of the political and ritual art of ancient Egypt. Texts painted on tombs walls often related biographical details about the deceased, with the deep religious purpose of persuading the gods of judgment that the deceased was worthy of the afterlife.

RIGHT A Chinese oracle bone from the Shang dynasty c.1500 BCE. Many of these characters bear resemblance to marks incised on pottery a thousand years earlier, suggesting that early scribes created a writing system from intellectual materials that were already on hand.

c.2,600 y.a. South Arabian alphabet adopted in Ethiopia

c.3,500–2,700 y.a. Hittite hieroglyphic in use

c.3,000 y.a. Hebrew, Phoenician, Aramaic and South Arabian alphabetic scripts in use

c.2,800 y.a. Greek alphabet in use (later transmitted to Etruscans and Romans)

c.1,700 y.a. Runic alphabet (possibly derived from Etruscan) in use among Germanic peoples

c.2,600 y.a. Aramaic alphabet adopted throughout Iran; origin of many South and Southeast Asian scripts

c.1,600 y.a. Chinese ideographs introduced to Korea and Japan

c.2,200–2,100 y.a. Pictorial writing in Mexico; Maya hieroglyphs

3,000 y.a. 2,500 y.a. 2,000 y.a. 1,500 y.a. 1,000 y.a.

Part Three

THE RISE OF CIVILIZATIONS

*The great standing stones of the inner sanctuary
of Stonehenge, southern England*

EUROPE & WESTERN ASIA

ARCHAEOLOGY HAS a distinguished tradition in Europe and Western Asia. From its antiquarian roots in the Renaissance, it passed through a period of science and romanticism in the 19th century and a fascination with classification and cultural diffusion in the early 20th century to emerge as a mature research discipline after World War II, and now embraces a variety of fieldwork techniques, scientific analytical methods and interpretive frameworks to trace the development of human society.

The history of archaeology in Europe may perhaps be dated from the excavation of Hadrian's villa at Tivoli in the 16th century, an important landmark in the revival of interest in the sculptures and monuments of the Classical world. At about the same time, the voyages of discovery to Asia and the New World brought Europeans into contact with peoples whose customs and practices were very different from their own; some lacked metal tools. In Europe, mysterious structures like Stonehenge and chance finds of artifacts such as burial urns and flint handaxes began to capture the curiosity of antiquarians. Their imagination, however, was tempered by the Biblical account of the creation of humankind. All antiquities could date only from Adam, whose appearance was calculated in 1650 by James Ussher, the archbishop of Armagh in Ireland, to have been in 4004 BCE.

During the 18th century, it became increasingly apparent that there was a buried past, and promising localities were investigated with the shovel. Since systematic methods of archaeological investigation had not yet been developed, these excavations were generally haphazard. Mounds, called "barrows", were opened throughout northwestern Europe and were discovered to be burial sites of ancient peoples. Tunneling through the volcanic mud at Herculaneum and Pompeii yielded sculptures and traces of the Roman towns destroyed in the eruption of 79 CE. A surge of enthusiasm for collecting the art of the Classical world led to the retrieval (some might say plunder) of artifacts and statues from sites in Greece and Italy. Travelers through the lands of the Ottoman empire noted down cuneiform inscriptions and captivated the romantic imagination of the age with descriptions of forgotten cities such as Petra.

By the first quarter of the 19th century, it was becoming increasingly clear that there was a human past not documented by written records or whose records were in languages not completely understood. Moreover, this past, at least as it was manifested in the buried record of Europe and Western Asia, was far more complicated and confusing than had been hitherto imagined. Tools and pottery occurred in a bewildering array of shapes and sizes. Chipped stone, specifically flint, had clearly been used much more extensively in the past for making tools, even predating the use of metals. Geologists and archaeologists made the observation that the stratification, or layering, of soil held considerable significance for establishing the historical sequence of events. The Principle of Superposition, which states that lower layers are older than the ones that lie above them, provided the key that unlocked human prehistory.

The Three Age System

A critical breakthrough in understanding how the prehistoric past was organized came in about 1817 when Christian Jurgensen Thomsen (1788–1865) classified the ancient tools in the Danish National Museum according to whether they were made from stone, bronze, or iron. The idea of three successive ages of stone, bronze and iron had been around for some time, but Thomsen took it a step further by using the same framework to organize the pottery and other finds associated with these tools. Thus, for the first time, it was seen that a specific sort of pottery was made when people used tools of stone, while different kinds of pottery were used in the other periods. Glass artifacts did not appear until iron was used for tools. The Principle of Association, which states that finds from the same

c.400,000 y.a. *H. erectus* at Zhoukoudian, China

c.30,000 y.a. Panaramittee rock carvings in Australia

Regional Timeline

c.800,000 y.a. Archaic humans at Atapuerca (Spain)

c.200,000–30,000 y.a. Neandertals in Europe

c.30,000–10,000 y.a. Rock and cave art of Ice Age hunters

c.9,000–7,500 y.a. Pottery in Near East and Balkans; copper at Çatal Höyük (Turkey)

c.1.8–1.4 m y.a. Archaic humans at Dmanisi (Georgia) and Ubeidiyah (Israel)

c.90,000 y.a. Modern humans at Skhul and Qafzeh (Israel)

c.13,000–10,000 y.a. Domestication of wild cereals in Near East

200,000 y.a.

10,000 y.a.

layer or similar context are contemporaneous, permitted the development of a chronology, albeit a rough one, for prehistoric Europe.

The Principles of Superposition and Association were only useful, however, if archaeological materials were excavated carefully. As it gradually came to be realized that haphazard digging into ancient sites destroyed irreplaceable information about the layers in which objects and their associated artifacts were found, so the techniques of excavation and recording the position and association of finds gradually improved over the course of the 19th century. When, for example, Johann Georg Ramsauer (1797–1876) excavated the early Iron Age cemetery at Hallstatt (Austria) in the 1850s, each grave was meticulously cleaned, drawn in watercolor, and described in writing (see page 9). His record is still of immense value to archaeologists.

Uncovering past civilizations

In the Near East, the civilizations of Mesopotamia, Egypt, and Palestine were coming into sharper focus. The English archaeologist Austen Henry Layard (1817–1894) excavated the palaces of Nineveh and Nimrud, revealing the sculptures and reliefs of the

ABOVE A photograph of Maiden Castle (1926) shows the grid system of excavation devised by English archaeologist Mortimer Wheeler (1890–1976). The site is divided into square blocks with baulks left between, recording the stratigraphic sections.
FAR LEFT Gold funerary mask excavated from a 16th-century BCE grave at Mycenae.

Assyrian empire, while the decipherment of Akkadian cuneiform script by Henry Rawlinson (see page 106) made it possible to read ancient records on clay tablets. Mounds (tells) in the Near East were found to have been the sites of ancient settlements, formed by the constant replenishment of mud-brick buildings and the accumulation of debris over thousands of years. By digging down through the layers of occupation, archaeologists could recover traces of life from the ancient cities of Babylon and Sumer.

By the last decades of the 19th century, the classification and chronological organization of artifact types (typology) had resulted in the ability to position new finds in relation to others in time. Although there were no methods yet of connecting this system to a scale of years, this relative chronology permitted archaeologists to build regional sequences of artifact types from the Stone Age

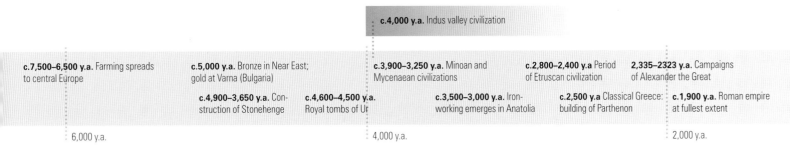

c.4,000 y.a. Indus valley civilization

c.7,500–6,500 y.a. Farming spreads to central Europe

c.5,000 y.a. Bronze in Near East; gold at Varna (Bulgaria)

c.4,900–3,650 y.a. Construction of Stonehenge

c.4,600–4,500 y.a. Royal tombs of Ur

c.3,900–3,250 y.a. Minoan and Mycenaean civilizations

c.3,500–3,000 y.a. Iron-working emerges in Anatolia

c.2,800–2,400 y.a Period of Etruscan civilization

c.2,500 y.a Classical Greece: building of Parthenon

2,335–2323 y.a. Campaigns of Alexander the Great

c.1,900 y.a. Roman empire at fullest extent

6,000 y.a.

4,000 y.a.

2,000 y.a.

through the Iron Age. At points where the Iron Age finds were connected with historically-known peoples like the Romans and Greeks, these chronologies could be anchored in time at their recent end. The more distant that these sequences became in space and time from historical dates, the more uncertain and arbitrary became the duration assigned to particular artifact types. Nonetheless, it was a start in expanding prehistory from being a way of organizing museum collections to telling a story about the human past.

In the 1870s, the German businessman Heinrich Schliemann (1822–90) began digging at Hissarlik in Turkey, which had putatively been identified as the site of ancient Troy. Schliemann was determined to find the city described by Homer. Despite his amateurish and destructive methods , his efforts were rewarded by the discovery of a multilayered site. The second level had been destroyed by fire, in the ruins of which he found an immense treasure of gold and silver vessels. Schliemann triumphantly (but inaccurately) claimed this to be the city sacked by the Greeks, and then shifted his efforts to Mycenae in Greece, where he found royal tombs with masks of hammered gold; evidence of a civilization a thousand years older than that of Classical Greece. The display and publication of these finds perhaps did more to fire the public imagination than any other discoveries, and provided a stimulus to archaeological investigation that reverberated throughout Europe and the Near East. Twenty years later Arthur Evans (1851–1941), excavating at Knossos on Crete, uncovered the remains of the Minoan civilization, the earliest in Europe.

By the early decades of the 20th century, the age of the amateur was almost ended. Increasingly, archaeological activity was organized through European and American museums and universities, who maintained overseas "schools of archaeology", especially in the countries of the Classical world, Egypt and the Near East. Important excavations in the 1920s and 1930s included Ur, where the tombs of the royal cemetery were uncovered by Leonard Woolley (1880–1960), Mari and Megiddo in the Near East, and the excavation of the agora at Athens.

Cultural preoccupations

In northern and central Europe, investigations of large sites like the early agricultural settlement of Köln-Lindenthal (Germany), the lake village of Biskupin (Poland) and the hillfort of Maiden Castle (England) enlarged the picture of European prehistory and fed the debate about cultural diffusion. It had long been recognized that objects changed in form gradually and that the geographical ranges of certain types of artifacts expanded and contracted with time. Certain types of tools, pottery and ornaments consistently occurring together were defined as archaeological "cultures", and change in archaeological cultures was attributed to the movement of people and ideas, through a vaguely understood process called "diffusion".

BELOW Tollund Man, whose well-preserved body was found in a peat bog in Denmark in 1950. Analysis of his stomach contents showed his last meal had been a gruel of barley, linseed, knotweed and other seeds – a pioneering example of paleobotanical investigation.

The problem was that archaeological cultures came to be equated in the minds of archaeologists with peoples who had a common ethnic identity and who behaved collectively, a leap of faith that was not entirely justified. From here it was a short step to view these cultures as the prehistoric precursors of modern ethnic and national groups. In the political and social climate of the 1920s and 1930s, this connection between archaeology and nationalism was especially pernicious.

Archaeologists also came to recognize that the association between prehistoric sites and their environment was an important clue to the understanding of how people lived in the past. In 1931, the crew of the trawler *Colinda* found a block of peat from the bottom of the North Sea caught in their nets. On deck, the peat broke open to reveal an antler harpoon, now known to be about 11,000 years old. From this it was clear that this area of the North Sea had once been dry land and that the environment of the Stone Age had been very different from that of the present. The emerging technique of pollen analysis, which permitted the reconstruction of past vegetation, was widely used in Europe to provide the environmental context for archaeological finds.

Carbon-14 and after

The advent of radiocarbon (carbon-14) dating in the 1950s allowed prehistoric archaeology in Europe and the Near East to move forward as a mature research science. By providing archaeologists in all parts of the world with a method of establishing a firm chronology for events in prehistory, it helped to eradicate some of the misconceptions of cultural diffusion. At the same time, Aegean archaeology was transformed in 1952 by the decipherment of the Linear B script by Michael Ventris (1922–56). The ranks of professional archaeologists swelled, and the field was established as a discipline at many additional universities and research institutions. Collaborations were sought with botanists, zoologists and other scientists to characterize as completely as possible the technology and economy of ancient societies.

The 1960s and 1970s saw a major refocusing of the aims of prehistoric archaeology. Although processual archaeology was never so wholeheartedly embraced as in North America, archaeologists in Europe and the Near East came to concentrate in very great measure on large problems of social change and development rather than questions of chronology and culture history and the minutiae of typology. Two major research problems came to dominate archaeological research: the origin and dispersal of agriculture, and the origin and development of complex societies such as chiefly polities and urban states. Attempts were made to identify specific causal factors in these processes. In the case of agriculture, climatic change and population growth were seen as important factors, whereas trade, religion and warfare were viewed as critical for the emergence of chiefdoms and states. These explicit research aims had the benefit of leading to an explosion of archaeological research conducted in a very systematic and orderly fashion with high

ABOVE Archaeological investigations continue at Arslantepe, a tell site (*tepe* means mound) in Anatolian Turkey. Urban life began here in the 4th millennium BCE, but its history of occupation stretches back nearly 8,000 years to its habitation by pottery-using farmers.

standards of recording and publication. Unfortunately, despite the ambitious goals of archaeology to find the underlying causes of social change, it was difficult to demonstrate the primacy of any one factor over another in most situations.

New interpretations

During the last two decades, modern archaeology in Eurasia has embraced a much larger variety of interpretive frameworks. At one extreme, a reaction to processual archaeology has led to approaches rooted in literary and social theory that see the archaeological record as a text to be "read" with multiple interpretations. A somewhat more temperate view sees culture change in prehistory as the interplay among many different factors, many of which are based in the decisions and choices made by individuals and families, within the constraints imposed by the environment. The continual development and refinement of techniques for finding, excavating, and dating archaeological sites have permitted new insights into the human past and the revision of old positions. Yet even in the well-explored archaeological terrain of Europe and the Near East, many discoveries remain to be made in the century to come ◆

Foragers of the Mesolithic

The European Mesolithic – the period between the retreat of the ice sheets about 10,000 years ago and the introduction of farming – is now recognized by archaeologists as a period of productive change when the environment provided populations of hunter–gatherer–fishers with a reasonably comfortable way of life. As the climate began to warm, forests sprang up where previously there had been cold, dry tundra or steppe. The migratory herds of reindeer shifted northwards, to be replaced by woodland game such as deer and wild pig, and human territories became smaller as hunting groups no longer had to follow the seasonal migrations of herds over vast distances.

BELOW The skeleton of a 50-year-old female from Vedbæk, Denmark. Her head is resting on a red deer antler. It is one of 22 bodies excavated from a cemetery of 17 graves belonging to a forager group of the Ertebølle culture who lived along the coastlines of southern Scandinavia some 6,000 years ago. Analysis of their bones shows that fish and shellfish featured heavily in their diet. Food resources were so plentiful in some spots that foragers remained in the same settlement for long periods and buried their dead in cemeteries. As well as deer antlers, shells, animal bones and teeth, and flint blades were found with many of the bodies at Vedbæk.

Abundant forest resources offered rich new possibilities for exploitation. Analysis of pollen from bog and lake sediments from this period suggests that postglacial foragers altered the forest by burning it to create artificial clearings where hazel and other shrubs could flourish and to which small game animals would be attracted. Edible wild plants such as nuts, berries, fungi, and fleshy roots and tubers became an important source of diet. They could be collected by members of the community, such as children, who previously would not have contributed to the family's food supply.

Harpoons, nets and traps

By now, stone tools had become tiny flint triangles and rhomboids that were inserted into handles of wood and antler to form composite spearpoints and knives. A wide variety of harpoons were made, including a particularly effective and clever fishing tool called a "leister", in which two curving serrated pieces of antler were attached to the end of a handle and thrust down over the back of a fish to seize it. Trees and shrubs provided materials for larger devices. Dugout canoes came into use, while willow and hazel branches were woven into conical fish traps. These were set into streams and estuaries to harvest the seasonal migrations of salmon. The trapped fish would be preserved for future eating by smoking them. During underwater archaeological investigations undertaken in conjunction with the building of a bridge from Zealand to Fyn in Denmark, a great number of such traps were found preserved in the estuarine mud, hinting at trapping activity on a level that was almost industrial in scale.

The presence of such facilities points to the existence of recognized property rights; a community – or even a single household – would not invest time and effort in constructing large installations if their yield could be claimed by others. A number of Mesolithic burials discovered in the last few decades provide further evidence of communal organization. Cemeteries at sites like Vedbæk (Denmark), Skateholm (Sweden), and Oleneostrovskii Mogilnik (Russia) are strongly indicative of ritual behavior, and perhaps social differentiation. They suggest, too, that where resources were constantly on tap, settlements were occupied for longer periods of time.

Diverse resources

In central and southern Europe, foragers congregated around lake basins in the Alpine foreland and took advantage of the vertical distribution of resources in mountainous areas: fish and waterfowl from the lakes and rivers; small game, nuts, and berries from the

Ferri
C

Douro

Cabeço da *Tagus*
Arruda
Muge
Cabeço do Pez

Hoyo de la Mi

Ivanovskoye III
Zamostye II
Nizhneye Veretye
Veretye I
Suhoye
Oleneostrovskii Mogilnik
Popovo
Sandermokha
Lake Onega
Jönjas
Kunda
Narva
Lake Ladoga
Pulli
Zvejnieki
Lake Peipus
Abora
Baltic Sea
Zvidze
Dvina
Øvre Storvatnet
Viste
Tørkop
North Sea
Aggersund
Ertebølle
Meilgaard
Agerød V
Ringkloster
Vedbæk
Saltbæk Vig
Tybrind Vig
Halsskov
Skateholm
Strøby Egede
Møllegabet II
Zedmar
Dudka
Duvensee
Lille Knabstrup
Dąbki
Ulva
Oronsay
Lussa Bay
Morton
Star Carr
Rough Island
Bergumermeer
Pesse
Friesack
Poznan-Strarołęka
Chwalim
Konin
Ostrów
Janisławice
Zátyní
Bug
Vistula
Aveline's Hole
Peacock's Farm
Broxbourne
Farnham
Herdinxveld-Giessendam
Hengistbury Head
Fère-en-Tardenois
Seine
Henauhof-Nord
Lautereck
Rhine
Danube
Sered
Oder
CARPATHIAN MTS
Tisza
Soroki
Prut
Dniester
Vasil'evka, Voloshsky
Téviec
Hoëdic
Loire
Birsmatten
Villar-sous-Dampjoux
Schötz
Baulmes
Sous-Balme
Rouffignac
ALPS
Mezzocorona
Monderal de Sora
Romagnano
Col du Coq
Rhône
Po
Colli Berici
Kraske Spilje
DINARIC ALPS
Iron Gates gorge
Lepenski Vir
Vlasac
Padina
Danube
Mirnoe
Laspi
Sauveterre-la-Lémance
Balma Abeurador
Arene Candide
Châteauneuf-les- Martigues
APPENNINES
Mas-d'Azil
La Crouzade
PYRENEES
Ebro
Cogul
Perelló
Cueva Remigia
Llatas
Parpalló
Grotta Maritza
Crvena Stijena
BALKAN MTS
Riparo Blanc
Positano
Grotta delle Mura
Cipolliane di Novaghie
Sidhari
Grotta della Madonna
Corsica
Sardinia
Balearic Islands
Mediterranean Sea
Grotta
Termini Imerese
Sicily
Grotta Corruggi
Franchthi Cave
Crete

shell midden site
mortuary site
site with dugout canoe
site with fish trap
other Mesolithic site
northern limit of wooded steppe, c.10,000 BCE

vegetation zones, c.7,000 BCE
boreal forest
mixed forest
steppe
semi-desert

ancient coastline, c.7000 BCE

0   600 km
0   400 mi

ABOVE At the end of last Ice Age land-bridges dammed the southern end of the Baltic Sea, making it a freshwater lake. Southern Britain was joined to the European mainland. The Black Sea had no outlet to the Mediterranean. As the ice sheets melted, sea levels rose and eventually inundated these land bridges. Land that had been compressed under millions of tons of ice began to spring back upward. Sites that were once on dry land are now under water. Elsewhere, places once on the coast are now a considerable way inland.

wooded slopes; wild goats from the alpine meadows above the treeline. Caves along the Mediterranean coasts and in the karst limestone landscapes of the Adriatic were attractive locations. Franchthi Cave in southern Greece was used as a seasonal camp by groups of foragers throughout this period. As sea levels rose at the end of the Ice Age it came closer to the coastline, and by 8,500 years ago was only about 0.62 mi/1km away – a fact reflected in the increasing amounts of fish and shellfish remains found at the site, along with many different plant species.

An important series of Mesolithic sites have been investigated in the Iron Gates gorge of the Danube, where the river cuts through the Carpathian mountains. The forests contained game, while the

turbulent river provided favorable conditions for fishing, attracting forager groups to settle permanently along the river. Lepenski Vir is the best-known of a number of settlements dating from around 8,000 years ago. Several dozen houses with plastered floors and a central stone-lined hearth were built on a low river terrace. Almost every one contained a limestone sculpture, often in the form of a human head.

When agriculture began to penetrate southeastern Europe about 8,000 years ago, many hunter–gatherer–fisher communities were slow to abandon their traditional way of life. After some delay, however, they either integrated cultivated crops and domestic livestock into their diet, or were eventually assimilated by farming peoples (see pages 58–59) ◆

First Farmers of the Near East

Until about 13,000 years ago the Near East was occupied by mobile groups of hunter–gatherers who lived in small groups and moved from place to place across the landscape in a regular cycle determined by seasonal abundances of wild foods. This millennia-old way of life began to alter as the climate became warmer and wetter at the end of the Ice Age. Forests of oak and pistachio began to spread, together with grasses like wild barley and wheat. Seasonal supplies of edible plants became more reliable, enabling people to adopt a more sedentary way of life.

The transition from hunter–gathering to settled agriculture took place very gradually, over a period of about five millennia. As climatic changes took hold, in some favorable parts of the environment wild grasses grew so densely that enough grain could be harvested to sustain a family group for much of the year, provided it could be stored. With greater assurance of a steady food supply, people could form larger groups able to remain in the same place for longer periods of the year. Released from the pressure of having to move so frequently, they began to turn their energies to constructing more permanent dwellings for themselves.

The first villages

It was a natural development to begin to form small clusters of houses close to the places where food plants grew most abundantly. The first known villages were built by the Natufians, a people who occupied the wooded hilly corridor along the eastern coast of the Mediterranean Sea (the Levant). They lived in round pit houses and dug silos to store the wild grain they gathered, but still made use of temporary campsites, which were occupied by work parties at particular times of year to hunt migrating herds of animals or harvest the annual crop of acorns.

A parallel development was taking place to the north, in the Taurus and Zagros mountains of eastern Turkey, northern Iraq and western Iran. Here hunter–gatherers began to herd wild animals: pigs that inhabited the wooded slopes and sheep that lived at higher altitudes. Wild cereals played a less important part in their diets. Animal bones from Zawi Chemi and Shanidar suggest that sheep were being herded around 8500 BCE, while at Hallan Chemi pigs seem to have figured more.

The beginnings of farming

Once communities took steps to improve their food supply by planting wild cereals in a particular favored spot – perhaps at first merely to augment their provisions – they had initiated a new economic system, in which people manipulated nature and the environment for their own benefit. The earliest domesticated cereal grains, from Abu Hureyra (Syria), date to c.11,000 BCE but many groups in the Near East continued to rely on wild harvests long after this. Where cultivation was adopted, it became a key element in people's lives, tethering them more firmly to specific localities. This important step toward a food-producing economy is evident at sites like Jericho and Netiv Hagdud in the southern Levant, and at Tell Aswad (Syria). Archaeologists refer to this period as the Pre-Pottery Neolithic A (PPNA), thus acknowledging the absence of pottery that scholars once believed to be a hallmark of Neolithic agricultural societies.

ABOVE Bone sickle handle belonging to the Natufian culture, from a cave on Mount Carmel, 4 in/10.5 cm high. It is carved in the shape of an animal and may have had a ritual function.

Jericho: enigmatic structures

When a British-led excavation at Jericho in the 1950s uncovered the remains of a stone town wall dating from the PPNA (c.8300–7300 BCE) it showed that the town was already thousands of years old when the Israelites captured it to the sound of Joshua's trumpets, an event described in the Bible that probably took place c.1150 BCE. The wall had been built around a farming settlement of some 500 or more people that had grown up near a permanent spring in the Jordan valley. The wall still stands almost 13 ft/4 m high in places and is nearly 10 ft/3 m thick. A ditch once ran around the outside, while just inside stood a circular tower, over 26 ft/8 m high, with an interior staircase leading through solid stone masonry to a flat roof. When these discoveries were first made, it was thought that the massive stone wall and tower were defensive in purpose, but more recent opinion suggests that the wall was built as a water-diversion scheme to protect the village from flash floods – indeed, the wall was eventually covered by water-borne silts and gravels. This explanation does not account for the tower, however, the purpose of which remains enigmatic. Whatever their function, the sheer scale and sophistication of these early construction projects command our respect and curiosity ◆

ABOVE THE TOWER WITHIN THE STONE WALL AT THE EARLIEST SETTLEMENT AT JERICHO.

BELOW Farming began to develop at sites across the Near East between 11,000 and 7000 BCE as hunter–gatherers turned to the cultivation of wild cereals, such as einkorn, emmer wheat and barley. Over time, selection produced higher yielding domesticated strains of these crops. Animal husbandry was also initiated during this period, with increasing management of wild goats, sheep and pigs, especially in the north of the region. By 7000–6500 BCE, the successful integration of the newly domesticated plants and animals formed the basis of village and town life in many parts of the Near East. This revolutionary economic movement set the stage for the later emergence of civilization, and of the world we still know today.

Agricultural communities

During the period from c.7600–6300 BCE (PPNB), the farmers of the Near East developed domesticated plant and animal species by selectively breeding the genetic characteristics that made them useful to humans as sources of food or for other products such as wool, milk, or traction power. These species were introduced into areas where their wild progenitors did not naturally occur – sheep and goats into the southern Levant, and various species of cereals into the drier habitats of the Near East.

Trade in raw materials like obsidian began to grow, linking regions and giving farming communities access to desirable commodities. Village settlements increased in size and number. Some, such as Ain Ghazal and Basta in the southern Levant, formed settlements of several thousand people. Throughout the western Near East buildings were constructed with firm foundations, and with plastered or terrazzo floors. Some dwellings even had two storeys. Shrines with impressively sculptured steles appeared at sites like Nevali Chori and Göbekli in southeastern Turkey, and statues modeled in lime plaster at the southern Levantine sites of Ain Ghazal and Jericho. Burial practices thought to have been associated with an ancestor cult accorded special prominence to the skull. This rite took a number of different forms; in the southern Levant plastered skulls depicted the faces of dead relatives, while in Syria and Turkey the dead, or sometimes just their skulls, were interred in communal burial chambers.

These momentous developments transformed the Near East into a landscape of farming villages and small towns, running in a crescent from the Mediterranean coast through the Taurus and Zagros mountains to the Persian Gulf. Seen against this backdrop, the town at Çatal Höyük (c. 6300–5400 BCE) in central Turkey, once considered an anomaly for its large size and rich murals, appears in its proper light as a descendant of earlier Pre-Pottery Neolithic towns ◆

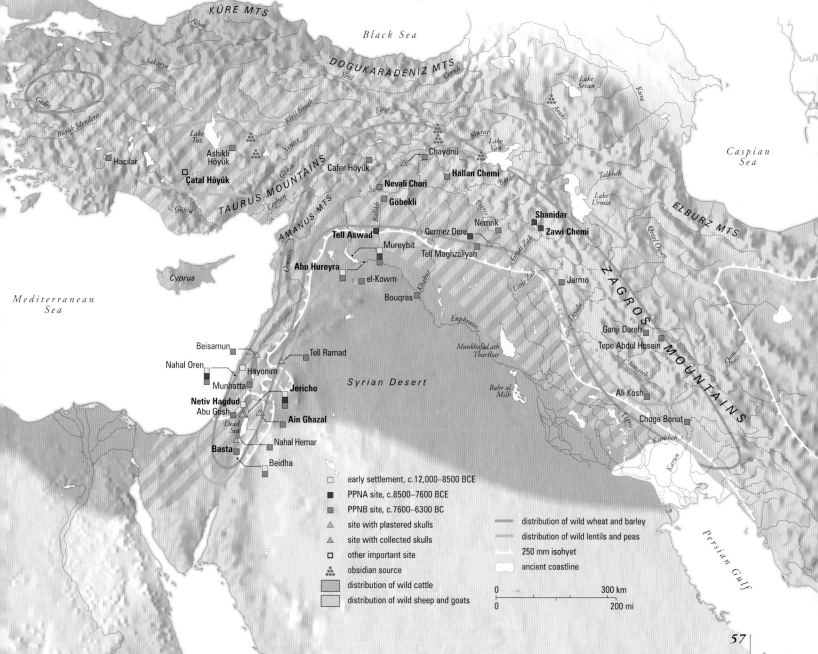

early settlement, c.12,000–8500 BCE
PPNA site, c.8500–7600 BCE
PPNB site, c.7600–6300 BC
site with plastered skulls
site with collected skulls
other important site
obsidian source
distribution of wild cattle
distribution of wild sheep and goats

distribution of wild wheat and barley
distribution of wild lentils and peas
250 mm isohyet
ancient coastline

0   300 km
0   200 mi

Early Farmers of Eurasia

The relatively rapid spread of agriculture in Europe between c.6500 and 5000 BCE was a complex process. In some cases it took place through the dispersal of farming populations, with their crops and livestock, into new habitats. Elsewhere, farming was adopted by local groups of foragers, eventually replacing their traditional way of life. Differentiating between these two processes, and explaining why farming populations dispersed and foragers began to farm, is a fundamental research challenge for archaeologists. Although the earliest farming communities in southeastern Europe were very similar to their precursors in the Near East, those to the north and west developed their own particular character.

ABOVE The fertile alluvial plains of Thessaly. Farming was probably introduced into the Balkans by immigrants from Anatolia who brought domesticated cereal crops such as emmer and einkorn with them, as well as sheep and goats.

Farming made its appearance in southeast Europe a little after 7000 BCE. Although the early agricultural communities of Thessaly and northern Greece share many similarities with contemporaneous settlements in the Near East, there are significant differences. For example, mud-brick houses at Nea Nikomedeia and Sesklo (Greece) are freestanding one-room structures instead of being joined together, as in many Near Eastern sites like Çatal Höyük.

The archaeological record from Franchthi Cave and other occupation sites in Greece shows that local communities of foragers were taking up agriculture very soon after its introduction into Europe, and farming seems to have spread west from Greece through the Mediterranean basin, following coastal routes that were familiar to indigenous hunter–gatherers. Evidence for crops and livestock, together with

BELOW A Linear Pottery bowl from the Rhineland, Germany. The early farmers who made wares like these lived in small clusters of timber longhouses, sometimes 100 ft/30 m in length, which stood in forest clearings in the midst of small fields. Domestic cattle bones are most frequently found on Linear Pottery sites, in contrast to southern Europe where sheep and goats remained the major livestock species.

Impressed Ware pottery, appears at places like Arene Candide (Italy) and Châteauneuf-les-Martigues (southern France) that had long been visited by forager groups. Early farming sites differ little from forager settlements, suggesting that crops and livestock were passed along from group to group and adopted into the hunter-gatherer economy.

Northward dispersal

As farming moved north through the Balkans, it seems likely that some population dispersal of farming groups took place. Elsewhere, however, existing forager groups appear to have adopted domestic plants and animals into their economy (see page 55). There are firmer grounds for arguing that central Europe was colonized by groups of farmers moving along the major rivers, who settled on hillsides covered with fine-grained loess soils, which could be tilled year after year without much loss of fertility. By c.5300 BCE early farming communities, known from their incised ceramics as Linearbandkeramik (LBK) or Linear Pottery, are found as far west as the Seine valley and the Netherlands.

From foraging to farming

The adoption of domestic plants and animals by the Ertebølle fisher–hunter–foragers of coastal northern and western Europe was a much more gradual process, lasting several centuries. A similar pattern is observed in the Alpine regions of central Europe. It is almost always clear that the last hunters were also the first farmers, as crops and livestock initially caused few changes in other aspects of the archaeological record. The forest peoples of northern and eastern Europe were even slower to abandon fishing and hunting as their primary source of food. However, they readily adopt pottery, which provided them with improved means of storage and food preparation ◆

Corut Calde

Gruta de Furninha

Ponte de Sa

site with evidence of early farming
- □ before 6000 BCE
- ■ 6000–5000 BCE
- ▩ 5000–4000 BCE

- ▨ area of later Ertebølle sites
- ▢ area of early Balkan farming cultures

- ▨ area of Impressed Ware pottery
- ▨ area of Linear Pottery culture
- ▨ area of La Hoguette Ware
- ▨ area of Limburg Ware
- ⇒ spread of agriculture by 6000 BCE
- ⇒ spread of agriculture by 5000 BCE
- ⇒ spread of agriculture by 4000 BCE
- ▨ area of loess soils

ABOVE Farming expanded east from the Levant to beyond the Iranian plateau and the oases of Central Asia at the same time as it spread into Europe. There is evidence of farming and local domestication of animals at Mehrgarh (Pakistan) before 6000 BCE, when farming communities were also present at Djeitun and neighboring oases in Turkmenistan. In both areas, rectangular mud-brick houses constituted the primary domestic architecture of small hamlets.

ABOVE Agriculture moved into Europe along two paths out of the Balkans, one going west across the islands and peninsulas of the Mediterranean, the other north along the major rivers of central Europe.

Bylany: an early farming settlement

The Linear Pottery settlement complex at Bylany (Czech Republic), which has been the focus of archaeological research since 1953, has proved to be one of the most important early farming sites in central Europe. Dated to c.5400–5000 BCE, the settlement is spread out over a loess-covered landscape on both sides of a small stream. Excavations at several locations have revealed dozens of superimposed longhouse outlines and storage pits. These have proved a challenge for archaeologists to unravel, but based on changes in pottery styles and the overlapping of houses and pits, five major occupation phases have been proposed. However, it is clear that houses were continually being built, abandoned, and rebuilt on these sites. The soil is very acidic and consequently few animal bones have been preserved, though it appears that domestic cattle were most commonly kept. The discovery of many other Linear Pottery sites close by suggests that this area was particularly favored by the earliest farmers of central Europe ◆

ABOVE PART OF THE EXCAVATED SITE AT BYLANY, SHOWING SEVERAL STORAGE PITS.

First Cities of the Near East

Almost three millennia (c.6500–3500 BCE) separate the early farming villages of the Near East (see pages 56–57) from the emergence of its first cities and states. This period witnessed the growth of many different prehistoric societies, characterized by distinct types of pottery, dwellings, and other aspects of material culture. In the north, where there was adequate seasonal rainfall, dry-farming carried on more or less as before. Early in the 6th millennium, however, farmers discovered ways of diverting river waters to irrigate their fields. This allowed them to cultivate more arid areas, and they gradually began to colonize the fertile plain between the Euphrates and Tigris rivers. This basic technological and environmental difference between the early agricultural societies of northern and southern Mesopotamia laid the groundwork for their divergent histories. It was in the south during the Uruk period (c.4000-3100 BCE) that a momentous change in social organization took place and the world's first cities arose.

Because the early farmers of northern Mesopotamia relied on rainfall to sustain their fields and pastureland, they were not tied down to living in a particular area, unlike the farmers of the south, and their settlements were able to spread out widely across the landscape. Each family was able to supply its own wants in most things, at least under normal circumstances: they did not have to share resources as farmers employing irrigation systems did, or pool their efforts to enhance community survival. Rather different forms of communal organization emerged among the farmers of the south, where irrigation was in use. As irrigated farming relies on the cooperative use of land and labor, larger social units are essential. Typical settlements (at sites like Tell es-Sawwan, Tell Abada, and Tell Madhhur) contained large houses with a block of rooms on each side of a central hall, probably to house extended families. At some sites, such as Choga Mami, excavation has actually uncovered the irrigation canals associated with these early settlements.

Temple-building

These communities give the appearance of social equality: there are no obvious signs of differences in wealth or status. The role of maintaining social and economic stability seems to have fallen increasingly to religious institutions. Excavations at Eridu (identified in later Mesopotamian myth as the first city) have uncovered a succession of 16 temples built one on top of the other. The earliest temple was a simple square room with an altar fitted into a niche in the back wall.

Over time the shrine became more complex as additional rooms were built around the altar room. These findings are repeated at other sites. Finally, as certain settlements acquired political, religious and economic significance, they developed from villages into towns.

The urban explosion

These quiet changes set the scene for the transformations that reshaped southern Mesopotamian societies during the Uruk era of the 4th millennium BCE. As towns increased rapidly in size – several now topped 123 acres/50 hectares – the temples within them grew correspondingly larger and more elaborate. There is some evidence to suggest that farmers and other workers delivered a proportion of their produce – be it grain, wool, fish, or other goods – to the temple precincts, partly to feed the temple personnel and partly to create a central store or bank from which the temple could distribute commodities to certain people in the community. The temples' economic and social role may have helped attract people to town life and in time created the basis for state organization. However, we do not really understand the nature of the temples' political authority, and it is clear that other political institutions existed alongside them.

The temple personnel (and presumably those at other institutions) developed systems for recording economic transactions, which laid the foundations for writing (see pages 46–47). These scribes possessed special skills and knowledge that set them apart from the farmers and herders who still made up the majority of the population. Others began to specialize in particular arts and crafts, such as pottery, weaving, seal cutting, metalworking, and sculpting. These craftspeople may have been directly employed (and fed) by the temples, or supplied items for the growing networks of trade. By the mid 4th millennium BCE,

ABOVE Excavations at Warka, the most important city of southern Mesopotamia in the 4th millennium, also known as Uruk, the name given by archaeologists to this period of Mesopotamian prehistory. By about c.3000 BCE, Warka had a population approaching 50,000 and covered an area of around 500 acres/200 hectares. Although the precise role of temples in early Mesopotamian civilization is unknown, they clearly lay at the heart of the urban impulse. At Warka, the sacred precinct of the goddess Inanna covered 10 acres/ 25 hectares and contained large, lavishly appointed buildings set on platforms.

RIGHT A pottery figurine (c.5000 BCE) belonging to the late Halaf period. The Halaf culture, noted for its exceptionally fine painted pottery, developed about 5500 BCE and expanded across a vast area of northern Mesopotamia. Pottery first came into use in northern Mesopotamia in the mid-7th millennium. The earliest style, which was decorated with simple incised or painted designs, is known as Hassuna. The farmers who made it lived in small villages of multi-roomed houses. By contrast, Halaf families often lived in round houses.

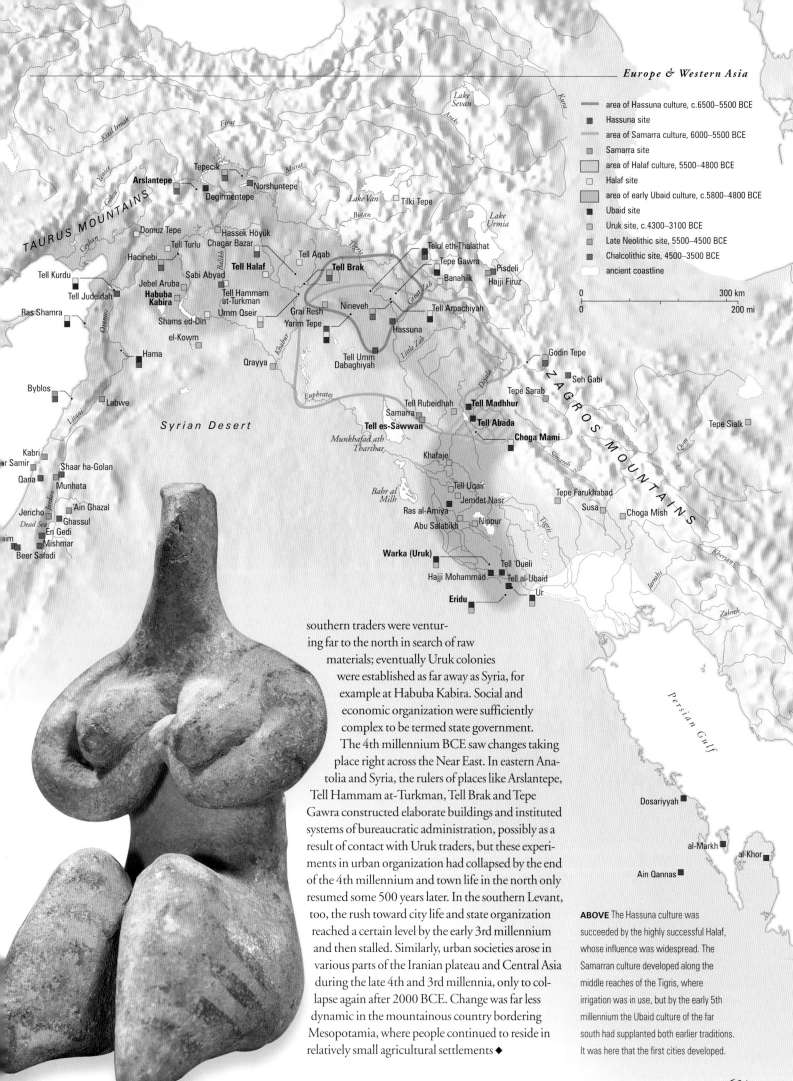

TAURUS MOUNTAINS

ZAGROS MOUNTAINS

Syrian Desert

Persian Gulf

Dead Sea

Lake Sevan

Lake Van

Lake Urmia

Bahr al Milh

Munkhafad ath Tharthar

Kizil Irmak

Firat

Murat

Botan

Great Zab

Little Zab

Diyala

Tigris

Euphrates

Khabur

Balikh

Orontes

Litani

Jordan

Ceyhan

Yenice

Gelbsu

Kura

Araks

Simareh

Khersan

Jarrahi

Zohreh

Qom

Map labels:
Arslantepe · Tepecik · Norshuntepe · Degirmentepe · Domuz Tepe · Hassek Höyük · Chagar Bazar · Tell Turlu · Tell Aqab · Telul eth-Thalathat · Tepe Gawra · Pisdeli · Banahilk · Hajji Firuz · Tilki Tepe · Hacinebi · **Tell Halaf** · **Tell Brak** · Sabi Abyad · Jebel Aruba · **Habuba Kabira** · Tell Hammam at-Turkman · Umm Qseir · Grai Resh · Nineveh · Tell Arpachiyah · Shams ed-Din · el-Kowm · Yarim Tepe · Hassuna · Tell Kurdu · Tell Judeidah · Ras Shamra · Hama · Qrayya · Tell Umm Dabaghiyah · Godin Tepe · Seh Gabi · Tepe Sarab · Tell Rubeidhah · **Tell Madhhur** · Samarra · **Tell es-Sawwan** · **Tell Abada** · **Choga Mami** · Khafaje · Tepe Farukhabad · Tepe Sialk · Tell Uqair · Jemdet Nasr · Ras al-Amiya · Nippur · Susa · Choga Mish · Abu Salabikh · **Warka (Uruk)** · Tell 'Oueli · Hajji Mohammad · Tell al-Ubaid · **Eridu** · Ur · Byblos · Labwe · Kabri · Shaar ha-Golan · Qana · Munhata · Jericho · 'Ain Ghazal · Ghassul · En Gedi · Mishmar · Beer Safadi · ar Samir · Dosariyyah · al-Markh · al-Khor · Ain Qannas

southern traders were venturing far to the north in search of raw materials; eventually Uruk colonies were established as far away as Syria, for example at Habuba Kabira. Social and economic organization were sufficiently complex to be termed state government. The 4th millennium BCE saw changes taking place right across the Near East. In eastern Anatolia and Syria, the rulers of places like Arslantepe, Tell Hammam at-Turkman, Tell Brak and Tepe Gawra constructed elaborate buildings and instituted systems of bureaucratic administration, possibly as a result of contact with Uruk traders, but these experiments in urban organization had collapsed by the end of the 4th millennium and town life in the north only resumed some 500 years later. In the southern Levant, too, the rush toward city life and state organization reached a certain level by the early 3rd millennium and then stalled. Similarly, urban societies arose in various parts of the Iranian plateau and Central Asia during the late 4th and 3rd millennia, only to collapse again after 2000 BCE. Change was far less dynamic in the mountainous country bordering Mesopotamia, where people continued to reside in relatively small agricultural settlements ◆

ABOVE The Hassuna culture was succeeded by the highly successful Halaf, whose influence was widespread. The Samarran culture developed along the middle reaches of the Tigris, where irrigation was in use, but by the early 5th millennium the Ubaid culture of the far south had supplanted both earlier traditions. It was here that the first cities developed.

Developed Farmers of Europe

Around 4500 BCE a number of changes took place among the Linear Pottery farming communities of central Europe, reflected in the development of new pottery styles and house types. The next thousand years saw the emergence of much greater regional variation and the rise of hierarchically structured societies. In western Europe, agriculture was gradually taken up by local indigenous populations and had been established as far as the British Isles and southern Scandinavia by 4000 BCE.

The new pottery styles that developed among the farmers of the Linear Pottery (LBK) area after 4500 BCE are used by archaeologists to identify emerging regional cultures such as the Lengyel in the east and the Rössen, which developed in the area of the Rhineland. By about 4200 BCE the Funnel Beaker or *Trichterbecher* (TRB) culture had developed among farmers on the northern edge of the area of loess soils and extended to the Baltic coast as settlement expanded out of the river valleys on to the northern European plain. Farther west, the Michelsberg culture succeeded the Rössen between the Rhine delta and the Alps, and the Chasséen culture was dominant over much of France.

Between 4500 and 3500 BCE there is evidence of increasing social differentiation among the farming societies of central Europe, perhaps due in part to the increased emphasis on cattle (see pages 42–43). Plowmarks and other signs that animals were being used for traction are found as far north as Denmark

ABOVE Stone "eye idols", perhaps representing goddesses, are associated with the Late Neolithic/early metalworking period at Los Millares and other Iberian sites. Staring eyes also appear on statue-menhirs from France and Italy, and as motifs on pottery vessels and bone ritual objects from elsewhere in western Europe.

by 3500 BCE but are much less common in western Europe. New house types came into use and copper-working, which emerged among the Vinča and Tripolye-Cucuteni cultures of the Balkans and Carpathians (see pages 66–67), spread quickly into central and northern Europe. The appearance of defended hilltop settlements such as one at Dölauer Heide (central Germany) are indicative of increasing social tensions as populations rose, putting pressure on available land.

In the Alps, distinctive settlements developed after c.4000 BCE, often deliberately located on lake shores or in marshy areas, with buildings raised on wooden stilts. Such locations were easily defensible, allowed easy communication by means of dugout canoe, and provided convenient access to a wide range of aquatic and dryland resources. The exceptional preservation of timbers from these waterlogged settlements allows the detailed histories of occupation, abandonment and occasional conflagration to be built up through the use of dendrochronology. One of the best preserved of these sites is Egolzwil (Switzerland), where the timber floor and central hearth of a longhouse about 32 ft/10 m long have been uncovered.

Communication and exchange

Clearance of woodland and movement through the landscape were important aspects of Neolithic life. In southwest England, archaeologists have discovered a well-preserved wooden trackway, the Sweet Track, that allowed people to travel across the marshy Somerset Levels; its construction can be precisely dated by dendrochronology to 3807/6 BCE. A greenstone ax

Skara Brae: a Neolithic village

Between 3100 and 2500 BCE a village of stone-built houses was constructed at Skara Brae on the north coast of Mainland, one of the Orkney Islands off the northeast coast of Scotland. The site, originally excavated by V. Gordon Childe in the 1920s, shows how sophisticated domestic life could be at the northern edge of Neolithic Europe; joined by covered passage ways, the houses boasted built-in stone furniture including beds, dressers, wall-cupboards and limpet tanks. The people of Skara Brae raised sheep and cattle and hunted or scavenged whales and other marine mammals – whale jawbones found at the site may have helped to support the earthen roofs of the buildings, and hollowed whale vertebrae were probably used as querns for grinding cereals. The uniform structure of the houses at Skara Brae and other newly discovered Orcadian settlements such as Barnhouse suggests that there were cultural restrictions on architecture and the ways in which people entered and moved around their homes. The crouched burials of two elderly women were found under the walls of one of the houses, but for the main part the residents of Skara Brae were probably buried in megalithic tombs ◆

ABOVE SKARA BRAE, ONE OF THE BEST PRESERVED NEOLITHIC SETTLEMENTS IN NORTHERN EUROPE.

BELOW As farming communities settled across Europe, a series of distinct regional cultures developed, replacing the more homogenous styles of the earliest agricultural colonists. Long distance trade increased, and large enclosed settlements came to dominate the landscape.

found near the Sweet Track has been shown to come from a source in the Alps, and there are many other indications of long-distance exchange.

Large collective sites have been excavated in Denmark, for example at Trelleborg, dating from the Late Neolithic period. These may not have been fixed settlements but were places where groups came together at certain times. Many Neolithic groups in Britain also followed a relatively mobile lifestyle. A large pit, the Coneybury anomaly, in southern England contained the bones of cattle, deer and pigs and a large number of broken pottery vessels – perhaps the remnants of repeated periodic feasting. From about 3500 BCE ditched enclosures become common in Europe. Examples are found at Sarup (Denmark) and Lublin-Volhynian (Poland), where a 10 ft/3 m deep ditch enclosed an area 186 x 230 yds/170 x 210 m in extent. An enclosure at Windmill Hill (England)

gradually developed a series of concentric ditches over time. These enclosures were locations for large, possibly seasonal, gatherings during which great feasts and other social activities took place.

Southern Iberia

In the Late Neolithic (c.3000–2200 BCE), some farming communities in southern Iberia fortified their settlements with concentric drystone walls and built outlying bastions, probably to protect their irrigated fields and crops. They buried their dead in megalithic communal graves (see pages 64–65) with rich grave goods. Investigations of the walled sites at Los Millares (southeastern Spain) and Zambujal (Portugal) have found evidence of craft specialization, including pottery and copper-working, which probably developed here independently. There were also areas for processing and storing cereals ◆

area of farming cultures

- area of Alpine lakeside settlements
- area of Iberian farming groups
- area of Rössen culture
- Chasséen culture, c.4200 BCE
- Lengyel culture, c.4200 BCE
- Michelsberg culture, c.4200 BCE
- Vinča culture, c.4200 BCE
- Tripolye-Cucuteni cultures, 4200–3800 BCE
- Funnel Beaker cultures, 4200–2800 BCE

- site with enclosure
- site with evidence of animal traction, c.3500 BCE
- site of ax factory
- other Late Neolithic site

0   600 km
0   400 mi

The Megalith Builders

Early archaeologists believed that the megalithic culture of prehistoric western Europe, characterized by large communal tombs, standing stones and stone circles, could only have derived from early Mediterranean societies: it was assumed that the building of such complex architectural forms must have been diffused from more "civilized" cultures. The advent of scientific dating methods in the 1950s transformed these views, demonstrating that the megaliths were the product of indigenous European traditions that predated the building of the pyramids.

ABOVE Huge sarsen (sandstone) slabs block the entrance to West Kennet long barrow, southern England (c.3500 BCE). Beneath a mound some 330 ft/100 m long, the tomb consists of five burial chambers leading off a central passage. It held the disarticulated remains of at least 46 people.

Megalithic tombs were of several types. One of the earliest was the passage grave, comprising a stone burial chamber (with a corbelled or stone-slab roof), entered through a passage, the whole structure being covered with an earth or stone mound. Even though the passage was often low and narrow, it allowed repeated access to the tomb. Similar to passage graves are gallery graves, also known as *allées couvertes*, consisting of a corridor with lateral chambers, covered by an elongated mound or long barrow. In Ireland, access to the burial chamber was sometimes by an open semicircular forecourt (the court cairn). Round stone chambers known as dysser are found in association with passage graves in parts of northern Europe. Where stone was in short supply, some long barrows contain wooden burial chambers, as at Haddenham (England) and Sarnovo (Poland).

Many of these megalithic tombs were in use for decades, even centuries. The great necropolis of Bougon (western France), for example, was used for more than 2,000 years. Some tombs may contain the bones of hundreds of individuals. Very often the skeletons have

BELOW A figurine of a sleeping woman, from the hypogeum, or underground tomb complex, at Hal Saflieni, Malta, c.3400 BCE. Malta's Neolithic inhabitants carved burial chambers into solid rock, complete with roof beams, lintels and other features of buildings above ground. The tomb at Hal Saflieni consisted of 20 interconnected chambers and contained the remains of up to 7,000 people, so is likely to have been in use for a considerable time. Female figures popularly known as "fat ladies" occur at many sites in Malta.

been disarticulated. Earlier burials may have been moved to make way for new arrivals. Sometimes skulls and long bones were displayed in particular parts of the tomb, possibly in connection with ancestor rituals.

Many megalithic monuments have incised designs carved into the surface of the stones. The earliest examples are simple motifs of axes and crosses restricted to early passage graves in Brittany (4800–4000 BCE), but during the classic period of passage grave building (4000–3200 BCE), abstract designs including circles, spirals and meandering lines are found all along the Atlantic coast, but especially in Ireland (see box) and Brittany, most notably at Gavrinis. Some megalithic tombs in Portugal appear to have been painted. Later still, new representational forms appear in megalithic art: human-like figures in the rock-cut tombs of the Marne region of eastern France, and pairs of breasts and necklaces in Brittany.

Territorial markers

Some archaeologists believe that the megalithic long barrows were funerary representations of Neolithic longhouses. They would have stood out in the early agricultural landscape and may have acted as territorial markers in a world of increasing population and resulting pressure on land. Megalithic architecture was not confined to monumental tombs; during the later Neolithic, standing stones, stone circles and stone alignments set up in many parts of Europe may have been used as calendrical observatories or regional ceremonial centers. Sites like Avebury (southern England) and Carnac (Brittany), with their great stone avenues and circles, would have required great investment of labor over long periods of time, witnessing to the technological ingenuity and social power of the Neolithic societies that created them ◆

RIGHT From the 5th to 3rd millennium BCE, many prehistoric societies across Europe expressed their beliefs through the construction of massive stone monuments. The labor invested in these megalithic tombs and stone circles was enormous, and archaeological investigation has shown that many of the monuments in their present form are the result of long and often complex developmental histories. The earliest tombs are at Hoëdic and Téviec off the Brittany coast (c.5800 BCE).

area of megalithic monument building, 5800–2000 BCE

■ megalithic tomb

□ stone circle or alignment

▣ hypogeum

▢ other burial site

0   400 km

0   300 mi

Map labels

Ring of Brodgar · Rousay · Maes Howe · Quanterness · Callanish · Broubster · Leacach an Tigh Chloiche · Camster Long · Clava · Cullerie · Ballymeanoch · Monzie · Carn Ban, Monamore · Cairnpapple · Drumskinny · Lochhill · Carrowmore · Long Meg & Daughters · Dowth, Knowth, Newgrange · Castlerigg · Masonbrook · Barclodiadd y Gawres · Bryncelli Ddu · Derrynahinch · Arbor Low · Kealkil · Belas Knap, Hazleton · Notgrove · Haddenham · Mynydd-bach · Stony Littleton · Rollright Stones · Ty Isaf · West Kennet · Avebury · Fussells Lodge · Kit's Coty · Stonehenge · Merry Maidens

Haga · Jordhøj · Tustrup · Grønhøj · Knebel · Ramshög · Kong Askers Høj · Rügen Island · Putlos · Gnewitz · Liepen · Exlo · Oldendorf · Havelte · Emmen · Sarnovo · Wietrzychowice · Rimbeck · Altendorf · Ellenberg · La Chausée-Tirancourt · Weris

Les Fouaillages · Guennoc · Barnenez · Fontenay le-Marmion, La Hogue · Carn · Tressé · Coizard · La Madeleine · Colpo · Le Mesnil sur Oger · St Just · Carnac · Téviec · Gavrinis · Neuy-en-Dunios · Aillevans · Hoëdic · Pornic · Bagneux · Noisy · Auvernier · Bougon · Chenon · Sion

Puy de Paulhiac · L'Aumede · Roaix · Lamalou · Fontvieille · Coutignargues · La Halliade · Pepieux · Ponte San Pietro · Pouey-Mayou · Perarine · Artajona · La Clape · Cova d'En Daina · Puig Roig · Corsica · Cauria

Pedra Coberta · Cangas de Onis · Antela de Portelagem · Viseu · Carapito · Vila Nova de São Pedro · Cabeço da Arruda · Zambujal · Alapraia · Palmella · Anta da Marquesa · Pedra Branca · Poço da Gateira · Nora Velha · Anta das Gorgions · Alcalá · Alcaide · Dolmen de Soto · Cueva de la Menga · Romeral · El Barranquete

Sant Vincens · Son Baulo · Balearic Islands · Arzachena · Anghelu Ruju · Sa Coveccada · Santu Pedru · Sant Andrea Priu · Sardinia · Bou Nouara · Dougga · Bisceglie · Giovinazzo · Gaudo · Laterza · Cellino San Marco · Conca d'Oro · Sicily · Castelluccio · Pantelleria · Ggantija · Ta Hammuti · Hal Saflieni · Tarxien

North Sea · *Baltic Sea* · *Vättern* · *Elbe* · *Oder* · *Rhine* · *Danube* · *Sava* · *Seine* · *Loire* · *Rhône* · *Po* · *Ebro* · *Douro* · *Tagus* · *ALPS* · *PYRENEES* · *Mediterranean Sea*

Newgrange: stones with an enigma

At the end of the 4th millennium BCE, a cemetery of passage graves came into use in the Boyne Valley, Ireland. The largest, with a mound 330 ft/100 m in diameter and 43 ft/13 m high, is at New-grange. The cruciform-plan, corbelled-roofed burial chamber is 20 ft/6 m high. As well as its sophisticated structure, Newgrange (like neighboring Knowth) is noted for its megalithic art. Intricate designs of spirals, triangles, lozenges, concentric circles and wavy lines have been etched over the entire surface of the stones in the chamber and passage, and on the curbs of the mound. Archaeologists have proposed a number of interpretations for these designs. Some suggest they symbolize celestial bodies. Many Neolithic monuments have astronomical alignments, and Newgrange is constructed so that the midwinter sunrise illuminates the passage and chamber through a small aperture above the entrance (the same phenomenon occurs at Maes Howe in the Orkneys). An alternative view argues that they reflect images seen in narcotic-induced trances or altered states of consciousness. We shall never know ◆

ABOVE THE DECORATED ENTRANCE STONE AT NEWGRANGE. THE APERTURE IS ABOVE THE LINTEL.

Copper Age of Eastern Europe

The period from 4500 to 2500 BCE witnessed the transformation of prehistoric Europe into a society of developed farming communities that invested time and material wealth in ceremonial burials. Livestock became important as providers of milk, wool and power, and the first clear evidence for horse domestication is found on the Eurasian steppes. At the same time copper, the first metal to be smelted, came into use for the manufacture of ornaments and simple tools. It was most widespread in southern and eastern Europe, where this period is often referred to as the "Copper Age".

Although copper working first appeared in the Near East, it had its most pronounced social and economic effects in Europe, where it figured very prominently in personal ornamentation and in mortuary ritual. Copper use reached a remarkable peak in eastern Europe between 4500 and 3000 BCE, when it appears very commonly in burial finds. Mines have been discovered at several locations, including Rudna Glava (Serbia) and Aibunar (Bulgaria). Seams of copper ore were followed by miners who heated the rock and then dashed cold water on it to fracture the metal-bearing stone. The copper that appears in rich burials at Varna in northeastern Bulgaria (see box) came from a source about 125 mi/200 km away. The copper used in items found at Osłonki and Brześć Kujawski in north-central Poland was transported at least 310 mi/500 km from the Carpathians.

Most copper artifacts have been recovered as a result of deliberate burial in graves or hoards. Large cemeteries of several hundred burials in the Balkans have yielded graves that contain staggering amounts of copper, gold and other luxury items, and hoards of copper axes have been found throughout the region. Skeletons from great Copper Age cemeteries

like Tiszapolgár-Basantanya (Hungary) in the Carpathian Basin are accompanied by hammered copper bracelets and massive copper axes cast in molds. Graves at Brześć Kujawski and Osłonki (Poland) have yielded thousands of copper beads in belts and necklaces; one burial at Osłonki featured a diadem made from strips of copper that had been wrapped around a hide or fabric core. As far east as the Caucasus, rich Copper Age burials are found at sites like Maikop, where a massive timber-lined tomb contained several burials with an enormous number of gold and silver objects, many of them representing animals.

Cultural patterns

Archaeologists have tended to see the rich Copper Age cemeteries of the Balkans and the megalithic mortuary structures of Atlantic Europe (see pages 64-65) as distinct phenomena, but it is possible to view them as separate manifestations of a general trend toward elaborate mortuary ritual. The impact of this behavior was the creation of a landscape marked with large permanent monuments, clearly visible by later generations. In Central Europe, ditched sites known as "rondels" also appear at this time. They seem to have had a ceremonial function similar to that of the ditched enclosures or causewayed camps such as Windmill Hill that are found in western Europe.

Settlements at this period become increasingly diverse. Large settlements of densely packed houses like Poljanica and Ovčarovo (Bulgaria) are in marked contrast to the sprawling settlements of the Tripolye culture that overlooked river valleys in Ukraine. Traces of trapezoidal longhouses have been found at Brześć Kujawski and Osłonki in northern Poland. As cattle came to be used for traction and valued for their milk and secondary products, it is likely that the ownership of large herds conferred status and prestige. On the steppes of southern Russia and Kazakhstan, at sites like Botai, new evidence of wear on horse teeth caused by bits indicates that horses were used for transport during the 4th millennium BC. This development had profound implications for subsistence, warfare and human mobility throughout subsequent prehistoric periods on the Eurasian steppes and eventually throughout the world ◆

ABOVE The earliest copper artifacts were hammered from smelted copper, but craftsmen in the Balkans soon developed the ability to cast the molten metal into complex shapes such as this axadze from Belgrade (Serbia), which has a central hole for a shaft. The molds had to be carefully designed to avoid imperfections from bubbles trapped in the molten copper.

RIGHT Southeast Europe was a major center of metallurgical innovation between 4500 and 3000 BCE due to the availability of copper ores and the local mastery of pyrotechnology through experience in pottery manufacture. Demand for copper ornaments and weapons to demonstrate status and wealth fueled this innovation. Copper from the Carpathians and eastern Alps reached distant locations such as the lowlands of central Poland and Germany through trade along major waterways.

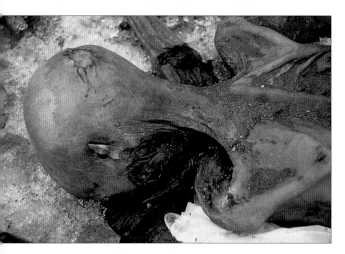

LEFT The 5,300-year-old body popularly known as the Iceman, which emerged from a glacier in the Ötztaler Alps in 1991. The high concentrations of copper found on his hair have led to speculation that he was a metalworker who died on the mountain while prospecting for ore. His clothes and possessions, preserved by the ice, are a "time capsule" of information. They include leather leggings, shoes, leather trousers or skirt, a cloak of woven grass, a fur cap, and a fur and hide jacket. He carried with him a copper ax on a yew handle, a yew bow, a deerskin quiver with 14 arrows, a flint dagger and a backpack.

Stora Köpinge

Osłonki   Brześć Kujawski

Wahlitz

Haldorf   Schafstädt

Bronicice

Bylany

Tripolye   Derievka

Těšetice-Kyjovice   Tibava   Vladimirovka

Friebritz

Branč   Tiszapolgár-Basatanya

Hornstaad   Svodin   Bodrogkeresztúr

Mondsee   Budakalász   Békásmegyer   Cucuteni
Szigetszentmárton   Hăbăşeşti

Ötztal   Öcsöd-Kováshalom   Usatovo
Val Camonica   Tirpeşti   Karbuna
Molino Casarotto   Hódmezővásárhely

Petit-Chasseur

Lagozza
Remedello   Vučedol   Cernica   Cernavodă
Vinča   Belgrade   Danube
Prljusa-Mali Struac   Sălcuta   Gumelnitsa   Ovčarovo
Selevac   Rudna Glava   Poljanica
Bubanj   Goljamo Delčevo   Varna
Aibunar   Karanovo

Rinaldone

Corsica

Black Sea

ALPS
APPENNINES
DINARIC ALPS
CARPATHIAN MTS
BALKAN MTS

Rhine   Danube   Oder   Vistula   Bug   Desna   Dnieper   Dniester   Prut   Tisza   Sava   Po   Elbe

Gaudo
Buccino,
Tufariello

□ site with burial or cemetery
■ major settlement
▣ site with rondel
▪ rock carving or carved standing stone
⬚ other important site
▨ area of copper using cultures, c.4000 BCE
— probable trade route
⁙ source of copper
⁙ source of gold

0 ——————————— 400 km
0 ——————————— 300 mi

Varna: a rich Balkan cemetery

Construction of drainage ditches on the outskirts of the Black Sea resort of Varna in 1972 led to the discovery of one of the richest Copper Age cemeteries in Europe, dated to c.4000 BCE. Excavations led by Ivan Ivanov revealed over 280 graves. Many contained skeletons (mostly interred on their backs), while others were cenotaphs (empty tombs) in which burial goods had been placed as if a body were present: in some, a clay mask represented the absent corpse. The rich graves in the Varna cemetery represent an unparalleled accumulation of wealth, reflected in the quantity and quality of artifacts made from gold, copper, shell and stone. Two of the graves each contained over 3.3 lb/1.5 kg of gold, while another contained over 850 separate objects. Many of the materials and worked goods came from a considerable distance, indicating that Varna was part of a trade network covering much of southeastern Europe and the Aegean. Its coastal location would have made it an important gateway for trade in precious metals and prestige goods, and inland settlements such as Poljanica and Ovčarovo indicate increasing social differentiation during this period ◆

ABOVE THIN GOLD PLAQUES DEPICTING CATTLE (2.5 IN/6.5 CM AND 1.5 IN/3.8 CM HIGH).

Sumerians and Akkadians

The phase of Mesopotamian civilization that followed the Ubaid and Uruk periods (see pages 60–61) is known as the Early Dynastic (3000–2300 BCE). Archaeology reveals it to have been a time of political fragmentation and conflict between competing city-states. It was also a period of great artistic and intellectual creativity when the Sumerians and Akkadians laid the foundations of what would become one of the world's great early civilizations, the Mesopotamian. Sumerian and Akkadian are languages, not distinctive cultures: Akkadian was a Semitic tongue, the origins of Sumerian are uncertain. In spite of their linguistic differences, Sumerians and Akkadians shared a closely intertwined cultural and political history.

The Early Dynastic period saw the development of cuneiform writing, which had been invented in the late Uruk period (see pages 46–47). The earliest inscriptions, from c.3300 BCE, are mostly terse administrative records; the first examples of Sumerian literature are about 500 years later. Early Dynastic texts suggest that people with Akkadian names lived mainly in the north, at places like Kish, Jemdet Nasr, and Abu Salabikh, while Sumerians lived south of Nippur (an important religious center) in towns such as Ur, Lagash, Uruk and Umma. But this linguistic and geographic distinction was not a real boundary; even the earliest Sumerian texts contain Semitic words and scribes with Akkadian names recorded much of the later Sumerian literature.

In the Early Dynastic period as many as four out of every five people in southern Mesopotamia lived in a city or large town. Some of the more prominent cities, including Uruk, Ur, Lagash, Umma, Adab, and Kish, were the capitals of small kingdoms, or city-states, each of which encompassed subsidiary settlements and a rural hinterland. The principal city housed the court of the ruling elite as well as the temple of the city's chief tutelary god. Temples to other deities were also built in the capital and in secondary cities.

Both palace and temples wielded considerable economic power, controlling extensive farmlands with a large agricultural workforce and employing artisans, craftsmen and traders. Although temples may once have been autonomous, and perhaps even preceded the palace as the source of political authority, by late in the Early Dynastic period the palace had come to control temple assets. Literary and material evidence provides a picture of constant rivalry between city-states, often leading to war. One of the best recorded of these conflicts, which persisted over many generations, was between Umma and Lagash over the control of land and water in a district along their frontier.

Uncovering the past

Over the last 150 years archaeologists of all nationalities have dug in many of the Early Dynastic cities and towns of Mesopotamia. Most excavations have concentrated on temples and palaces; consequently, our knowledge of the non-official aspects of city life is much less complete. At the center of the temple precinct was the shrine, which was set upon a platform to raise the god's abode above the rest of the city. The most exhaustive excavation of an Early Dynastic temple site has been at Khafaje. Included within the precinct were the living quarters for the director of the temple, storage rooms, workshops, and extensive plazas, enclosed within an oval wall. This arrangement is repeated in the cities of Tell al-Hiba and Tell

RIGHT Southern Mesopotamia (Sumeria and Akkadia) was a country of low relief defined by the levees and backslopes of rivers, a landscape of canals, irrigated farmland, dry pastureland and marshes. Its cities, the crowning glory of early Mesopotamian civilization, lay along the river courses and main canals that sustained settled life in this arid region. Many places could trace their beginnings back to the first permanent occupation of the region during the 6th millennium BCE, becoming cities two or three thousand years later. These urban places formed the political, social and cultural heart of the Mesopotamian civilization, the city-states of which perceived themselves to be culturally united but rarely achieved, or even desired, political integration during the 3rd millennium BCE.

Ur: An Opulent Royal Cemetery

Excavated by a British team in the 1920s, the royal cemetery at Ur was found to contain over 2,000 graves of people interred there over five centuries. Of these, only 16 or 17 may truly be called "royal". Dating from around 2600–2500 BCE, these tombs are not just simple pits but constructed chambers with an entrance ramp, and may hold the bodies of as many as 75 people in addition to the central figure. The grave goods they contain are of fabulous opulence: helmets, daggers, spears, cups and other vessels as well as lamps, headdresses, jewelry, and toiletry kits made of gold, silver, electrum and copper; necklaces of lapis lazuli and carnelian; carved jars, cups, bowls, lamps and cosmetic containers. Objects such as the so-called Standard of Ur, which is decorated with scenes of warfare and ritual celebration composed of lapis lazuli and mother-of-pearl inlays; two small statues of gold and lapis lazuli known as the "rams in the thicket", ornamented lyres, a gold headdress and an ornate helmet from the tomb of Meskalamdug have all acquired world fame. In the tombs, archaeologists also found the remains of ox-drawn carts and their drivers, along with guards and ladies-in-waiting. These burials graphically demonstrate the absolute authority wielded by the Sumerian elites ◆

ABOVE THE ROYAL CEMETERY AT UR, EXCAVATED IN THE 1920S BY SIR LEONARD WOOLLEY.

al- Ubaid to the south, but in some other places residential quarters and workshops stood outside the walls that formally demarcated sacred space.

Fewer Early Dynastic palaces have been excavated. Two of the earliest are at Kish and date from around 2700 BC. Another building identified as a palace has been found at Eridu, and others dating from toward the end of the period can be seen at Mari and Ebla in Syria, a region open to Mesopotamian influence but nonetheless distinctive in cultural practices. These palaces are modestly proportioned compared to later royal buildings. As well as a reception room and other areas for the king's public duties, the palace complex included suites for the royal family, offices for scribes and the bureaucratic staff, the royal treasury and kitchens and facilities for food storage. Though self-contained, these public buildings often lay in the midst of residential quarters with the surrounding houses pressing up close against the enclosing palace wall.

RIGHT The victory stele of Naram-Sin. Around 2300 BCE the kings of Agade (Akkad) became the dominant power in southern Mesopotamia and extended their influence beyond it. Naram-Sin, the fourth king of the Akkadian empire, was the first to declare himself a god. This is indicated by his horned helmet and his superhuman size as he tramples the heads of his enemies.

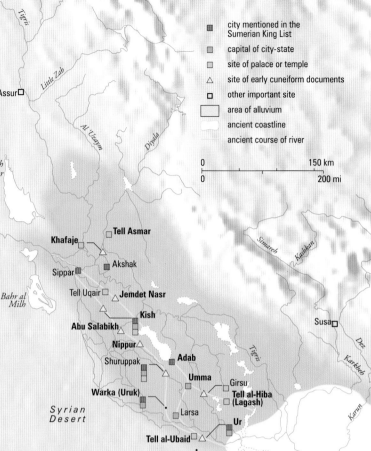

Objects of wealth

Although a great part of their resources would have been spent on weapons and defense, the ruling elites of the early Mesopotamian city-states devoted a considerable proportion of their treasuries to adorning their palaces and temples. The purpose of much of this art was to glorify the power of individual kings or the mythical deeds of ancestors like Gilgamesh, the legendary founder of Uruk. Successful military campaigns were celebrated on carved victory stelae or shown in mother-of-pearl inlaid furnishings of palaces, as at Mari and Ebla. Kings and other wealthy citizens showed religious devotion by placing statues of themselves praying to the gods in the temples: typically – as in a famous series of statues found at Tell Asmar – supplicants were portrayed with clasped hands and staring eyes.

Other products reveled in ostentatious displays of material wealth. The wealth of magnificent grave goods discovered in the Royal Cemetery at Ur (see box) serves as the outstanding example of the variety and splendor of luxurious objects that the ruling elite was able to commission from Mesopotamian craftsmen, magnificently worked in gold and silver, semiprecious stones, copper and other materials ◆

69

Bronze Age Trade of Western Asia

The alluvial plains in which the great early civilizations of the Near East developed supported sufficient abundance of natural resources to satisfy most basic requirements of life: water for drinking, watering livestock and irrigating fields; fertile soils for growing cereals; riverine mud that could be sun-dried as bricks for building and used for pottery; shrubs and reeds to provide construction poles and roofing materials. But they yielded few of the luxury materials used to ornament the palaces and persons of their ruling elites and confer political and social status. Exotic goods such as metals, brightly colored minerals like lapis lazuli, scented woods, and hard stones for carving had all to be obtained through contact with neighboring societies. During the 3rd and early 2nd millennia BCE, a vast network of trade opened up in western Asia that linked Afghanistan with Anatolia, 2,500 mi/4,000 km away.

The city-states of southern Mesopotamia were particularly well placed to benefit from the many trade routes that converged in the region. Barges laden with merchandise from eastern Anatolia, Syria and the northern plains floated down the gently flowing Euphrates and the more turbulent Tigris, while donkeys carried goods northward along the river banks. Important towns such as Mari, Emar, Carchemish, Sippar, Assur and Nineveh grew up along these rivers at major intersections with the overland trade routes that led westward across Syria via Ebla and Aleppo, or through Palmyra and Qatna toward the Mediterranean Sea. Other routes headed in a more northerly direction into central Anatolia, while to the east, mountain passes gave access to the Iranian plateau and beyond. Several major routes led directly through the Zagros mountains into southern Mesopotamia. One

of them entered the area of Babylon and Sippar, while another ran farther south through Susa. They linked Mesopotamia with the mineral-rich areas of Iran, Afghanistan and Turkmenistan, where Bronze Age civilizations flourished at places like Malyan, Shahdad, Shahr-i Sokhta, Altyn-depe and Namazga.

The trading network

A huge variety of goods moved through the western Asian network of exchange. Profitable items on overland routes were typically those that combined high value with low bulk. Transportation of bulky staple goods by water was usually restricted to local trade, and distant commerce along the long trade routes of the ancient Near East concentrated on metals and luxury goods: copper from eastern Anatolia, western Iran, Oman and Cyprus; tin from Afghanistan and eastern Anatolia; silver and gold from eastern Anatolia; lapis lazuli from northeastern Afghanistan; carnelian from eastern Iran and northern India; mother-of-pearl from the Persian Gulf and Indian Ocean; cedar and other scented woods (used to grace the walls of palaces and temples), aromatic resins and oils from the Amanus mountains and Lebanon; soapstone vessels from Central Asia, Iran and Oman; wine from Syria; textiles from Mesopotamia.

ABOVE Beehive tombs, c.3000 BCE, from the eastern foot of Jebel Hafit in southeastern Arabia. There are hundreds of such tombs in the area, many containing grave goods of imported pottery as well as locally manufactured copper artifacts. This region, known as Magan in cuneiform texts, was an important producer of copper for the Mesopotamian market. Tons of smelting slags can still be seen at places in the interior of Oman, showing how great was the copper production that fed this trade in ancient times.

RIGHT Archaeological finds and the details of trading transactions given in contemporary cuneiform texts provide evidence of the extensive network of land and sea routes that connected the far-flung Bronze Age civilizations of western Asia. Goods might flow from Afghanistan and the Indus valley to the Mediterranean coast, but the traders themselves worked only certain stretches of these routes, meeting in important entrepôts to exchange commodities for further distribution and profit.

RIGHT A silver model of a barge from the King's Tomb in the Royal Cemetery of Ur. Boats of this type are still used by the Marsh Arabs of southern Iraq today. The rivers and canals of Mesopotamia were important arteries for shipping bulk cargoes of foodstuffs and other goods within the region.

Ancient trade was not a single integrated system, but consisted of a number of small, geographically delimited spheres, each focused on particular exchanges. Wider trade took place where one sphere intersected with another. These spheres were not permanent, but shifted in scope and organization according to the prevailing social and political circumstances. Surviving cuneiform texts tell us much about the goods and conditions of trade in one such commercial sphere, Cappadocia (central Anatolia), around 1800 BCE. The network of exchange was controlled by Assyrian trading firms who had established colonies in the region through commercial treaties with local rulers. Excavations at places like Kültepe have recovered remains of these colonies. Assyrian merchants mostly brought textiles and tin, which they traded for silver to take back to Assur. Some of the textiles for trade were made at home, but others came ultimately from Babylonia. The tin was shipped from the east, probably Afghanistan.

Legendary lands

We also know about Babylonian trade in the Persian Gulf from around 2500 to 1750 BCE. It is apparent from cuneiform texts that kings, temples and private entrepreneurs invested in cargoes of textiles and other goods that were shipped to the societies along the Arabian shore of the Persian Gulf. Here they were exchanged for copper from Oman and luxury goods from more distant regions.

References to the lands of Dilmun, Magan and Meluhha in Mesopotamian texts describe them as semi-legendary places. Dilmun, which is mentioned in early Akkadian epics recounting the journeys and exploits of the hero Gilgamesh, was clearly regarded as a particularly pure and holy place, a place of eternal life. Archaeological research has shown that Dilmun was the island of Bahrain and the adjacent coastal areas of the Persian Gulf. Magan is identified as southeastern Arabia (Oman and the United Arab Emirates), and Meluhha as the Indus valley civilization (see pages 114–115). Each of them were separate civilizations but they were all part of the same trading network. Excavations in Bahrain have uncovered pottery and other artifacts from Mesopotamia, southeast Arabia, Iran and the Indus valley, while objects from these same places, and from Bahrain itself, have been found in southern Mesopotamia ◆

BELOW The splendid grave goods from the Royal Cemetery at Ur are striking evidence of the extent of Bronze Age trade in the Near East and beyond. The gold for this jewelry probably came originally from Anatolia, the lapis lazuli from as far away as eastern Afghanistan. Mesopotamian rulers had to import all the raw materials that their craftsmen manufactured into superb weapons and luxury items, or used to embellish palaces and temples.

Black Sea

KÜRE MTS

CAUCASUS MOUNTAINS

Caspian Sea

Sakarya • Boghazköy
Alishar
Kültepe
Acem Höyük
TAURUS MTS

Lake Tuz

Lake Sevan

Lake Van

Lake Urmia

Marlik

ELBURZ MTS

KOPET DAGH

Shah tepe
Tureng
Hissar
Altyn-depe
Namazga
Shortugaï

Amu Darya

Panj

ASHIYA
Ugarit
Cyprus

AMANUS MTS
Carchemish
Aleppo
Ebla **Emar**
Qatna
Byblos **Palmyra**
Hazor

Syrian Desert

Nineveh
Assur

ZAGROS MOUNTAINS

Mari

Munkhafad ath Tharthar
Tell Asmar
Khafaje
Sippar
Babylon Kish
Nippur
Lagash
Ur

Bahr al Milh

Susa
ELAM

Malyan
ANSHAN

Tepe Sialk

MARHASHI

Dasht-e Kavir

Dasht-e lut
Shahdad

Shahr-i Sokhta

Mundigak

MELUHHA

Mehrgarh

Zohreh

Tepe Yahya

Nindowari

Shahi Tump

Sutkagen Dor
Sotka Koh

Sinai

major source of commodity

- bitumen
- copper
- marine shells
- obsidian
- semi-precious stone
- silver
- soapstone
- tin

—— trade route
□ Indus site
△ site with Indus style find
□ other site
▨ alluvial valley
▨ ancient coastline

0 ———— 400 km
0 ———— 300 mi

Persian Gulf

Failaka

Qala'at al Bahrain
DILMUN

Tell Abraq Ajman
Umm an-Nar Hili

Gulf of Oman

MAGAN

Maysar
Ras al Junayz

Arabian Sea

Early Empires of Mesopotamia

The urban-based character of early Sumerian and Akkadian civilization (see pages 68–69) continued later in the Bronze Age. The archaeological record supports the literary texts in showing southern Mesopotamia divided into numerous city-states perpetually at war with one another or forming temporary coalitions. From time to time certain cities managed to rise above the rest, temporarily holding sway over their neighbors and even over adjacent regions. During this period, three ruling families gained control of territories large enough to be termed empires: the dynasty of Sargon at Agade (c.2350–2230 BCE), of Ur-Nammu at Ur (2112–2004 BCE), and of Hammurabi at Babylon (1792–1595 BCE). These cycles of empire building and collapse altered the Mesopotamian political landscape but never fully succeeded in supplanting cities as the ultimate sources of authority and power, or in creating a lasting sense of political unity.

Sargon (whose name in Akkadian literally means "the true king") was the first of these empire builders, and his career served as the exemplar of imperial ambition over the next two millennia. He brought the cities of southern Mesopotamia under his control, led military campaigns into Syria as far as the Amanus and Taurus mountains (the "Cedar Forest" and "Silver Mountain" of his inscriptions) and ventured into the highlands of Iran to the east. Wishing perhaps to avoid being drawn into the traditional conflicts of the Mesopotamian city-states, Sargon founded a new capital at Agade (believed to be near modern Baghdad), to which he diverted trade and tribute. His successors also undertook frequent military expeditions. In the course of one such campaign, probably led by Sargon's grandson Naram-Sin, the palace at Ebla was destroyed; the recently excavated royal archive there throws fascinating light on the Syrian politics and society of the day. Naram-Sin left carved inscriptions on cliff faces in eastern Turkey and Kurdistan commemorating his victorious progress through these lands. The kings of Agade established garrisons and administrative centers throughout their empire at places like Susa, Assur, Nineveh, Nuzi and Tell Brak. At home they built palaces and temples and employed artisans to produce outstanding sculpture, metalwork and engraved seals.

The Third Dynasty of Ur

The Agade empire broke apart, partly under pressure from mountain peoples invading from Gutium to the east. Gutian rulers became established in territories in the north of Mesopotamia, while the southern city-states were governed by local dynasties for about a century until a new power arose in the region, based on the city of Ur. Known as the Ur III dynasty from its position in the Sumerian King List, it was founded by Ur-Nammu in 2112 BCE and reached its height during the reign of his son Shulgi (2094–2047 BCE). Though his empire was not as extensive as some of those that came before or after him in Mesopotamia, Shulgi consolidated his hold on the provinces along the Tigris river and established vassal states in the Zagros mountains of western Iran. He set up an efficient system of bureaucracy that enabled him to extract huge surpluses from farmers, animal herders and craftsmen,

RIGHT Sargon of Agade and his successors were the first ruling dynasty to extend their power beyond the Mesopotamian heartland. Their military conquests carried their influence as far as the Mediterranean Sea and northwards into Anatolia, and they established garrisons throughout the Near East. A hundred years after the dynasty's demise, the principal power in Mesopotamia was based at the southern city of Ur. The influence of the Ur III dynasty ran from north of Nineveh to the eastern shore of the Persian Gulf. The city-states of Sumer and Akkad formed the core of its empire; the periphery lands to the north and east were controlled by military officers who paid an annual tax in livestock, while farther east, in the Zagros mountains, the Ur rulers gained influence by forming close alliances with local states. Although the Babylonian empire of the early 2nd millennium established by Hammurabi was not long lasting, it altered the political landscape of Mesopotamia by permanently shifting the focus of power away from the deep south to Babylon.

RIGHT A fragment of a wall-painting from Mari, possibly depicting a sacrificial procession. It hints at the former glories of the palace that was destroyed by Hammurabi in 1757 BCE.

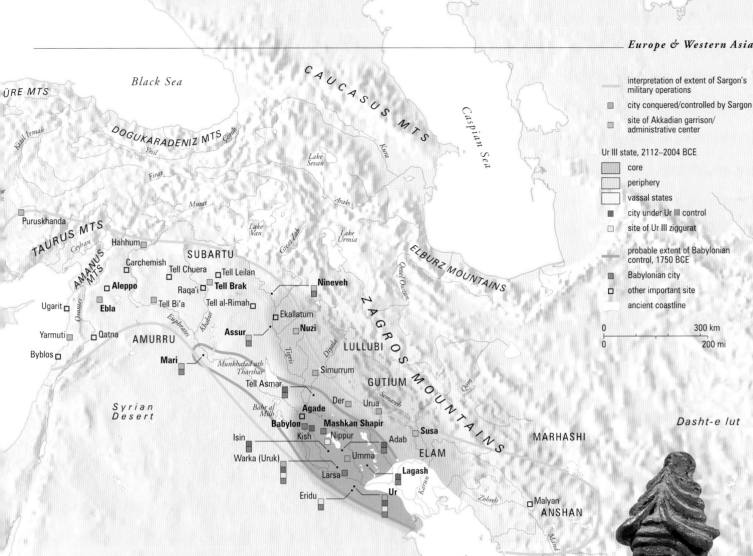

and also promulgated a law code, which is the earliest example that survives from Mesopotamia, predating Hammurabi's more famous document by about three hundred years.

The Ur III kings, and especially its first two rulers, used part of their wealth to finance great building projects, particularly temples. The ziggurat – the distinctive architectural form of ancient Mesopotamia, which has entered western consciousness as the tower of Babel described in the Bible – attained its classic shape in the structures built by Ur-Nammu at Ur and other Mesopotamian cities. They consisted of three, and eventually as many as eight, stepped platforms, lifting the temple shrine high above the ground. The Ur III kings also constructed elaborate buildings to house the gods' priests and servants, as well as palaces for their own households and officials.

Hammurabi and Babylon

The third great empire of the early Bronze Age Near East was that of Hammurabi (1792–1750 BCE), who transformed Babylon from a minor city-state to the dominating political and religious power of both northern and southern Mesopotamia, extending right to the borders of the Syrian kingdom of Aleppo. It has not been possible to excavate Hammurabi's palace at Babylon, which lies buried beneath centuries of later occupation, and we can only speculate

RIGHT A copper nail commemorating a temple foundation depicts Gudea, governor of Lagash c.2130 BCE, who claimed to have rebuilt many temples out of reverence to the gods and styled himself "lord of the four quarters", a title formerly used by the kings of Agade. He almost certainly exaggerated his real power as ruler of a small southern city-state.

on its appearance from our knowledge of other palaces of the same period. At this time, the Near East was a patchwork of small kingdoms. The degree of power their rulers wielded varied enormously but all were driven by pretensions to greatness. Many kings turned to palace-building to project their ambition, and some palaces gained an international reputation for size and elegance. Perhaps the most famous of these was the palace at Mari, an immense edifice with several hundred rooms, corridors and courtyards, its walls decorated with painted scenes of royal authority. Archaeological investigation of sites like Ur and Mashkan Shapir gives us a good impression of the crowded urban landscape of the Babylonian era, with twisting streets and small houses, while canals and main thoroughfares gave more direct access to the major temples and palaces ◆

Bronze Age Social Elites

The Bronze Age in northern Eurasia traditionally covers the period from c.2500-1000 BCE, which saw the rise of societies based on institutionalized, probably hereditary, distinctions of status, power and wealth. The rise in elite burials right across the region from the Atlantic coast to Siberia is evidence for this change. Bronze was used for a wide variety of artifacts that accompanied important burials and was clearly a major medium for the accumulation and display of wealth. The term Bronze Age, nevertheless, is a somewhat arbitrary one, as many of the economic, social, and technological developments that characterize the period began in the preceding millennium and continued on afterward.

Bronze is an alloy of copper and tin, and deposits of these ores usually lie a long way apart. Thus bronze-working would have been restricted to individuals or communities that had connections to long-distance exchange networks. It would have been impossible for any person who did not have regular access to supplies of the raw material to learn metalworking skills. Although with time there may have been sufficient quantities of bronze in circulation to be melted down and reworked into new articles, it is highly probable that specialist bronze-working was supported by the patronage of wealthy sponsors.

The ritual landscape

Study of the European Bronze Age has concentrated primarily on burials. Small earthen mounds or "barrows" are found almost everywhere from the Atlantic coast to Siberia. In western Europe, the switch from a practice of communal burial in megalithic tombs (see pages 64–65) to one of single burials may reflect increased emphasis on the status of the individual, but single burial had been customary in eastern Europe since the Neolithic. The end result of this ritual activity was the creation of a ritual landscape of monuments to individual ancestors – especially important in a society where status and prestige was determined by membership in genealogical line.

The area around Stonehenge in southern England contains a concentration of round barrows. Though the construction of Stonehenge itself began in the late Neolithic, it reached its final form in the early Bronze Age. The raising of its massive stone blocks would have required great organizational capacities. It is one of a series of earth, timber and stone enclosures that served as ceremonial centers in the midst of the ritual landscape of mortuary barrows. It is possible that the rebuilding of such centers was one of the ways by which local elites reaffirmed their authority.

Wealthy burials

Individual burials were often accompanied by grave goods that took considerable effort to produce. The single male interred in Bush Barrow (southern England) c.2000 BCE was buried with a gold belt-fastener and breastplate, a copper dagger whose handle had been inlaid with thousands of tiny gold nails, a bronze dagger, and a bronze flanged ax. Barrows of the Únětice culture (central and east Europe) are notable for their high-value burial goods and distinct architecture: fourteen tumuli at Łęki Małe (Poland) have a cairn of boulders at their center, within which is a wooden-roofed burial chamber containing the skeleton of a man lying on his back in an extended position. At Leubingen and Helmsdorf (southeastern Germany), barrows concealed mortuary structures with pitched roofs. Horses appear to have had considerable ritual importance: a number of burial mounds from the Urals contain lavish grave goods and horse sacrifices. A striking find from Trundholm (Denmark) is a bronze statue of a horse pulling a sun disk mounted on a chariot. It has obvious ritual significance and was found deliberately broken up.

Late in the Bronze Age, c.1300 BCE, cremation began to replace inhumation as the predominant form of burial. Urns containing cremated ashes were placed in pits located in defined cemetery areas or "urnfields". Buried with them were various objects like knives, pottery cups, bronze pins and rings. The vast numbers of urn burials in many cemeteries suggest that population densities rose in the Late Bronze Age. The practice continued in some areas into the Iron Age (see pages 96–97).

Settlement sites

Information concerning settlement sites is limited, but indicates that people lived in hamlets of dispersed farmsteads, much as their predecessors had. In southern Scandinavia, the principal dwelling was a longhouse. In Britain, hamlets of small circular houses containing between two to ten households have been excavated at sites like Itford Hill and Black Patch. Palisaded lakeside villages in southern Germany and Switzerland continued a tradition of settlement that had begun in earlier periods. At some sites, like Iwanowice in Poland, no evidence of buildings has survived, but storage pits identify the locations of individual households. In east-central Europe fortified settlements at places like Nitriansky Hrádok and Spišský-Štvrtok controlled major trade routes in the Carpathians. Beyond the Urals, Bronze Age settlements in the Yenisei valley are characterized by large semi-subterranean cabins built from logs ◆

RIGHT A bronze socketed spearhead from a hoard found at Arreton Down, southern England, 9 in/22.5 cm.

RIGHT Archaeological investigation over the last 200 years has identified several areas of temperate Europe in which rich burials reflect the ritual practices and wealth of Bronze Age societies. The Wessex culture of southern England, the Únetice culture of central Europe, and the peoples of Denmark buried their dead under mounds that reflected their social status. Later in the Bronze Age, the Urnfield peoples cremated their dead and buried them in urns in shallow pits.

Knocknalap

Gwithi

Kerno

■ fortified settlement
□ barrow burial
▪ other burial site
▪ site of rock art
▪ ceremonial site
▪ other Bronze Age settlement or site

▨ area of lakeside settlement
▨ area of Únětice culture, c.1800 BCE
▨ area of Wessex culture, c.1800 BCE
▨ area of urnfield burials, c.1200–800 BCE

— major trade route

major source of commodity
▲ amber
▲ copper
▲ tin

0   400 km
0   300 mi

North Sea

Baltic Sea

Rickeby
Tromøy
Tanum
Hallunda
Vänern
Kvarnby
Vättern

Thy Island
Egenhøj Hemmed Church
Muldbjerg
Borun Eshøj
Højgard
Egtved Trundholm
Trappendal Kivik

Reznes

Memsie

Brenig ■ Mam Tor
Dinorben
Irthlingborough Flag Fen
Avebury, bury Hill *Thames*
Bush Barrow
Jpton Stonehenge
Lovell
gh Moor Itford Hill Black Patch
Arreton Down

npatrick

Elp
Perleberg
Gustorzyn

Wassenaar
Toterfout

Helmsdorf
Weser
Grossbrembach Leubingen
Nieder-Neundorf
Łęki Małe
Elbe
Oder
Vistula
Postoloprty
Rhine
Únětice
Meuse
Bug
Nieman

Iwanowice-Babia Gora

Ivanja
Moska

Fort Harrouard
Aulnay-aux-Planches
Hagenau Forest
Seine
Danube
Straubing
Velké Pavlovice
Nitriansky Hrádok
Spišsky-Štvrtok
Branč
Barca
Čaka Malé Kosihy
Loire
Wasserburg, Buchau, Forschner
Boheimkirchen
Füzesabony
Mitterberg

CARPATHIAN MOUNTAINS

Dniepr
Dniester
Prut
Usatovo
Tudoromo

Chalain Cortaillod Baldegg Wittnauer Horn
Clairvaux
Petit Chasseur *ALPS* Crestaulte
Ledro
Val Camonica
Polada
Rhône
Po
Tószeg
Nagyrév
Periam
Mokrin
Tisza
Drava
Sava
Gomalava
Vattina
Monteoru

DINARIC ALPS

APPENNINES

Monte Bego

PYRENEES

Luni
Narce
Filitosa
Corsica

Mediterranean Sea

Danube
Tarnava
Donja Slatina
Ezerovo
Ezero

BALKAN MTS

Scandinavia: log coffin burials

Late Bronze Age burial mounds in southern Sweden and Norway, Denmark, and parts of northern Germany provide unique evidence of Bronze Age life. The mounds, which are particularly large, contain coffins hollowed out from oak trunks. The tannic acid of the oak has preserved woolen clothing, hides, and even the hair, nails and skin of the dead. One of the best known of these burials is at Egtved, Jutland, where archaeologists in the 1920s discovered the body of a young woman who died one summer over 3,000 years ago (we know this because a flower was placed in her coffin). She wore a woolen tunic and short cord skirt bound with a belt decorated with a large disk of engraved bronze. Close to her lay a birch-bark container holding the remains of a fermented beverage and a small bag with the burnt bones of an 8-year-old child. Another container held the woman's personal effects, including bronze pins and a hair ribbon. Under the large mound at Borun Eshøj, which was excavated in the 1870s, three oak coffins were found. In one, an old man lay on his back with a cowhide beneath him and a woolen cloak over him, while in another a woman wore a woolen hairnet and bronze ornaments ◆

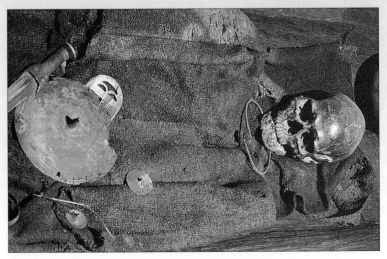

ABOVE THE BODY OF A MAN FOUND LYING WITHIN AN OAK COFFIN PRESERVED IN A DANISH BOG.

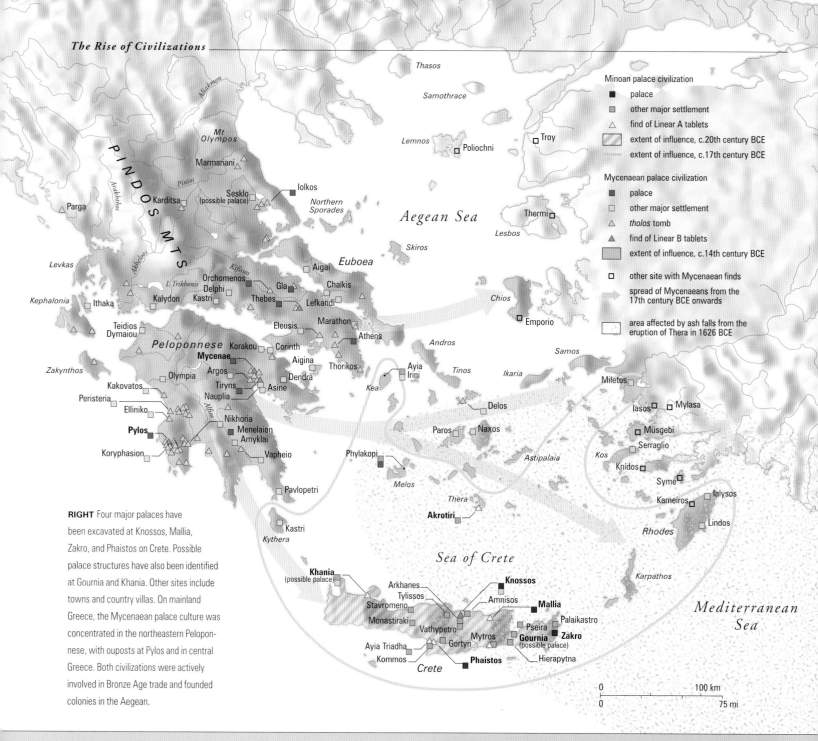

Minoan palace civilization
- ■ palace
- ■ other major settlement
- △ find of Linear A tablets
- ▨ extent of influence, c.20th century BCE
- extent of influence, c.17th century BCE

Mycenaean palace civilization
- ■ palace
- □ other major settlement
- △ *tholos* tomb
- ▲ find of Linear B tablets
- ▨ extent of influence, c.14th century BCE
- ▢ other site with Mycenaean finds
- ⇨ spread of Mycenaeans from the 17th century BCE onwards
- ▢ area affected by ash falls from the eruption of Thera in 1626 BCE

RIGHT Four major palaces have been excavated at Knossos, Mallia, Zakro, and Phaistos on Crete. Possible palace structures have also been identified at Gournia and Khania. Other sites include towns and country villas. On mainland Greece, the Mycenaean palace culture was concentrated in the northeastern Peloponnese, with outposts at Pylos and in central Greece. Both civilizations were actively involved in Bronze Age trade and founded colonies in the Aegean.

| 0 | | 100 km |
| 0 | | 75 mi |

Akrotiri: beneath the volcano

In the 17th century BCE the volcanic island of Thera erupted, spewing vast quantities of tephra and pumice into the atmosphere, causing widespread destruction: palace buildings on Crete collapsed under the fallout of ash. In the late 1960s, excavations began at Akrotiri, a town on Thera that lay buried beneath layers of volcanic deposits. The discovery of several large public buildings and town houses gave archaeologists a unique insight into the everyday life of a prosperous Aegean town of the Late Bronze Age. The main source of the town's wealth most probably came from trade, though there was agricultural activity as well. It occupied a site of around 50 acres/20 ha and supported a population of several thousand. No bodies and few artifacts have been found, suggesting that most of the inhabitants had fled before the final eruption blew the island apart. The presence of Linear A writing and Minoan discoid lead weights indicate that Akrotiri lay within the Minoan orbit of economic influence in the Aegean, and there are marked cultural influences as well. Elegant wall-paintings in a naturalistic style, some of which depict scenes of island life (see page 81), share strong iconographic similarities with those on Crete ◆

ABOVE ONE OF THE EXCAVATED HOUSES AT AKROTIRI.

Aegean Palace Civilizations

Two civilizations developed in the Aegean in the Late Bronze Age (c.1900–1250 BCE): the Minoan on Crete and the Mycenaean on the Greek mainland. Both may be defined as hierarchical, politically complex societies, dominated at their apex by a large bureaucratic and governmental system, which was located within an architecturally distinctive building, the palace. The palace commanded the surrounding area and in addition to its political and economic activities served as the residence of the ruling elite; it possibly also had an important religious role. Some scholars argue that the political and bureaucratic structures of the Aegean palace societies evolved naturally through gradual economic, technological and social change. Others believe they had their origins in the political systems of the older palatial states of Egypt and the Near East, and came about as the result of increased trading contact in the eastern Mediterranean.

The four major Cretan palaces, located within large unfortified towns, emerged shortly after 2000 BCE as the center of Minoan economic, diplomatic and religious life. All share the same basic ground plan and architectural features, and were built around a large rectangular open area: the central court. The main approach to the palace was from the west, through a stone-faced facade overlooking an outer court. Large store-rooms or magazines were located behind this facade, where agricultural produce (grain and olive oil) was kept in large clay storage jars (*pithoi*), and beyond them a series of small shrines ran along the western side of the court. Also at ground level were the workshops for specialist craftsmen. The upper storeys of the palace buildings housed the reception halls and residential rooms, and possessed sophisticated drainage and sanitation systems.

Extensive use was made of cut stone masonry and gypsum slabs, and particular attention was paid to the facing of the western facade, presumably to impress visitors. The walls of public areas and residential rooms were decorated with fine paintings. The subject matter and style of these frescoes varied, but many show scenes of palace life. One of the best known is the bull-leaping fresco from Knossos, which may represent a religious ritual or a sporting activity.

The palaces supported scores of specialist workers, chief amongst whom were the scribes who oversaw the laborious bureaucratic system. Administrative records were kept on clay tablets, many of which have survived because they were baked in the fires that destroyed the palaces. Three separate scripts have

been identified: Hieroglyphics, Linear A, and Linear B. The first two remain undeciphered. Linear B was used for an early form of Greek, and its use dates to the final occupation of Knossos.

The final destruction of palaces by fire is usually dated to 1450 BCE (based on synchronisms with the Egyptian chronology) but radiocarbon dates from Thera (see box) place the destruction at the end of the 17th century. Only the palace at Knossos was rebuilt, but was abandoned c.1360 (traditional chronology).

Mycenaean palaces

Powerful aristocratic warrior clans emerged on the Greek mainland during the 16th–15th centuries BCE, as is evident from the presence of rich grave goods in shaft-grave burials. Later *tholoi*, beehive chamber tombs, were used for elite burials at Mycenae and elsewhere. Palaces do not appear until the14th and 13th centuries, usually built on an acropolis, or rocky outcrop, surrounded by massive walls of large uncut blocks of stone. The palace structure dominated a complex of subsidiary buildings. It consisted of a large megaron, a rectangular building comprising porch, vestibule and square hall, in the center of which was a large circular plaster hearth. Immediately in front was a large porticoed court. These elements formed the nexus of royal life, where the king received local dignitaries and foreign embassies. The megarons were richly decorated with wall-paintings, and scenes of hunting and warfare were favored. The royal residences were located nearby and the palaces were equipped with large storage facilities, best preserved at Pylos. The writing system used to adminster the palace bureaucracy was Linear B, suggesting that Mycenaeans may have taken over as rulers at Knossos in its latter days ◆

ABOVE A gold seal-ring from Mycenae, 1.3 in/2.5 cm in length. It shows a warrior overcoming three assailants. The Mycenaeans placed high value on gold: the earliest rulers of Mycenae were buried with magnificent gold death-masks, and other grave goods include finely wrought cups and weapons with blades and handles inlaid with gold. They loved to embellish their art with warlike subjects, or with aristocratic scenes of hunting or feasting. In style, however, this ring is wholly Minoan – rings like it from Crete often depict cultic images of priestesses – and it may have been made by a Cretan craftsman working for a Mycenaean ruler. Minoan art was highly developed. Specialist artisans employed in the palaces produced high-quality gold and faience work, as well as the distinctive polychrome "Kamares" pottery, examples of which have been found at sites throughout the eastern Mediterranean.

Rival Empires of the Near East

A number of imperial powers contested power and influence in the Near East during the Late Bronze Age (c.1550–1200 BCE). The Hurrian people, who had migrated into the region from the north in earlier centuries, formed the loose-knit state of Mitanni, about which little is known. It lost ground to the New Kingdom rulers of Egypt, who extended their control into the Levant at this time, and was weakened still further by the Hittites, who burst forth from their Anatolian heartland to embark on a series of wars of conquest. The Hittites dismembered the Mitanni federation and reduced much of Syria to the condition of client states, clashing with Egypt over domination of the petty kingdoms between the rivers Orontes and Euphrates. The battle of Qadesh (1285 BCE) between the Hittites and an Egyptian army resulted in a short-lived period of peaceful coexistence in the Near East, which was ended by the rise of a new aggressive power in northern Mesopotamia, the Assyrians. Having freed themselves from subjection to the Mitanni, they began expanding westwards at the expense of the Hittites and by the end of the 13th century their influence reached as far as the Euphrates. This background of warfare and rivalry did not prevent commerce, trade and culture from flourishing across the region, and new technologies such as glassmaking developed.

ABOVE The Lion Gate from the Hittite capital of Hattusas (Boghazköy) in central Anatolia. It was an immense city ringed by multiple defensive walls and boasted many large temples, including the Great Temple of the Hittite weather-god.

RIGHT A *kudurru*, a type of stone document commonly used by the Babylonian kings of the Late Bronze Age to record royal grants of land. They were often elaborately carved, as here, with symbols of the gods and astronomical signs. Babylonia at this time was ruled by a Kassite dynasty. How they came to power, probably about 1570 BCE, is unknown, but they may originally have been a tribal people from the Zagros mountains. Although they appear never to have fully integrated into Babylonian society, the legitimacy of Kassite rule was universally accepted throughout southern Mesopotamia. The dynasty enjoyed close relations with Egypt, regularly exchanging brides and diplomatic gifts.

The Amarna letters – an archive of clay tablets addressed to the New Kingdom pharoahs of Egypt – throw considerable light on the lively diplomatic contacts that existed between the great powers of the Late Bronze Age. Most of the letters, which are written in Akkadian, the lingua franca of the day, are from the rulers of vassal states in Palestine and Syria. The archive also contains a few missives from kings of other Near Eastern powers, including Mitanni, Hatti (home of the Hittites), Assyria, Babylonia, Arzawa (western Anatolia) and Alashiya (Cyprus). Most of the latter are concerned with the exchange of sumptuous gifts as a mark of amity or coalition, or with arrangements for diplomatic marriages to consolidate political alliances. These documents, and others like them, reveal a busy circulation of objects, ideas and peoples back and forth across the Near East.

Continuity and stability

The archaeological record suggests that the impact of the Late Bronze Age empires on the local cultures of their vassals states was not profound. The Egyptians, certainly, created a military and administrative machinery of empire in the southern Levant, building garrisons, residencies and temples in styles that were alien to the local architectural tradition. Clay sarcophagi have been found at places like Beth Shean and Deir el Balah containing the remains of Egyptian officials stationed abroad and of local elites who wanted to emulate the customs of their Egyptian masters. But by and large the cities of the region remained largely unaffected by foreign encroachment, and the ruling elites, once they had subordinated themselves to Egyptian suzerainty, continued to hold the reins of local

area of control, c.1500 BCE

Egypt

Kassite Babylonian

Hittite

Mitanni

area of control, c.1250 BCE

Assyrian

Egypt

Hittite

Kassite Babylonian

Assyrian site

site with Egyptian settlement

Kassite Babylonian site

Hittite site

Mitanni site

site of Levant vassal state

NIYA ancient region

ancient coastline

authority. The ruler of Megiddo, for example, occupied a palace built in the local style just inside the city gates.

The Mitanni left behind few traces of their presence, the most common being a distinctive style of cylinder seal and a type of very elegantly painted goblet. Their vassal kings in Syria continued to build in the architectural style of earlier times, the palace and temple at Alalakh providing clear evidence of such continuity. The nature of the Mitanni heartland remains largely undiscovered, although towns like Nuzi to the east do give an impression of the wealthy landowners of the time. We have greater material evidence from the Hittite civilization, thanks to excavations at the Hittite capital at Hattusas (Boghazköy) and at numerous imperial cities like Alaca Höyük, Arslantepe and Carchemish. Under the Hittites, Syrian vassal states like Ugarit, a trading kingdom with a rich religious tradition and striking palace, were allowed to retain their local character.

Assyrian growth and decline

The Assyrians, by contrast, ruled as occupiers and not as distant overlords. As they pushed westward into Hittite territory, they established garrisons at frontier towns like Sabi Abyad and promoted the growth of settlements in newly conquered lands nearer to home, such as Dur Katlimmu. This policy implanted Assyrian culture so deeply in the region that it never entirely disappeared, despite the disasters that overwhelmed the Near East shortly after 1200 BCE (see pages 80–81). The Assyrians lost control of their western territories to a succession of nomadic invaders from the north. Although the advances of Tiglath-pileser I (1114–1076) temporarily halted the decline, the empire was reduced to its original heartland and a series of petty Aramaean and Neo-Hittite kingdoms emerged in Syria and northern Mesopotamia. But when their fortunes revived in the 9th century BCE the Assyrians were able to restore their former garrisons and settlements and pick up the reins of power again (see pages 86–87) ◆

ABOVE The Late Bronze Age (c.1550–1200 BCE) was a time of intense competition among the rival imperial powers of the Near East for control of what is now Syria, Lebanon, Israel and Jordan. At first Egypt was the dynamic force, driving northward to contest Mitanni control in Syria. We know from the Amarna letters and other sources that three Egyptian provinces were established in the Levant under Egyptian governors who exercised authority over local vassal-kings. Then the Hittites, and later the Assyrians, established their imperial rule in parts of the same region, restricting Egyptian influence to the south. Babylon, which had gone into decline after the fall of Hammurabi's dynasty in the 16th century, emerged as the dominant power in southern Mesopotamia under the Kassite kings.

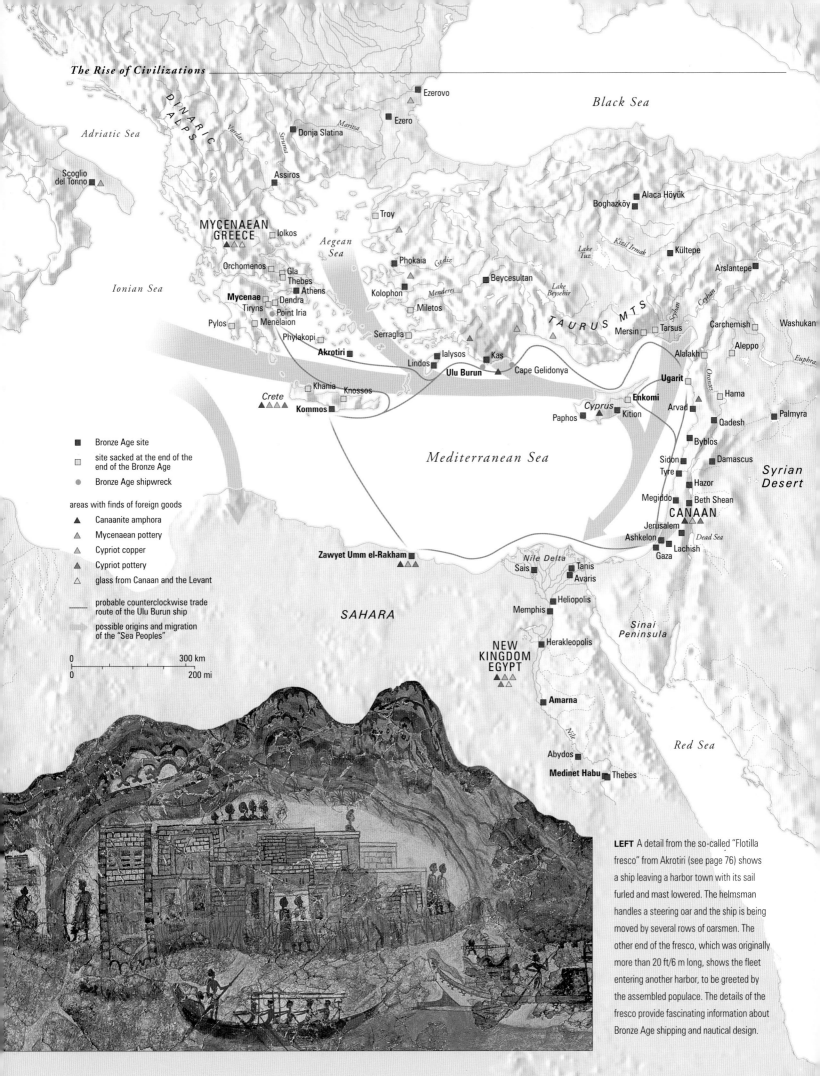

Ezerovo
Ezero
Donja Slatina
Marisa
Strnma
Vardar
Assiros
Black Sea
Alaca Höyük
Boğazköy
Kültepe
Arslantepe
Troy
Phokaia
Gediz
Beycesultan
Lake Tuz
Kizil Irmak
Lake Beyşehir
Washukan
Orchomenos
Gla
Thebes
Athens
Kolophon
Menderes
Miletos
Mycenae
Tiryns
Dendra
Point Iria
Menelaion
Pylos
Phylakopi
Akrotiri
Serraglia
Ialysos
Lindos
Kas
Ulu Burun
Cape Gelidonya
Khania
Knossos
Crete
Kommos
Mersin
Tarsus
Alalakh
Ugarit
Carchemish
Aleppo
Euphra
Hama
Orontes
Enkomi
Arvad
Cyprus
Kition
Qadesh
Palmyra
Paphos
Byblos
Sidon
Tyre
Damascus
Syrian Desert
Hazor
Megiddo
Beth Shean
CANAAN
Jerusalem
Ashkelon
Dead Sea
Lachish
Gaza
Scoglio del Tonno
MYCENAEAN GREECE
Iolkos
Aegean Sea
Ionian Sea
Adriatic Sea
DINARIC ALPS
TAURUS MTS
Mediterranean Sea

Zawyet Umm el-Rakham
Nile Delta
Sais
Tanis
Avaris
Heliopolis
Memphis
SAHARA
Sinai Peninsula
Herakleopolis
NEW KINGDOM EGYPT
Amarna
Nile
Abydos
Medinet Habu
Thebes
Red Sea

■ Bronze Age site
□ site sacked at the end of the end of the Bronze Age
● Bronze Age shipwreck

areas with finds of foreign goods
▲ Canaanite amphora
△ Mycenaean pottery
△ Cypriot copper
▲ Cypriot pottery
△ glass from Canaan and the Levant

—— probable counterclockwise trade route of the Ulu Burun ship
—— possible origins and migration of the "Sea Peoples"

0   300 km
0   200 mi

LEFT A detail from the so-called "Flotilla fresco" from Akrotiri (see page 76) shows a ship leaving a harbor town with its sail furled and mast lowered. The helmsman handles a steering oar and the ship is being moved by several rows of oarsmen. The other end of the fresco, which was originally more than 20 ft/6 m long, shows the fleet entering another harbor, to be greeted by the assembled populace. The details of the fresco provide fascinating information about Bronze Age shipping and nautical design.

Trade in the Late Bronze Age

The Late Bronze Age was a period of unprecedented wealth and long-distance exchange that involved all the great powers of the eastern Mediterranean world. A great deal of information about this trade comes from documentary sources such as the Amarna letters, which give details of the exchange of luxury goods in gold, silver, ivory and faience, and of raw materials of real economic value, such as copper. Inscriptions on Egyptian tomb walls concerning foreign emissaries amplify this information, as do a number of Babylonian and other Near Eastern texts. These suggest that trade was not organized solely for the benefit of rulers: private merchants and sea captains traded profitably on their own account. In the 12th century BCE cataclysmic upheavals affected all the societies around the eastern Mediterranean, sweeping away the the Hittite empire and Syrian city-states, curtailing Assyrian and Egyptian power, and destroying the Mycenaean civilization. Maritime trade all but vanished until its revival by the Phoenicians in the 10th century (see pages 84–85).

LEFT The long-distance exchange between the great empires of Egypt, the Near East, Anatolia and the Aegean funnelled raw materials and finished goods into a circular coastal maritime trading system around the eastern Mediterranean. The cargo discovered on the Ulu Burun shipwreck (see box) provides striking evidence of this trade, allowing archaeologists to reconstruct the possible route of the ship's final journey. Finds of foreign objects, particularly pottery, at urban sites and cemeteries also make it possible to trace the long-distance movement of goods. This exchange system, which pulled in goods from Persia and Afghanistan in the east, Africa in the south, Italy in the west, and central Europe in the north, came to an end shortly after 1200 BCE. The most likely cause of its collapse was an influx of invaders, usually grouped together under the name of the Sea Peoples. They probably originated in the northern Aegean, though it is thought that some may have come from as far west as Sicily and Sardinia.

During the reign of Ramesses III (c.1194–1163 BCE) a new threat was added to that of the Libyans: the "Sea Peoples". They were probably a disparate collection of marginal peoples from the northern Aegean, especially from the Turkish coast, but whatever their origins, their damaging raids around the eastern Mediterranean effectively destroyed the great Late Bronze Age world system. They may have been responsible for repeated raids against Mycenaean strongholds, including a well-documented attack on Pylos, which brought an end to the palatial culture of mainland Greece (see pages 76–77) and led to the abandonment of many settlements. More certainly, they overran the Hittite empire and caused the destruction of coastal cities like Enkomi and Ugarit.

Only Egypt withstood their onslaught. An inscription on the walls of Ramesses III's temple at Medinet Habu celebrating a victory over the Sea Peoples provides our best textual and graphical evidence of these raiders. The destruction levels discernible at many Near Eastern sites c.1200 BCE provide the most striking archaeological evidence of the Late Bronze Age collapse. The Sea Peoples themselves may be seen in the presence of a new Iron Age population, the "Peleset", in southern Levant (see pages 82–83) ◆

Archaeological confirmation of extensive seaborne trade is found around the eastern Mediterranean. The most common container for the transportation of goods was the two-handled "Canaanite amphora", wide at the shoulder and narrow at the base. Such vessels have been recovered in large quantities, especially from important ports and trading centers such as Ugarit on the Syrian coast, which was at the height of its influence in the Late Bronze Age. Larger *pithoi* were also used to carry consignments of goods: one such storage jar raised from the Ulu Burun wreck was found to contain 18 close-packed pieces of Cypriot pottery.

The island of Cyprus was the chief source of copper and was fully integrated into the Mediterranean trading network under the control of the Mycenaeans who came here as traders and settlers. The coastal town of Enkomi flourished as an entrepot between the Levant and the Aegean. Similar evidence of international maritime trade has been uncovered at Kommos, southern Crete.

Raiders and invaders

As in most periods of history, pirate ships were a constant threat to the safety of trading fleets in the eastern Mediterranean: Zawyet Umm el-Rakham, a fortress-town some 186 mi/300 km west of the Nile delta, seems originally to have been built to protect mariners crossing the seas from Crete to Egypt. Later it also defended the Nile delta against Libyan raiders.

Ulu Burun: an underwater excavation

In 1982, a sponge diver discovered an ancient shipwreck at Ulu Burun, off the coast of Turkey. Underwater excavation of the site began two years later. The ship lay at a depth of 150 ft/45 m, which meant that divers could remain on the site for periods of no more than twenty minutes, and the rocky seabed shelved steeply, adding to the difficulties of excavation. The international team of underwater archaeologists was led by George Bass, whose knowledge of Mediterranean shipwrecks was unsurpassed. It quickly became apparent that the site was of major importance and work continued at the site for many seasons. Radiocarbon dating of the timber from the small section of the hull that had survived, together with other organic material on board, showed that the ship had sunk in the 14th century BCE. It was carrying a mixed cargo of valuable goods, including 250 copper ingots from Cyprus, Anatolian tin, terebinth resins for making perfume, ebony from Egypt, ivory and ostrich eggs, gold and silver jewelry, bronze tools and weapons, glass ingots and beads. The crew's personal possessions were also recovered. A rare find was a hinged wooden writing tablet: its waxed pages could have been used by a merchant traveling on the ship for keeping

records of transactions and shipments. The remains of foodstuffs such as almonds, figs, olives, and pomegranates were probably the crew's rations. The quality and number of exotic items on board the ship suggest its cargo was intended for a royal sponsor, and archaeologists speculate that the ship had sailed from North Africa and Egypt to Cyprus and the Levant, picking up cargo as it went. It was probably on its way to the Aegean, perhaps to a Mycenaean palace, when it was shipwrecked ◆

BELOW AN ARCHAEOLOGIST EXAMINES A CONSIGNMENT OF AMPHORAS FOUND LYING ON THE SEABED.

Philistines and Israelites

The origins and later history of the Israelites and Philistines attract more attention than almost any other area of Near Eastern archaeology. The early books of the Bible (written down centuries after the events they describe) recount the story of the arrival of God's chosen people, the Israelites, in the Promised Land of Canaan after their escape from captivity in Egypt. According to these accounts, the Philistines already inhabited the coastal plains of the southern Levant and opposed the expansion of the early Israelite leaders. For many believing Jews and Christians, this scriptural account is sufficient and true. However, the archaeological evidence would appear to place the origins of both peoples in the period of confusion and upheaval in the eastern Mediterranean that lasted from c.1200–1000 BCE and was inaugurated by the invasion of the Sea Peoples (see pages 80–81). When the dust lifted, one group of invaders, known as the Peleset, had settled in the Gaza area of the southern Levant; they gave their name to the land known in the Bible as Philistia. The Israelites seem to have emerged from among a number of small village communities in the central hill country west of the Jordan River that developed characteristics of a shared culture at about this time. Meanwhile, traditional Canaanite elements persisted for a time in some parts of the south such as Megiddo, but Canaanite culture found its main continuation in the Phoenicians of the Lebanon coastal region (see pages 84–85). The Egyptians still maintained several garrisons in the deep south.

BELOW Philistine pottery of the 12th–11th century BCE, from Ashkelon and Ashdod. These fine pieces are typical of the handsome ware, decorated with geometric patterns and bird-like designs and usually painted in one or two colours, that is found throughout the southern Levant. Other pieces have been discovered beyond the limits of the Biblical Philistia, probably as a result of trade. The similarity of this pottery to Mycenaean painted wares (see pages 76–77) leads many archaeologists to conclude that the Peleset originally came from the Aegean, a view that is upheld by other facets of Philistine culture. For example, excavations at Tel Miqne, Biblical Ekron, have uncovered a large public building with a hall, which has at its center a circular hearth, an architectural feature that belongs to the Aegean.

According to the Bible, the Philistines occupied five major towns: Ashkelon, Ashdod, and Gaza on the coast, and Ekron and Gath farther inland. The archaeological record shows evidence of a characteristic culture, which is called Philistine, at all these places and at a number of other sites in the region. Much of the evidence suggests that the Philistines were an elite ruling over a larger indigenous population. For example, the characteristic Philistine pottery is mostly a fine table ware, while ordinary kitchen wares recall the local Canaanite pottery of the Late Bronze Age.

The early Israelites

Archaeologists have identified a number of distinctive features that appear in several small highland villages west of the Jordan valley late in the 2nd millennium BCE. The dwellings commonly have a floor-plan known as the "four-room house"; among the domestic pottery is a particular form of storage jar with a thickened collar-shaped rim; and the householders did not keep pigs – a break with earlier Canaanite practice. Open-air cult centers also appear at Mount Ebal and other hilltops in the area; in one of these the bronze figure of a bull was found.

These characteristics have been equated with the settlement of the early Israelites from Egypt as described in the Book of Judges. But most are not unique to this place and time – four-room houses and collared storage jars appear elsewhere in the southern Levant, and they probably represent a continuation of Canaanite traditions, albeit with certain new features, rather than an influx of people from outside. The origins of these settlements may lie in the turbulent times of the Late Bronze Age, perhaps among animal herders living on the fringes of the city-states to avoid political control and tax obligations, who reverted to a settled life as the imperial order collapsed. Alternatively, they may have been established by refugees and fugitives (referred to in the cuneiform texts of the time as *habiru*) who escaped to the hills from oppressive Late Bronze Age regimes.

The Jewish kingdoms

These settlements laid the foundations of the societies that later became the early Jewish kingdoms. The Bible describes how Israelite leaders like Saul overcame local opposition and gained regional authority. Around 1000 BCE David solidified this fledgling state organization. The construction of the first temple at Jerusalem by Solomon was a further act of political consolidation, as the rituals of the priests lent authority to the secular power. Although the remains of his temple remain buried inside the Temple Mount, the Biblical description of the temple tallies closely with the layout of temples that have been excavated in Syria. Solomon also built provincial centers, and evidence of strong walls and three-chambered city gates dating to around this time has been uncovered at towns like Hazor, Megiddo and Lachish.

On Solomon's death in 922 BCE, his kingdom split into two quarrelsome halves: Israel in the north with its capital at Samaria, and Judah in the south centered on Jerusalem. The northern kingdom struggled to gain equilibrium for several generations. Excavations at Samaria, Jezreel and several other royal centers have revealed large walled palaces, storehouses and bureaucratic offices. Samaria was rich in administrative *ostraca* (brief documents written in ink on potsherds) and elaborate carved ivory inlays for furniture; the latter throw light on the Biblical reference to the ivory house at the capital of Israel. Important centers like Megiddo were rebuilt as military garrisons.

Similar works have been uncovered in the south. While Jerusalem remains largely unavailable for excavation, other sites reveal the scale of Judaean building programs: a royal country retreat at Ramat Rahel, an impressive administrative complex at Lachish, and a string of fortified garrisons in the Negev. The town walls, street layouts and everyday dwellings of more ordinary settlements have been found at Tel Beit Mirsim, Tel Batash, Tel Beer-Sheba and elsewhere ◆

RIGHT For such a small region, the southern Levant contains an impressive diversity of terrain, economic activity, and cultural traditions. The cultural legacy of Late Bronze Age Canaan was directly perpetuated by the Phoenicians of the northern coast and town dwellers of the interior. The Philistine newcomers of the south adopted elements of Canaanite culture, while the emerging Israelites of the central hill country reshaped this tradition into a new form.

□ Phoenician site
□ Philistine site
■ early "Israelite" site
▨ town of the divided kingdom
▨ site with evidence of Solomonic building project
■ other early Iron Age site
▢ kingdom of Israel, 920–721 BCE
▢ kingdom of Judah, 920–587 BCE

0 _____ 60 km
0 _____ 40 mi

The Phoenician Empire

The Phoenicians were the Iron Age (1st millennium BCE) inhabitants of the narrow but fertile strip of land between the Lebanon mountains and the Mediterranean roughly equivalent to the modern state of Lebanon. The Bronze Age peoples of this region were part of the Canaanite cultural tradition of the Levant, and it is not until around 1200 BCE that a distinctive Phoenician civilization emerges. The Phoenicians most probably identified themselves simply as belonging to a particular city such as Sidon, Tyre or Byblos: the name Phoenician, related to the word "phoenix", is known from Greek texts of the 8th century BCE and means "purple-red". A similar term (*po-ni-ki-ja*), likewise meaning red, appears in the Linear B tablets of Mycenaean Greece, and the names apparently refer to one of the major Phoenician industries of antiquity – textile dyeing.

The mountains of Lebanon are rich in timber, particularly cedarwood, a valued trading commodity in the ancient Near East (see pages 70–71). In places the mountains reach down nearly to the sea, and the narrow coastal plain is dissected by a series of rivers, hindering overland communication. This encouraged the development of numerous small, independent city-states and the people of the region became skilled sailors. They usually built their trading cities on rocky promotories jutting out to sea , or on small islands off the coast, presumably because they were easier to defend.

With the collapse of the Late Bronze Age world in c.1200 BCE, international trade in the eastern Mediterranean all but ceased. Gradually, however, we find signs of a revival with the export of distinctive Phoenician pottery to Cyprus, where it is present in tombs at Salamis and Paphos in large quantities. By the 10th century a Phoenician colony had been established on the southern coast of Cyprus at Kition – its name, like that of Carthage (see box), derives from the Phoenician word for "New Town". Trade had begun with small

RIGHT This ivory panel of a lioness attacking a Nubian, found at Nimrud, is a fine example of Phoenician work showing strong Egyptian influence.

Greek communities such as Lefkandi on Euboea (see page 90). Kommos on Crete seems to have been an important trading post: in addition to large quantities of Phoenician ceramics, excavation has revealed the site of three consecutive Phoenician temples, the earliest dating to around 900 BCE.

Skilled craftsmen

The Phoenicians were renowned for producing high-quality craftwork that built upon and continued the artisanal traditions of the Bronze Age Near East. Of particular note are elaborately carved ivory plaques used to decorate furniture. Ironically, such pieces are rarely found in Phoenicia. An important group, for example, was discovered in the Assyrian palace at Nimrud (Kalhu). Others are known from Samaria, the Neo-Hittite city of Zincirli in Syria, and Salamis on Cyprus, and they have also been found in the west, at Tas Silg on Malta, Carthage, Tharros, and in Spain. Phoenician artisans also made finely worked bronze statuettes. These derive from a Bronze Age tradition, perhaps best typified by a group of gold-plated votive statues from Byblos. The original range of subjects was very limited, reflecting a strong egyptianizing influence: smiting god, enthroned god, and female figure. However, statuettes of the 1st millennium BCE found in Phoenician colonies on Sicily, Sardinia and in Spain are more varied in form. Bronze votive

BELOW The Phoenicians first established a trading presence in the eastern Mediterranean in the 10th century BCE. However, the main thrust of their westward expansion dates from the 8th century. To meet the demand for luxury objects created by the Assyrian empire (see pages 86–87) Phoenician traders exploited the abundant copper and silver reserves of Cyprus, Sardinia and Spain. Intermediary trading stations provided convenient ports of call for their vessels.The Phoenicians appear to have met with little local opposition, but rivalry with the Greeks in Sicily and Italy (see pages 90–91) was inevitable. Colonies at Utica, Carthage and Hadrumetum gave the Phoenicians control of the narrow strait between Sicily and North Africa, protecting their route to the west. Phoenician explorers ventured down the Atlantic coast of Africa and may have sailed as far northwest as Britain.

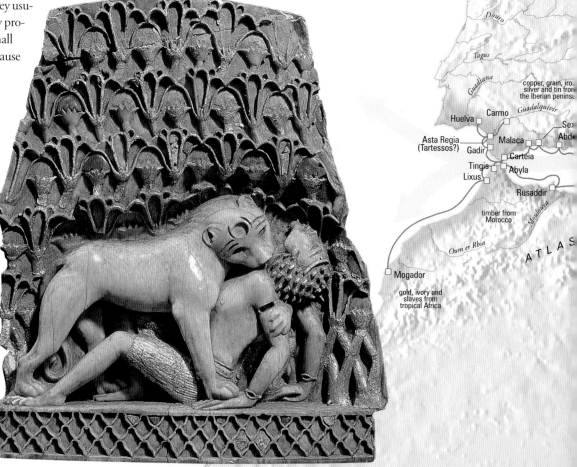

razors dating mainly from the 7th to 2nd century BCE are found at funerary sites throughout the western Mediterranean; they appear to have been high status, prestige objects associated with purification and religious ritual. Phoenician bowls of gold, silver or bronze decorated with elaborate figured scenes were highly prized objects and were widely distributed throughout the ancient world. Examples have been found at Nimrud (Assyria), Amathus and Idalion (Cyprus), Olympia (Greece), and at several Etruscan sites in Italy, most notably Praeneste.

The alphabet

Classical writers such as Herodotus and Pliny the Elder attributed the invention of the alphabet to the Phoenicians. It is now thought that the earliest alphabetic scripts developed in the Sinai and the Canaanite Syrian kingdom of Ugarit between the 15th and the 13th centuries BCE. However, by 1000 BCE the Phoenicians were using a simplified form of the alphabet. This is known to us from funerary inscriptions like that on the coffin of Ahiram, king of Byblos, or from short inscriptions on bronze weapons. It is this alphabet that was transmitted to Greece at some point in the 8th century, and is the ancestor of the modern Latin alphabet ◆

Carthage: capital of the Punic west

Carthage (Phoenician *Kart-Hadasht*, meaning "New Town"), home of the legendary queen Dido, is the most famous of the Punic or western Phoenician colonies. According to Greek and Latin sources, it was founded in 814–813 BCE, but the earliest archaeological remains date to the 8th century. The site – on a triangular peninsula between the lagoon of Sebkhet er-Riana to the north and Tunis to the south – was easily defensible and provided safe anchorage for ships on the trade route between Phoenicia and Spain. Excavations have uncovered substantial evidence of Carthage's Phoenician origins. The focus of city life was the the acropolis or Byrsa, which was protected by a complex line of fortifications. At the top was a city temple dedicated to the Phoenician god Eshmun; the main square, or city forum, lay at its foot. Carthage became the center of a commercial maritime empire, and an artificial harbor (*cothon*) was later built on the south side of the peninsula. This comprised a rectangular dock for mercantile vessels and a circular harbor for warships, surrounded by arsenals. A number of cemeteries have been exavated in the city. The usual burial rite was inhumation accompanied by a fine range of grave goods. In the *tophet* sanctuary of Salammbo, child sacrifices to the god Baal Hamman were cremated and marked by funerary stelae (*cippae*) ◆

RIGHT A GLASS PENDANT FROM CARTHAGE IN THE SHAPE OF A MAN'S HEAD, ONLY 1.8 IN/4.5 CM HIGH.

Black Sea

PYRENEES

Corsica

Praeneste △

APPENNINES

DINARIC ALPS

BALKAN MTS

KÜRE MTS

Kizil Irmak

lead, marble, and wine from the Balearics

grain and silver from Sardinia

Palma — Mago

Tharros

Sardinia

Lake Tuz

Ebusos

Balearic Islands

ntum

Sulcis

Caralis

Nora

Panormos — Soluntum

Motya

Sicily

Lefkandi

TAURUS MTS

Zincirli

Rusucurru

Hippo Diarrhytus

Olympia △

Rhodes

Salamis

Ugarit

Cartenna

Hippo Regius

Utica

Kerkouane

Cossyra

Amathus

Idalion

Kition

Arvad

copper, marble and timber from Algeria

Carthage

Hadrumetum

Leptis Minor

Tas Silg

Malta

Kommos

Paphos

Cyprus

Byblos

Sidon

Berytus

MOUNTAINS

Thapsos

Acholla

Usilla

Mediterranean Sea

Crete

Tyre

Sarepta

dyes, grain and olive oil from Tunisia

Girba

'Atlit

Akhziv

dye, glass, metalwork, textiles from Phoenicia

Sabrata

Oea

Leptis Magna

Jerusalem

gold, ivory and slaves from tropical Africa

Gaza

gold and slaves from tropical Africa

SAHARA

Sinai Peninsula

Nile

Red Sea

■ Canaanite Bronze Age city, from 2nd millennium BCE

■ Phoenician colony or trading post established in the 11th–9th centuries BCE

□ Phoenician colony or trading post established in the 8th–6th centuries BCE

△ other site with Phoenician finds

Phoenician expansion, 11th–6th centuries BCE

▨ Phoenician heartland

▨ coast under Phoenician influence by the 6th century BCE

▢ coast under Greek influence by the 6th century BCE

— Phoenician trade route

0 ___ 600 km

0 ___ 400 mi

The Assyrian Empire

Assyria took some time to recover from the political and economic collapse that engulfed the Near East at the end of the Bronze Age (see pages 78–79). Its influence was reduced to its heartland around the cities of Assur and Nineveh on the river Tigris, but by the late 10th century BCE it had begun to rebuild its former empire and was pushing westward again to the Euphrates. This phase of expansion culminated in the middle decades of the 9th century under the ambitious rulers Assur-nasir-pal II and Shalmaneser III, but Assyria's grip on its western provinces later weakened as the pace of imperial expansion was halted by internal power struggles. These problems had been overcome by the mid 8th century and a series of militaristic kings began a new round of conquests. At its greatest extent, around 650 BCE, the Assyrian empire stretched from Elam and Babylonia in the southeast to Anatolia in the west, and throughout the Levant into Egypt. Although the Assyrians dealt ruthlessly with rebellion, the frontiers of the empire were never secure. The invasion of Egypt proved short-lived, and the empire collapsed at the end of the 7th century BCE when Babylonia overthrew its Assyrian masters.

Several of Assyria's great conquering kings, such as Tiglath-pileser, Sargon, Sennacherib, Esarhaddon, and Assur-bani-pal, figure in the Bible, which paints a harsh picture of the tyranny of the Assyrians. Their own annals delight in recounting the sack of cities and the flaying or slaughter of rebellious subjects. For all this, the Assyrians built palaces and cities that were without rival in the ancient Near East and commissioned works of art from those they conquered, like the Phoenician ivories that decorate the palace at Nimrud (Kalhu; Calah of the Bible).

Building on a grand scale

Archaeologists first began investigating the great monuments of the Assyrian kings in the 1840s, when the great British archaeologist Austen Henry Layard, who excavated Nimrud and Nineveh, brought the achievements of the Assyrians to the attention of the world. They built on a grand scale. Their capital moved several times: Nimrud was succeeded by Khorsabad (Dur-Sharrukin) and then by Nineveh, which was reconstructed for Sennacherib at the end of the 8th century and held up to 100,000 inhabitants. The cities were supplied with fresh water through a system of dams and canals, fed from mountain streams, and they were surrounded by massive walls, interrupted at intervals by many gates that allowed entry to a steady flow of traffic bringing food from the provinces.

Palatial compounds

Archaeological research has so far revealed little information about the life of the ordinary inhabitants of these cities, but a considerable amount is known about the organization of government. The royal palaces and main temples lay within an enclosed compound, while military officials and their arsenals were housed in a second compound, both being set into the city wall. Each of these compounds was the size of a small town.

The sprawling palaces were entered through portals guarded by immense statues of human-headed winged bulls. They contained an entire world in themselves. The official, public areas, where the king held audiences and his officials discharged their duties, were separated from more private interior spaces, where the royal families and their servants

BELOW The wall reliefs that graced Assyrian palaces glorified the deeds and functions of the monarch, representing him as the war leader responsible for expanding the rightful bounds of the empire, the peace-keeper whose role was to maintain tranquility and harmony within the empire, and the performer of rituals that kept the cosmic order in balance. Four-winged protective spirits were common figures in Assyrian art, like the one shown here holding a pollinating cone (ordinarily used to fertilize date palms) to symbolize fertility and the rejuvenation of the world.

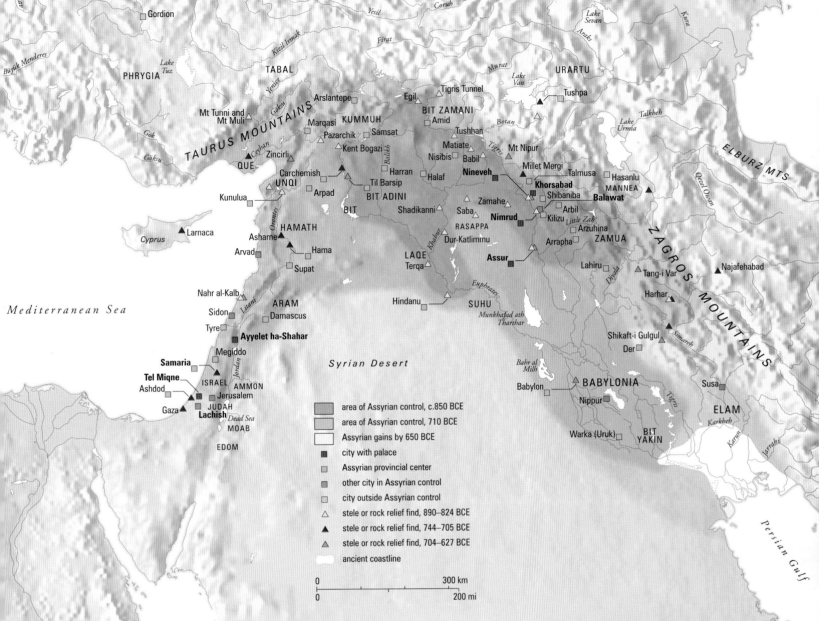

Mediterranean Sea

Syrian Desert

▪	area of Assyrian control, c.850 BCE
	area of Assyrian control, 710 BCE
	Assyrian gains by 650 BCE
◼	city with palace
◼	Assyrian provincial center
◻	other city in Assyrian control
◻	city outside Assyrian control
△	stele or rock relief find, 890–824 BCE
▲	stele or rock relief find, 744–705 BCE
△	stele or rock relief find, 704–627 BCE
	ancient coastline

0   300 km
0   200 mi

lived and worked. Decorative bas-reliefs carved on alabaster panels and fixed to the walls of rooms and corridors depicted military campaigns, royal lion hunts and court ceremonies. Temples were also elaborately decorated. The famous temple gates from Balawat were covered with sheets of bronze showing Shalmaneser's military victories. Similarly, military arsenals contained not only functional elements such as parade grounds and weapons stores, but also splendidly appointed palaces and offices for army officials.

The profits of war

This extensive building program was funded by taxes, tributes, and war booty. Conquered peoples were forcibly deported from their homes and resettled in the Assyrian heartland by imperial decree, providing builders and laborers to construct the new temples and palaces, and craftsmen to produce carved ivory, metal wares, cloth, and other luxury goods for the court. Other deportees became agricultural colonists, resettled in new farming villages in Assyria or the

provinces, where they grew food to supply the imperial capitals and regional centers. Yet others entered the service of their conquerors, forming foreign auxiliary cavalry or other units in the Assyrian army. The Biblical story of the ten lost tribes of Israel is based on the forced deportation of people from the Jewish kingdom of Samaria (see pages 82–83).

The Assyrians ruled their conquered lands from provincial administrative centers. In Syria they took over existing Neo-Hittite and Aramaean structures, but excavations at several sites in Israel have found evidence of large buildings with floor-plans typical of Assyrian palaces; in some instances, such as Ayyelet ha-Shahar near Hazor, these buildings probably housed imperial officials. However, at Tel Miqne the local ruler – an Assyrian vassal – built himself a palace in the Assyrian style. At Lachish, remains have been found of the siege ramp the Assyrians built to approach the city walls: this was one of the best documented events in Near Eastern history, depicted in wall paintings and described in Assyrian annals ◆

ABOVE The Assyrian empire expanded out of its northern Mesopotamian homeland, eventually coming to dominate the entire world of the Near East. At its height it extended from the mountainous country of western Iran to the Mediterranean coast, and for a time even ruled Egypt. Imperial expansion came in fits and starts, according to prevailing political conditions at home and the vigor exercised by individual kings. The most impressive territorial gains took place during the first half of the 9th century BCE, and again in the hundred years between 745 and 650 BCE.

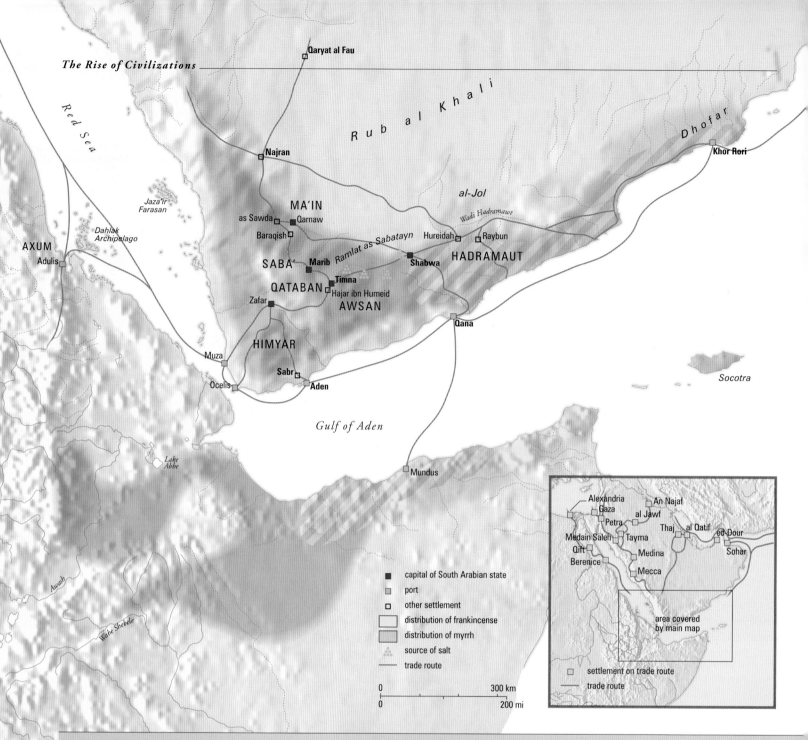

capital of South Arabian state
port
other settlement
distribution of frankincense
distribution of myrrh
source of salt
trade route

settlement on trade route
trade route

area covered
by main map

0   300 km
0   200 mi

Marib: a massive earthen dam

After the monsoon rains strike the high elevations of the Yemeni mountains, torrential streams pour down the normally dry lower slopes to the east. For more than 4,000 years the farmers of the region have found ways of trapping these floodwaters and diverting them to profitable use. Water engineering techniques grew more complex, reaching their height with the building of a massive earthen dam at Marib, the Sabaean capital, which was constructed across a narrow point in the valley to restrain the floodwaters; two stone sluices channeled a manageable flow through a network of long

canals to irrigate vast expanses of cultivated land downstream. In the city's heyday, the inhabitants of Marib numbered several tens of thousands, a figure only made possible by the life-sustaining dam. The dam was breached many times in antiquity by the force of the floodwaters and rebuilt, so that the remains seen today date mostly from the 4th century CE. According to later tradition, the final catastrophic breaching of the dam in 570 CE resulted in the dispersal of tribes to other parts of Arabia, and to this day some tribes in Oman trace their genealogy to ancient South Arabia. This legendary tradition aside, the South Arabian cities of the desert fringe did not survive the destruction of their agricultural foundation ◆

ABOVE RUINS OF THE ANCIENT SLUICE-WORKS THAT DIRECTED WATER INTO IRRIGATION CANALS.

Southern Arabia

Saba', or Sheba – modern Yemen in the southwest corner of Arabia – was renowned for its riches throughout the ancient Near East. The Bible boasts of the sumptuous gifts of incense, gold, and precious objects presented by the queen of Sheba to king Solomon, and an Assyrian inscription from around 800 BCE reports a caravan of Sabaean merchants carrying incense, iron, and other commodities. Greek and Roman writers knew of Saba' as the source of frankincense and myrrh. It was the most famous of a number of small Iron Age kingdoms strung out along the wadis of the southern Arabian peninsula that grew prosperous through control of the lucrative overland and maritime trade that passed through the region.

Dominating the southwest corner of southern Arabia is a mountain chain running parallel to the Red Sea. Monsoon rains make these high mountains green and fertile, and recent archaeological work suggests that terraced farming began here in the 3rd millennium BCE. Small, walled towns developed, laying the foundations for more advanced Iron Age societies, culminating in the rise of Himyar in the 1st millennium CE. The foothills east of the mountains are drier, merging gradually into the arid wastes of the Empty Quarter. Irrigation schemes may have started in these lowland valleys by 2500 BCE. At first farmers diverted water to their fields through a series of check dams. Later, they built sophisticated barrages with sluices and canals (see box).

It was here that the kingdom of Saba' developed early in the 1st millennium BCE. Temples and other monuments mark the beginning of state organization, and carved rock inscriptions give us a general, if somewhat hazy, picture of Saba's relations with neighboring kingdoms such as Ma'in, Qataban, and Awsan. Throughout the period these small, independent kingdoms were involved in an almost constant struggle for regional domination. What was at stake was control over the caravan routes that served the profitable incense trade.

Sweet smells of success

Frankincense and myrrh are aromatic resins obtained from various small, thorny trees of the Burseraceae family that grow in the Hadramaut hills of eastern Yemen and Dhofar (today part of Oman). Incisions are made in the trunks of the trees to tap the resin, which then hardens into lumps and globules on exposure to the air and is easily harvested. Aromatics were highly

LEFT The South Arabian civilization developed around the overland and maritime trade routes that connected this region in antiquity with the Near East and eastern Mediterranean, East Africa, the Persian Gulf and India. Control of the profitable incense trade played a key role in shaping the internal political history of the area, brought fabled wealth to its kingdoms, and opened the region to important artistic and cultural influences from the Classical Mediterranean world. The survival of the inland kingdoms was dependent on the continuation of this overland trade, as on the maintenance of irrigation works to support marginal agriculture. When both came to an end in the early 1st millennium CE, political power had already passed to the coastal cities.

BELOW Incense burner from Shabwa, 3rd century CE. Camels had come into use as riding and pack animals by the 1st millennium BCE, promoting the commerce in incense and other valuables for which South Arabia was famous.

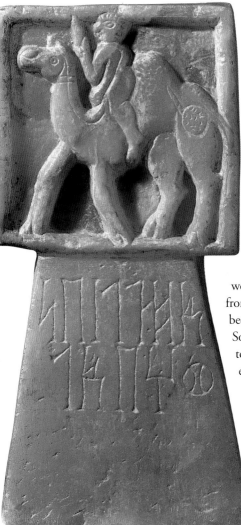

prized throughout the ancient Near East and Mediterranean for use in religious ceremonies and embalming. They were also added to pharmaceuticals, perfumes and cosmetics, and used to flavor wine. Demand for such luxury items from the citizens of Rome increased the value of the trade at the end of the 1st millennium BCE, intensifying regional rivalry.

Caravans carrying incense and other goods north from Hadramaut had first to travel west, keeping the Yemen mountains on their left and the deserts of the Empty Quarter on their right. This geographical bottleneck was occupied by the southern Arabian kingdoms. The city of Najran stood at an important crossroads where caravans diverged northwest to the Mediterranean or northeast to Iraq and the Persian Gulf. A caravanserai, (overnight stopping place) has been excavated at Qaryat al Fau on this latter route.

Whichever kingdom had control of the caravan routes was able to skim off rich dividends in the form of taxes and other imposts from the merchants and camel drivers traveling along them. Some of this surplus wealth was diverted into grandiose building projects: the spectacular temples of Mahram Bilqis and Awwam near Marib, the palace at Timna, the temple at Sirwah and many other monumental buildings give us some idea of the profits passing through the hands of local rulers. A distinctive artistic tradition emerged among the artisans of the region, which was influenced by the styles of the Mediterranean world with which the incense trade brought them into contact.

Seafaring trade

Recent excavations at Sabr, near Aden, have uncovered warehouses filled with elephant tusks, copper, and other precious goods dating to c.1200 BCE. Over time, the rise of states in the South Arabian interior seems to have attracted commercial enterprise away from the coastal routes into the caravan trade, but during the late 1st millennium BCE maritime trade revived in the northern Indian Ocean as profitable routes connected the Mediterranean world with India. Pottery and other goods imported from both east and west dating to this period have been found at such ports as Qana and Khor Rori. Some of these foreign goods found their way inland to the traditional centers at Timna, Shabwa and elsewhere. As the coastal routes grew in importance, the regional balance of power shifted away from the interior kingdoms, and by about 100 CE, Himyar in the southern highlands had assumed dominance. When the Marib dam (see box) was breached for the last time in the 6th century CE, the Sabaeans could no longer afford to repair it ◆

The Expanding Greek World

Between the 9th and 7th centuries BCE, Greece emerged from the period of relative obscurity that followed the collapse of Mycenaean civilization (see pages 80–81). Although often called the "Dark Age", many archaeologists prefer the description of Early Iron Age, reflecting the replacement of bronze by iron during this period, perhaps introduced by the Dorians, migrants into Greece from the Balkans. Ionia on the coast of Anatolia was settled by Greek-speaking peoples at this time, possibly as a result of the Doric invasions. Much remains uncertain about the Early Iron Age, but it appears that fundamental social transformations had resulted in the development of independent city-states (*poleis*) as the prevailing form of political organization by the 8th century BCE. The adoption of the Phoenician alphabet, and the adding of separate symbols for vowels, was of major importance. Not least, the revival of literacy preserved the Homeric epics, the greatest achievement of the so-called "Dark Age".

By the 8th century BCE, the new social elites of the emerging city-states were keen to establish their rights over the surrounding countryside, or *chora*. This may explain the introduction of what appear to be "hero-cults", often focused on remains of the Bronze Age past. Mycenaean *tholoi* (beehive-shaped chamber tombs) have been found to contain later Greek material, leading archaeologists to suggest that the "heroes" they were thought to commemorate continued to influence land-holding patterns. One such *tholos* at Menidhi, Attica, contained pottery decorated with scenes of chariot-racing, echoing the heroic funeral games described in Homer's epic poem, the *Iliad*, composed in the 8th century but preserving earlier oral traditions.

Excavations at Lefkandi, the main settlement on Euboea from c.1000–c.800 BCE, throw considerable light on the period. An apsidal structure, measuring c. 164 x 33 ft/ 50 x 10 m, contained the bodies of a man and a woman: the early date of the find and the importance given to the burials indicate they were high-ranking personages, possibly the founders of the settlement. A very high number of graves in the cemetery at Lefkandi contain gold jewelry or faience objects – including some Egyptian-style scarabs. There is also evidence of metalworking and other industrial activity at the site. All this points to

Lefkandi having been a prosperous trading center. Finds of 9th-century Euboean pottery at Al Mina, a trading settlement in Syria, reinforce the island's connections with the Near East.

Greek colonies

By the end of the 8th century the Greeks had become major participants in the revival of long-distance Mediterranean trade in iron ore, luxury goods, wine and other commodities. One of the earliest Greek settlements in the western Mediterranean was Pithe-koussai on the island of Ischia, possibly founded for its proximity to the iron reserves of Etruria.

Over the following centuries colonies were established around the Mediterranean and Black Seas by most of the major city-states of Greece and Ionia, with Corinth and Chalkis on Euboea leading the way. It is not immediately clear why such widespread

| | Greek settlement, 10th century BCE |
| | Mycenaean tomb reused from the 8th century BCE |

Greek colony founded by the
	8th century BCE
	7th century BCE
	6th century BCE

	Greek influence, 10th century BCE
	coast under Greek influence by the 6th century BCE
	Greek trade route

0   200 km
0   150 mi

ETRURIA
copper, iron
and metalwork

DINAR

timber and horses
from the northern Adriatic

APENNINE MTS

Adriatic Sea

tin from western
Europe

Tiber

Cumae Neapolis
Pithekoussai
Poseidonia   Metapontion   Satyrion
Elea   Skidros   Siris   Taras
Laos   Sybaris
Tyrrhenian Sea   MAGNA GRAECIA
timber, grain, meat, pottery
and textiles
Terina   Kroton
Lipara   Medma Hipponion
Mylai   Metauros
Zankle Rhegion Lokri
Himera   *Sicily*   Naxos
textiles   Selinos   grain, cheese, textiles Katana
from Carthage   Minoa   and hides
Akragas   Leontini   Megara Hyblaea
Gela   Syracuse
Kamarina   Akrai
Kasmenai

Kinyps

LEFT Decorated ceramic jug found on Aegina but originating from the Cycladic islands, 7th century BCE. The griffin head spout is influenced by the Near East.

colonization took place. Later literary sources hint at famines and food shortages, but archaeological field-surveys show that the fertile areas of Greece were relatively under-exploited during the main period of colonization, so population growth is unlikely to have been a major cause. The oracle of Apollo at Delphi seems to have played a part in the planting of new colonies; for example, the historian Herodotus relates that the colony of Cyrene (Libya) was founded by the people of Thera on the advice of the Delphic oracle. However, research carried out in Sicily and Libya to try to match early pottery finds with the chronological accounts of foundations given in literary sources has failed to provide any firm conclusions.

According to Herodotus, a Greek colony was founded at Naukratis in the Nile delta at the instigation of the 6th-century Egyptian pharaoh Amasis. Excavations at the site have uncovered inscribed

Greek pottery, and similar contacts may explain the presence of Egyptian objects at the sanctuary of Hera on the island of Samos: Polykrates, the island's ruler, is said to have had regular correspondence with Amasis. The life-size stone statues of naked striding youths (*kouroi*) that begin to appear in Archaic Greek art of the late 7th century show the influence of Egyptian sculpture. The formal Geometric pottery of earlier times began to incorporate stylized animal and human figures, displaying Near Eastern influences ◆

BELOW The initial phase of colonization was in southern Italy and Sicily, and later extended to the northern Aegean and Black Seas. Colonies were also founded in Cyrenaica and Egypt. The dominance of Phoenician traders restricted activity further west (see pages 84–85), though an important colony at Massilia (Marseilles) was founded for trade with central Europe.

The Western Mediterranean

The presence of Phoenician and Greek colonies in the western Mediterranean had important cultural and economic consequences. By c.500 BCE Carthage (see page 85) had assumed leadership of the Phoenician (Punic) settlements in the west and established colonies of its own in southern Spain, the Balearic islands and Sardinia. Its domination of the southern sea routes confined Greek influence outside southern Italy and Sicily (Magna Graecia) to the northern Mediterranean coast: the Greek colony at Massilia (Marseilles) was a major conduit for trade with Iron Age Europe (see pages 94–95). Also involved in this widening trade were the Etruscan city-states of central Italy, whose wealth was based on rich mineral reserves. Their unique civilization reflected both Punic and Greek influences.

Evidence for wide networks of trade and cultural interchange in the western Mediterranean is plentiful. For example, Greek pottery as well a faience vessel bearing the cartouche of the Egyptian pharaoh Bocchoris (717–712 BCE) have been found at the site of the Carthaginian harbor at Motya, western Sicily. A similar vessel was present in an Etruscan tomb at Tarquinia, and a scarab of Bocchoris in a Greek grave on Ischia in the Bay of Naples. Oriental objects, including decorated ostrich eggs, bronze griffins, silver jugs and gilded silver bowls (some showing scenes of hunting on the Nile) have been found in several Etruscan sites. A battered Corinthian helmet from Jerez (southern Spain) as well as quantities of Greek pottery are also probably explained in terms of Phoenician trade. Athenian pottery has even been found on the west African coast. In the Guadalquivir valley north of Gades (Cadiz), interaction with the indigenous peoples led to the appearance of oriental metalworking techniques, sculpture and an incised script; it seems likely that the city of Tartessos, mentioned by Herodotus and others, was located here.

The Etruscans

The Etruscans were the inhabitants of the region of central Italy known as Etruria, roughly equivalent to modern Tuscany. After c.800 BCE a number of city-states emerged in the region. Although they were politically independent and culturally distinct, the twelve major city-states formed a loose political confederation. In the 7th and 6th centuries BCE, Etruscan influence expanded northward into the Po valley and south into Campania. Close contact with the Greek cities of southern Italy led to the absorption of many aspects of Greek civilization into Etruscan culture, including the alphabet, decorative arts, monumental temple-building and mythology.

Inscriptions are generally short, hindering decipherment of the non-Indo-European Etruscan language. However, three gold plaques with parallel Punic and Etruscan texts were discovered at Pyrgi in 1964. The inscription refers to the dedication of a temple to the Etruscan deity Uni, who appears to be equated with the Phoenician Astarte.

Few Etruscan cities have been excavated, but extensive cemeteries of chamber tombs, laid out and furnished like houses, offer substantial evidence of the daily life of their aristocratic occupants (see box). Enormous numbers of Greek vases have been found in these tombs, and the presence of chariots and imported gold, ivory and amber goods from the 7th century onwards is evidence of growing involvement in trade. Iron, mined on Elba and smelted in the coastal town of Populonia, was probably exported in

LEFT A bronze helmet of late 8th century date belonging to the Villanovan culture of central and northern Early Iron Age Italy (c.1000–800 BCE), which preceded the Etruscan civilization. It is characterized by cremation burials in terracotta urns (often hut-shaped or with a helmet-shaped lid), rich metalwork and dark, burnished pottery.

Douro

Tagus

Guadiana

Guadalqu

Carambolo ▪   ▪ Cruz del Ne
         ▪ Carmona
Tartessos? ▫   ▪ Osuna
      Mainake
Gades ▪   Malaca ▪ ▪ ▪ S
    Carteia ▪   ▪ Abdera
   Tingis ▪
Djebila ▪ ▪ Tamuda
     ▪ Lixus
          Rusade

Sala ▪

Monlouya

▪ Carthaginian site
▪ Etruscan site
▫ Greek site
▫ other site
● site of shipwreck

finds outside areas of influence
△ Carthaginian
△ Egyptian/Oriental
▲ Etruscan
△ Greek
▭ main distribution of Greek finds

── trade route
▨ maximum extent of Carthaginian empire
▨ Etruria, late 7th century BCE
▥ probable area of Tartessos, late 7th century BCE
▭ Greek influence, 6th century BCE
▥ Etruscan domination, late 6th century BCE

0   300 km
0   200 mi

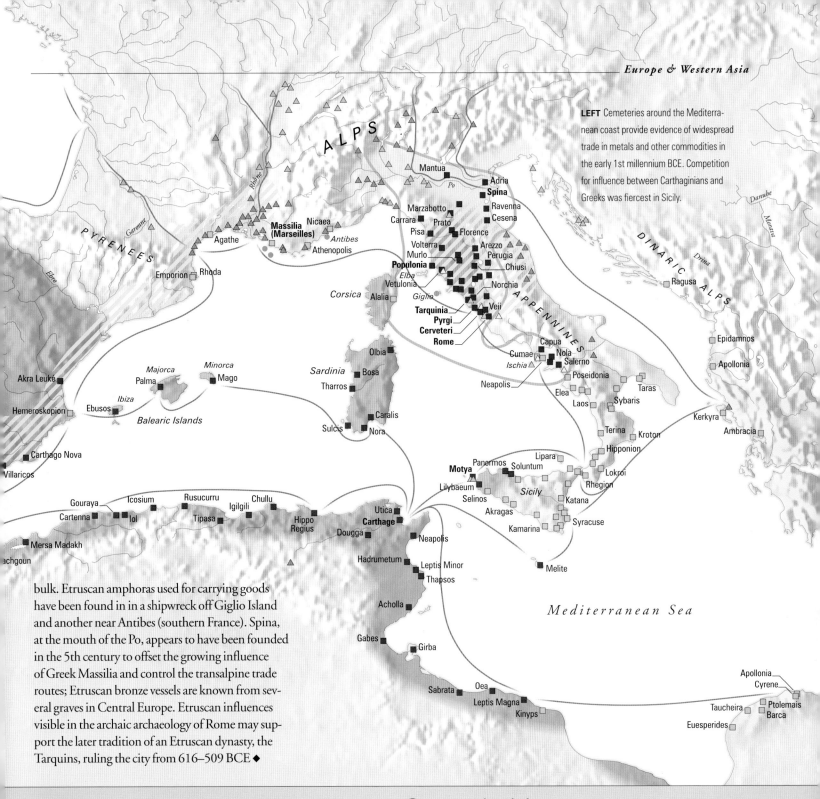

LEFT Cemeteries around the Mediterranean coast provide evidence of widespread trade in metals and other commodities in the early 1st millennium BCE. Competition for influence between Carthaginians and Greeks was fiercest in Sicily.

ALPS

Mantua
Adria
Spina
Marzabotto
Ravenna
Carrara
Cesena
Prato
Pisa
Florence
Volterra
Arezzo
Murlo
Perugia
Populonia
Chiusi
Elba
Vetulonia
Norchia
Giglio
Corsica
Alalia
Veii
Tarquinia
Pyrgi
Cerveteri
Rome
Capua
Cumae
Nola
Ischia
Salerno
Poseidonia
Neapolis
Elea
Taras
Laos
Sybaris
Terina
Kroton
Hipponion

PYRENEES
Massilia (Marseilles)
Nicaea
Antibes
Agathe
Athenopolis
Emporion
Rhoda

Majorca
Minorca
Palma
Mago
Akra Leukê
Sardinia
Bosa
Hemeroskopion
Ibiza
Tharros
Ebusos
Balearic Islands
Caralis
Carthago Nova
Sulcis
Nora
Villaricos

Gouraya
Icosium
Rusucurru
Chullu
Lipara
Soluntum
Cartenna
Iol
Igilgili
Panormos
Motya
Tipasa
Hippo Regius
Lilybaeum
Sicily
Mersa Madakh
Utica
Selinos
Katana
achgoun
Carthage
Akragas
Syracuse
Dougga
Neapolis
Kamarina
Hadrumetum
Leptis Minor
Thapsos
Melite
Acholla

Mediterranean Sea

Gabes
Girba

Sabrata
Oea
Leptis Magna
Kinyps

DINARIC ALPS
Ragusa
Epidamnos
Apollonia
Kerkyra
Ambracia

Apollonia
Cyrene
Taucheira
Ptolemais
Barca
Euesperides

Danube

bulk. Etruscan amphoras used for carrying goods have been found in in a shipwreck off Giglio Island and another near Antibes (southern France). Spina, at the mouth of the Po, appears to have been founded in the 5th century to offset the growing influence of Greek Massilia and control the transalpine trade routes; Etruscan bronze vessels are known from several graves in Central Europe. Etruscan influences visible in the archaic archaeology of Rome may support the later tradition of an Etruscan dynasty, the Tarquins, ruling the city from 616–509 BCE ◆

ABOVE CHAMBER TOMBS IN THE CEMETERY AT BANDITACCIA, NEAR CERVETERI.

Cerveteri: cities of the dead

Some of the most extensive Etruscan cemeteries, laid out like cities of the dead, are found at Cerveteri (ancient Caere) in southern Etruria, where rounded chamber tombs were carved out of the soft volcanic tufa rock and covered with mounds of earth. The magnificent sculptural art from these tombs is now displayed in museums and collections throughout the world, removed as the result of excavation or looting. They provide evidence of an aristocratic society that gave status to husband and wife, who were interred together in houselike-tombs containing their terracotta effigies. The Tomb of the Reliefs at Cerveteri, for example, represented a dining-room, with carved reliefs of armor and drinking-cups appearing to hang on the walls. The deceased couple were reclining on couches, as if for a banquet, equipped with stone cushions for extra comfort. At Tarquinia, also in the south, many tombs were decorated with elaborate painted frescoes depicting banquets with dancers and musicians, funerary games and scenes of fishing ◆

Iron Age Europe

During the 1st millennium BCE, most people in Europe lived in farming communities, much as their Bronze Age predecessors had. Iron was increasingly used after 700 BCE, but did not entirely replace bronze. Technical expertise in other materials, such as glass and gold, developed at around the same time. Contact with Greek trading colonies from around 500 BCE had dramatic impact, creating powerful elites in central Europe and east of the Carpathians. Large, semi-urbanized settlements (*oppida*) emerged in western Europe in the last two centuries BCE. The Roman conquest brought profound changes. Within the empire itself, Roman camps and villas were established alongside native settlements, and the two societies slowly blended together. Beyond its frontiers, the influx of Roman goods had economic and social impact as far as Poland and Scandinavia.

In the Low Countries, northern Germany and southern Scandinavia, the common type of farmhouse was a long structure with two rows of interior posts to support the roof. The farming family lived in one end; the other end provided shelter for stalled livestock. At some sites like Hascherkeller in Bavaria there is evidence of metalworking and other crafts, though farming remained the principal activity. A number of fortified towns were built in northern Poland about 700 BCE. At Biskupin, waterlogged soil has preserved evidence of timber-paved streets. The inhabitants were still primarily farmers, but a range of cloth, wood, bone and metal artifacts shows that they engaged in small-scale craft production.

Industrial Centers

Between about 700 and 500 BCE, several "industrial" centers arose in central Europe at places where the extraction of raw materials was combined with their manufacture into finished products. These were then traded over long distances. Two such centers are Stična (Slovenia), and Hallstatt (Austria). At the first of these sites, high-grade iron was smelted and forged. Hallstatt was a center for mining rock salt. Timber shoring, wooden tools and leather backpacks used by prehistoric miners have been found preserved by the salt deposits. Rich burials demonstrate the tremendous wealth that long-distance trade brought to these communities.

ABOVE Maiden Castle is one of a large number of small enclosed sites, known as "hillforts", found in southern and central Britain. The earliest date from the end of the Bronze Age. They were not all continuously occupied, or in use at the same time. Many were abandoned during the 3rd century BCE, while a few sites became dominant; these may have had a similar role to the continental *oppida*, serving as regional centers of production and trade. Later, true *oppida*, much larger than hillforts, were established in Britain as on the continent. Many subsequently became Roman towns, as at Camulodunum (Colchester) and Verulamium (St Albans). Maiden Castle was probably captured by the Romans in 43 CE.

Hochdorf: an elite burial

One of the most impressive finds of European Iron Age archaeology was made at Hochdorf (western Germany), in the late 1970s. Excavation of a tumulus (originally 20 ft/6 m high, but now much eroded) revealed an immensely rich Iron Age burial of about 550–500 BCE. Unlike many other such tombs, it had not been robbed at any time. At the center of the tomb, within a timber-lined burial chamber, the body of a man was found lying on a bronze recliner. This object has no known parallel in Iron Age Europe. Shaped like a bathtub with one side removed, it was lined with furs and textiles. The clothes and shoes of the dead man were decorated with gold ornaments. Nearby was a large bronze kettle, believed to be of Greek origin, from southern Italy; laboratory tests revealed that it had once contained mead. A large four-wheeled wagon of iron-sheathed wood, with harnesses for two horses, was on the other side of the chamber. Hochdorf is one of a number of sites that point to the emergence of wealthy chiefdoms in an area lying between the rivers Rhône, Rhine and Danube. Based on trade with the Mediterranean, they collapsed when this trade was interrupted about 400 BCE ◆

LEFT BRONZE ORNAMENT FROM WAGON (4 IN/10.5 CM).

Map labels:

North Sea · Baltic Sea · Mediterranean Sea · Corsica

Vendel · Gamla Uppsala · Helgö · Borre · Morgedal · Klepp · Torsburgen · Ismantorp · Borremose · Hørby · Grauballe · Tollund · Dankirke · Åhus · Hjortspring · Gudme · Sorte Mulde · Korselitse · Haithabu · Western Dvina · Neman

Castlerock · Magheralin · Lindow Moss · Maiden Castle · Danebury · Elp · Scharmbeck · Sobiejuchy · Biskupin · Rudki · Vistula · Bug · Dnieper

Weser · Rhine · Elbe · Oder · Thames · Seine · Soissons · Würzburg · Podbaba · Lodenice · Závist · Paris · Hochdorf · Staré Hradisko · CARPATHIAN MOUNTAINS · Dniester · Mont Lassois · Nagold · Kelheim · Manching · Vix · Breisach · Heuneburg · Hascherkeller · Kyberg · Danube · Bourges · Mont Guérin · Üetliberg · Hellbrunner Berg · Hallstatt · Sopron · Velemszentvid · Camp de Chassey · Loire · Châtillon-sur-Glâne · Klein-Klein · Tyras · Mâcon · Montmorot · ALPS · Stična · Novo Mesto · Gergovie · Vienna · Milan · Aquileia · DINARIC ALPS · Drava · Sava · Puy d'Issolu · Garonne · Rhône · Po · Spina · Bologna · Danube · Istros · Toulouse · APPENNINES · Pisa · PYRENEES · Marseilles (Massilia) · Ebro · Corsica · Alalia · Cerveteri · Epidamnos · Tissa · Prut

Legend:

- spread of iron working, 12th–8th century BCE
- spread of iron working, 8th–5th century BCE
- area of Greek influence, 6th century BCE
- area of west Hallstatt chiefdoms, 6th century BCE
- area of Etruscan city states, c.450 BCE
- area of Scythian influence, c.450 BCE
- ◼ industrial center
- ◻ fortified settlement or stronghold
- ◼ site of grave
- ▲ site of Etruscan find
- △ site of Greek find
- ◻ site of bog find
- ◻ other settlement or trading colony
- area of *oppida*, 1st century BCE
- main trade route

major source of commodity

- amber
- copper
- gold
- iron
- salt
- tin

0 ____ 400 km
0 ____ 300 mi

From 500 BCE, extensive trade with the Mediterranean passed through the Greek colony at Massilia (Marseilles) at the mouth of the Rhône, which was a convenient corridor into central Europe. Sites like Mont Lassois and the Heuneburg became the seats of powerful and wealthy elites (see box). At the Heuneburg, mudbrick walls were even built in the style of the Mediterranean, though the climate was hardly suitable for such construction. The Scythians (horse-riding pastoral nomads of the steppes of southern Russia and Ukraine) also had lively trade contacts with Greek Black Sea colonies (see pages 128–129).

The increasing volume of trade in Italian products may have played an important part in the emergence of *oppida*, the urbanized communities described by Caesar in his account of the conquest of Gaul (France and Belgium). They varied in area between 75 and 815 acres/30 and 300 hectares, and were surrounded by substantial stone or earth walls enclosing close-packed dwellings and industrial workshops.

Almost perfectly preserved human bodies of Iron Age date have been dug out of peatbogs at Tollund and Grauballe (Denmark) and at Lindow Moss (England). None had died a natural death and they appear to have been ritually sacrificed. The throat of the Grauballe man had been slit, the Tollund man had been strangled, and the Lindow victim subjected to both these methods of killing. The contents of the Tollund man's stomach showed that his last meal had been a gruel containing barley, linseed, knotweed, dock and camomile. At Hjortspring (Denmark), a large canoe built of planks, which apparently carried a party of warriors, was found preserved in a bog, where it had been ritually deposited as an offering of war booty. Bogs, ponds and springs were clearly sacred locations in prehistoric northern Europe ◆

The Classical Age of Greece

The Persian wars (499–435 BCE) shaped and defined the world of Classical Greece. Three attempts by Persia to invade the mainland between 490 and 479 were defeated by an Hellenic alliance headed by Athens and Sparta, and by 448 the Greek cities of Ionia had been won back from Persian rule by the Athenian-led Delian League. The wealth accruing to Athens from control of what was in effect an empire allowed it to embark on a major building program, but the tensions created by its power gave rise to the Peloponnesian war, won by Sparta in 404 BCE. The struggles for supremacy among the Greek city-states continued throughout the 4th century until all were subsumed by the emergent dominant power of Macedon under Philip II (see pages 98–99).

For a 5th-century Athenian or Spartan there was no such concept as Greece, except in terms of a shared language (though there were regional variations of the alphabet) and deities: the Greek city-states were autonomous and independent. However, a Panhellenic identity was expressed through common sanctuaries, whose importance as religious centers extended back at least as far as the 8th century BCE; the traditional foundation date of the great athletic festival held in honor of Zeus at Olympia, which was open to competitors from throughout the Greek world, was 776 BCE. As well as Olympia, Panhellenic games were held at two other sanctuaries in the Peloponnese, Nemea and Isthmia (near Corinth), where an early 7th-century stone temple was discovered in the 1950s, and a fourth in central Greece at Delphi. In addition, oracles at shrines such as Dodona, the

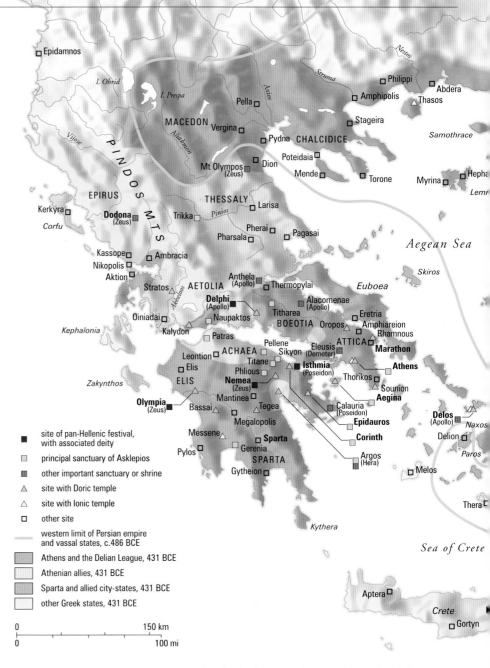

■ site of pan-Hellenic festival, with associated deity

▫ principal sanctuary of Asklepios

▣ other important sanctuary or shrine

△ site with Doric temple

△ site with Ionic temple

▫ other site

western limit of Persian empire and vassal states, c.486 BCE

Athens and the Delian League, 431 BCE

Athenian allies, 431 BCE

Sparta and allied city-states, 431 BCE

other Greek states, 431 BCE

0 ———————— 150 km
0 ———————— 100 mi

ABOVE The Parthenon, the temple of Athena on the Acropolis, was built at the height of Athens' fame and wealth.

island of Delos (sacred to Apollo), and Delphi attracted pilgrims from all over Greece. Many cities sent embassies to the Delphic oracle for advice before embarking on their colonizing expeditions.

Wealthy dedications

The Panhellenic sanctuaries were endowed with rich gifts and buildings dedicated by city-states from Sicily and North Africa and throughout the Greek islands and mainland. Archaeologists have been assisted in their identification of these monuments by the descriptions left by the Roman travel writer Pausanias, writing in the 2nd century CE. Some celebrated sporting successes, such as the statue of the bronze charioteer at Delphi, which was part of a large group erected to commemorate a win in the chariot race by the city of Gela in southern Sicily. Others were placed there as dedications for military victory: Pausanias records that the Athenian treasury (or store house) at

Byzantium
Perinthos · Chalkedon

Sea of Marmara

Lampsakos
Cyzicus

Mytilene
Pergamon

**PERSIAN
EMPIRE**
after peace of Kallias, 448 BCE

Gediz

Sardis

Smyrna
Klazomenai
Teos
Kolophon
Lebedos
Ephesos
(Artemis)
Klaros
(Apollo)
Menderes
Magnesia
Samos
Priene

Miletos
Didyma
(Apollo)

Mylasa

Myndos
Halikarnassos

Kos

Kephalos
Knidos
(Aphrodite)

Ialysos · Rhodes

Kameiros
Lindos
Rhodes

Karpathos

Mediterranean Sea

Delphi, commemorating the city's role in defeating the Persians at Marathon (490 BCE), was built with the booty taken in the battle. French archaeologists have discovered the base of a monument erected by the cities of the alliance that defeated Xerxes in 480 BCE; the monument itself, a huge cauldron supported by intertwined bronze snakes, was taken from Delphi in late antiquity and set up in the Hippodrome in Constantinople, where it can still be seen.

The inscription on a gold cup found at Olympia shows that it was dedicated by the Kypselid family of Corinth after the sack of a Greek city referred to as Herakleia (location unknown). The sanctuary at Olympia contained one of the seven wonders of the ancient world, the gold and ivory cult-statue of Zeus by the Athenian sculptor Pheidias (who also created a similar statue of Athena for the Parthenon in Athens). It has not survived, but German archaeologists have uncovered the site of the workshop where it was made; the excavators even claimed to have found a clay drinking mug inscribed "I belong to Pheidias".

The Athenian achievement

Athens was the largest of the Greek city-states, covering an area of approximately 960 sq mi/2,400 sq km. At its height in the 5th century BCE it perhaps had a population of around 350,000, of which possibly 50,000 were full citizens (men over 18 years of age born into an Athenian family). Athenian democracy (which excluded women and slaves) had been established late in the 6th century, and was strengthened by reforms during the Persian wars. Through its leadership of the Delian League Athens promoted democratic factions elsewhere in the Greek world, but many forms of political and social systems were found among the Greek city-states: Sparta, for instance, had a narrow oligarchy based on serf labor.

Athens was sacked by the Persians in 480 BCE. The destruction of the city allowed for an extravagant program of rebuilding, financed by the subscriptions of the members of the Delian League after the treasury, previously housed in the sanctuary of Apollo on Delos, was moved to Athens in 454 BCE, ostensibly to protect it from Persian attack. The debris from the destroyed buildings was used to build a defensive wall, 7 mi/11 km long, to protect the city (now at war with Sparta) and its port of Piraeus. New temples were constructed on the Acropolis, including the Parthenon (begun in 447 BCE), the Propylaea, the temple of Athena Nike, and the Erechtheum.

The political life of the city was conducted in the agora, an open space that was both marketplace and civic center. Excavations of this area since the 1930s have revealed the layout of the agora, with the bouleuterion, the council chamber, on the west side. Elsewhere were located the law courts, where bronze ballots used to give the decision of the jurors were found. Stoas, open-sided colonnades where business was done, lay on the north and south sides of the agora, and the area was bisected by the processional Panathenaic Way leading from the city gates to the Acropolis ◆

ABOVE The division of the Greek world into two main cultural groupings, Dorians in the west and Peloponnese and Ionians in the east, is reflected in architectural terms in the Doric style (used for the great temples of Zeus at Olympia and Apollo at Delphi) and the Ionian of the east Greek world (as in the temples of Hera on Samos and Artemis at Ephesos). Later the styles were often mixed, for example, in the 5th-century rebuilding of the Acropolis. The cult of Asklepios, centered at Epidauros, grew in importance in the 4th century.

LEFT A *kore* (draped female figure), one of many such 6th- and early 5th-century statues found on the Athenian Acropolis. These statues were deliberately buried, either after the Persian destruction of the Acropolis in 480, or in subsequent political upheavals. As a result, many still retain their painted decoration, as on the patterning on their dresses. Other significant areas producing lifesize sculptures of this kind included Samos, Paros and Aegina.

The Hellenistic Near East

Through the ambitious policies of Philip II (r.359–336) Macedon, a small kingdom on the periphery of the Classical Greek world, won control of most of the mainland city-states by 338 BCE. Philip was assassinated before he was able to undertake a planned invasion of the Persian empire, leaving his son Alexander the Great (r.336–323) to complete the task. This he did with phenomenal success, creating a vast empire that stretched from Greece across Asia to the Indus, and included Egypt. On his death, his possessions broke up into a number of successor states. The Hellenistic kingdoms of the Near East blended Greek cultural traditions with extravagant militarism and a lavish court life. Most were later incorporated into the provincial structure of the Roman empire (see pages 100–101).

One of the most striking archaeological discoveries of recent years was made at Vergina (northern Greece), identified as the site of Aigai, the ancient Macedonian capital. Excavation of a large tumulus some 46 ft/14 m high and 360 ft/110 m in diameter revealed an unplundered tomb containing many items of bronze armor, bronze and silver vessels, and wooden furniture. A marble sarcophagus was found to hold a gold box (larnax) bearing the royal Macedonian symbol of a star-burst. Inside were the cremated remains of a male, originally wrapped in a purple cloth. Whether or not the excavators are correct in their belief, based on medical forensic reconstruction of the skull and other bones, that this was the body of Philip II himself, it was clearly an important royal burial, dating from the mid-4th century BCE, the formative period of Macedonian power.

The legacy of Alexander

Alexander's conquests amazed his contemporaries. His victories were celebrated in art; the clash with Darius's army at Granikos was commemorated with a group sculpture by Lysippos of Sikyon, later looted and set up in the portico of Metellus in the Campus Martius at Rome. The "Alexander mosaic" from the House of the Fauns at Pompeii showing him in head-long charge at the battle of Issos is thought to be a copy of a 4th-century painting by Philoxenos of Eretria. Coins struck in Alexander's lifetime showed him as the Greek hero Heracles, a comparison also made in portraits after his death, such as the frieze on the Alexander Sarcophagus from the royal cemetery at Sidon (c.325–300 BCE).

In the wars following Alexander's death, his generals created independent kingdoms for themselves and

ABOVE The acropolis at Pergamon, perhaps the most stunning of the Hellenistic capitals of the Near East, built by Attalos I who broke away from Seleucid rule in the mid 3rd century BCE after defeating the Galatians (Gauls). The city, constructed on a steeply sloping hill with a theater cut into the side, was embellished with many monuments in celebration of his victories. They include the bronze statue of the "Dying Gaul" known today only from a Roman marble copy. The Great Altar of Zeus (now in the Berlin Museum) was decorated with a frieze in a free-flowing, grandiloquent style typical of Hellenistic sculpture. The library at Pergamon, the ruins of which can still be seen, was the largest outside Alexandria.

Alexandria: city of the Ptolemies

Alexandria, on the Nile delta, was the greatest of the cities named for Alexander. Under the Ptolemies, it was the largest Greek-speaking city in the world, excelling even Athens as a cultural center. Most of the Ptolemaic city is buried today beneath modern Alexandria, but underwater surveys of the eastern harbor have recorded over 2,000 granite blocks that almost certainly come from the Pharos, or lighthouse, built in 280 BCE and destroyed by an earthquake in the 14th century CE. A number of sculptures raised from the sea bed may once have been placed on or around this structure. Among them is a colossal pink granite statue, possibly that of the wife of a pharaoh in the garb of Isis, and a torso fragment from another colossal statue of a Ptolemaic pharaoh. Also found were the bases for six statues, so at least three royal pairs of statues may once have stood at the harbor entrance. Some of the sculpture seems to have been reused from earlier pharaohs, including sphinxes that date to the 26th dynasty pharaoh Psammetichus II. Divers have also located structural foundations in the eastern harbor. These have tentatively been identified as belonging to the royal palaces of the Ptolemies ◆

ABOVE A DIVER CONFRONTS A STATUE OF A SPHINX ON THE SEA BED OF THE EASTERN HARBOR.

RIGHT With the death of Alexander the Great, the conquered lands of the Near East were divided between the Greek kingdoms of the Seleucids and the Ptolemies. Ptolemaic influence included the new foundation of Arsinoë in the region of Argos in the northeastern Peloponnese of mainland Greece, where they had extensive estates. The Seleucids secured their possessions across Asia Minor by a number of foundations, including Antioch.

founded ruling dynasties, the most long-lasting of which were the Antigonid (Macedon), Seleucid (Syria and Mesopotamia) and Ptolemaic (Egypt). The Hellenistic kings had vast wealth at their disposal, and their patronage attracted Greek artists, intellectuals and mercenaries. They maintained large standing armies and built huge warships: war elephants were a feature of Hellenistic warfare. Sculptural art and architecture was characterized by flamboyance, extravagance, complexity and size: the Hellenistic period saw the construction of colossal temples in the Near East such as the rebuilt temple of Artemis at Ephesos. In Egypt, the Ptolemies consciously blended Greek and Egyptian culture, assuming the traditional religious functions of the pharaohs and promoting local cults. But here, as elsewhere, there appears to have been little cultural assimilation between Greeks and non-Greeks.

Priene in western Turkey, founded in the 7th century and substantially rebuilt in the 3rd century BCE, is one of the best sources of information on town planning and city life in the Hellenistic period. Laid out to a grid pattern, it was built on a steep hillside and excavations have revealed the careful use of terracing to create open spaces for the agora, the temple of Athena Polias, and other public buildings. Several private houses have also been uncovered ◆

BELOW In 334 BCE Alexander invaded Anatolia, liberating the Greek cities of the coast from Persian rule. He continued down the Mediterranean coast to Egypt before overrunning the Persian empire in 331. Six years of campaigning in the east followed, which left a string of cities in his name.

campaign of Alexander, 334–324 BCE
■ city founded by Alexander
□ other city

■ city founded under Greek influence, 3rd century BCE
■ Hellenised city, 3rd century BCE
△ site of temple founded 3rd century BCE
▣ other Greek settlement or site
▢ area of Macedonian control, c.270 BCE
▨ area of Ptolemaic control, c.270 BCE
▩ area of Seleucid control, c.270 BCE
▢ area of Celtic settlement, c.2nd century BCE
— trade route

0   400 km
0   300 mi

The Spread of the Roman Empire

The seat of Roman power was the city of Rome itself. Evidence of an early Iron Age settlement has been uncovered on the Palatine hill, but the transformation from village to city began under the Tarquin kings in the 6th century BCE when the forum and other marshy areas were drained by the construction of a drain, the Cloaca Maxima, into the Tiber. Under the Republic (509–27 BCE), Rome extended its power throughout Italy and acquired an overseas empire. The population of Rome rose to nearly 1 million and politicians vied for popular support by funding lavish building programs, a practice continued on an even more grandiose scale by the early emperors. The provincial structure of the empire was reorganized by Augustus (27 BCE–14 CE) to give the emperor direct control of the most newly acquired parts of the empire, which continued to expand for another century. By the 2nd century CE it extended from Scotland to Egypt and from Portugal to Syria.

ABOVE The Colosseum, Rome's great amphitheater, was imitated throughout the empire.

The spread of Roman power and influence throughout the Mediterranean world and western Europe is reflected in the archaeological record. The excavation of Roman towns and cities from Wroxeter (Viroconium) in England to Coimbra (Conimbriga) in Portugal, St-Rémy (Glanum) in France, Leptis Magna in Libya, Corinth in Greece or Caesarea in Israel shows the same pattern of temples, courthouses and markets, based on those to be found in the forum at Rome. Roman art and culture were disseminated through the empire both as a result of deliberate policy (for example, by the use of official portraits of the emperors for propaganda purposes) and through the projection of Roman tastes and fashions onto social elites. The building of aqueducts, amphitheaters (for animal games and gladiatorial shows) and public baths spread the "advantages" of Roman civilization. Even in Britain, at the northern

[Map labels: Flaviobriga, Douro, Zamora, Cala, Ta, Coimbra, Segovia, Toledo, Tágus, Mérida, Beja, Córdoba, Italica, Écija, Martos, Seville, Osuna, Guac, Car, Cádiz, Tangiers, Banasa, Malahala]

Pompeii: an Italian provincial town

The city of Pompeii, buried under ash and volcanic mud by a major eruption of Vesuvius in 79 CE, together with nearby Herculaneum, has been of unparalleled importance for the study of Roman archaeology since excavations began in the 18th century. Tunneling beneath the solidified layers of pumice, early excavators uncovered the street layout, municipal buildings and private houses of a typical provincial town of the early Roman empire. The sudden eruption left the fleeing citizens little time to save their belongings. Jewelry, household utensils, wax tablets, wooden furniture, foodstuffs, even garden plants have all been recovered from beneath the ash. Some people were trapped beneath falling timbers; others were overcome by poisonous fumes as they tried to escape in the last stages of the eruption and were buried where they fell, their body-shapes preserved as cavities in the hardened debris. The wall paintings found intact in many houses tell us much about the private life and tastes of the wealthy: a series in the Villa of Mysteries appears to show the initiation stages into a mystery cult. A number of houses contained bronze or marble portraits of their owners. One of these is of a woman, Eumachia, whose name appears on an inscription naming her as the benefactor of the meat-market. Thousands of graffiti, many of them passing on gossip and scandal, record the voices of Pompeii's ordinary citizens. Such personal insights into Roman life are seldom found elsewhere ◆

LEFT A PLASTER CAST CAPTURES THE LAST MOMENTS OF A MAN'S LIFE AS HE CROUCHES TO ESCAPE THE CHOKING FUMES.

limit of the empire, houses were
decorated with mosaic floors and wall
paintings that drew on Roman iconography (vines,
doves, dolphins, mythological scenes) and equipped
with the latest Roman technology of underfloor heating (hypocausts) and bath-houses.

The eastern Mediterranean

In the Greek-speaking parts of the empire, in contrast
to the west where urbanization was a recent development, Roman culture was imposed on urban societies
that had already existed for centuries. Excavations at
Roman Corinth, founded in 44 BCE on the site of
the Greek city destroyed by the Romans in 146 BCE,
have uncovered a Roman-style forum and a large
number of Latin inscriptions indicate that the social
elites of nearby cities moved to Corinth, capital of the
Roman province of Achaia, to benefit from a Roman
lifestyle. This is unlike the situation at Athens, where

Greek architectural styles and inscriptions in Greek continued in use throughout
the centuries of Roman rule.

In the east, Roman-style bath-houses were sometimes attached to the Greek gymnasia where young
men trained for athletic events. Often the benefactors
of these complexes, provincial officials or local pluto-
crats, were also benefactors of the games. Even in a
city like Jerusalem, with its strongly Jewish emphasis,
there was an attempt to introduce Roman culture.
Archaeologists have found theater tokens in a wealthy
Jewish house destroyed during the Roman sack of the
city in 70 CE, even though the public performance of
plays was linked to pagan religious festivals ◆

Communications and Trade

The administration of the empire was assisted by the highly efficient network of paved roads that linked Rome with the provinces. The earliest roads, built during the wars of conquest in Italy, played a crucial role in consolidating Roman control throughout the peninsula, and the road system continued to expand with the growing empire. Roads were constructed and maintained by the army and used to supply garrisons in distant parts of the empire from the Parthian frontier in the east to the north of Britain. They also served the empire's administrators: the orator Cicero's correspondence as governor of Cilicia in southeastern Turkey during the late Republic shows that he made his official visits only to those cities easily accessible by road. Although Roman roads were designed to take the most direct line over flat terrain, in mountainous areas such as Turkey they were carefully constructed to catch the early sunlight, thus ensuring that they remained usable in all weathers.

As Rome's empire grew, so did the volume of trade moving around it to supply its urban populations with foodstuffs and luxury goods. By the early empire, Rome alone needed to import around 400,000 tons of grain each year, most of which came from Egypt, North Africa and Sicily: it was cheaper to transport grain in bulk in huge seagoing ships than to cart it into the city from the surrounding countryside. In the early decades of the 1st century CE there were several disasters when the corn fleet was destroyed before it was able to unload at Ostia, Rome's port at the mouth of the Tiber, and several emperors, including Claudius, Nero and Trajan, undertook construction works to improve the facilities. Protective harbors were also created at other important ports by Roman engineers. The city of Corinth, at the strategic narrow isthmus between the Greek mainland and the Peloponnese, was provided with two of the largest harbors in the empire at Cenchreae (serving the Gulf of Corinth, and providing access to the Adriatic) and Lechaeum (serving the Saronic Gulf and with access to the east). An attempt was even made during Nero's reign to cut a canal through the isthmus itself, but the work had to be abandoned. An equally large harbor complex, partially submerged, has been located at Caesarea in Israel, a port initially built by Herod the Great and named in honor of the Roman emperor.

BELOW A selection of blown-glass vessels made in Italian or southern European workshops in the 1st century CE. The technique of glass-blowing was invented in the 1st century BCE, probably in Syria, but it reached its greatest early florescence in Italy, where the making of elaborate cameo-cut glass also developed into a fine art. Glass vessels were luxury items among well-off Romans (some fine examples are displayed on wall paintings at Pompeii) and were widely traded within and outside the empire. Excavations at Cologne have found evidence of a glass-making factory there from c.50 CE. Rhineland glass vessels were popular items of trade with Germanic tribes living beyond the frontier.

Roman shipwrecks

Marine archaeologists have identified numerous shipwrecks off the southern coast of France containing Roman amphoras for transporting goods like wine, olive oil, and even pickled fish. The ships seem to have come mostly from Spain, North Africa, Tuscany and Campania. Archaeologists are able to classify these amphoras by type and in some cases can even identify their place of origin. For example, "Dressel 1" type amphoras of late Republican date bearing the stamp of Sestius were found on the Grand Congloue shipwreck. They came from an estate near Ansedonia (Cosa), Tuscany, as presumably did their contents, which were probably of fish: excavations at Cosa have revealed the site of amphora workshops, together with fish processing facilities and fish tanks.

In 1999, nine well-preserved ships dating from between the 2nd century BCE and the 5th century CE were discovered in the silted up Roman harbor at Pisa – the largest collection of Roman vessels ever found. Study of their structure and cargoes (quantities of amphoras have been found) is providing new information about Roman seafaring and trade.

Rich profits

The demands made by the urban population of Rome on other parts of the empire were huge. At Rome itself a huge mound of discarded fragmentary transport amphoras, the Monte Testaccio, bears witness to the movement of Spanish

La Coruña

Douro

Tagus

Lisbon

Mérida

Córdoba

Cádiz

ATLANTIC OCEAN

Tangiers

Mondeg

RIGHT Basic commodities such as metals, pottery, foodstuffs (grain, oil and wine) flowed to Rome from around the empire or were sent to the frontier provinces to supply garrison towns, which became active centers of cross-border trade. Most goods traveled by sea and along navigable rivers such as the Rhine and Danube.

olive oil. In North Africa, where the olive was intensively cultivated, recent surveys have detected the presence of large oil factories. The urban elite of the region grew rich on profits from the oil trade. They included the family of the emperor Septimius Severus (r.193–211), who later endowed his native city of Leptis Magna with a new forum and basilica.

In the northwestern empire (Britannia and Gaul), towns did not dominate the economy to the same extent, and country houses (villas) became the centers of large, virtually self-sufficient farming estates ◆

ABOVE A painted fresco showing farmworkers outside a country villa in northern Gaul.

North
Sea

Inveresk
York
Chester
Lincoln
London
Dover
Exeter
Chichester
Boulogne
Cherbourg
Rouen
Paris
Nantes
Saintes
Bordeaux
Nijmegen
Cologne
Trier

Elbe
Rhine
Danube
Loire
Rhône

Regensburg
Augsburg
Carnuntum
Budapest
Virunum
Aquilèia
Milan
Genoa
Ravenna
Ancona
Po
Sava
Tisza
Salonae
Belgrade
Kostolac
Sarmizegethusa
CARPATHIAN MTS
Dnieper
Dniester
Prut
Don
Donets
Olbia
Kerch
Constanta
Danube
Nis
BALKAN MTS
Black Sea
Sinope
Trabzon
Byzantium
Perinthos
Izmit
Ankara
Sivas
Kayseri
Lake Van
Yesil
Kizil Irmak
Lake Tuz
Diyarbakir
Urfa
Tarsus
Antakya
Dura Europus
Palmyra
Euphrates
Orontes
Tigris

Thessalonica
Bergama
Izmir
Ephesos
Pisidian Antioch
Laodicea
Corinth
Athens
Rhodes
Myra
Crete
Gortyn
Paphos
Salamis
Cyprus
Tyre
Damascus
Syrian Desert
Busra ash Sham
Caesarea
Jerusalem
Gaza
Petra

ALPS
PYRENEES
Lyon
Arles
Narbonne
Marseilles
Tarragona
Cartagena
Cherchell
Annaba
Carthage
Tebessa
Corsica
Sardinia
Balearic Islands
Ansedonia
Rome
Ostia
Pozzuoli
Pompeii
Pisa
Brindisi
Durrës
Messina
Palermo
Reggio
Syracuse
Sicily

Mediterranean Sea

Leptis Magna
Cyrene
Alexandria
Memphis
Clysma
Nile
Myos Hormus
Berenice

ALPS

Durrës

area of Roman influence, 117 CE
city with population over 100,000
city with population over 30,000
city with population under 30,000
area of heaviest urbanization
area of villa economy
site of Dressel amphora find, c.1st century BCE

olives
pottery

main road
sea route
navigable river
area of shipwreck

source of traded goods
grain
glass
metal ores

0   600 km
0   400 mi

The Frontiers of the Empire

Rome acquired its empire through a combination of accident, greed and ambition: punitive wars had to be undertaken to defend its existing interests; fresh territorial conquests brought a flood of treasure and slaves to Rome; success in war was the surest route to political power at home. After a humiliating defeat in Germany in 9 CE, Augustus called a halt to expansion, but the desire for military glory led his successors to further territorial conquests. Hadrian (117–138), perhaps in reaction to his predecessor Trajan's costly wars of expansion, was the first to create permanent frontiers in Britain and Germany.

Hadrian decided to build a stone wall in northern Britain after undertaking a tour of the empire in 121 to inspect troops and examine frontier defenses. Recent excavations at the pre-Hadrianic fort of Vindolanda, lying just to the south of the later line of the wall, have uncovered a structure tentatively identified as a temporary imperial palace, which is perhaps linked to this visit.

Running for 70 mi/113 km from coast to coast across northern England, Hadrian's Wall is one of the most impressive and fully excavated Roman archaeological sites in western Europe. The wall is best preserved in its central sector, which was built along the edge of a limestone outcrop, giving it a dominant view to the north; there is evidence that it was originally painted white to make it clearly visible. Small forts and gates were built at mile intervals along the wall regardless of terrain: as a result, the entrances of some of these milecastles give access to a sheer drop.

Wooden writing tablets and slivers of wood with written messages have been discovered at Vindolanda, preserved by the damp conditions of the site. This unique archive provides remarkable insights into army life on the northern frontier. Some letters contain information about the secondment of troops and supplies. Others are more personal – an invitation to a birthday party from the wife of a neighboring garrison commander, or a request to send more beer.

The Rhine-Danube frontier

One of the most sensitive areas in the empire's defenses lay between the rivers Rhine and Danube. In the late 1st century military campaigns in the Black

ABOVE The fortress on the rocky outcrop of Masada (Israel), besieged by a Roman force after the Jewish revolt of 66 CE. The Romans encircled the fortress with a series of forts connected by walls to prevent a break-out and to stop supplies reaching the defenders. The logistics of such a siege in desert conditions reflects Rome's resolve to eliminate all pockets of resistance in this vulnerable frontier region. A siege ramp built up the cliff towards the ramparts still provides the easiest access to the site.

The Jewish historian Josephus records the story that the defenders killed themselves just before the troops broke in rather than become slaves to Rome. The fortress was built originally as a palace for king Herod (40–4 BCE) and excavations have revealed the remains of buildings decorated with paintings in the Roman style.

Hoxne: a buried silver hoard

By the early 4th century the empire had split into eastern and western halves and imperial control was crumbling in the west. The uncertainty of life in the provinces may be reflected in the number of buried coin and silver hoards that have been discovered in eastern England from the last two centuries of Roman occupation. One of the largest, consisting of around 200 gold and silver objects and 14,865 coins, was uncovered in a plowed field at Hoxne, Suffolk, in 1992. It was probably buried some time between 408 and 450, and traces of organic material, probably straw, and textiles indicate that the objects had been carefully wrapped before being placed in a wooden chest. At least 24 of the objects bear Christian symbols or inscriptions. A late Roman hoard from Water Newton, Cambridgeshire, also contained silver items associated with Christianity, including several vessels belonging to a Eucharist set ◆

ABOVE A PRANCING TIGRESS OF SILVER FROM THE HOXNE HOARD (6.25 IN/15.9 CM LONG). IT MAY HAVE BEEN A MOUNTING FROM A LARGE VESSEL.

area of Roman control, c.235 CE
market zone close to Roman frontier
legionary camp
frontier fort founded before 85 CE
frontier fort founded 85–138 CE
fontier fort founded 138–192 CE
Saxon shore fort, 3rd and 4th centuries CE
Roman find outside area of control
site of silver hoard
other settlement
Roman wall or rampart
main road
expansion of Germanic peoples

0   300 km
0   200 mi

Antonine Wall
Inveresk
Newstead
Hadrian's Wall
Newcastle
Bowness
Vindolanda
Ebchester
Brough
York
Caernavon
Manchester
Brough
Chester
Lincoln
Wroxeter
Brancaster
Water Newton
Leicester
Hoxne
Burgh Castle
Carmarthen
Brecon
Godmanchester
Mildenhall
Swansea
Neath
Gloucester
Caerleon
Bath
Silchester
London
Reculver
Exeter
Dorchester
Chichester
Dover
Portchester
Pevensey
Marck
Boulogne
Tournai
Cherbourg
Port en Bessin-Huppain
Rouen
Lisieux
Rennes
Paris
Le Mans
Angers
Nantes
Tours
Bourges
Autun
Poitiers
Saintes
Clermont-Ferrand
Lyon
Langres
Besançon
Tournus
Avenches
Geneva

North Sea

Voorburg-Arentsburg
Nijmegen
Xanten
Tüdden
Neuss
Tongeren
Cologne
Meuse
Bonn
Trier
Bingen
Reims
Mainz
Metz
Speyer
Öhringen
Strasbourg
Regensburg
Passau
Augsburg
Danube
Weis
Lorch
Vienna
Bregenz
Rosenheim
Carnuntum
Windisch
Innsbruck
Lind
Szombathely
Szöny
Budapest
Chur
Lake Balaton
Rhône
Lake Geneva
Augst

Weser
Elbe

Saône
Rhine
Seine
Marne
Loire
Creuse
Saône

Forest pushed the frontier forward beyond both rivers, a line made permanent by Hadrian with the construction of a wooden palisade (later strengthened with stone forts and watch towers) that ran from just south of Bonn (Bonna) on the Rhine to a point west of Regensburg (Castra Regina) on the Danube. Colonies of veteran troops all along the German frontier acted as the foci for urban growth, drawing trade into the area, and *vici* (trading villages) sprang up outside the garrison forts, as they did in northern Britain. As cross-border incursions increased in the 3rd and 4th centuries, towns and bridges along the Rhine and Danube were fortified.

In this same period, sea-raiders from north Germany began to attack the prosperous settled areas of southeast Britain and northern Gaul, where there were few army garrisons. To meet this threat, a series of fortified camps, commonly known as Saxon shore forts, were built to house mobile quick-response troops, and a number of towns were walled ◆

ABOVE AND RIGHT Vulnerable frontiers were demarcated by a *limes* consisting of a military road flanked by ramparts and ditches. Legionary troops were stationed in fortress towns behind the frontier line: Chester and York in Britain; Cologne, Mainz and Strasbourg in Germany. In Britain, a turf rampart – the Antonine Wall – was built some way north of Hadrian's frontier by his successor Antoninus Pius; the motive may have been to win acclaim at Rome. It was shortlived, and the frontier soon returned to Hadrian's Wall. Outside Britain and Germany, the most elaborate border defenses were in the east, where a network of roads and forts was designed to guard against attack from the Parthians and Sassanians.

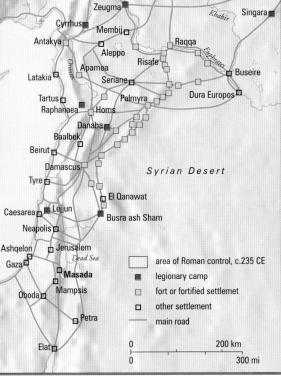

Zeugma
Khabir
Singara
Cyrrhus
Membij
Antakya
Raqqa
Aleppo
Risafe
Latakia
Apamea
Euphrates
Seriane
Buseire
Tartus
Palmyra
Raphanaea
Homs
Dura Europos
Danaba
Baalbek
Beirut
Syrian Desert
Damascus
Tyre
El Qanawat
Caesarea
Lejjun
Busra ash Sham
Neapolis
Ashqelon
Jerusalem
Gaza
Dead Sea
Masada
Oboda
Mampsis
Petra
Elat

Orontes

area of Roman control, c.235 CE
legionary camp
fort or fortified settlemet
other settlement
main road

0   200 mi
0   300 km

CENTRAL, SOUTH & EAST ASIA

CONCERN WITH THE WAYS of the past has always characterized the traditionally minded societies of Asia. When, in 1079, a violent storm exposed part of the great Shang dynasty capital near Anyang, it brought about a major upsurge of interest in things past, and collecting and cataloguing ancient bronzes became a popular pursuit in China. Likewise in 17th-century Japan, people investigated antiquities, collected jade ornaments and occasionally excavated ancient tombs.

As in other parts of the world, the peoples of the east often sought to explain ancient monuments by attributing them to a mythical past. For example, the megaliths – *pandavaragudigallu* – of south India were credited to the Pandavas, heroes of legendary Mahabharata wars. Early artifacts discovered by chance might be attributed to supernatural forces – stone axes were venerated in Indian shrines; oracle bones, the earliest Chinese documents, considered to be dragons' bones. But from early times, there was also more academic speculation about the past. As long ago as the Eastern Zhou period (475–221 BCE), a Chinese philosopher proposed that humanity had passed through four ages, in which tools had been made of stone, jade, bronze and, in his own times, of iron.

China's long historical tradition began with the Shang dynasty, said to have been founded in 1766 BCE, and by the period of the Han (206 BCE– 220 CE), detailed records of their own history were being augmented by ethnographic accounts of their neighbors to the south and in Central Asia. In India, historical records began around the time of the Buddha, in the 5th century BCE. Some 1,500 years ago, Chinese pilgrims were braving the hazards of the Central Asian deserts and the stormy Southeast Asian seas to to visit the monuments erected by the great Indian emperor Ashoka (3rd century BCE) to mark the holy places of Buddhism. Their accounts were a major source of information when scholars began investigating the historical treasures of these regions in the 19th century.

From the 16th century on, Europeans became established in many parts of India and Southeast Asia as traders, administrators, soldiers and travelers. Steeped in the Classical traditions of their own past, they seldom credited native peoples with the ability to create the spectacular works of art they observed, be it the Buddhist and Hindu rock-cut temples of western India or the monuments of Angkor in Cambodia, and attributed them instead to Alexander the Great or to the wandering tribes of Israel. The works of the alien cultures they encountered, and especially the "licenciousness" of sculptures on Indian and Southeast Asian temples, often appalled them . "All those who enter...say it makes their flesh creep, it is so dreadful", wrote the 16th-century Portuguese doctor, Garcia da Orta, of the rock-cut shrines near Bombay.

Antiquarians and early excavators

Westerners felt more at home with the monuments of ancient Iran, as the history of the Persian empire was known to them from Classical sources. Travelers such as Pietro della Valle, who visited Persepolis in 1615, were zealous in copying down ancient inscriptions, though the cuneiform scripts, which initially were not even recognized as writing, were not fully understood until the 1830s, when the English diplomat Henry Creswicke Rawlinson (1810–95) copied the long trilingual inscriptions carved on an inaccessible cliff-face at Behistun. One was written in an alphabetic cuneiform text in the known Old Persian language, another in Akkadian, the unknown language of early Mesopotamia. Once he had deciphered the first, he had the key to understanding the second.

In India, the Asiatic Society of Bengal was founded in 1784 by Sir William Jones (1746–94), a leading Calcutta judge and eminent Orientalist who established the existence of the Indo-European family of languages through his observation that Sanskrit, the classical language of India, shared a common ancestry with Greek and

Regional Timeline

c.60,000 (?)–40,000 y.a. Modern humans in Australia

c.400,000 y.a. *H. erectus* present at Zhoukoudian (China)

c.1.8 –1.5 m y.a. *H. erectus* at Longgupo (China) and Javanese sites

c.53,000–27,000 y.a. Possible late *H. erectus* at Ngandong (Java)

c.40,000 y.a. Modern human skull, Niah Cave (Borneo)

c.12,000 y.a. World's earliest pottery at Fukui Cave (Japan)

c.9,000 y.a. Rice farming at Pengtoushan (China)

c.8,000 y.a. Pottery and farming at Mehrgarh (Pakistan)

100,000 y.a.

10,000 y.a.

ABOVE Early European travelers were often horrified by the alien exuberance of India's ancient architecture. This rock-cut temple, open to the sky, is at Ellora, central India.

ABOVE LEFT Wheel-shaped bronze mounting, 33 in/85 cm in diameter, excavated from a sacrificial pit at Sanxingdui, China, c.1200–1000 BCE. Its purpose is unknown.

with Avestan, the ancient language of Persia. Over the following century members of the Asiatic Society surveyed and excavated monuments, studied epigraphy, numismatics, art and architecture, and deciphered Kharoshti and Brahmi, the scripts in which the edicts of Ashoka, the earliest classical Indian texts, were inscribed.

The megaliths of India were among the first monuments in the subcontinent to attract the serious attention of excavators. Their similarity to European dolmens and cists gave rise to speculation on the culture that had produced them, and for many decades they were regarded as the tombs and altars of a "Celtic Scythian race". Finds of Roman coins in the south were more intelligible, pointing

to the existence of wide networks of trade 2,000 years ago. In the 1840s, excavation of the Amaravati stupa and the retrieval of its elaborate sculptures (which were shipped to England and deposited in the British Museum) aroused an interest in Buddhist art and architecture, which continued with the discovery of the Greek-influenced Gandharan art in the northwest in the 1850s.

India's Archaeological Survey

In India, as in other parts of the world, ancient remains were wantonly plundered and vandalized: among the treasures that suffered were exquisite paintings in the rock-cut monasteries at Ajanta. In 1870, the Archaeological Survey of India was instituted with the purpose of recording and preserving India's ancient heritage. Archaeologists still believed that India was a cultural backwater at the time that early states and civilizations were known to be emerging in Egypt and Mesopotamia. In the 1890s and early 20th century, French excavations at sites like Tepe Sialk and the long-lived city

c.4,000–3,450 y.a. Minoan civilization in Crete			**c.2,200–1,300 y.a.** Teotihuacán state in Mexico	
c.3,700 y.a. Shang dynasty in China	**c.3,500 y.a.** Bronzeworking in Thailand	**c.2,400 y.a.** Steppe nomad burials in Altai mountains	**c.2,200 y.a.** Burial of terracotta army at Xian (China)	**c.1,600–1,200 y.a.** Period of *kofun* tomb-building, Japan
c.4,000 y.a. Indus valley civilization; bronzeworking at Erlitou (China)		**c.2,500 y.a.** Achaemenid rule extends across Iranian plateau	**c.2,250 y.a.** Mauryan empire at height under Ashoka	**c.2,000 y.a.** Early kingdoms of Korea; Kushans dominate Silk Route trade
4,000 y.a.		2,500 y.a.		2,000 y.a.

of Susa, where finds included the spoils of Elamite victories over Mesopotamian cities, began to reveal the part that the Iranian plateau had played in the civilized life of the 3rd and 2nd millennia BCE. India's place in this world was suddenly made apparent when, in 1924, Sir John Marshall (1876–1958), excavating on behalf of the Archaeological Survey, announced the discovery of an ancient civilization in the Indus valley, which Mesopotamian scholars were quick to recognize as the source of various Sumerian imports. In 1944 Sir Mortimer Wheeler (1890–1976) was appointed to breathe new life into the Archaeological Survey. He made further discoveries at Harappa and instituted his famous grid technique of excavation as well as training and reorganizing staff, and establishing a chronological framework that now incorporated prehistoric times.

Central and East Asia

More rigorous excavation techniques were also revealing new and often unsuspected aspects of the past in Central and East Asia. A landmark dig was conducted by Schmidt and Pumpelly into the ancient mounds of Anau in Turkmenistan from 1902 to 1904. Specialists were employed to investigate the plant, animal and human remains, and meticulous attention was given to artifacts and to precise horizontal and vertical recording. The archaeological treasures of the Silk Route were brought to light early in the 20th century by Aurel Stein (1862–1943), who undertook a series of expeditions into Chinese Turkestan and Central Asia. Among the discoveries he made, preserved by the dry conditions, were magnificent Buddhist silk banners, precious manuscripts in many languages, and the invaluable everyday paraphernalia of the unfortunate Chinese officials who ran the Han empire's Silk Road outposts.

Research and excavation flourished in Japan, and in 1913 its first Department of Archaeology, at Kyoto, came into being under Hamada Kosaku. In Korea, prehistoric dolmens, the golden tombs of the Shilla and the monuments of the Lelang commandery dating from China's domination of the region were also excavated under Japanese auspices following the peninsula's annexation in 1911. The first cord-decorated Jomon pottery had been discovered in 1877 by Edward Morse while excavating a Japanese shell midden. It was initially attributed to the ancestors of the surviving Ainu people, but by the 1930s the Jomon culture was recognized as the work of the prehistoric inhabitants of Japan.

The first systematic excavations in China were undertaken in 1928 at the early Shang capital, Anyang, by the newly founded Academica Sinica. China's earlier past had been revealed a few years before when the Swedish geologist, J. Gunnar Andersson (1874–1960), excavated Neolithic remains at Yangshao, and in 1929 he uncovered far earlier remains in the now famous Palaeolithic cave of Zhoukoudian. Here he found bones of the hominid now known

LEFT Excavators at work measuring and recording the tumbled soldiers and horses of China's "terracotta army" prior to their restoration. The complex of pits containing the buried army was discovered accidentally by peasants digging a well in 1974.

ABOVE A photograph from the 1880s shows workers restoring the Great Stupa at Sanchi for the Asiatic Society of Bengal. Stupas were originally funerary mounds enclosing holy relics of the Buddha or his followers. The one at Sanchi was built by the emperor Ashoka.

as *Homo erectus*, whose remains had first been discovered in Java in 1887, but had not initially been accepted by science.

Among the most dramatic Asian discoveries of recent times are the terracotta army of the First Emperor of China, and the frozen tombs of the steppe nomads of the Altai region of Central Asia. In the latter case, the excavation team led by Sergei Rudenko (1885–1969) had to use boiling water to thaw the frozen deposits, but the discomfort of the digging conditions was compensated by the magnificent state of preservation of the graves' organic contents, including silk, leather, wood and felt textiles and horsetrappings.

Origins of agriculture

Since the 1950s, the establishment of chronology, the major pre-occupation of earlier years, has been made possible by radiocarbon and other absolute dating techniques. From this has arisen a much clearer sense of the timetable of human existence, pinpointing gaps in our knowledge. A major area of investigation has been the origins of agriculture. Excavations in the 1950s at Banpo, a village on the Yellow River (c.5000 BCE), began to fill in the picture of China's early millet farmers, and farming is now known at several sites in northern China by the 7th millennium BCE. Early rice farming communities of about the same period were discovered on the Yangzi River, and traces of Southeast Asia's early rice farmers have also been uncovered. South Asia presented an anomaly, with farming communities apparently emerging only in the 5th millennium BCE, several thousand years after their counterparts in western and southern central Asia. The discovery in the 1970s of early Neolithic deposits at Mehrgarh (Pakistan) has transformed the picture, showing that farmers were also present here by the 7th millennium BCE ◆

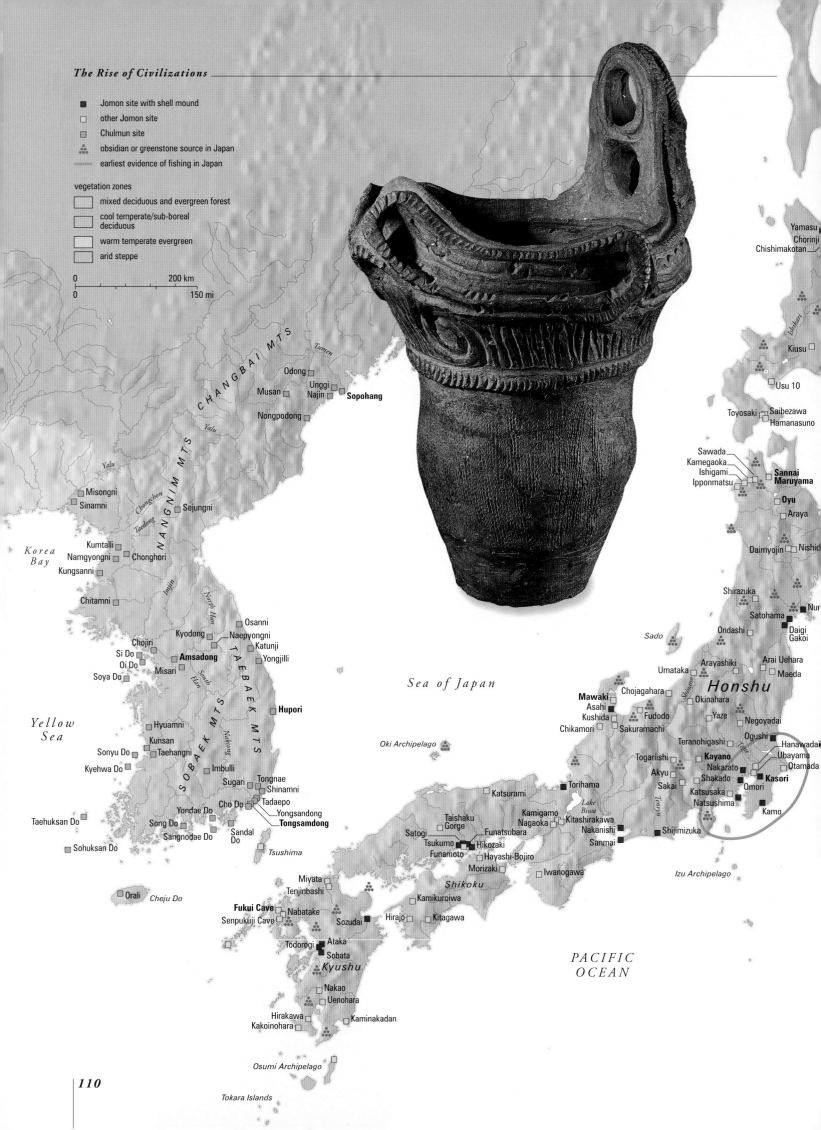

■ Jomon site with shell mound

□ other Jomon site

▨ Chulmun site

⚘ obsidian or greenstone source in Japan

⌇ earliest evidence of fishing in Japan

vegetation zones

☐ mixed deciduous and evergreen forest

☐ cool temperate/sub-boreal deciduous

☐ warm temperate evergreen

☐ arid steppe

0   200 km
0   150 mi

CHANGBAI MTS

Tumen

Odong

Musan   Unggi
                Najin   **Sopohang**

Nongpodong

Yalu

NANGNIM MTS

Chongchon

Misongni

Sinamni

Taedong

Sejungni

Korea Bay

Kumtalli
Namgyongni   Chonghori

Kungsanni

Injin

Chitamni

North Han

Osanni
Kyodong
        Naepyongni
Chojiri   Katunji
Si Do   **Amsadong**   Yongjilli
Oi Do   Misari
Soya Do

South Han

TAEBAEK MTS

Hupori

Yellow Sea

Hyuamni
    Kunsan
Sonyu Do   Taehangni

Naktong

SOBAEK MTS

Kyehwa Do
        Imbulli
Taehuksan Do
        Sugari   Tongnae
Yondae Do   Shinamni
Song Do   Cho Do   Tadaepo
Sangnodae Do   Yongsandong
Sohuksan Do   Sandal   **Tongsamdong**
              Do

Tsushima

Orali   *Cheju Do*

Miyata
Tenjinbashi

Fukui Cave   Nabatake
Senpukuji Cave

        Sozudai   Hirajo
Todorogi   Ataka
        Sobata
        Kyushu

Nakao
    Uenohara
Hirakawa
Kakoinohara   Kaminakadan

Osumi Archipelago

Tokara Islands

Sea of Japan

Oki Archipelago

Katsurami

Torihama

Taishaku
Gorge   Funatsubara
Satogi   Hikozaki
Tsukumo   Funamoto
        Morizaki
        Hayashi-Bojiro
Shikoku
Kamikuroiwa
        Kitagawa

Kamigamo
Nagaoka
        Kitashirakawa
Nakanishi
        Sanmai

Iwanogawa

Lake Biwa

PACIFIC OCEAN

Izu Archipelago

Yamasu
Chorinji
Chishimakotan

Ishikari
        Kiusu

        Usu 10

Toyosaki   Saibezawa
        Hamanasuno

Sawada
Kamegaoka
Ishigami   **Sannai**
Ipponmatsu   **Maruyama**

        Oyu
        Araya

Daimyojin   Nishio

Shirazuka

        Nur
Satohama
        Daigi
Ondashi   Gakoi

Umataka   Arayashiki   Arai Uehara
                Maeda

Honshu

Chojagahara   Okinahara
Mawaki
Asahi   Yaze
Kushida   Fudodo   Negoyadai
Chikamori Sakuramachi
                Ogushi   Hanawadai
Shinano   Ubayama
Teranohigashi   *Tone* Otamada
Togariishi **Kayano**   Nakazato **Kasori**
Akyu   Shakado   Omori
Sakai   Katsusaka
        Natsushima   Kamo
        Shijimizuka
Tenryu

110

*Sea of
Okhotsk*

Yubetsu-Ichikawa
Tosamporo
Kunashir
Tokoro
Mokoto

kkaido

LEFT With the creation of new forest, river and coastal environments some 10,000 years ago, the people of East Asia turned from highly mobile hunting to foraging and fishing. The year-round availability of marine resources, combined with the ability to store vegetable foods such as nuts, meant that communities could settle permanently in one location. Villages of foragers thus appeared from the subtropical areas of southern Kyushu to the subboreal landscape of Hokkaido. Exchange routes for commodities such as obsidian and greenstone developed along coast, rivers and mountain paths. Dugout canoes have been recovered from many Jomon sites, used not only for traveling but also for exploiting marine resources off the coasts.

TOP LEFT The pottery-making foragers who occupied the Japanese archipelago from 11,000 years to just over 2,000 years ago took the art of decorating their vessels to remarkable lengths. The creativity of these early potters is witnessed in the diversity of pottery styles – over 70 major types are now recognized by Japanese archaeologists. The earliest vessels were used for cooking, and transformed the diet across the archipelago, as boiling and steaming made previously indigestible vegetables and shellfish edible. As Jomon culture developed, other pottery forms were made, including a range of vessels for the presentation and consumption of food. Heavily inscribed rims became a characteristic form around 5,000 years ago, bold incised and appliqué decoration complementing the cord-marking (*jomon*) from which the period takes its name.

Forager Groups of East Asia

The great climatic and environmental changes that took place at the end of the last Ice Age brought about broadly the same transformations in human society in East Asia as occurred in western Eurasia (see pages 54–55). As sea levels rose, large areas of the coastal plains were flooded, submerging the land bridges that had joined the islands of the Japanese archipelago to the mainland. The forests that replaced the Pleistocene tundra brought new opportunities for exploitation: instead of grazing herds of reindeer and bison, woodland species such as wild boar and deer were hunted, and plants (especially nuts), fish and shellfish became major components in the diet. A notable development in East Asia was the markedly early use of pottery by forager groups well before the emergence of agriculture.

Shell middens, mounds of discarded shellfish remains, are full of information about the diet of the coastal-dwelling Holocene foragers of East Asia. Some of the largest are in Japan. Middens at Kasori (Honshu) were used over a period of 2,000 years; they now form low circular banks more than 328 ft/100 m in diameter. Shellfish, notably clams, were clearly an important food source, but fish such as salmon and trout, available in large numbers at particular times of year, were also eaten. At Mawaki on the Japan Sea coast of Honshu, dolphins were captured in large numbers, while quantities of whale and sea lion bones have been found at Sopohang and Tomgsamdong on the Korean peninsula.

Early use of pottery

Middens also provide evidence for the very early manufacture of pottery. The oldest reliably dated pottery in the world (c.10,700 BCE) comes from Fukui Cave (Kyushu), but recent discoveries in northern Japan and the east coast of Siberia show that pottery was being made very early across a wide area and in disparate environmental zones. The characteristic Jomon pottery of the foragers of the Japanese archipelago (c.10,000–400 BCE) was decorated by pressing twisted fibers into the clay prior to firing. The Chulmun foragers of the Korean peninsula (c.6000–2000 BCE) used a similar cord-marked pottery, and textured pottery was also made by foragers on the southern coast of China and on Taiwan.

Pottery is more usually associated with settled farming communities than with forager societies as it is easily broken and difficult to transport. In East Asia, however, the abundance of natural resources in coastal and inland forest areas enabled foragers to lead relatively sedentary lives, possibly supplemented by

small-scale horticulture. At Amsadong, an inland site in the Korean peninsula, for example, people living in pit houses collected quantities of wild nuts, which they stored in deep storage pits in large pottery vessels.

Forager cultures

The Jomon people's rich material culture included clay figurines, wood carving and lacquerwork. Some Jomon settlements were large and long-lived. Sannai Maruyama (northern Honshu) was occupied for more than 1,000 years; in this time at least 1,000 houses were built, along with some large communal structures. The settlement was at the center of an extensive trading network for the exchange of valuable commodities such as greenstone and obsidian.

In northern Japan, the construction of stone circles marked out burial grounds across the landscape: the most famous are the twin circles of Manza and Nonakado at Oyu. Stone circles are also found at Hupori and other places on the Korean peninsula. With the exception of bank-enclosed cemeteries that appear on Hokkaido in the 1st millennium BCE, in which the dead were buried with a rich array of grave goods, there is little to suggest institutionalized social differentiation in either Jomon or Chulmun societies. However, rank may have been manifested in ways that are not visible in the archaeological record. The high standard of ceramics and woodworking possibly indicates a degree of craft specialization, and the development of Sannai Maruyama and other regional centers suggests the presence of some form of leadership. Bodily ornamentation was important to many Jomon people. Skulls show clear evidence for tooth filing, perhaps related to life-cycle rituals, and decoration on clay figurines is suggestive of elaborate clothing, hairstyles and tattooing. Fragments of hundreds of ornate clay earrings found at Kayano (Honshu) may point to the presence of specialized manufacturing centers for Jomon fashion accessories.

The Jomon preserved their foraging lifestyle for longer than people on the East Asian mainland: rice cultivation, which was established in China by 5000 BCE, did not reach Japan until the 1st millennium BCE (see pages 122–123). The intensification of ritual activity (involving clay figurines, pottery masks, and stone bars) in the southwestern archipelago just before the appearance of the first rice paddies possibly suggests that the Jomon actively resisted the spread of agriculture and the different way of life it brought. The hunting and gathering of wild food resources continued to play an important role in the Japanese archipelago even after agriculture took hold. The *matagi* hunters of northern Honshu and the Ainu of Hokkaido are the latest representatives of a tradition of fishing, gathering and hunting that has lasted in the northern islands off East Asia since prehistory ◆

The Origins of Rice Cultivation

The transition to settled agriculture in Asia has only recently begun to be understood, with increasingly clear evidence that rice cultivation began in the lakeland of the middle Yangzi valley and radiated out from there into the rest of China and Southeast Asia. As in the Near East, the other region of the Old World that witnessed a Neolithic revolution, the necessary environmental conditions that brought about the shift from nomadism to permanent settlement were laid down during the periods of climatic change that followed the end of the last Ice Age.

As the climate began to warm up, the zone in which wild rice flourishes moved north from its tropical refugium into the rich marshlands of the Yangzi valley. Between 9000 and 8000 BCE, however, the climatic phase known as the Younger Dryas brought a sharp deterioration in temperature. This period saw the deposition of loess, a fine wind-blown dust, over the plains of China. Glaciers advanced once more, and plants and animals that were adapted to living in warmer conditions retreated south. The Younger Dryas had run its course by 8000 BCE, and there is some evidence that hunter–gatherers began to live in semi-permanent settlements during the subsequent long period of increasing warmth. This was followed by another cooling phase, less severe than the Younger Dryas, and it is then that permanent villages first appear in East Asia. The dead were interred in communal burial sites, pottery vessels were manufactured, and new stone artifacts for processing grains were in use.

At Pengtoushan, near Lake Dongting, rice has been found as a temper in pottery vessels dated between 7500 and 6500 BCE. It is not yet known if this rice was cultivated or collected, but it seems reasonable to suppose that hunter–gatherer groups had become accustomed to gathering wild rice in the warm period before the Younger Dryas. As the temperature cooled, these hunter–gatherer groups increasingly tended the plant, perhaps by selective burning or by removing competitors, to ensure its annual regeneration.

As the transition to rice cultivation took place, permanent villages like Pengtoushan proliferated up and down the course of the Yangzi. Hemudu, a lakeside settlement dating from about 5000 BCE, provides abundant evidence for life in such a village. The people made spades by lashing the shoulder blades of cattle to wooden hafts. They built wooden houses of excellent and sophisticated joinery. Immense quantities of cultivated rice were grown, and they supplemented their diet with fish and birds from the lake.

The spread of rice farming

As centuries turned into millennia, agricultural communities spread out from the Yangzi. By the 3rd millennium BCE, rice farmers were settling in the lowlands south of the Nanling range: grave goods found at Shixia, dated to about 2800 BCE, have similarities to artifacts found in Yangzi sites. From there they spread to the Red River valley and onto the plains of Vietnam, where they interacted with large, prosperous coastal-dwelling groups of hunter–gatherers. The presence of rice and of domestic dogs (descended from the gray wolf of Asia) in archaeological sites is an indication of the route taken by incoming farming groups, as is the present-day distribution of Austroasiatic languages, spoken in Vietnam, Cambodia, Thailand, Burma and eastern India. These agricultural villages represent the basic building blocks for the early states of the the Yangzi valley, as well as for the Bronze and Iron Age peoples of Southeast Asia ◆

ABOVE Intensive rice cultivation today in the Yangzi valley of southern China, where rice farming began around 8,000 years ago. The transition to farming from a hunting–gathering existence led to permanent settlement. Population numbers began to rise, and farming spread outwards as small family groups traveled away from the main village to clear a new area of forest for cultivation.

RIGHT This three-legged pottery vessel comes from a 4,000-year-old burial at Ban Kao, a small inland settlement in Thailand extensively excavated in the 1960s, which has revealed rich pottery finds. Tripod pots are found at many other sites in western Thailand, and vessels similar to those excavated at Ban Kao have been discovered as far south as Malaysia.

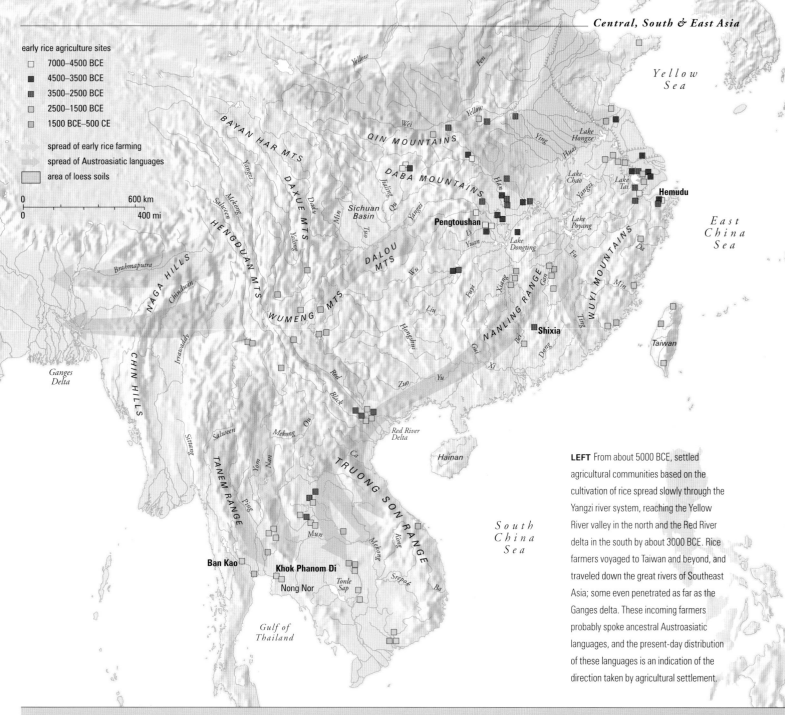

early rice agriculture sites

- ☐ 7000–4500 BCE
- ■ 4500–3500 BCE
- ■ 3500–2500 BCE
- ☐ 2500–1500 BCE
- ☐ 1500 BCE–500 CE

spread of early rice farming
spread of Austroasiatic languages
☐ area of loess soils

0 ____ 600 km
0 ____ 400 mi

LEFT From about 5000 BCE, settled agricultural communities based on the cultivation of rice spread slowly through the Yangzi river system, reaching the Yellow River valley in the north and the Red River delta in the south by about 3000 BCE. Rice farmers voyaged to Taiwan and beyond, and traveled down the great rivers of Southeast Asia; some even penetrated as far as the Ganges delta. These incoming farmers probably spoke ancestral Austroasiatic languages, and the present-day distribution of these languages is an indication of the direction taken by agricultural settlement.

Khok Phanom Di: a rich coastal site

Khok Phanom Di in Thailand is located in one of the world's richest natural habitats, the tropical estuary. A sequence of 17 to 20 generations of graves dated from c.2000–1500 BCE has been excavated here. The hunter–gatherer community who occupied the site made superb decorated pottery vessels, adorned themselves with shell ornaments, and enjoyed a marine-based diet. Rice was eaten, but as their estuarine location would have made local cultivation hazardous, it was probably obtained through exchange with incoming groups of farmers, with whom they may also have traded goods, ideas and possibly even people. A series of environmental changes took place during this period of occupation, and a temporary reduction in sea level may have permitted rice-growing for a time: stone hoes and shell harvesting knives came into use but they were no longer being fashioned in the high sea-level phase that followed. Burials now became enormously wealthy, perhaps due to new trading relations with rice farmers in the hinterland. The site was abandoned by 1500 BCE, by which time the millennia-long hunting and gathering tradition had given way to the remorseless advance of rice farming ◆

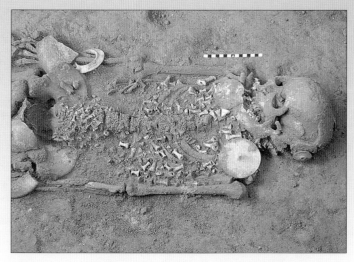

ABOVE THIS FEMALE WAS BURIED WITH NUMEROUS ORNAMENTS, INCLUDING 120,000 SHELL BEADS.

The Indus Civilization

In the early 1920s large-scale excavations were carried out at Harappa and Mohenjo-Daro, two sites in the northwest of the Indian subcontinent, now modern Pakistan. Both revealed evidence of large, well-planned cities. They were the first indication that a major Bronze Age civilization – known to archaeologists as the Indus or Harappan civilization – had existed in the Indus valley more than 4,000 years ago. Its cities and towns were dependent on farming and herding and were home to craftsmen, priests and merchants who traded with Mesopotamia and neighboring lands. Quantities of soapstone stamp seals found at Indus sites frequently bear inscriptions a few signs long, probably giving the name or title of the owner. However, the Indus script has not been deciphered and little is known about the civilization's social, religious and political organization. One puzzling aspect is that it appears to have lacked a ruling elite: there are no palaces or richly furnished burials, though there is some indication that authority may have rested in the hands of a priesthood. Cohesion had broken down by 1800 BCE. There does not seem to have been a sudden collapse; writing, craft mass-production and townlife gradually disappeared as settlements became isolated from one another.

ABOVE At Mohenjo-Daro, the Great Bath was the main feature of the citadel, or public area of the city. It was probably used for ritual ablution and was surrounded by a complex of smaller rooms with bathrooms. The lower town, which may have housed more than 100,000 people, was organized on a grid pattern of streets. The houses, often several storeys high, were usually laid out around a courtyard. Most had a well and a brick-paved bathroom; many also had a toilet connected by drains to the city's sewerage system.

Early communities of farmers first appeared in the Indo-Iranian borderlands that fringe the Indus river system around 9,000 years ago. By 4000 BCE, many villages and towns had developed in the area, forming the eastern end of an exchange network that extended across the Iranian plateau to Mesopotamia. In this dry region, intensive agriculture relied on the building of dams and other technology for conserving water.

Farmers did not begin to move into the region of the Indus valley proper, formerly the home of nomadic hunter-gatherers and fishers, until the 4th millennium BCE. At this time a complex of rivers known as the Saraswati flowed south of the Indus, and a great concentration of prosperous farming villages developed here. It has long since dried up and today the region is largely desert.

Cities of the Indus

The cities and towns of the Indus civilization have been much better studied than its rural villages and hamlets. Around 2600 BCE many were rebuilt to a more formalized design. They were usually divided into separate public and residential sectors.

The public buildings were generally located on a higher mound or "citadel" and probably had religious significance. However, the great diversity in the type of buildings found suggests that religious practice varied from place to place. Baked brick was the principal building material, and standard units of measurement were in use. Great importance was attached to sanitation and water supply. Mohenjo-Daro, the most extensively explored Indus site, was built on giant brick platforms and had massive walls to protect it from flooding. It was probably occupied from the late 4th millennium on, but the high water table (which has risen 26 ft/8 m since 1922) has prevented investigation of its substantial lower levels.

LEFT This terracotta camel head is typical of the high-quality objects produced by Indus craftsmen. Industrial workshops for the manufacture of pottery, seals, shell ornaments, stone beads and metalwork were housed in separate areas of the cities.

Map labels

pre or early Indus site
major city of the Indus civilization
other settlement of the Indus civilization
contemporary non-Indus settlement

ivory
marine shells
trade route
area of dense settlement
ancient river course of Saraswati and Indus systems
conjectural ancient coastline, c.3rd millennium BCE

major source of commodity

copper, gold and tin
lapis lazuli
agate and carnelian
flint
timber

0   300 km
0   200 mi

HINDU KUSH
KARAKORAM
HIMALAYAS
CHAGAI HILLS
ROHRI HILLS
Thar Desert
ARAVALLI RANGE
Rann of Kutch

Amu Darya
Pyandch
Indus
Khash Rud
Helmand
Arghandab
Jhelum
Chenab
Beas-ancient
Beas-modern
Ravi
Beas-ancient
Sutlej-modern
Saraswati
Indus
Saraswati-ancient
Saraswati-modern
Yamuna-modern
Luni
Mahi
Baddo
Hingol

Shortugai
Sarai Kola
Tarakai Qila
Lewan
Musa Khel
Manda
Rahman Dheri
Hathala
Gumla
Periano Ghundai
Ropar
Shahir-i-Sokhta
from Mesopotamia
Mundigak
Damb Sadaat
Rana Ghundai
Jalilpur
Harappa
Dadheri
Dhalevan
Mehrgarh
Dabar Kot
Kalapar
Kalibangan
Banawali
Hulas
Naushero
Ahmadwala
Sandhanwala
Kudwala
Sothi
Rakhigarhi
Alamgirpur
Anjira
Judeirjo-Dara
Derawar
Siswal
Mitathal
Shikhai
Ganweriwala
Nal
Sukkur
Khetri
Nindowari
Mohenjo-Daro
Kot Diji
Shahi Tump
Lohumjo-Daro
Kulli
Ghazi Shah
Chanhu-Daro
Ganeshwar
Sutkagen Dor
Damb Bhuti
Amri
from the Persian Gulf
Sotka Koh
Balakot
Bagor
Allahdino
Nuhato
Gilgund
Ahar
Dholavira
Desalpur
Surkotada
Kotada
Langhnaj
Nageshwar
Lothal
Rangpur
Rojdi
Bhagatrav
gold from Karnataka
115

Farming and trade

Arable agriculture, irrigated from the rivers, was the mainstay of the Indus economy. Wheat, barley, pulses, fruits and cotton were grown. Only toward the end of the civilization were rice and millets introduced. Marginal land between the fertile areas was used as seasonal grazing by pastoralists. The main herd animals were zebu cattle, but water buffalo, sheep and goats were also kept. River and sea fish were important in the diet.

The Indus people enjoyed a high standard of living and were skilled craftsmen, making tools of high-grade flint or copper and jewelry of shell, carnelian and agate. Some settlements were situated to exploit particular local resources, such as marine shells for making bangles and other ornaments. Raw materials might be processed at source, but much of the finishing and specialist manufacturing took place in towns, from where the finished objects were distributed throughout the Indus area. Then as now, mobile pastoralists probably played a major role in distribution. Local transport used bullock carts, while rivers and the sea provided longer distance communications. Ivory and gold were obtained through trade with neighboring hunter-gatherer groups. Lothal, in the south, was apparently such a center.

Mesopotamian texts give details of international trade at this time (see pages 70–71). We do not know what goods the Indus people imported, but their ships carried timber, ivory, carnelian beads and other luxuries to Gulf and Sumerian ports. Lapis lazuli from Badakshan was supplied to the west through the Indus outpost colony at Shortugai on the Amu Darya (Oxus) river ◆

ABOVE The Indus civilization covered an area of 262,000 sq mi/680,000 sq km. Within this vast region, five major cities, spaced fairly evenly apart, and numerous towns, villages and farming hamlets have been found. The river courses of the Indus and Saraswati systems and the coastline have altered very considerably in the intervening millennia, and archaeologists conjecture that the drying up of the Saraswati river played a major role in the decline of the civilization. As arable land became unusable, farmers growing rice and millets – the crops upon which later Indian civilizations depended – moved out of the region, traveling east into the Ganges valley and south to the Deccan.

Earliest Dynasties of China

Around 9,000 years ago, millet farming began on the loess soils of the Yellow River in northern China at sites such as Qishan. As irrigated rice farming spread north from the Yangzi River in the late 4th millennium (see pages 112–113), populations rose, copper came into use and elite Neolithic societies such as the Longshan, Liangzhu and Hongshan emerged. Jade was a valued commodity. Stamped earth fortifications give evidence of warfare, and the first cities developed. Shortly after 2000 BCE, bronze wine vessels were being cast at Erlitou, the probable capital of the Xia dynasty. Founded c.2205 BCE, the Xia was traditionally the first of the Sandai, the three dynasties with which the history of China begins.

Three-legged wine vessels from Erlitou are the oldest bronze objects yet found in East Asia and mark the start of Chinese Bronze Age civilization. Around 1700 BCE, the Shang dynasty emerged as the preeminent power in north China. According to the early histories, the Shang occupied seven successive capitals. One of these sites is the modern city of Zhengzhou, where the early Shang city walls of stamped mud are still visible. By this stage, the influence of the Shang civilization was felt far to the south, for example at Panlongcheng.

Oracle bones – scapulae from cattle and tortoise shells used for divination by the Shang – bear the oldest true examples of Chinese ideographic script. Some oracle bones are known from Zhengzhou, but most are from Anyang (see box). The precursers to this script are potters' marks found on Neolithic ceramic vessels. Divination, asking the gods about the outcome of events such as military campaigns, hunting trips and royal births, was an important aspect of Shang elite life. The questions were written on the bones and shells; these were then heated, and the answers provided by interpreting the resultant cracks. Remains of over 10,000 oracle bones have been found at Anyang.

In the southwest, the state of Shu was producing bronzes very different in style to those of the north. At Sanxingdui the remains of a city have been discovered with stamped earth walls and many buildings, one of which is over 2,150 sq ft/200 sq m in area. A series of pits contain sacrificial deposits, including large bronze statues and masks perhaps representing gods or spirits, along with stone, jade and gold objects, and elephant tusks. Sanxingdui appears to be contemporary with the Shang, and these discoveries confirm the presence of other Bronze Age centers in China.

The Zhou dynasty

In 1027 BCE the Shang were defeated by the Zhou, a people who originated further to the west and had for a long time formed part of the Shang domain. The Zhou established their dynastic capital at Hao near modern Xian and built a center for ancestor worship at Baoji. For some 300 years (the Western Zhou period) the Zhou ruled a relatively unified domain. Much information about the Western Zhou is contained in long inscriptions cast on bronze vessels, and in one of the oldest surviving long texts, the *Shu Jing* (Book of Documents). Many Western Zhou cities and lavishly furnished elite tombs have been located.

In 771 BCE hostile invaders forced the Zhou to establish a new capital at Luoyang (the Eastern Zhou

ABOVE A ritual *gong* vessel, consisting of a jug with a lid decorated with a tiger head at the front and an owl at the rear, height 9.5 in/24.1 cm. Shang bronzeworkers were expert in using ceramic piece molds to cast sets of highly decorated bronze vessels; these were used in rituals propitiating ancestors. The tiger and other motifs were borrowed from central southern China; their appearance at Anyang represents a cosmopolitan phase in Shang art.

Anyang: the last Shang capital

Excavations near the present-day city of Anyang have uncovered substantial remains of the city of Yin, founded around 1400 BCE by the Shang ruler Pan Geng; they provide the first archaeological proof in support of traditional Chinese histories. The site, covering an area of 24 sq mi/62 sq km, is not within a city wall and is more a cluster of urban facilities than a true city. It includes the remains of royal cemeteries, palaces, temples, elite and artisan residences, and workshops. Inscriptions on oracle bones found in the city provide invaluable evidence for life at the dawn of Chinese civilization. The Shang kings were buried in great shaft tombs. Most were looted in antiquity but one, that of Fu Hao, the consort of King Wu Ding, has survived intact. The tomb's contents included over 440 bronzes, 590 jades, 560 bone artifacts, and 7,000 cowrie shells, the currency of the Shang state – giving some idea of the treasures that have been lost to archaeology from the other royal graves. Fu Hao's identity was revealed by inscriptions on some of the bronze vessels. She is recorded as having taken part in battles against barbarian tribes and was accompanied in death by human sacrifices, a widespread practice among the Shang ◆

ABOVE AN EXCAVATED CHARIOT BURIAL FROM YIN, NOW IN ANYANG MUSEUM.

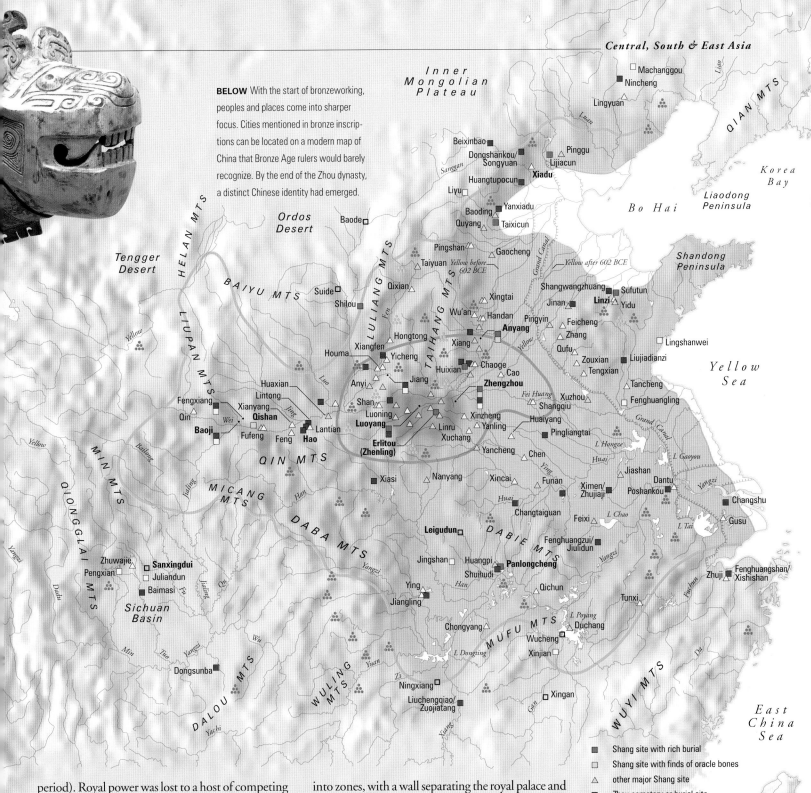

BELOW With the start of bronzeworking, peoples and places come into sharper focus. Cities mentioned in bronze inscriptions can be located on a modern map of China that Bronze Age rulers would barely recognize. By the end of the Zhou dynasty, a distinct Chinese identity had emerged.

period). Royal power was lost to a host of competing small kingdoms during the "Spring and Autumn Period", named after a chronicle of the state of Lu. After 500 BCE, power consolidated in the hands of a few major states, notably Qi, Chu and Qin, during the Warring States period (481–221).

War and prosperity

The growing use of iron after the 6th century led to the development of new weapons and armor. States built defensive walls around their borders and siege warfare developed. Cities became much larger: Linzi, the Qi capital, had a population of hundreds of thousands. The sites of many cities have been investigated. One such, Xiadu, a city of the Yan state, was divided into zones, with a wall separating the royal palace and government area, built on a raised platform, from the city's workshops, markets and residential areas.

Iron tools improved agricultural productivity to support these large urban centers. Commerce flourished, profiting rulers who imposed taxes on trade and tolls on travelers, and issued their own currency from over 140 mints across China. Despite endemic warfare, it was a time of great philosophical and artistic activity. The lavish 5th-century BCE burial of the Marquis Yi of Zeng at Leigudun (Hubei province) included a carillon of bronze bells, as well as silks, jades and gold; his armory of dagger-axes, halberds, spears, chariot fittings and over 3,000 arrowheads is witness to the troubled times in which he lived ◆

Bronze and early Iron Age site
△ source of copper
△ source of tin
▢ area of Shang bronze-working
⫼⫼⫼ most likely route of exchange

0 _____ 500 km
0 _____ 400 mi

Ban Chiang: a dating puzzle

Excavations at the site of Ban Chiang, carried out in the narrow lane of a modern Thai village, attracted great attention in the mid 1970s when burials yielded quantities of red-painted pottery. Apparently associated with some of the early graves – given radiocarbon dates of c.4500 BCE – were cast-bronze spearheads, bangles, and anklets, making them among the earliest known bronze objects anywhere in the world. If this chronology was accurate, bronze-working must have developed independently in the region long before it did in China. It was also suggested that iron was in use here not long after 2000 BCE. Because of the nature of the site, however, the radiocarbon dates from Ban Chiang were notoriously difficult to interpret. Since then well-provenanced material dated by AMS (accelerator mass spectometry) indicates that the site is much later than first proposed. The two Bronze Age burials have been given revised dates of 1740–1450 and 1320–1000 BCE. These accord with sets of AMS dates obtained from other Bronze Age burial sites such as Non Nok Tha and Nong Nor, and suggest that bronze-working in Southeast Asia should now be dated to after 1500 BCE ◆

ABOVE QUANTITIES OF POTTERY FOUND WITH IRON AGE BURIALS AT BAN CHIANG.

The Bronze Age of Southeast Asia

French archaeologists working in Indochina (Laos, Cambodia, and Vietnam) in the 19th century were among the first to identify the existence of a Bronze Age in Southeast Asia. Recent excavations at copper mines in Thailand and findings from a considerable number of graves in the region indicate that metal smelting had begun here by about 1500 BCE – a later date than was once believed. The Bronze Age of Southeast Asia lasted a millennium. Less than 15% of graves from this period contain bronze offerings, suggesting that metal was never in common use. Nor is there evidence for the existence of complex social hierarchies. Individuals were buried without the mortuary wealth seen in later Iron Age cemeteries.

Much of our information about metal-working in Southeast Asia comes from excavations at Phu Lon and the Khao Wong Prachan valley, two copper mining areas with associated ore processing sites that have been intensively investigated. Findings suggest that mining and processing copper was a dry season activity. The ore was extracted from galleries that followed the ore veins before being crushed, concentrated and smelted in small bowl furnaces to produce round copper ingots.

These ingots then entered established exchange networks. Bronze casting took place at local sites by the participating communities in the exchange. The ingots were mixed with tin, then liquefied in small clay crucibles and cast into stone or clay bivalve molds. Castings included socketed axes, spears and arrowheads, but quite the commonest bronze artifacts were decorated bangles. These were usually made by the sophisticated lost wax technique, which allowed ornamentation to be incorporated into the finished form. Bronze was also cast into thin tie-wires to repair stone or shell ornaments.

Bronze Age burials

Excavations of cemeteries provide compelling evidence of life during the Bronze Age. The best documented of these are all from Thailand. The dead were buried in inhumation graves, face up and in an extended position. In some cemeteries, a sufficiently large area has been uncovered to suggest that the graves were arranged in rows, and that men, women, infants and children were buried next to each other.

Thailand's Bronze Age cemeteries are very diverse in character, but share some common features. As well as pottery vessels and stone, shell and bronze jewelry, grave goods often include the remains of animals that were slain during the ritual feasting that

LEFT A distinct province of bronze-working technology, stretching from Hong Kong in the east to Nyaunggan in the Chindwin valley of Myanmar in the west, can be recognized in Southeast Asia. Copper ore is relatively common throughout this area, and the richest known deposits of tin ore in the world extend from Malaysia into peninsular Thailand. Early copper smelting skills may have developed independently within the region itself, or were introduced from north China, where the vibrant Shang tradition of bronze casting was in existence. Late Neolithic graves in southern China contain a number of Shang bronzes, together with Shang jades, which are also found in contemporaneous burials in Vietnam.

BELOW A serpentine bangle from a Bronze Age grave at Nong Nor (4.3 in/11 cm wide). The bronze tie wires used to repair it can be clearly seen. Most individuals in the cemetery at Nong Nor were buried with a dog's skull, probably from an animal consumed during the ritual graveside feasting.

accompanied the burial. At Ban Na Di, several generations of villagers were buried with the left forelimb of a cow or pig. In one grave a child had been buried under a crocodile skin shroud. It was lying beside a woman who wore a large bone pendant fashioned from crocodile skull. Other graves contained clay figurines of cattle, deer, elephant and humans.

Analysis of the skeletal remains from Ban Na Di shows robust bone development, indicating a healthy diet: rice, meat and fish were all eaten. Nevertheless, few people lived beyond 35 years of age, and infant mortality was high. Although groups of relatively wealthy graves, measured in terms of shell and stone ornaments, have been found, no Bronze Age site in Thailand provides evidence for an entrenched social hierarchy. The exotic materials such as shell, carnelian, agate, serpentine and talc used to fashion these grave goods must have reached these villages via distant exchange networks. However, the copper socketed implements found in two graves at Nong Nor almost certainly came from the Khao Wong Prachan valley 112 mi/180 km to the northwest, where matching molds have been found ◆

First Empires of China

During the Warring States period of Chinese history (see page 117), war became the subject of learned treatises, the most famous of which is the *Art of War* by Sun Zi (c.500 BCE). Increased agricultural productivity had brought about rapid population growth, as a result of which rulers were now able to mobilize huge armies. Chariots were replaced by troops of cavalry. Under these circumstances, great advantage was had by those states that developed the highest degree of organization. From 361 BCE the state of Qin in the northwest underwent a series of reforms. Power was taken away from the feudal aristocracy, control centralized in the hands of the government, and the army strengthened, laying the foundations for steady territorial expansion in the late 4th and early 3rd centuries. In 256 BCE the Qin deposed the last of the Eastern Zhou rulers based at Luoyang. The remaining states were conquered in a series of lightning campaigns between 230 and 221, when the Qin king Zheng took the title of Qin Shi Huang Di, the First Emperor of China.

Under the First Emperor, China underwent a series of reforms that have set the tone of Chinese history to the present day. Centralized totalitarian government with regional bureaucracies replaced the defeated feudal power structures. To assist in controlling the new empire, writing, coinage, weights and measures – even the axle sizes of wagons – were standardized right across the country. Large-scale irrigation schemes had already been put in place in Qin by Zheng to improve agricultural productivity, and as First Emperor he undertook vast engineering projects across the whole of China by mobilizing vast teams of conscript laborers. Roads and canals were built and the various frontier walls built by the Zhou states to keep

RIGHT The First Emperor created a strong infrastructure with roads and defensive walls, and his Han successors extended Chinese rule into Central and Southeast Asia, creating the conditions for flourishing trade within the empire and along the Silk Route (see pages 134–135). Chinese goods reached the Roman empire, and western goods and new ideas, most importantly Buddhism, flowed back into China itself.

ABOVE SOME OF THE TERRACOTTA SOLDIERS AND HORSES SET TO GUARD THE BODY OF THE FIRST EMPEROR.

Xianyang: burial place of an emperor

Qin Shi Huang Di, the First Emperor of China, was obsessed with immortality. He died while on a tour of the provinces in 210 BCE, but preparations for his life in the afterworld had begun soon after he unified China. About 25 mi/40 km east of his capital at Xianyang, close to the modern city of Xian, a great burial mound was erected within sight of Mount Li. Squarish in shape, it is 164 ft/50 m high with a circumference of over 4,593 ft/1,400 m: history records that some 700,000 men were conscripted to build it. The mausoleum is still intact, protected by the fear inspired by the First Emperor during his life. The tomb itself is only part of a wider mortuary landscape, which includes a funerary palace, a temple and a series of at least four large pits. In 1974, an army of terracotta warriors, horses and chariots was discovered in the largest of these structures. Further excavations showed that it extended 689 ft/210 m east–west and 197 ft/60 m north–south, and was divided into 11 corridors, with galleries at the eastern and western ends and five earthen ramps leading up to the surface. The 3,200 soldiers were made with great attention to detail; officers are distinguished by headgear and badges of rank. Weapons are still sharp, and the faces of the figures are all individually modeled, giving the army an uncanny realism ◆

Excavations of a number of tombs in the 1960s and 70s revealed something of the lives of high-ranking individuals in the Former Han period. The Marquis of Dai, who died in 186 BCE, was buried in a shaft tomb at Mawangdui (modern Changsha). Waterlogging had preserved quantities of lacquer, basketry and wooden artifacts, as well the earliest examples of Chinese cartography preserved on three pieces of silk. Jade suits, thought to preserve the body of the deceased, were worn by a Han prince, Liu Sheng, and his wife, discovered in a tomb at Mancheng. Each one, consisting of about 2,500 jade plaques sewn together with gold thread, must have taken 10 years to make.

Expansion and collapse

Successive Han rulers extended the boundaries of the empire into central and southeast Asia. Under a program of peasant colonization more than two million people were moved to the northern frontiers between 127 and 92 BCE. The Xiongnu, the most implacable of the northern nomads, were finally pacified in 36 BCE. As wealthy landowners became increasingly powerful, political and economic strains led to the revolt of Wang Mang, who established the short-lived Xin dynasty (9–23 CE).

During the Eastern or Later Han period (25–220 CE) a new capital was established at Luoyang, the former Zhou capital. Grand military expeditions were revived but failed to halt economic decline or curb the importance of large private estates. There was a large population shift southward. From the middle of the 2nd century peasant unrest increased, and political revolts often contained elements of messianic religious fervor, cults based on Daoism finding favor with the disaffected populace. Over half a million people died in 184 during the largest of these rebellions, the revolt of the Yellow Turbans. The empire was severely weakened, independent generals took power for themselves, and at the end of the reign of Xian Di (189–220), the Han dynasty collapsed ◆

out the nomads to the north were brought together into a continuous defensive system. Opposition was ruthlessly suppressed, protestors were executed and "subversive" books destroyed. The First Emperor ruled for just over a decade. He was buried under a huge mausoleum near his capital of Xianyang (see box).

The Han dynasty

On the First Emperor's death, war broke out and the entire Qin royal family massacred in 206 BCE in reaction against his harsh rule. However, his empire did not break up and in 202 a former Qin official, Liu Bang, became emperor under the title of Gaozu and established the Han dynasty. The modernizing administration of the Western or Former Han period (202 BCE–8 CE) created an enlightened state bureaucratic organization underpinned by a stringent examination system for the civil service.

Map legend:

- ☐ Qin frontier fort
- ▦ Han trade emporia
- ■ Qin or Han site with burial
- ☐ other Qin or Han settlement

growth of Qin and Han empires

- state of Qin, c.350 BCE
- Qin gains by 221 BCE (unification of China)
- further Qin gains by 206 BCE
- gains under Western Han, 202 BCE–8 CE
- gains under Eastern Han, 25–220 CE
- Han protectorate of the Western Regions
- area of intensive agriculture during the Western Han period
- frontier wall
- main road during the Han period
- ancient course of the Yellow river
- ancient coastline during the Han period

0   500 km
0   400 mi

Map labels:

GOBI DESERT · Xiongnu nomads · Inner Mongolian Plateau · Tengger Desert · LANG MTS · Jiayuguan · Zhangye · Ordos Desert · Wuyuan · Holingol · Diangxiang · Shanggu · Dabaotai · Youbeiping · Xiadu · Xuantu · Xiangping · Chiao-li · NANGNIM MTS · Sea of Japan · Korea Bay · Bo Hai · Liaodong Peninsula · Lelang · Wuwei · Mancheng · Wangdu · Yellow before 11CE · Yellow from 11 CE · Shandong Peninsula · Jincheng · Taiyuan · Anping · Qinghe · QI · Zichuan · Linzi · Yellow Sea · Xianyang · Qin · Li Shan · Zofengyi · Lintong · Yu-fu-feng · QIN MOUNTAINS · Anyi · Wei · Luoyang · Julu · Jinan · Handan · Puyang · Qufu · Yinan · Langya · Nanzheng · Nanyang · Runan · Linhuaiguan · Shouxian · Nanjing · Guangling · Sichuan Basin · Guanghan · Chengdu · SHU · Chongqing · Dangyang · Ying · DABA MTS · Shuihudi · CHU · L Tai · Wu · Chengyang · Guiji · Xichang · Yibin · Nan · Jiangling · L Poyang · Pengli · Fuchun · Mawangdui · L Dongting · WUYI MOUNTAINS · DALOU MTS · WULIANG MTS · Lingling · Guiyang · NAN MTS · Chengjiang · Jiaozhi · Gulf of Tonkin · Zhuyai · Hainan · Nanhai · Panyu · South China Sea · Xianyang · Xinzheng · Chenliu · Daliang · Shangqiu · Xie · Linyi · Donghai · Huai · Zhangye · Qinghai · Jinan

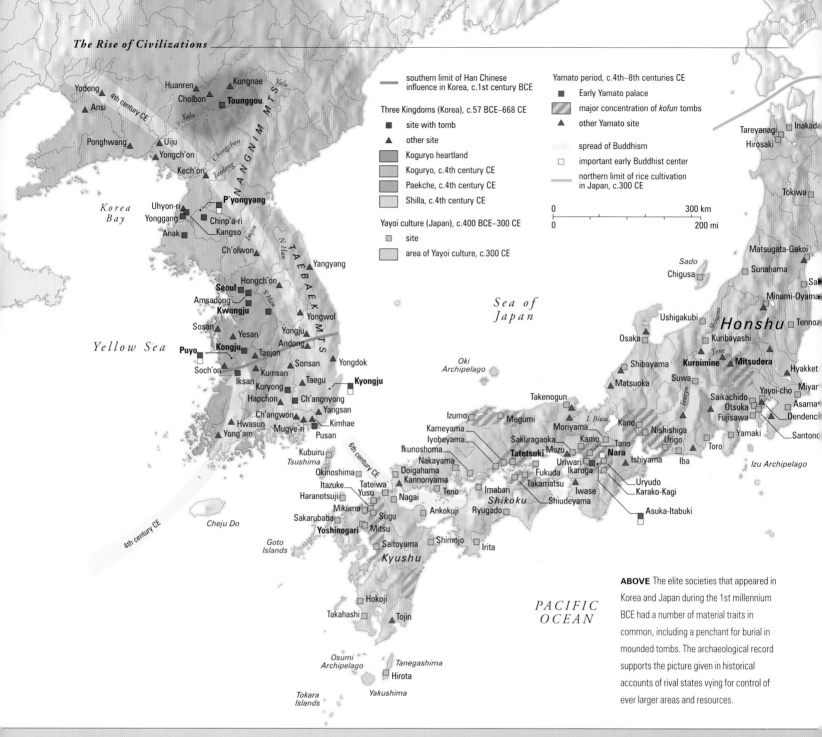

southern limit of Han Chinese
influence in Korea, c.1st century BCE

Three Kingdoms (Korea), c.57 BCE–668 CE

■ site with tomb

▲ other site

Koguryo heartland

Koguryo, c.4th century CE

Paekche, c.4th century CE

Shilla, c.4th century CE

Yayoi culture (Japan), c.400 BCE–300 CE

□ site

area of Yayoi culture, c.300 CE

Yamato period, c.4th–8th centuries CE

■ Early Yamato palace

▨ major concentration of *kofun* tombs

▲ other Yamato site

spread of Buddhism

□ important early Buddhist center

northern limit of rice cultivation
in Japan, c.300 CE

0 ——— 300 km
0 ——— 200 mi

ABOVE The elite societies that appeared in Korea and Japan during the 1st millennium BCE had a number of material traits in common, including a penchant for burial in mounded tombs. The archaeological record supports the picture given in historical accounts of rival states vying for control of ever larger areas and resources.

Kyongju: "gold-glittering" city

The capital of Shilla at Kyongju, then known as Kumsong ("the Golden City"), was one of the great cities of the ancient world with a population at its height of a million. Parts of the city were laid out like Chang-an, the great Chinese capital that also provided the model for Nara, the early capital of the Yamato state in Japan. It had no city wall, unlike many Chinese cities, but was protected by five fortresses, including Panwolsong, the Half Moon Fortress, enclosed by an earthen wall 2,525 ft/800 m in diameter. Within the city limits lay

palaces, Buddhist temples, parklands with landscaped gardens, an artificial "sea" at Anap-chi, and the great Ch'omsong-dae observatory built in 640 by King Sondok. There are over 150 mounded tombs in Kyongju belonging to the Shilla elite, many of which appear to have survived intact from antiquity. The rulers of Shilla were buried in lavish style, and excavations of tombs such as the Tomb of the Heavenly Horse and the Gold Crown tomb have yielded quantities of exquisite gold, including crowns and other regalia. The goldwork produced by Korean craftsmen was well-known along the Silk Route, and 9th-century Arab traders knew Shilla as the "gold-glittering nation" ◆

ABOVE ROYAL TOMBS AT KYONGJU OFTEN CONTAIN GREAT TREASURES FROM THE SHILLA KINGDOM.

Early States of Korea and Japan

During the early 1st millennium CE a series of states developed in the Korean peninsula and, slightly later, in the Japanese archipelago, on the peripheries of China. This period of protohistory is described in later Korean and Japanese literary works such as the *Samguk Sagi* ("History of the Three Kingdoms", dated 1146) and the *Nihon Shoki* ("Chronicles of Japan", dated 720), as well as in a number of contemporary Chinese chronicles. It should be viewed in the context of Chinese fragmentation following the demise of the Wei dynasty in the early 3rd century when local rulers seized the new opportunities to increase their power base through alliance and warfare.

The protohistoric period saw greatly increased levels of communication and interaction between competing states. The new elites shared a taste for prestige items, and artisans were brought from far afield to establish centers for the production of stoneware ceramics and metalworking, introduced from China. Into this context of competing state organizations came Chinese ideas of government based on Confucian principles, the use of the Chinese writing system, and from the 4th century CE, a new religion, Buddhism.

The Korean peninsula

According to the *Samguk Sagi,* the three kingdoms of Korea – Paekche, Koguryo, and Shilla – were founded in 18, 37 and 57 BCE respectively. Koguryo, however, was the first to emerge as a developed state and during the 1st and 2nd centuries CE it came to dominate a large area in the north from its first capital at Tounggou on the Yalu River. Particularly important rulers were buried in splendidly painted tombs, the details of which provide a vivid picture of elite life at this time , such as hunting, feasting and courtly pursuits including music, dancing and watching acrobats. During the eastern Han period of expansion (see pages 120–121), a Chinese colony was established at Lelang in the northern part of the Korean peninsula. In 313 CE it was overrun by mounted troops from Koguryo, but the influence of Chinese culture persisted in the northern part of the Korean peninsula. Buddhism arrived in 366, and a Confucian school was established soon afterwards. In 427, the capital of Koguryo was moved to P'yongyang, the site of the old Lelang commandery.

In the southwest, the kingdom of Paekche had its successive capitals at Wiryesong (near modern Seoul), Hansan (modern Kwangju), Ungjon (modern

ABOVE A *haniwa* (terracotta tomb guardian) of a seated man. Many Japanese *kofun* were surrounded by hundreds of these figures: the tomb of the emperor Nintoku had up to 20,000 arranged in seven rows. Some *haniwa* were shaped as simple cylinders, while others depict people (warriors, singers, dancers), animals (dogs, wild boar, birds) and buildings; *haniwa* on the summit of one tomb represent an elite residential compound with model buildings and enclosures resembling those excavated at Mitsudera. These representational *haniwa* are a source of valuable information about everyday life at the time that the first Japanese states were coming into being.

Kongju) and Puyo. The wealth of its rulers is indicated by the opulent contents of the tomb of King Munyong (501– 523). Frequent attempts were made to strengthen its position against Koguryo through alliances with China and the early Yamato state in Japan, but no amount of diplomacy could save Paekche from the rising power of Shilla. This small state, based on the southeastern city of Kyongju (see box), became the paramount power on the Korean peninsula in the 7th century, conquering first Paekche (663) and then Koguryo (668). Power was highly centralized and exercised through a rigidly ordered social hierarchy.

Japanese protostates

Rice agriculture, metalworking and other new technologies arrived all at one time in the Japanese archipelago, introduced from the mainland after c.400 BCE. The intensive production of rice and control of new, prestigious materials, particularly metal, marked a radical break with the lifestyles of the Jomon foragers (see pages 110–111) and laid the foundations for a new social and cultural order during the Yayoi period (c.400 BCE–c.300 CE). During these centuries, through a mixture of aggressive warfare and advantageous alliances, regional chiefs gained control over progressively larger territories. Large defended settlements such as Yoshinogari in northwestern Kyushu give a good idea of what life was like for these leaders and their followers. Bronze items such as bells, spearheads, halberds and swords were prized as status objects and are found in significant numbers in burials of this period. In some areas, chiefs were buried in large mounded tombs that foreshadow the great tombs of the Yamato emperors, as at Tatetsuki in the Kibi region of Honshu.

Between the 4th and 8th centuries the local chiefs of the Yamato area of Honshu, at the eastern end of the Inland Sea, gradually extended their control throughout most of the Japanese archipelago. As in Korea, these early elites found expression for their newfound power in the construction of massive burial mounds, called *kofun* in Japanese, the biggest of which are known as "keyhole tombs" from their shape (round at the back and square in front). The largest, traditionally said to belong to Nintoku, one of the early emperors mentioned in the *Nihon Shoki*, covered an area of more than 80 acres/32 hectares and probably dates from the early 5th century. Survivals of everyday life from the *kofun* period are fewer, but a mid-6th century volcanic eruption in the region of Mount Haruna in Gunma prefecture preserved a farming village and an elite residential compound at Kuroimine and Mitsudera in a thick layer of mud and ash. Excavation of these sites has led to their being described as the Pompeii of Japan ◆

The Iron Age of Southeast Asia

The Iron Age, which began in Southeast Asia about 500 BCE, saw marked changes in social organization. A series of luminous and wealthy kingdoms arose across the rich agricultural lands of southern China and in the region of the Red River delta. The stimulus for this development appears to have been competition for the control of exchange with the powerful state of Chu, centered on the middle Yangzi valley. This process intensified during the 1st century CE as the region came under the influence of the expansionist Han dynasty (see pages 120–121). South of the Truong Son mountains, there was growing exchange in exotic goods with India as Iron Age farming communities grew wealthier. New religious ideas incorporating features of Hinduism and Buddhism made their appearance and social differentiation increased. Both may have been factors in the transition to early states that took place in the lower Mekong valley from about 200 CE. The first civilizations of Southeast Asia, such as Angkor, were to emerge from among these Iron Age chiefdoms over the course of the next thousand years.

Two cultures – Dian and Dong Son – appear to have stood out from the rest of the rival chiefdoms that occupied southern China and Vietnam at the beginning of the Iron Age. In large part, however, this is because archaeological investigation has been more intense in those areas than elsewhere.

Aristocratic burials

The chiefdom of Dian in Yunnan dominated the lake that bears the same name and whose rich sedimentary soils and gentle climate made it a prosperous center of rice production. Shizhaishan (Stone Fortress Hill) rises up from the plain on the southeastern edge of the lake. Archaeologists have uncovered a royal necropolis here, in which the dead aristocrats were interred in lacquered wooden coffins that contained a remarkable array of mortuary offerings. One burial includes a golden seal that bears the inscription "the seal of the King of Dian" and was a gift from the Han emperor. A feature of these burials are miniature figures, cast in bronze and often gilded, which were then placed on top of bronze drums or containers holding cowrie shells. These small figures enact scenes of aristocratic life – women are seen performing the seasonal rituals, while men are often depicted in battle scenes. At Lijiashan, a second royal necropolis, aristocratic women were buried with exquisite bronze weaving tools, while male burials contained weaponry.

The Red River, which originates in Yunnan, links the territory of Dian with that of Dong Son. Here again aristocratic graves have been investigated at several sites. The bodies were often interred in wooden coffins that contained elaborate bronzes. Ornate ceremonial drums are frequently found. Many have decorative friezes that depict plumed warriors, music making, rice threshing, and domestic houses; others bear geometric patterns. These bronzes were of local manufacture, but at Viet Khe a particularly large boat coffin contained local bronzes together with imported southern Chinese forms. Similar graves at Xuan La included clothing, wooden hafts for bronze weapons, and a number of Chinese coins.

Iron Age farmers

Beyond the Truong Son mountains, the development of iron-working after 500 BCE brought significant change to the cultural and social fabric. Iron ore for smelting was readily available over much of northeast and central Thailand. Tools made from forged (heated and hammered) iron vastly increased agricultural efficiency: trees were more easily felled and the soil was turned with less effort. Iron-smelting furnaces required a constant supply of fuel wood, opening more land to agriculture. As population levels rose settlement sites sprang up in areas where there was

Noen U-Loke: a rich burial site

Excavations in 1997–98 at Noen U-Loke in Thailand uncovered the largest area of an Iron Age settlement yet investigated in Southeast Asia. Occupation lasted from about 400 BCE to at least 400 CE. Some 125 inhumation graves were revealed, together with much evidence of iron-working, glass making and domestic activities. There are five distinct burial phases. Iron ornaments are present in the earliest graves. During the fourth phase, c.100–200 CE, people were interred in clusters; the graves were filled with burnt rice and lined and capped with clay. The clusters include men, women, infants and children. Three of them contained a particularly rich burial. One man wore three bronze belts, 150 bronze bangles, bronze finger and toe rings, and silver ear coils sheathed in gold. Another wore four bronze belts as well as heavy bronze earspools, while the necklace of a woman included gold, agate and glass beads. All were buried with an iron knife ◆

RIGHT ONE IRON KNIFE WAS STILL WITHIN ITS BAMBOO SHEATH (5.5 IN/14 CM).

RIGHT Two distinct spheres of influence developed in Southeast Asia during the early Iron Age. Exposure to the expansionist Chu and Han states of northern China encouraged a sharp increase in social ranking among the rice farmers of southern China and Vietnam, leading to the emergence of rival militaristic states in the region of the Red River. Imperial influence did not extend south of the Truong Son range, however. Instead, as agricultural prosperity increased through the use of iron, the farming communities of Cambodia and Thailand were drawn into closer cultural and trading contact with India.

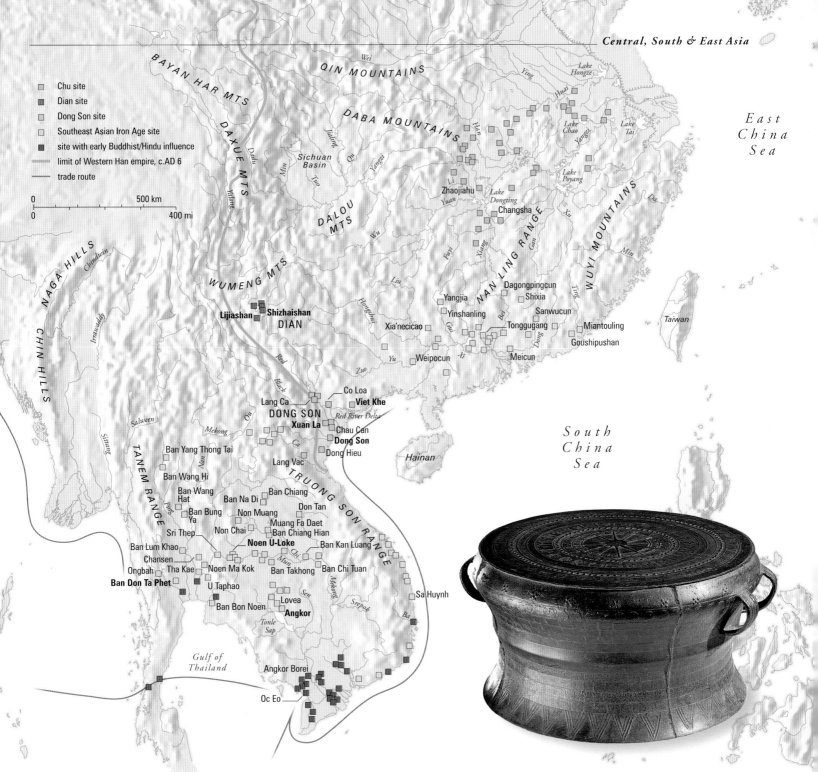

Chu site
Dian site
Dong Son site
Southeast Asian Iron Age site
site with early Buddhist/Hindu influence
limit of Western Han empire, c.AD 6
trade route

0 ——— 500 km
0 ——— 400 mi

East China Sea

South China Sea

BAYAN HAR MTS

QIN MOUNTAINS

DABA MOUNTAINS

DAXUE MTS

SICHUAN BASIN

DALOU MTS

NAGA HILLS

CHIN HILLS

WUMENG MTS

NANLING RANGE

WUYI MOUNTAINS

TANEM RANGE

TRUONG SON RANGE

Zhaojiahu
Changsha
Li
Yuan
Lake Dongting
Lake Chao
Lake Tai
Lake Hongze
Lake Poyang

Dagongpingcun
Yangjia
Yinshanling
Shixia
Sanwucun
Xia'necicao
Tonggugang
Miantouling
Goushipushan
Weipocun
Meicun

Lijiashan Shizhaishan
DIAN

Taiwan

Co Loa
Lang Ca
Viet Khe
DONG SON
Xuan La
Chau Can
Dong Son
Dong Hieu
Red River Delta

Hainan

Lang Vac
Ban Yang Thong Tai
Ban Wang Hi
Ban Wang Hat
Ban Na Di
Ban Chiang
Don Tan
Non Muang
Muang Fa Daet
Ban Chiang Hian
Ban Bung Ya
Non Chai
Sri Thep
Noen U-Loke
Ban Kan Luang
Ban Lum Khao
Chansen
Tha Kae
Noen Ma Kok
Ban Takhong
Ban Chi Tuan
Ongbah
Ban Don Ta Phet
U Taphao
Lovea
Ban Bon Noen
Angkor

Sa Huynh

Tonle Sap

Gulf of Thailand

Angkor Borei

Oc Eo

ABOVE A ceremonial Dong Son drum (height 11.8 in/30 cm; diameter 20.8 in/ 53 cm). Early Chinese accounts relate that the chiefs of the people living in the region to the south beat drums in time of war. A large number of these impressive instruments have been discovered, mostly from the Red River delta and Yunnan province in China. They are often decorated with scenes of war. Others depict ritual processions with figures of musicians and dancers.

previously little evidence of occupation. Some of these settlements grew to be considerably larger than their Bronze Age predecessors.

Iron was used for a wide range of practical implements such as knives, socketed spades, hoes, and sickles. Iron weapons came more slowly into use but are present in burials by the Late Iron Age: a man with an iron arrowhead lodged in his spine was found in excavations at Noen U-Loke (see box). The new wealth of these Iron Age settlements can be seen at Ban Don Ta Phet in central Thailand in the form of carnelian, agate and glass jewelry, new iron artifacts including spears and billhooks, and decorated bronzes portraying languid scenes of lotuses, structures, and elegant women with elaborate coiffures.

There are indications of increasing trade and cultural contact with India: a carnelian lion, in a site dated within the 4th century BCE, could only have originated in the subcontinent, where the lion was used as a symbolic representation of the Buddha. Bronze bowls found at sites in India could well have come from places in Thailand like Ban Don Ta Phet. Such finds point to the growing presence of Indian merchants in Southeast Asia, who exchanged exotic goods for spices, bronzes and gold, and transmitted cultural ideas. The leaders of the local communities controlling the distribution networks for these goods, or those who ventured overseas on trading expeditions, would have acquired wealth and standing, encouraging the formation of powerful social elites ◆

Later States of South Asia

During the 2nd millennium BCE, horse-riding nomads from Central Asia entered the Indian subcontinent. The Indo-Aryan languages they introduced gradually gained dominance, and a hybrid culture developed with the local successors of the Indus civilization. Iron-working spread rapidly as easily worked ores were widely available. With iron tools, forests could be felled and land cleared for farming. Towns began to appear in the Ganges valley, and a vigorous indigenous culture emerged, continually enriched by contact with incoming groups and societies of traders and invaders.

BELOW Buddhism provided a major stimulus to art and architecture. Stupas such as this one at Sanchi, built to house the corporeal relics of the Buddha and later saints, became the vehicle for lavish sculptured decorations. Temples were also constructed, often associated with monasteries. These were initially founded to house monks during the rainy season, but by the 2nd century BCE they had developed into large, affluent establishments. The monasteries served as centers of learning and provided hospitality and patronage for socially important guilds of merchants and craftworkers.

The spread of settled farmers into the Ganges valley and the transition from an agrarian village-based society to the emergence of small rival kingdoms can be traced in the stories of warring peoples contained in the Vedas and other religious epics. The Vedic religion, from which Hinduism is descended, crystallized in the mid-1st millennium BCE. It probably combined elements of Indo-Aryan culture with the religious practice of the Indus people (see pages 114–115), hinted at on their seals and citadel mounds. The earliest Vedic texts were written down in the syllabic Brahmi and Kharoshti scripts, based on western Semitic scripts.

The Mauryas

By the time of the great religious reformers, Mahavira (the founder of Jainism) and Siddharta Gautama, the Buddha, in the 6th and 5th centuries BCE, tradition recounts that there were sixteen major kingdoms, or regional states, spread across northern India. The most prominent of these was Magadha, which gradually expanded its influence through conquest, dynastic marriages and diplomacy. By the late 4th century, under the Magadhan king Chandragupta Maurya (r.321–c.293), most of the subcontinent had been brought together in the Mauryan empire.

The towns and cities of the Ganges region were prosperous centers of craft activity, producing both tools and luxury goods such as jewelry. Coinage came into use in the 6th century BCE, appearing at around the same time both here and among the trading cities of the Punjab, such as Taxila. These were absorbed into the Persian empire until its conquest by Alexander the Great. After Alexander's death, the Mauryas made substantial gains in the northwest.

Contemporary texts, such as that of Megasthenes, an ambassador from one of Alexander's successors to the court of Chandragupta Maurya, describe the magnificence of the public architecture, including a pillared hall at Pataliputra, the Mauryan capital. Archaeology has revealed traces of this hall, as well as a huge wooden rampart that defended the city. Here and elsewhere huge ringwells were particularly impressive features of domestic architecture, reminiscent of the attention given to sanitation and water supply in the Indus civilization. Although there was no direct link between the Indus civilization and the later Gangetic states, many cultural features survived, including the basic units of measurement.

The Mauryan empire reached its greatest extent under Chandragupta's grandson, Ashoka (r.272–231). A great patron of Buddhism, he sent missions to neighboring regions, including Sri Lanka where it took firm root. A number of the carved edicts that Ashoka commanded to be set up in the frontier regions of his empire can still be seen today.

RIGHT The agrarian settlements of the Ganges plain emerged as the focal point of South Asian civilization a thousand years after the eclipse of the Indus civilization. From here the Mauryan rulers of Magadha extended their influence over northern and central India in the late 4th century BCE. Trade and cultural contact with Central Asia was through the mountain passes of the northwest, providing a stimulus to urbanization here. Buddhist monasteries were founded along trade routes through-out the subcontinent: in the Western Ghats richly decorated temples were carved into the soft laterite rocks.

▲ important urban center
■ Buddhist stupa, temple or monastery
□ other important Buddhist site
▪ Mauryan rock or pillar edict
— trade route
heartland of Mauryan empire, c.324 BCE
probable maximum extent of Mauryan empire, c.260 BCE
formative area of Vedic culture
formative area of Buddhism
expansion of Indo-Aryan peoples
ancient river course
ancient coastline around Rann of Kutch

0   400 km
0   300 mi

Successor states

After the fall of the Mauryas in 192 BCE the Ganges region was fragmented among a succession of weak dynasties. In the 1st century CE the Kushans incorporated northern India into their vast trading empire, which prospered through control of the western portion of the Silk Route (see pages 134–135). Roman and Arab commerce reached India by sea, and coastal towns in South India were trading with the emerging states of Southeast Asia.

South of the Kushan sphere of influence, local dynasties flourished: chief among these were the Satavahanas who established a powerful kingdom in the Deccan in the 1st and 2nd centuries CE. Following the collapse of Kushan rule the Guptas emerged after a further period of fragmentation to create a unified state that dominated the subcontinent (4th to 5th centuries). They were a native dynasty and their reign is regarded as India's Golden Age. Arts and sciences flourished and many features of classical Indian culture, including the caste system, came into being; Buddhism declined. The late Gupta empire was weakened by internal feuding and it fell easy victim to the latest wave of Central Asian invaders, the Hephthalites or White Huns, who differed from their predecessors in their savagery and failure to become assimilated to the native culture ◆

Scythians and Steppe Nomads

Nomadic pastoralism seems to have emerged among the horse-raising inhabitants of the steppe grasslands of central Eurasia early in the 1st millennium BCE. Their wealth lay in their vast herds of animals, and they followed a seasonal pattern of migration between areas of pasture land, often covering vast distances. Because they were constantly on the move their equipment was generally light and portable, consisting of carts and wagons for transporting domestic goods and tents for shelter. The spread of a characteristic "animal style" of art from the eastward end of the steppe corridor into the lands north of the Black Sea during the 8th and 7th centuries BCE provides evidence of a substantial migration. The incomers mingled with the local population to became the people known to Herodotus and other Greek writers as the Scythians. Close relations were established with the Black Sea Greek colonies (see pages 90–91), which grew into substantial trading centers with multicultural hinterlands. For the next 500 years, until their defeat by Philip II of Macedon in 339 BCE, the Scythians were a powerful and wealthy people: the landscape of southern Russia and Ukraine is littered with burial mounds concealing the tombs of elite warriors, some of which have yielded astonishing collections of gold and silver artifacts, along with the horse furnishings, weapons and wagons that characterize the nomadic life. Far to the east, on the high plateau of the Altai mountains, pastoral communities related to the Scythians lived a similar nomadic life and buried their dead in timber-lined tombs. The Altai nomads likewise accumulated great wealth through exchange in horses with their settled neighbors in Persia, India and China.

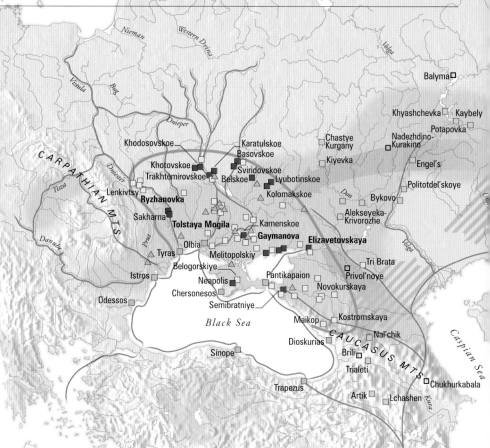

Our primary sources of archaeological information about the Scythians are their spectacular burials. A central shaft, 33–50 ft/10–15 m deep, was dug into the loess subsoil and a cavern-like chamber, often reinforced with timbers, was then hollowed out at the base to hold the main burial. Additional alcoves sometimes branched off from this chamber to contain the bodies of the servants and relatives who accompanied the deceased personage to the grave. A variety of grave goods was also placed inside and the grave shaft was then filled with earth

ABOVE The steppes of Eurasia were the home of horse-riding pastoralists during the 1st millennium BCE. Greek trading colonies established on the north coast of the Black Sea around 600 BCE brought the people known as the Scythians great wealth, which is reflected in the numerous rich burials from this period. To the east, among the Altai mountains, other pastoralists were in contact with China, Persia and India at around this date.

ABOVE ARCHAEOLOGISTS EXAMINE THE EXCAVATED PAZYRYK TOMB AT UKOK.

The Lady of Ukok: frozen in time

The pastoral nomads of the high Altai mountains on the border of Russia with China and Mongolia are frequently called "Pazyryk", the local name for "burial mound". Because the moisture that accumulated in their timber-lined tombs froze almost immediately, the contents have been preserved in extraordinary condition, providing archaeologists with fascinating information about the Iron Age peoples of this cold and remote region. One of the most remarkable discoveries was made at Ukok in the summer of 1993, when the tattooed body of a woman about 25 years old was found lying in a log coffin, along with textiles and leather items. Accompanying her was a meal of mutton and horsemeat laid on wooden plates. Six horses had been buried just outside the timber chamber, each killed by a blow to the head. The woman's clothes were exceptionally well-preserved. She wore a hair-and-felt headdress decorated with gold-covered carved cats, a silk blouse with maroon piping, a woolen dress, and felt boots. The silk found in the Pazyryk tombs was long presumed to have come from China, but examination of the fibers of the Ukok blouse suggest that it may have come from elsewhere, possibly India ◆

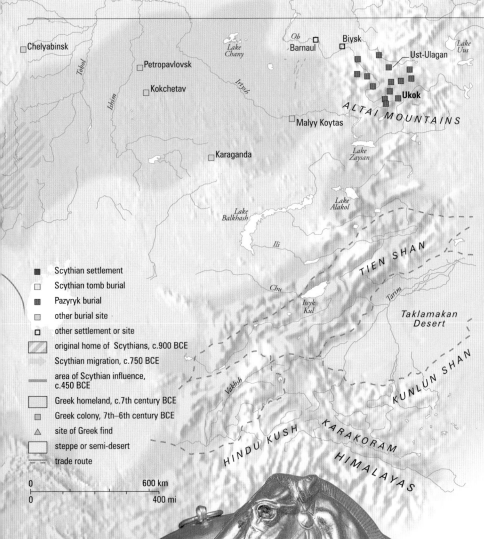

Scythian settlement
Scythian tomb burial
Pazyryk burial
other burial site
other settlement or site
original home of Scythians, c.900 BCE
Scythian migration, c.750 BCE
area of Scythian influence, c.450 BCE
Greek homeland, c.7th century BCE
Greek colony, 7th–6th century BCE
site of Greek find
steppe or semi-desert
trade route

and rocks. The burial mound was heaped up over the top, sometimes to a height of 66 ft/20 m. Later burials might be added by digging adjacent shafts into the mound and then tunneling into the original burial chamber or hollowing out another.

Spectacular artifacts

Tolstaya Mogila is a classic Scythian tomb. The main grave, that of a male about 50 years old, was robbed in antiquity, but the thieves overlooked a sword within its gold scabbard and a gold pectoral. A secondary burial shaft was intact. The side grave contained five burials: a young woman and infant laid side-by-side with rich burial goods, a young man with a bow-and-arrow, a young woman beside a niche with food offerings, and a male next to a complete wagon and several horses. Bones of horses, boar and deer found in the perimeter ditch, together with shards of wine vessels, were presumably the remains of a funeral feast.

The Scythians typically decorated their gold and silver ornaments and vessels with representations of wild animals or with figurative scenes of battle. Some motifs, however, are more peaceful. For example, a silver bowl excavated at Gaymanova was decorated with a gold-plated frieze showing two elderly warriors engaged in relaxed conversation; they are wearing Scythian tunics of fur-trimmed leather. The gold pectoral found at Tolstaya Mogila, which is perhaps the finest known example of Scythian goldwork, depicts a child milking a sheep and two men making a hide garment. It was probably the product of a Greek colonial workshop in which the Scythian themes were interpreted by Greek artisans.

Permanent settlement

Despite the nomadic roots of the Scythians, their contact with the Greeks seems to have led to the emergence of permanent settlements. Elizavetovskaya, on an island at the mouth of the river Don, had certainly developed into a center of craft production and trade in the second half of the 4th century BCE, and was surrounded by fortification walls and ditches. Although other Scythian settlements are rare, a remarkable tomb excavated by a team of Polish and Ukrainian archaeologists at Ryzhanovka, south of Kiev, in 1996 hints intriguingly at sedentism. The tomb was arranged like a two-room house. One chamber represented a kitchen with a mock hearth with bronze kettles containing boiled horse and lamb bones, the other a bedroom, in which the chief's body lay on a wooden platform. The late date (c.300 BCE or later) and "domestic" nature of this grave have led archaeologists to speculate that the Scythians were in transition from nomadism to a settled life ◆

RIGHT The base of a Scythian gold cup is decorated with a repeating pattern of horses' heads.

The Persian Empire

After 1000 BCE, Iranian-speaking peoples, originally from Central Asia, emerged as the dominant force on the western Iranian plateau south of the Caspian Sea and began moving west and south through the Zagros mountains. One group, the Medes, benefited from the collapse of Assyrian power in the 7th century BCE briefly to create an empire that reputedly extended from Anatolia to Afghanistan, with its capital at Ecbatana (Hamadan). A related branch settled in the area of Persis (modern Fars or Shiraz) in the uplands of southwestern Iran. In the mid 6th century, under their king Cyrus the Great of the Achaemenid dynasty, the Persians conquered the empire of the Medes, their former overlords, then overran the wealthy Anatolian kingdom of Lydia and the Greek cities of Asia Minor before turning on Babylonia. Cyrus's successors added Egypt and northern Thrace. Only the Greeks, by turning back the armies of Xerxes in the 470s (see page 96–97), called a halt to Persian expansion. Having conquered lands on an unprecedented scale, the Achaemenid kings united them by creating a shrewd and flexible system of government that allowed room for local custom and religious tolerance within the structures of a centralized state bureaucracy and imperial army. The empire they created lasted for two centuries before being conquered by Alexander the Great.

The architect of the Achaemenids' political and administrative system was Darius (r.522–486 BCE), who divided the empire into provinces and appointed Persian nobles as governors. Prime agricultural land throughout the empire was parceled out as noble estates or military smallholdings in return for army service and the payment of taxes in silver. The Persians were the first Near Eastern power to impose taxation in this form. They minted gold and silver coins, an innovation they took over from the Lydians. The Persian kings also constructed an elaborate network of roads, roadhouses and checkpoints to communicate with their far-flung possessions. The fastest couriers might take only a week to travel the "Royal Road" from Susa to Sardis, the former Lydian capital, a journey of 1,600 mi/2,575 km.

Tombs and palaces

The Shiraz region of Iran contains many visible reminders of the Achaemenids' power. The original capital was at Pasargadae. Although little remains of the buildings erected by Cyrus, his tomb – a simple stone crypt raised on a stepped plinth – is impressive. Darius founded a new capital at Persepolis, which was completed by his successors Xerxes and Artaxerxes (see box). He also constructed the first of the royal tombs cut into the cliff-face at Naqsh-i Rustam near Persepolis. The entrances were carved with columned facades with reliefs and inscriptions. Darius is portrayed on his worshipping at a fire-altar; he is standing

RIGHT The empire created by the Achaemenid dynasty of Persia was the largest in the ancient world. Its rulers developed new strategies for organizing and administering such large territories, providing a model for later empires of the Near East.

BELOW A frieze of polychrome glazed brick, which has been molded with reliefs depicting archers from the Persian royal guard. From the palace of Darius at Susa, c.500 BCE.

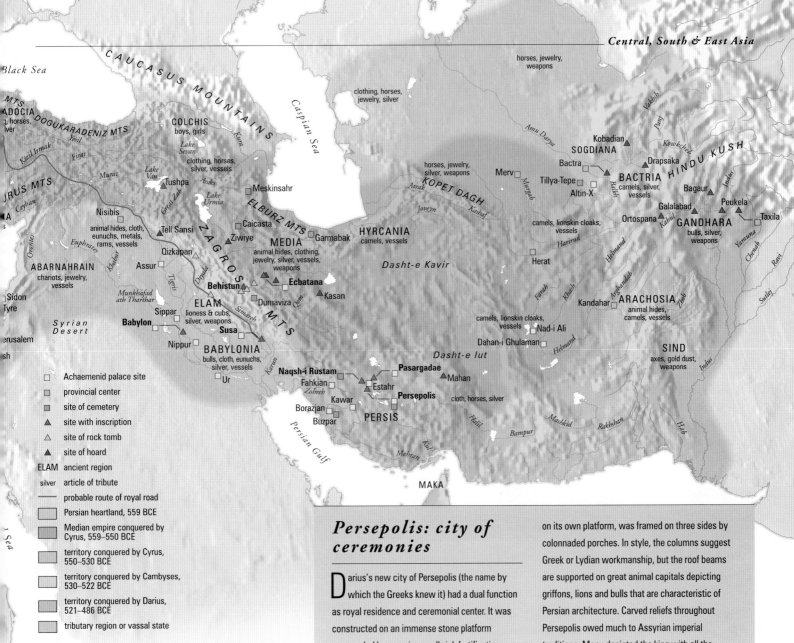

Black Sea

CAUCASUS MOUNTAINS

Caspian Sea

horses, jewelry,
weapons

clothing, horses,
jewelry, silver

DOGUKARADENIZ MTS

COLCHIS
boys, girls

Lake
Sevan

clothing, horses,
silver, vessels

Kobadian

SOGDIANA

Drapsaka

Kowkcheh

HINDU KUSH

Bactra

BACTRIA

Lake
Van

Murat

Lake
Urmia

ELBURZ MTS

horses, jewelry,
silver, weapons

KOPET DAGH

Merv

Tillya-Tepe
Altin-X

camels, silver,
vessels

Bagaur

Peukela

Meskinsahr

Tushpa

Nisibis

animal hides, cloth,
eunuchs, metals,
rams, vessels

Tell Sansi

Caicasta

Ziwiye

MEDIA

Garmabak

HYRCANIA
camels, vessels

Dasht-e Kavir

Herat

camels, lionskin cloaks,
vessels

Galalabad

Ortospana

GANDHARA

bulls, silver,
weapons

Taxila

Euphrates

Qizkapan

Assur

animal hides, clothing,
jewelry, silver, vessels,
weapons

Ecbatana

ARACHOSIA
animal hides,
camels, vessels

ABARNAHRAIN
chariots, jewelry,
vessels

Behistun

Kasan

Kandahar

Sidon
Tyre

Munkhafad
ath Tharthar

ELAM
lioness & cubs,
silver, weapons

Dumaviza

camels, lionskin cloaks,
vessels

Nad-i Ali

Syrian
Desert

Sippar

Babylon

Susa

Dahan-i Ghulaman

SIND
axes, gold dust,
weapons

Nippur

BABYLONIA
bulls, cloth, eunuchs,
silver, vessels

Dasht-e lut

Ur

Naqsh-i Rustam

Pasargadae

Mahan

Fahkian

Estahr

Persepolis

cloth, horses, silver

Borazjan

Kawar

Buzpar

PERSIS

Persian Gulf

MAKA

Legend:

- ☐ Achaemenid palace site
- ☐ provincial center
- ☐ site of cemetery
- ▲ site with inscription
- △ site of rock tomb
- ▲ site of hoard
- ELAM ancient region
- silver article of tribute
- — probable route of royal road
- Persian heartland, 559 BCE
- Median empire conquered by Cyrus, 559–550 BCE
- territory conquered by Cyrus, 550–530 BCE
- territory conquered by Cambyses, 530–522 BCE
- territory conquered by Darius, 521–486 BCE
- tributary region or vassal state

upon a dais supported by figures representing the different peoples of the empire. At Behistun, a sacred spot in a pass through the Zagros mountains, a carved relief shows Darius receiving his defeated enemies after a civil war: the long trilingual inscription (in Old Persian, Akkadian, and Elamite) played a key role in the decipherment of cuneiform writing.

The Achaemenid kings displayed their power in large-scale building outside the Persian homeland. A second imperial capital was created at the Elamite city of Susa, with new palatial construction on a commensurate scale, and a palace was also maintained at Babylon, which remained an important imperial center. To create their grandiose monuments, the Achaemenids imported building materials, precious stones, gold, silver and ivory from all over the empire and summoned a multinational force of laborers and craftsmen: brickmakers from Babylonia, stonecarvers from Ionia and Lydia, wood and metalworkers from Egypt. So successful was the artistic representation of their power that rulers in neighboring regions and in later times copied many aspects of this new tradition ◆

Persepolis: city of ceremonies

Darius's new city of Persepolis (the name by which the Greeks knew it) had a dual function as royal residence and ceremonial center. It was constructed on an immense stone platform surrounded by massive mudbrick fortifications, the latter long since crumbled away. On the platform stood vast colonnaded halls and pavilions, ceremonial gates and stairways, storerooms and stables, together with Darius's palace, the Apadana or "Audience Hall". This large pillared hall, standing on its own platform, was framed on three sides by colonnaded porches. In style, the columns suggest Greek or Lydian workmanship, but the roof beams are supported on great animal capitals depicting griffons, lions and bulls that are characteristic of Persian architecture. Carved reliefs throughout Persepolis owed much to Assyrian imperial traditions. Many depicted the king with all the symbols and trappings of royal power, while the stairs that led up to the Apadana were decorated with tall carved figures of Persian soldiers and nobles, and of the different subject peoples of the empire bearing tribute and gifts ◆

ABOVE THE APADANA, SHOWING SEVERAL OF THE RESTORED COLUMNS IN THEIR ORIGINAL POSITION.

131

The Greeks in Asia

According to traditional western accounts, Alexander the Great's conquest of the Persian empire (see pages 98–99) resulted in the successful transplantation of Hellenistic culture across western Asia and into parts of northwestern India, a cultural triumph of west over east that left an enduring legacy. But the Greek (or Macedonian) experience in Asia was far more complex than this view suggests. It is true that Alexander and his successors settled veteran soldiers on lands across their new possessions from Syria to Afghanistan. In architectural style and layout, the cities and garrisons they founded or rebuilt bore the strong imprint of Greek ideas, and Greek material culture was widespread. But excavation of some of the widely scattered Hellenistic sites of western Asia indicates that in many of these settlements large local populations lived side by side with the new colonists. While outward observance was given to Greek practices, these populations continued to follow their own culture and customs, and the way of life of those of Greek origin often took on a strong local coloring.

Alexander won his vast empire from the Persians through unparalleled military genius: that he was able to hold on to it owed much to the administrative machinery created by the Achaemenid emperors. The long traditions of imperial rule in the Near East had weakened local identities and loyalties, and the provinces of the Persian empire were used to foreign rule. As Alexander respected local customs and did not make unreasonable demands for tribute, there was little popular opposition to his rule. The breakup of his empire was caused by the dynastic wars of his successors rather than internal rebellion.

Greek cities in Asia

Alexander founded cities (originally as colonies for veteran Macedonian soldiers) throughout his territories, a policy continued by the Seleucid kings who succeeded to his Asian provinces. Existing cities were enlarged. Occupation has continued to the present day at many of the Hellenistic cities of Turkey and the eastern Mediterranean, and visible traces of their early origins are few. Farther east, most Hellenistic foundations, including such famous centers as Seleucia-on-the-Tigris, have vanished in the course of time. It has

BELOW The Seleucid dynasty emerged as rulers of Alexander's vast possessions in Asia after the wars that followed his death in 323 BCE. The eastern frontier was not held for long: Gandhara and Arachosia in the Indus valley had been lost to the Mauryan rulers of the Ganges by 304, and Bactria soon broke away under the rule of independent Greek dynasts. In the mid 2nd century the Parthians began to expand west from their homeland in northeastern Iran and had replaced Seleucid rule in Babylonia by 130 BCE. The Romans, the recent conquerors of Greece and now the dominant power in the eastern Mediterranean, prevented their further advance by establishing a new east–west frontier in Syria. In the far east, the Bactrian Greek kingdoms and the Parthians were overthrown by fresh waves of nomadic invaders: the Sakas (1st century BCE) and the Kushans (1st century CE).

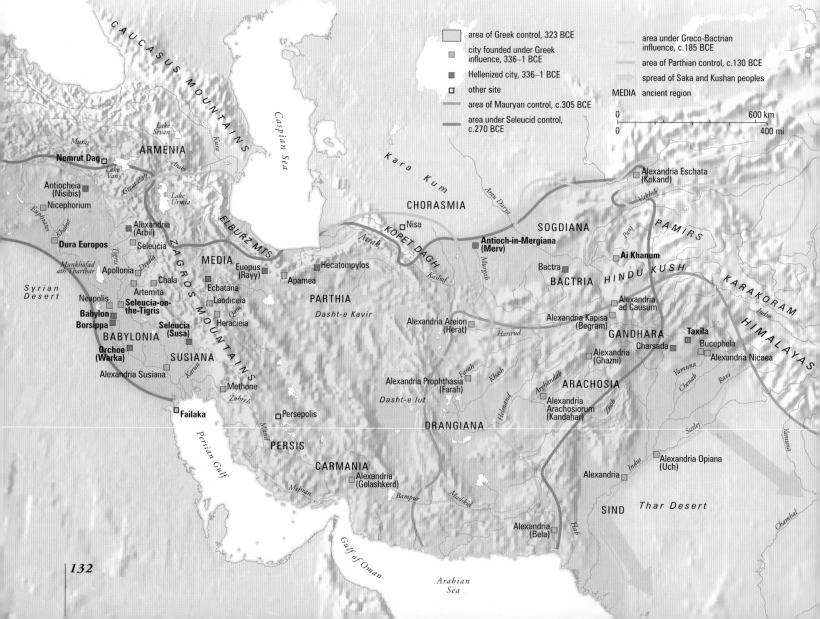

□ area of Greek control, 323 BCE
■ city founded under Greek influence, 336–1 BCE
■ Hellenized city, 336–1 BCE
□ other site
— area of Mauryan control, c.305 BCE
— area under Seleucid control, c.270 BCE

— area under Greco-Bactrian influence, c.185 BCE
— area of Parthian control, c.130 BCE
— spread of Saka and Kushan peoples
MEDIA ancient region

0 ———— 600 km
0 ———— 400 mi

palace at Susa, for example, was built in earlier Persian style. Seleucia-on-the-Tigris, a Greek foundation, may have contained a ziggurat. Hellenistic building projects in many places display influences from several traditions at once. Ai Khanum, one of the most remote outposts of Hellenistic culture, contains a mix of local Bactrian, Mesopotamian and Achaemenid Persian influences in the design and details of its buildings.

In Mesopotamia, parents with Babylonian names appear to have given their offspring Greek names in the hope of social and political advancement. People on the periphery of the Hellenistic world imitated Greek symbols of authority as an expression of their own ambitions: petty rulers along the Arabian coast of the Persian Gulf, for example, issued silver money resembling Hellenistic coins. In the 1st century CE the Nabataeans of Transjordan built extravagant rock tombs to designs that borrowed wholesale from the Mediterranean world. Greek contacts with northwest India led to the emergence of the Gandharan style of Buddhist art and architecture at places like Taxila, which Bactrian Greeks controlled for a time.

The Greek component thus was but a single element in the multicultural societies of western Asia. Nowhere better exemplifies this than Dura Europos. The city, which passed into Roman and then Parthian control in the 1st century BCE, contained Greek, Roman and Syrian temples, a synagogue, a church, and a shrine to Mithras. Official documents were written in Greek, Latin, Aramaic and other languages ◆

taken archaeological investigation to restore some of these sites to view, including Dura Europos on the Euphrates, the garrison sanctuaries of Failaka off the coast of Kuwait, Ai Khanum in Afghanistan, and Antioch-in-Mergiana (Turkmenistan). Most were laid out like Greek cities on a regular grid pattern of streets (called the "Hippodamian plan") with an agora (marketplace), gymnasia, theaters, temples and other architectural expressions of the Greek way of life.

Greek architecture also appeared in many long-established cities, for example at Babylon and other Mesopotamian sites. However, the great majority of people continued to live in traditional houses, use local pottery and other goods, worship familiar gods, and speak their parental language. Excavations at Susa and elsewhere have revealed Greek-style houses next door to traditional Mesopotamian dwellings. All across western Asia traditional pottery and other materials of daily life are found in juxtaposition with Greek influences and products.

Mix of cultures

The Hellenistic ruling elites appear to have accepted and even encouraged local customs, if only for reasons of political expediency. In Mesopotamia, they financed the rebuilding of the traditional temples at Babylon, Borsippa and Warka, subsidized the cults associated with them, and kept records in cuneiform. Even official secular architecture intended for the use of the ruling elite sometimes took on a local flavor; a Hellenistic-period

ABOVE Commagene, in the Taurus mountains of central Turkey, broke away from the decaying Seleucid empire about 162 BCE. It enjoyed a brief period of power during the reign of Antiochus I (c.69–c.34 CE), whose megalomaniacal tendencies led him to construct a splendid mausoleum to his own memory, together with a complex of temples, on the high summit of Nemrut Dag not far from Lake Van. These giant heads, formerly belonging to the immense statues of seated gods, portray both Greek and Persian deities.

ABOVE AND LEFT Bactrian coinage issues of the 3rd–1st centuries BCE reflect both the implantation of Greek practices and standards in Central Asia, and the local flavoring accreted to this Mediterranean tradition in its new locale.

Empires on the Silk Route

Between China and Iran lies an inhospitable region of deserts, mountains and high plateaus. The Silk Route, the ancient caravan route that traversed this forbidding landscape, was the fragile thread that connected the worlds of east and west. All kinds of valuable merchandise were carried along this road: not only the Chinese silk for which it is named, but also gems, pearls, ivory, perfumes, spices, finished goods of gold and silver, even slaves and horses. Oasis settlements had grown up along the most arduous stretch – the desert wastes of Xinjiang – by the Bronze Age or even earlier, and the discovery of 4,000-year-old silk in northern Bactria (Afghanistan) shows that even at this early date goods were being transported west from China. Over time, the Silk Route was the source of wealth for numerous cities, kingdoms and empires. Wall-paintings and sculptures from ancient settlements such as Afrasiab (Samarkand), Bukhara, Penjikent, Kashgar, Kucha and Turfan are evidence of the rich mix of cultures that met and interacted with each other on the Silk Route, and of the traffic in ideas and beliefs – including Buddhism and Christianity – passing along it.

Around 2,000 years ago trade along the Silk Route developed into a truly major enterprise as the empires and kingdoms of China, India, and the Mediterranean acquired a taste for imported luxuries. Warlike nomadic pastoralists from eastern Central Asia, attracted by this growing commerce, began to move west, sometimes just to raid and plunder, sometimes to found empires of their own. In the 2nd century BCE, the Sakas took control of trading towns like Khotan and then overran Greek Bactria, eastern Iran and northern India. Hard on their heels came a fearsome people whom the Chinese annals call the "Yueh-chih". The Kushans were one branch of these people. In the 1st century CE they established a sprawling empire along the Silk Route and into northern India (see box).

ABOVE At Bezeklik, in the foothills of the Tien Shan mountains near Turfan, Buddhist temples have been carved into the cliff-face above an oasis on the Silk Route. Few merchants traveled the entire length of the route, moving instead for short stages between market centers where middle-men exacted large sums of money for their services. Oasis settlements watered by the mountain rainfall provided overnight shelter for the camel caravans that carried silk and other luxury items from China to the west.

Begram: a Kushan treasure-house

Archaeologists in the 1930s, excavating the site of a royal palace at Begram dating to the early centuries of the 1st millennium CE, discovered treasury rooms that were brimming with exotic items: Chinese lacquers, Indian ivories, Roman glass and bronzes – eloquent testimony to the far-reaching nature of trans-Asian trade and to the wealth accumulated by the Kushans from their control of the traffic passing along the Silk Route. Begram (ancient Kapisa) is about 50 mi/80 km north of modern Kabul in the Hindu Kush range of Afghanistan. Sited on a pass through the mountains that connected the Silk Route with routes from India, it may have been established as a colony of Achaemenid Persia; in the 2nd century BCE Bactrian Greeks laid out a Hellenistic city here. However, Begram reached its greatest prosperity in the 1st and 2nd centuries CE when the

Kushans made it an important center of power. They built other imperial centers, for example at Surkh Kotal, and invested considerable resources in irrigation projects to feed the populations of the Bactrian cities and other places within their empire. The Kushans appear to have encouraged Buddhism, perhaps as part of a commercial policy to increase the flow of trade along the caravan routes. The famous monastery at Bamiyan, with its colossal images of the Buddha carved into the rock and wall paintings in a style that combines Indian and Iranian elements, shows the impact of Buddhism at this period. Wall paintings and sculpture at Khalchayan in northern Bactria likewise provide examples of Kushan patronage. Tragically, many of Afghanistan's archaeological sites, including the Begram treasure housed in the museum at Kabul, have been damaged or destroyed in recent fighting ◆

LEFT A PAINTED GLASS VASE MADE IN ALEXANDRIA, EGYPT, FOUND IN THE TREASURY AT BEGRAM, 4 IN/10 CM HIGH.

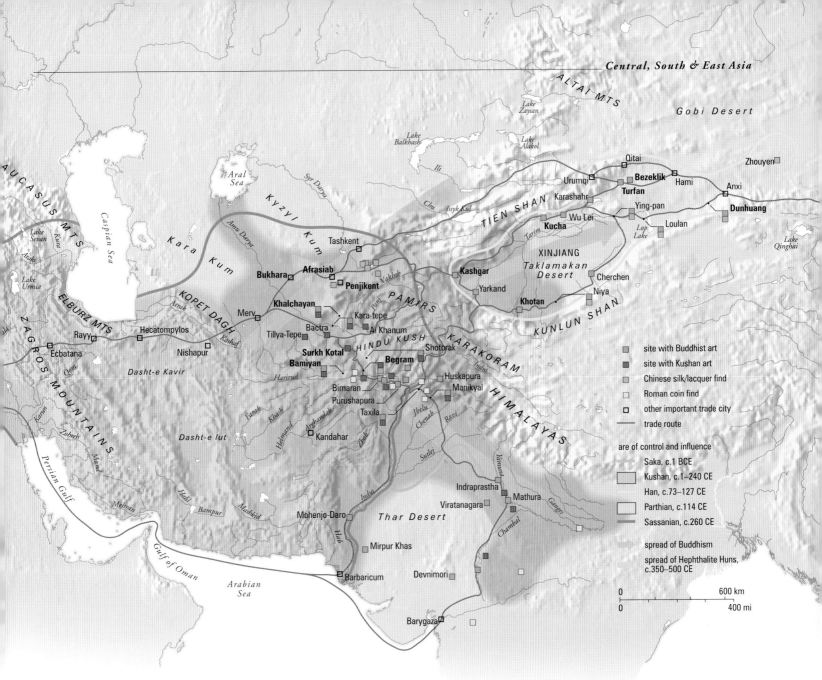

Map labels: ALTAI MTS, Gobi Desert, Lake Zaysan, Lake Alakol, Lake Balkhash, Qitai, Zhouyen, Urumqi, **Bezeklik**, Hami, Anxi, Karashahr, **Turfan**, **Dunhuang**, Ying-pan, TIEN SHAN, Wu Lei, Lop Lake, Loulan, Aral Sea, Syr Darya, Ili, Issyk Kul, Chu, Tarim, **Kucha**, Lake Qinghai, Caspian Sea, KYZYL KUM, Tashkent, XINJIANG, Taklamakan Desert, Cherchen, Niya, Kara Kum, Amu Darya, **Bukhara**, **Afrasiab**, **Penjikent**, Vakhsh, **Kashgar**, Yarkand, **Khotan**, KOPET DAGH, **Khalchayan**, Pamir, PAMIRS, ELBURZ MTS, Arak, Merv, Bactra, Kara-tepe, Ai Khanum, Kashaf, HINDU KUSH, KARAKORAM, KUNLUN SHAN, Lake Sevan, Lake Urmia, CAUCASUS MTS, Kura, Araks, Rayy, Hecatompylos, Tillya-Tepe, **Surkh Kotal**, Shotorak, Indus, HIMALAYAS, Ecbatana, Nishapur, **Bamiyan**, **Begram**, Huskapura, Qom, Zohreh, Dasht-e Kavir, Harirud, Bimaran, Manikyal, Purushapura, Ibelu, Chenab, Ravi, Karun, ZAGROS MOUNTAINS, Farah, Khash, Arghandab, Taxila, Zhab, Mand, Dasht-e lut, Helmand, Kandahar, Sutlej, Mehran, Hadh, Bampur, Mashkid, Mohenjo-Daro, Thar Desert, Indraprastha, Mathura, Ganges, Yamuna, Persian Gulf, Viratanagara, Chambal, Gulf of Oman, Arabian Sea, Hab, Barbaricum, Mirpur Khas, Devnimori, Barygaza

Legend:
- ◼ site with Buddhist art
- ◼ site with Kushan art
- ◻ Chinese silk/lacquer find
- ◻ Roman coin find
- ◻ other important trade city
- — trade route

area of control and influence
- Saka, c.1 BCE
- Kushan, c.1–240 CE
- Han, c.73–127 CE
- Parthian, c.114 CE
- Sassanian, c.260 CE

spread of Buddhism
spread of Hephthalite Huns, c.350–500 CE

0 ____ 600 km
0 ____ 400 mi

The Kushan empire was destroyed in the 3rd century by Sassanian Persia. Two centuries later, however, the Hephthalite Huns repeated the pattern of invasion from the east to overrun Bactria and Sogdiana in eastern Iran; at roughly the same period the western Huns were ravaging Europe. Another group whom the Chinese sources call the "Jouan-Jouan" controlled the oasis towns of Xinjiang at about the same time. The Sassanians regained Sogdiana from the Hephthalites in the 6th century but were themselves swept from power by the eastward advance of Muslim armies a century and a half later.

A rich mix of influences

The changing political landscape of Central Asia did little to stem the growing volume of trade along the Silk Route between the time of Alexander the Great and the arrival of Islam. Lively commerce and cultural exchange laid the foundations of a cosmopolitan civilization that combined Indian, Chinese and Iranian elements. Buddhism, traveling out of India, provided the merchant communities of the Silk Route with an ethical code that was appropriate to their way of life. Khotan, Kucha and Dunhuang became centers of Buddhist learning, where sacred texts were translated into many local tongues, including Khotanese, Kuchean and Uighur. The arid environment of the Taklamakan desert has preserved many beautiful Buddhist reliquaries, ornate silks, painted wooden panels and other fragile objects. Nestorian Christians (a Syrian sect that migrated east after being condemned for heresy) and Manichaeans (a religious movement that flourished in 3rd-century Persia) likewise traveled along the Silk Route: their sacred texts have also been preserved by the desert conditions.

Farther west, a similar multicultural environment developed in Sogdiana. Excavations at Afrasiab and Penjikent have uncovered houses decorated with beautiful wall paintings that are remarkably similar to those at Dunhuang and Turfan, though without the presence of Buddhist themes. Many of the old Silk Route cultures, including that of Sogdiana, were soon submerged by the pervasive spread of Persian influences encouraged by Islam ◆

ABOVE The Silk Route (in reality a series of ancient routes) followed a course westward from China through Xinjiang (Chinese Turkestan). It was here that the most perilous part of the journey lay. Travelers had to pass either side of the Taklamakan desert, an arid wasteland of sand some 600 mi/ 1,000 km long and 250 mi/ 400 km wide. The routes then met again at Kashgar, the great market town of the Silk Route, situated before a low pass through the Pamirs. Once across the mountains, traders could choose to take their merchandise west across Iran to the Mediterranean coast, north through Samarkand toward Russia and the Caspian Sea, or south into India.

AFRICA

CURIOSITY ABOUT THOSE who came before them inspired a remarkable heritage of African legends, beliefs and oral traditions about origins, ancestors and relics of the past. But archaeology in Africa began in earnest only after Napoleon's invasion of Egypt in 1798. His army included a small body of scholars who were ordered to record all the country's ancient monuments. The first serious attempts to unravel the buried history of sub-Saharan Africa waited still longer, until the end of the 19th century.

The individual who first brought the archaeological treasures of Egypt to the attention of the European public was Baron Vivant Denon, who accompanied Napoleon's ill-fated expedition to the Nile. His published sketches of the pyramids and other monuments inspired an enthusiasm for all things Egyptian that endures to this day. Egyptology, the study of ancient Egypt, was born in 1822 when Jean-François Champollion (1790–1832) successfully deciphered hieroglyphics with the help of the trilingual inscriptions on the Rosetta Stone, a basalt slab unearthed by the French in 1799.

As the fascination with ancient Egypt grew, the museums of Europe and North America began to fill with Egyptian antiquities that were either looted or at best collected in an unsystematic manner. The first attempt to regulate archaeological activities was the establishment of a national antiquities service and museum, the Cairo Museum, by Auguste Mariette (1821–81) in 1863. Even today, many African countries either lack laws regulating antiquities or, where they exist, they are inadequate or difficult to enforce.

Egyptology in its early years focused on large monuments, cemeteries and inscriptions of the pharaohs rather than the life and times of ordinary people. While the gold treasures and mummified remains of pharaohs and the upper classes continued to be found and reported with worldwide interest, Egyptologists later turned their attention to studying the origins of ancient Egypt, as well as describing the society and economy of all classes who constituted the fabric of this remarkable African civilization. Today, a huge investment is being made to preserve for future generations antiquities such as the sphinx and Great Pyramid at Giza, threatened by pollution and pressure from tourism.

South of the Sahara

Serious archaeology began in sub-Saharan Africa almost a century later than in Egypt, during the time of British and French empire-building towards the end of the 19th century. Its first practitioners were European settlers and visitors, whose interpretations mirrored prejudices grounded in their political, economic and social agendas. Many regarded the then non-industrialized African societies they encountered as "primitive" and "savage", if not actually "prehistoric". Examples of monumental architecture, such as the ruins at Great Zimbabwe, the capital of a vast Shona empire at its height in the 14th century CE, were dismissed as the work of non-African immigrants or, at best, the result of the diffusion of ideas from ancient Egypt, seen as the source of any African achievement. Astonishingly, despite decades of systematic archaeological research unequivocally demonstrating the medieval date and African origin of Great Zimbabwe, works describing the "mystery" and supposed extra-African origin of this indigenous state are still being published.

The first professional archaeologists to work in Africa almost invariably trained at European universities. They were interested mainly in the Stone Age and in establishing sequences of stone artifact industries that could be compared with those in Europe, regarded at this time as the source from which technology diffused. One of the first to appreciate the need for a local terminology was John Goodwin, the first professional archaeologist to be appointed in southern Africa. The classification of the southern African Stone Age into the Earlier, Middle and Later Stone Age, which he drew up with C. "Peter" van Riet Lowe, a civil engineer, in 1929, still forms the basis of Stone Age archaeology in much of sub-Saharan Africa.

Regional Timeline

c.1 m.y.a. *Homo erectus* present in Asia

c.2.5 m.y.a. First stone tools are being made

c.1.4 m y.a. Large (Acheulean) handaxes come into use

c.100,000 y.a. Emergence of modern *Homo* in Africa

c.7–6 m.y.a. Hominid line splits from ape line

c.2.3 m.y.a. First known *Homo* species present in Africa

c.28,000 y.a. Earliest dated rock art (Namibia)

5 m.y.a.

100,000 y.a.

LEFT The gold funerary mask of Tutankhamun. The discovery by Howard Carter of his treasure-filled tomb in 1922 was perhaps the greatest moment in Egyptian archaeology.

Fossils and feuds

Raymond Dart's pioneering research in the 1920s was the first to demonstrate the presence of early hominids in southern Africa, but his findings were widely ignored for several decades and few people would have accepted the idea of Africa as the "cradle of mankind" before Louis and Mary Leakey's headline-making discovery of an early australopithecine fossil in East Africa in 1959. Since then fossils like Lucy, the 3.18 million-year-old partial skeleton of an australopithecine discovered in Ethiopia by Donald Johanson and Tom Gray in 1974, have become celebrities all over the world. The discovery, also in Ethiopia, of a 4.4 million-year-old upright-walking creature by a team led by Tim White in 1994 firmly established Africa as the continent where humans and their immediate ancestors first evolved. Paleoanthropology, the study of early humans and their ancestors, has now developed into a very competitive and widely reported field in which personalities, rivalries and lively debates about interpretation sometimes outnumber the available specimens.

African archaeology today

The rise of African nationalism and the coming to independence of African states during the second half of the 20th century has led to the gradual training of Africans as archaeologists and to the placing of more emphasis on the archaeology of the recent past. Archaeological explanations take account of local African factors rather than looking for answers outside the continent. Since the 1960s, a great deal of research has concentrated on the last three millennia, especially on the origins of indigenous West African cities and states and on the migrations of Bantu-speaking black farmers from central Africa, responsible for taking iron and agriculture to many areas of the central and eastern sub-continent. In some places, particularly in South Africa, work is even being done on the historical archaeology of the impact of colonialism.

ABOVE The footsteps of *Australopithecus afarensis,* fossilized after walking upright through volcanic ash nearly 3.7 million years ago and discovered at Laetoli in 1978.

Only a few African countries, however, have the institutional facilities for active research programs, which many regard as a luxury on a continent plagued by poverty, famine and war, and most current archaeological and paleoanthropological work is funded from outside the continent. There is, however, a pressing need to inform a wide, often illiterate public about their heritage if Africa's unique past is to be protected and preserved in the face of rapid population growth, environmental destruction and increasing urbanization ◆

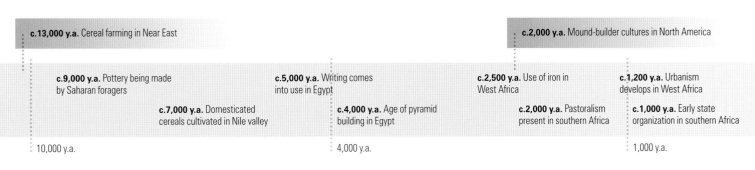

c.13,000 y.a. Cereal farming in Near East

c.2,000 y.a. Mound-builder cultures in North America

c.9,000 y.a. Pottery being made by Saharan foragers

c.5,000 y.a. Writing comes into use in Egypt

c.2,500 y.a. Use of iron in West Africa

c.1,200 y.a. Urbanism develops in West Africa

c.7,000 y.a. Domesticated cereals cultivated in Nile valley

c.4,000 y.a. Age of pyramid building in Egypt

c.2,000 y.a. Pastoralism present in southern Africa

c.1,000 y.a. Early state organization in southern Africa

10,000 y.a.　　　　4,000 y.a.　　　　1,000 y.a.

Hunters and Herders

Until cattle pastoralism began to spread into north Africa between 10,000 and 7,000 y.a., the inhabitants of Africa obtained their food by hunting birds, mammals and insects, fishing, and gathering edible wild plants. Their predominant tools were microliths, tiny worked flakes that were fitted onto wooden or bone handles, or used as spear or arrowheads, which came into use between about 40,000 and 20,000 years ago during the Late Stone Age. Other tools were used for specialized tasks, such as engraving designs on bone and shell. A few communities such as the Bushmen, or San, of the Kalahari desert in southern Africa continued to pursue a hunting and gathering existence well into modern times. Although none of them lived in complete isolation from outside influences, some preserved aspects of their millennia-old way of life. Cautious use of their records can help archaeologists in the task of interpreting the material remains of Africa's last Stone Age.

Although archaeologists categorize the Late Stone Age by reference to its tool technologies, the archaeological evidence is much greater than this suggests: artifacts made from perishable organic materials such as wood, leather and bone, as well as plant food remains (seeds and husks) and even bedding made from leaves and other plant materials, survive from the Late Stone Age, and radiocarbon dating makes it easier to pinpoint developments. Between 7,000 and 2,000 y.a., pottery was coming into use, and in later times iron and glass artifacts are also found in association with stone tool collections.

The staple diet was probably provided by plant foods, although Late Stone Age people ate a wide variety of hunted game as well. They were effective hunters whose equipment possibly by 14,000 y.a included the bow and arrow as well as the use of poison. Their hunting ability may have contributed to the extinction of a number of animals, such as the giant Cape horse, between 12,000 and 8,000 y.a.

Small groups of nomadic hunter–gatherers may have come together at certain times to cement social ties and obligations by exchanging gifts such as necklaces and headbands made of ostrich eggshell beads. The dead were buried, sometimes with similar articles or with stone tools; the graves were sometimes covered with painted stones, grindstones or cobbles.

A remarkable art tradition

These Stone Age hunters also painted and engraved on rocks and rock-faces. Rockshelters in southern and eastern Africa contain particularly rich collections of paintings, including depictions of animals, humans, combinations of animals and humans – known as therianthropes – handprints, geometric designs, and historical scenes.

The oldest known rock paintings in Africa are found on small fragmentary slabs from the Apollo 11 Cave in southern Namibia. These have been dated to between 27,000–19,000 y.a. As late as the 19th century hunter–gatherers in the area were painting historical scenes on rocks (datable from the inclusion of uniformed British soldiers), making this one of the longest and richest traditions of rock art anywhere in the world. Some anthropologists have suggested that much rock art in southern Africa is associated with the hallucinatory experiences of shamans during healing rituals: several painted scenes appear to show shamans entering a trance. Others argue that such scenes may be mythological in character.

RIGHT Late Stone Age tool technology changed over the passage of time, and distinct regional traditions were established. Tiny microliths belonging to the early Late Stone Age were widespread in south, central and east Africa from before 18,000 y.a. Large, side-struck flakes typified the tool collections of 12,000–8,000 y.a. in southern Africa, to be succeeded by fully developed microlithic industries. Pastoralism was well established in North Africa by 4000 BCE but was prevented from spreading by tsetse flies, which are woodland-dwelling and fatal to domestic cattle. The tsetse belt began to retreat south about 2,500 BCE as the Sahara became drier.

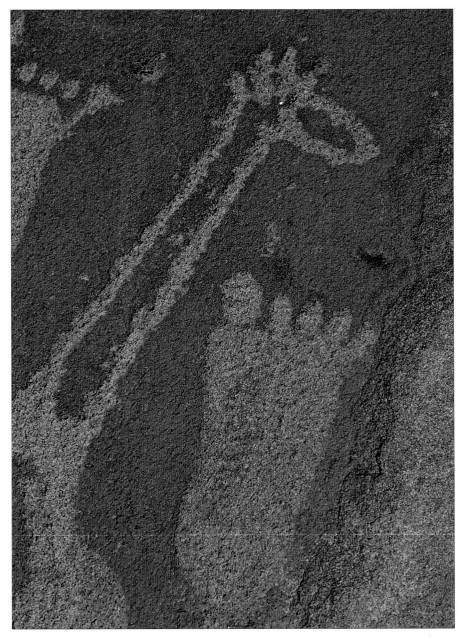

ABOVE Petroglyph of a giraffe and human foot from Twyfelfontein, Namibia.

Rock art is found all over Africa. Some of the most striking examples are paintings of wild and domestic animals as well as horse-drawn chariots found in the massifs of the central and western Sahara.

The spread of pastoralism

None of the economically important domestic animals of modern Africa was derived from indigenous African species, but were introduced to the continent from Asia. The earliest bone remains of domestic animals, dating to about 7000 BCE, come from sites in the Western desert of Egypt, wetter then than it is today. Herding societies do not begin to appear in east Africa until 2000 BCE. It was Iron Age farmers who introduced cattle and other domestic animals to central and eastern southern Africa little more than 2000 years ago (see pages 150–151).

By about 2000 y.a. the Khoekhoen (Khoikhoi), pottery-using Stone Age people living on the fringes of the Kalahari in western southern Africa, were herding domestic sheep, and later cattle and goats. Some anthropologists believe that domestic animals were brought into the region by incoming peoples rather than being adopted by hunter-gatherers already living there. The herding way of life, which regards animals as a form of personal wealth rather than an instant source of food, involves a different set of social values from those of hunter–gatherers. Research is still being carried out to establish whether this is the case, and if so what routes were followed by the groups migrating into the area.

Early European travelers to southern Africa have left descriptions of the large mobile camps of the Khoekhoen, which often contained 500 or more people. Their houses were made from a framework of poles covered with reed mats, which could be rolled up and carried on the backs of oxen when the group moved to new pastures. But there is no means of telling if such societies had developed comparatively recently or continued from the distant past ◆

selected Late Stone Age site

☐ 40,000–19,000 y.a.
■ 18,000–12,000 y.a.
■ 12,000–8000 y.a.
☐ post 8000 y.a.

selected Stone Age site with evidence of domestic animals

△ c.7000–3000 BCE
▲ c.3000 BCE–1000 CE

area of Saharan pastoral societies, 4500–2000 BCE

spread of animal domestication, 4000–2000 BCE

spread of animal domestication, 200 CE

approximate area of tsetse flies today

major rock art area

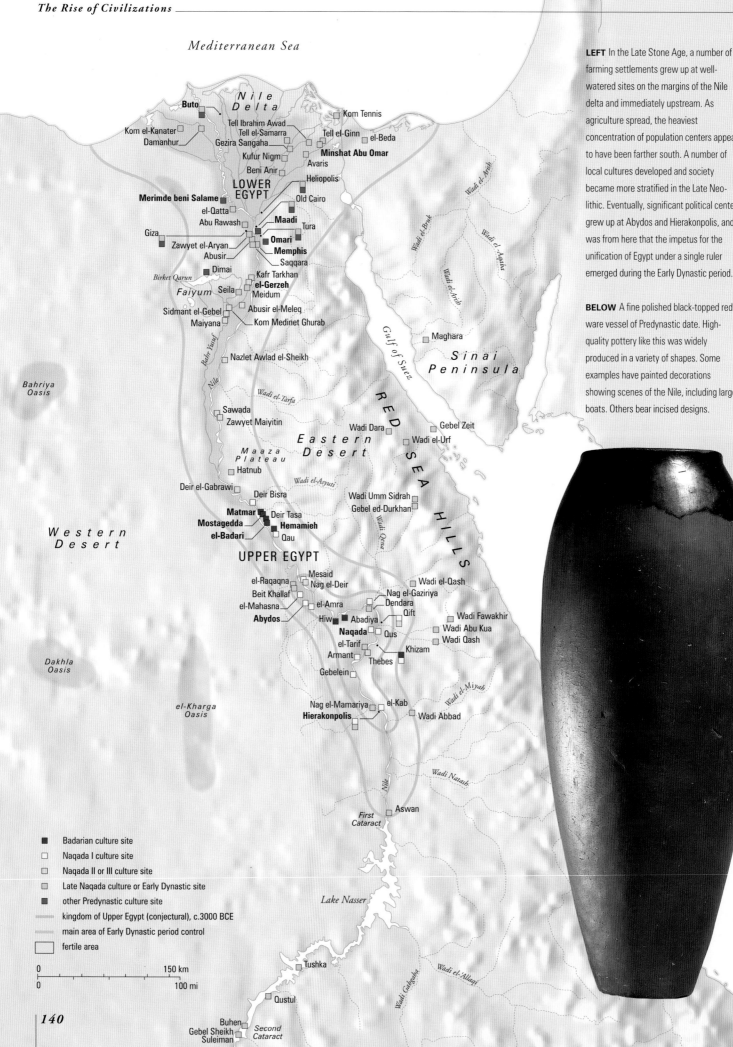

Mediterranean Sea

Nile Delta

Buto

Kom Tennis

Tell Ibrahim Awad
Kom el-Kanater
Tell el-Samarra
Tell el-Ginn
el-Beda
Damanhur
Gezira Sangaha
Kufur Nigm
Minshat Abu Omar
Avaris
Beni Anir
Heliopolis

LOWER EGYPT

Old Cairo
Merimde beni Salame
el-Qatta
Maadi
Abu Rawash
Tura
Giza
Omari
Zawyet el-Aryan
Memphis
Abusir
Saqqara
Dimai
Kafr Tarkhan

Birket Qarun
el-Gerzeh
Faiyum
Seila
Meidum
Sidmant el-Gebel
Abusir el-Meleq
Maiyana
Kom Medinet Ghurab

Bahriya Oasis

Nazlet Awlad el-Sheikh

Sawada
Zawyet Maiyitin

Bahr Yusuf

Nile

Wadi el-Tarfa

Maaza Plateau

Eastern Desert

Hatnub

Deir el-Gabrawi
Deir Bisra
Wadi el-Asyuti

Matmar
Deir Tasa
Wadi Umm Sidrah
Mostagedda
Hemamieh
Gebel ed-Durkhan
el-Badari
Qau

Western Desert

UPPER EGYPT

Mesaid
el-Raqaqna
Nag el-Deir
Wadi el-Qash
Beit Khallaf
Nag el-Gaziriya
el-Mahasna
el-Amra
Dendara
Abydos
Qift
Hiw
Abadiya
Wadi Fawakhir
Naqada
Qus
Wadi Abu Kua
el-Tarif
Wadi Qash
Armant
Thebes
Khizam
Gebelein

Dakhla Oasis

Sinai Peninsula

Maghara

Gebel Zeit
Wadi Dara
Wadi el-Urf

RED SEA HILLS

Gulf of Suez

Wadi el-Bruk
Wadi el-Arish
Wadi el-Agaba

Wadi Qena

Wadi el-Miyab

Nag el-Mamariya
el-Kab
Hierakonpolis
Wadi Abbad

el-Kharga Oasis

Wadi Natash

Nile

First Cataract
Aswan

Lake Nasser

Wadi Gabgaba
Wadi el-Allaqi

Tushka

Qustul

Buhen
Gebel Sheikh
Suleiman
Second Cataract

■ Badarian culture site
□ Naqada I culture site
□ Naqada II or III culture site
□ Late Naqada culture or Early Dynastic site
■ other Predynastic culture site
— kingdom of Upper Egypt (conjectural), c.3000 BCE
— main area of Early Dynastic period control
▭ fertile area

0 ____ 150 km
0 ____ 100 mi

LEFT In the Late Stone Age, a number of farming settlements grew up at well-watered sites on the margins of the Nile delta and immediately upstream. As agriculture spread, the heaviest concentration of population centers appears to have been farther south. A number of local cultures developed and society became more stratified in the Late Neolithic. Eventually, significant political centers grew up at Abydos and Hierakonpolis, and it was from here that the impetus for the unification of Egypt under a single ruler emerged during the Early Dynastic period.

BELOW A fine polished black-topped red ware vessel of Predynastic date. High-quality pottery like this was widely produced in a variety of shapes. Some examples have painted decorations showing scenes of the Nile, including large boats. Others bear incised designs.

Predynastic Egypt

Archaeologists give the name Predynastic to a succession of cultures that occupied the Nile valley in the Neolithic period before Egypt became a politically unified state under a hereditary kingship around 3000 BCE. During the Late Stone Age large herds of giraffe and elephant grazed the grasslands of what is now the Western Desert and hippopotami were plentiful in the Nile valley. Local populations supported themselves by hunting and by harvesting wild grasses, but as climatic change some 7,000 years ago altered the ecology of the region, forager groups began domesticating livestock and turned to settled agriculture. Eventually farming villages and small towns were established throughout the Nile valley.

Merimde beni Salame, on the western edge of the Nile delta, is a transitional early Neolithic site: excavations indicate that the inhabitants practiced a mixed economy of hunting and cultivation. The site was probably abandoned after the local branch of the Nile changed course, leaving the village with no river access and making it unviable as a major settlement. The importance of Merimde is all the greater for its being an isolated case. Predynastic sites are rare in the delta region where wetland conditions make excavation difficult; other early sites may be buried deep beneath layers of silt or lie under water.

Predynastic cultures

The great majority of surviving Predynastic sites are cemeteries on the desert edge in southern Egypt. A number of distinct local cultures have been identified, the earliest of which, Badarian (c.4500–3800 BCE), is named for the type-site of el-Badari in Middle Egypt. Badarian finds are also present at the nearby sites of Hemamieh, Mostagedda and Matmar, and are indicative of a small-scale, village-based culture.

The most important Neolithic cultural sequence is named for the type-site of Naqada and differentiated as Naqada I (also called Amratian), c. 4000–3600 BCE, Naqada II (or Gerzean), c. 3600–3200 BCE, and Naqada III, c. 3200–3050 BCE. Like the Badarian, Naqada I was local in scale, but Naqada II and III provide clear archaeological evidence of developing social and political stratification. Evidence from elite tombs suggests not only that such stratification grew more sophisticated over time, giving rise to local kingdoms, but also that it gradually spread north from the core area of Abydos–Hierakonpolis to the Faiyum, a lakeside oasis that was a center of early settlement, and el-Gerzeh. Some tombs contain objects of Mesopotamian origin, such as cylinder seals. These may have been acquired in exchange for gold from southern Egypt, an early indication of outside contact.

Although Predynastic sites are far fewer in Lower Egypt, there are clear signs of a distinct northern culture named for the type-site of Maadi, just to the south of Cairo. Related finds have been discovered at nearby Omari and at the settlement at ancient Buto (Tell el-Fara'in) on the northwestern edge of the delta, still being excavated. Maadi culture appears to have been less socially differentiated than Naqada.

The unification of Egypt

An important Predynastic cemetery has been found at Minshat Abu Omar in the northeastern delta. The presence of late Naqada artifacts here perhaps lends archaeological support to the view that the people of the delta were absorbed into a single unified state by the kings of southern or Upper Egypt. Corroborating evidence may be found at Hierakonpolis (ancient Nekhen, modern Kom el-Ahmar), which was one of the foremost political centers of Upper Egypt in the late Naqada and Early Dynastic period (c.3000–2650 BCE). Excavation of an early temple at the end of the 19th century uncovered a rich cache of ceremonial objects. Several of the items, which may have been buried at a time of political turmoil, appear to have been presented to the temple by Predynastic kings. An oversized slate palette commemorates king Narmer and shows him subduing his enemies in the north, leading to the suggestion – not capable of proof – that Narmer was the unifier of Upper and Lower Egypt. The Early Dynastic period was clearly a time of important cultural change: writing came into use, Memphis was established as the political capital, and a theocratic cult of kingship developed, which saw its culmination in the Old Kingdom monarchy ◆

ABOVE The Nile valley was a focal point for the development of agriculture in the Predynastic period. Until it broadens out into the delta,the valley is nowhere more than a few miles wide. Rainfall in the area is negligable and without the annual floods farming would have been impossible. The flooding of the Nile usually begins in the late summer, covering most of the valley floor and depositing fresh layers of fertile silts. Then, as now, the main crops were sown in October and November after the water level fell, and harvested in early spring. Cattle were probably grazed on marginal areas of swampy land, especially in the delta.

BELOW A slate palette in the shape of a ram, which would have been used for grinding cosmetics. Such items are among the most common funerary objects from cemeteries, which dominate the archaeological repertoire of the Predynastic period. Large worked flint knives and stone vessels are also widely found, together with quantities of pottery.

Egypt in the Old Kingdom

The Old Kingdom (c.2650–2150 BCE) has left one of the most instantly recognizable of all archaeological legacies, the great pyramids at Giza. The sheer scale and technical achievement of these structures suggest that Old Kingdom Egypt was technologically adept, economically buoyant and, in all likelihood, politically highly centralized. However, there is insufficient archaeological and textual evidence from the Old Kingdom to build up a coherent historical picture of the period. Most archaeological finds are in the form of tombs, both royal and private. Remains from sites other than cemeteries are rare; no substantial settlements have been excavated.

Pyramid building may well have been the defining activity for Old Kingdom Egyptians as it is for us today. From the reign of the 3rd Dynasty King Djoser (c.2630–2611 BCE) to the end of the Old Kingdom, all Egyptian kings were buried in monumental stone structures, most of which took the form of a pyramid. These tombs were built where the plateau of the Western Desert meets the edge of the Nile valley, a little to the west of (and many in sight of) the city of Memphis. Although nothing has been recovered of Memphis itself, the sheer quantity of royal and high-ranking private tombs in these cemeteries is a clear pointer to the city's importance as a center of royal administration.

Pyramid building peaked early. Djoser's step-shaped pyramid at Saqqara (see box) was soon superseded by the "true" pyramid design, and the 4th Dynasty King Snefru (2575–2551) put up at least two, and probably three, pyramids in the cemeteries of Meidum and Dahshur. His son Khufu (Cheops) built the largest of the pyramids (479 ft/146 m high) at Giza. Those of his son Khaefre and grandson Menkaure, also at Giza, are almost as large, but later Old Kingdom pyramids, mostly at Abusir and Saqqara, were smaller and more poorly constructed.

Private tombs

As pyramid construction declined, so the size and opulence of tombs belonging to high-ranking members of the government increased. These squat, rectangular buildings known as mastabas were probably, at least in part, a royal gift to favored courtiers, many of whom were themselves members of the royal family, bestowing on them the honor of lying in state near the king they had served in life.

Unlike the pyramids, the walls of private tombs were lavishly decorated with carved and painted scenes, whose function was to provide, magically, everything that the *ka* (soul) would need for life beyond the grave. Early tombs with limited wall space simply showed food being offered to the tomb's occupant, but as private tombs grew in size their walls were able to display much larger scenes showing the range of activities that the tomb-owner had pursued in daily life and would continue to enjoy for all eternity. Good examples of late Old Kingdom mastabas are those of Ti and Mereruka at Saqqara. They were government officials as well as major landowners, and the scenes on their tomb walls display the agricultural wealth that would sustain their souls in the afterlife.

Most texts on tomb walls consist of prayers and wishes for eternal feeding. Some provide autobiographies of the tomb-owner, usually a formulaic list of his sterling qualities, but others supply valuable archaeological and historical information. For example, the tombs of local officials near Aswan tell us much about Egypt's trading relationship with Nubia ◆

ABOVE DJOSER'S FUNERARY COMPLEX AT SAQQARA WITH THE STEP PYRAMID BEHIND.

Saqqara: burial place of kings

Saqqara, at the desert's edge a little distance from Memphis, was the chief burial place of kings and nobles during the 2nd Dynasty. The site is dominated by Djoser's step-shaped pyramid, 200 ft/60 m tall and the earliest monumental stone structure in the world. It is the most visible part of a complex of buildings including a mortuary temple where regular offerings were made for the benefit of the dead king's *ka*, and stands within an enclosure wall some 5,000 ft/1,600 m long. A unique feature of Djoser's pyramid complex is the *sed*-festival court, where the king had to perform a ritual race to show he possessed the vigor to rule: carved reliefs show Djoser running between markers as part of the ceremony. The cemetery at Saqqara contains some fifteen other Old Kingdom pyramids, many of which had long causeways linking the upper pyramid complex on the desert's edge to a lower valley temple, a standard feature of pyramid-building. Surrounding these pyramids are the associated tombs of nobles. Although these tombs were largely built and decorated as part of the pyramid project as a whole, they were only "occupied" as and when their owners were ready to take up residence ◆

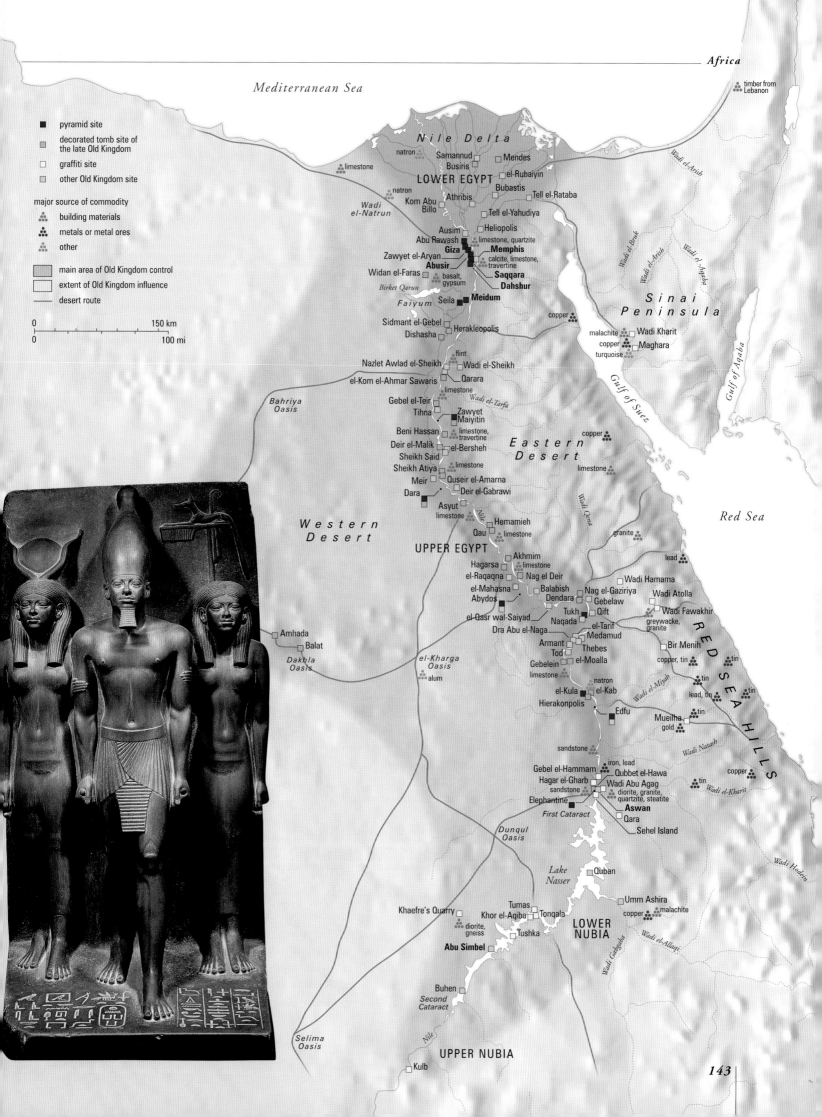

Mediterranean Sea

- ■ pyramid site
- ▪ decorated tomb site of the late Old Kingdom
- □ graffiti site
- ▫ other Old Kingdom site

major source of commodity
- ⋮ building materials
- ⋮ metals or metal ores
- ⋮ other

- main area of Old Kingdom control
- extent of Old Kingdom influence
- desert route

0 ————— 150 km
0 ————— 100 mi

timber from Lebanon

Nile Delta

natron

Samannud · Mendes
Busiris · el-Rubaiyin
LOWER EGYPT
limestone
natron · Tell el-Rataba
Kom Abu Bubastis
Billo · Tell el-Yahudiya
Athribis
Ausim · Heliopolis
Abu Rawash · limestone, quartzite
Giza · **Memphis**
Zawyet el-Aryan · calcite, limestone, travertine
Abusir
Widan el-Faras · **Saqqara**
· basalt, · **Dahshur**
Birket Qarun · gypsum
Faiyum · Seila · **Meidum**

Sidmant el-Gebel · copper
Dishasha · Herakleopolis
· malachite · Wadi Kharit
· copper · Maghara
· turquoise

Wadi el-Natrun

Wadi el-Arish

Wadi el-Bruk

S i n a i   P e n i n s u l a

Gulf of Aqaba

flint
Nazlet Awlad el-Sheikh · Wadi el-Sheikh
el-Kom el-Ahmar Sawaris · Qarara
· limestone
Gebel el-Teir · *Wadi el-Tarfa*
Tihna · Zawyet
· Maiyitin
Beni Hassan · limestone, travertine
Deir el-Malik · el-Bersheh
Sheikh Said
Sheikh Atiya · limestone
Meir · Quseir el-Amarna
Dara · Deir el-Gabrawi
· Asyut
· limestone
Hemamieh
Qau · limestone

Eastern Desert

Western Desert

copper · limestone

Wadi Qena

Red Sea

Bahriya Oasis

UPPER EGYPT
Akhmim
Hagarsa · limestone
el-Raqaqna · Nag el-Deir
el-Mahasna · Balabish
Abydos · Dendara · Nag el-Gaziriya
· Gebelaw
el-Qasr wal-Saiyad · Tukh · Qift
Naqada · el-Tarif
Dra Abu el-Naga · Medamud
Amhada · Thebes
Balat · Armant · Tod · el-Moalla
Gebelein
Dakhla Oasis · limestone
el-Kula · el-Kab
Hierakonpolis
· Edfu
· granite

· lead
Wadi Hamama
Wadi Atolla
greywacke, granite
Wadi Fawakhir
Bir Menih
copper, tin · tin
· tin
lead, tin · tin
Mueilha
gold

el-Kharga Oasis
· alum

RED SEA HILLS

Wadi el-Miyah

Wadi Natash

sandstone
Gebel el-Hammam · iron, lead
Hagar el-Gharb · Qubbet el-Hawa
· Wadi Abu Agag
sandstone · diorite, granite,
Elephantine · quartzite, steatite
First Cataract · **Aswan**
· Qara
· Sehel Island

· copper
· tin

Wadi el-Kharit

Dunqul Oasis

Wadi Hodein

Lake Nasser
· Quban

Tumas · Umm Ashira
Khaefre's Quarry · Khor el-Aqiba · Tongala · copper · malachite
· Tushka · **LOWER NUBIA**
diorite, gneiss
Abu Simbel · *Wadi el-Allaqi*

Wadi Gabgaba

Buhen
Second Cataract

Selima Oasis

Nile

UPPER NUBIA
· Kulb

143

Middle Kingdom Egypt

The Old Kingdom ended in an interval of political fragmentation known as the First Intermediate Period (c. 2150-2040 BCE). Central authority collapsed and Egypt was divided between rival dynasties based at Herakleopolis (modern Ihnasya el-Medina) in the north and Thebes (modern Luxor) in the south. Reunification was achieved by the 11th-Dynasty Theban King Nebhepetre Montuhotep (2061–2010 BCE), whose reign inaugurated the era of continuity and change known as the Middle Kingdom (c.2040-1640 BCE). Royal authority was restored and monumental building resumed throughout Egypt. This period saw Egypt extend its power into Nubia, which had extensive gold deposits, and an impressive line of fortresses was built beyond the Second Cataract.

LEFT The interior of a large rock-cut tomb at Beni Hassan, a substantial Middle Kingdom provincial cemetery. It belonged to a local overlord, Khnumhotep III, and many of the wall-paintings that decorate the tomb depict military scenes.

RIGHT Middle Kingdom rulers left many monumental sites, including pyramid groups in Lower Egypt and temples throughout the country. Perhaps the most striking legacy of their reign is the chain of frontier forts at the Second Cataract of the Nile, built largely under the direction of Senwosret I and Senwosret III. Many of these strongholds were submerged by the formation of Lake Nasser, following completion of the Aswan High Dam in 1970.

BELOW A superb collar of carnelian, feldspar and gold beads, with falcon terminals, from the tomb of a 12th-Dynasty princess at Dahshur, now in the Cairo Museum. Jewelry was worn on practically every part of the body and was part of the funerary equipment of the dead. This style of collar is highly characteristic of the Egyptian jeweler's craft.

Montuhotep, like his predecessors of the 11th Dynasty, was a local prince with a power base at Thebes (Waset to the ancient Egyptians). He was buried at Deir el-Bahri on the West Bank of the Nile opposite Thebes; his splendid colonnaded tomb served as the architectural inspiration for the magnificent neighboring mortuary tomb of queen Hatshepsut, built some 550 years later. Thebes remained the capital city until the reign of Amenemhat, a Theban vizier who became king as the result of a coup in 1991 BCE. Amenemhat transferred the royal capital north to the new city of Itj-Tawy. The location of his capital is uncertain but is thought to lie immediately east of el-Lisht.

Middle Kingdom pyramids

Amenemhat was the first of the powerful 12th Dynasty kings of Egypt. Under their rule, the Old Kingdom practice of pyramid building was revived, with considerable geographical overlap of cemeteries. For example, Dahshur, which stands at the southern end of the major Old Kingdom Memphite pyramid field, is also at the northern end of the Middle Kingdom group that contains the pyramids of Amenemhat II, Senwosret III and Amenemhat III. The Middle Kingdom pyramid builders generally used poorer construction materials and techniques than in the Old Kingdom, but incorporated greater security measures to protect the tomb from grave robbers.

Towns were built to house the workers employed on pyramid construction, as well as the personnel who ensured that the dead king's cult would continue at the site. Most of these towns have disappeared, but the one built by Senwosret II at el-Lahun (Kahun) has survived in good condition and has been excavated. Within a rectangular enclosure, more than 200 small houses are arranged in geometrical rows, providing space for a population of around 9,000. Seven much larger buildings probably served as dwellings for community leaders and contained workshops and storage areas for the use of the community at large. Quantities of administrative papyri and letters were excavated at the site, including building accounts, temple documents, and medical and veterinary works.

Unlike the Old Kingdom, Middle Kingdom pyramid sites no longer have a concentration of high-ranking tombs round the royal pyramid. This appears to be symptomatic of a greater provincialism that characterized the Middle Kingdom period. Important cemeteries containing tombs of both local rulers and officials are widely distributed, indicating that regional power-bases existed throughout the country. Such tombs were often cut into rockfaces overlooking the Nile. Noteworthy cemeteries of this type are to be found at el-Bersheh, Meir, Beni Hassan, and Sheikh Said in Middle Egypt, a short distance upstream at Asyut, Deir el-Gabrawi and Qau, and at Thebes and Aswan much farther to the south.

Temples and forts

Although the center of royal power had moved north, the Middle Kingdom rulers did not forget their southern origins. They added substantially to the temple of Karnak at Thebes, dedicated to Amen, the local deity. Much of this building work was swept away when the temple was extensively remodeled in the time of the New Kingdom. They also built major

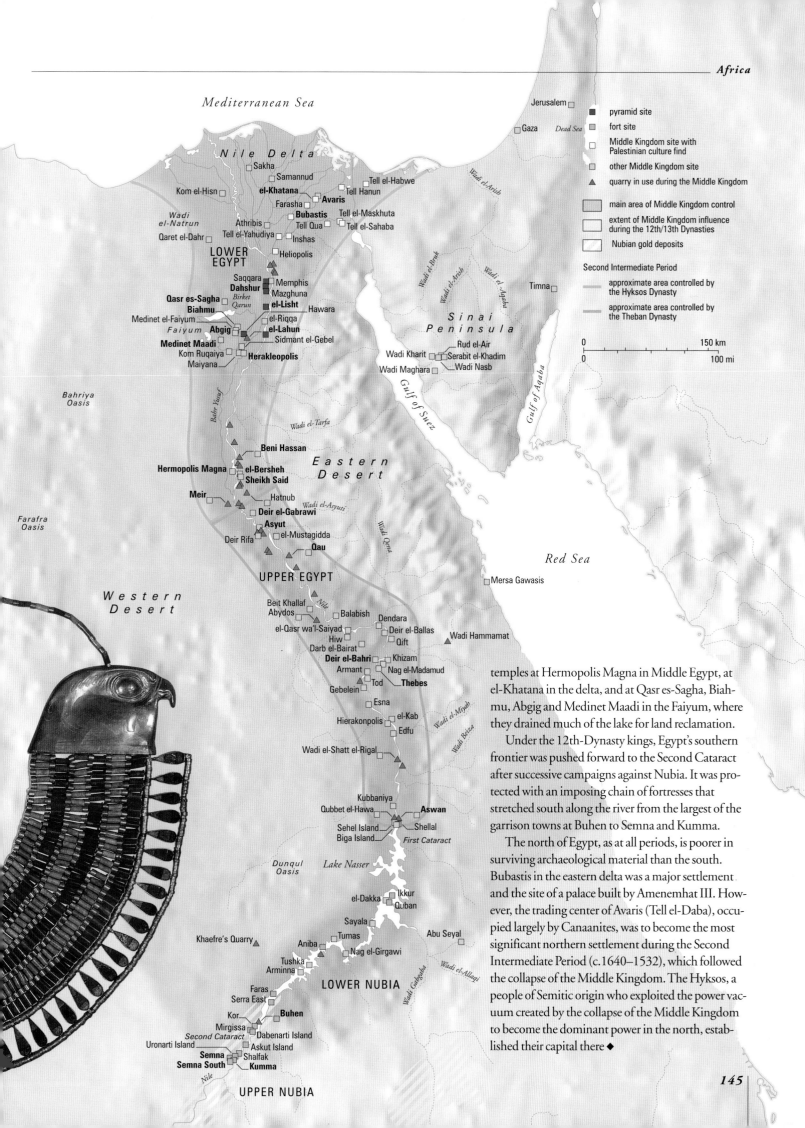

Mediterranean Sea

Legend

- ■ pyramid site
- ▢ fort site
- ▢ Middle Kingdom site with Palestinian culture find
- ▫ other Middle Kingdom site
- ▲ quarry in use during the Middle Kingdom
- main area of Middle Kingdom control
- extent of Middle Kingdom influence during the 12th/13th Dynasties
- Nubian gold deposits

Second Intermediate Period
- approximate area controlled by the Hyksos Dynasty
- approximate area controlled by the Theban Dynasty

0   150 km
0   100 mi

Nile Delta

Jerusalem
Gaza   *Dead Sea*

Sakha
Samannud
Kom el-Hisn
el-Khatana
Tell el-Habwe
Tell Hanun
Farasha
Avaris
Wadi el-Natrun
Bubastis
Tell el-Maskhuta
Athribis
Tell Qua
Tell el-Sahaba
Qaret el-Dahr
Tell el-Yahudiya
Inshas
Heliopolis

LOWER EGYPT

Saqqara
Memphis
Dahshur
Mazghuna
Qasr es-Sagha
Birket Qarun
el-Lisht
Biahmu
Hawara
Medinet el-Faiyum
el-Riqqa
Faiyum
Abgig
el-Lahun
Sidmant el-Gebel
Medinet Maadi
Kom Ruqaiya
Herakleopolis
Maiyana

Bahriya Oasis

Sinai Peninsula

Timna

Rud el-Air
Wadi Kharit
Serabit el-Khadim
Wadi Maghara
Wadi Nasb

Wadi el-Arish

Wadi el-Brak

Wadi el-Arish

Wadi el-Aqaba

Gulf of Suez

Gulf of Aqaba

Bahr Yusuf

Wadi el-Tarfa

Beni Hassan
Hermopolis Magna
el-Bersheh
Sheikh Said
Meir
Hatnub
Wadi el-Asyuti
Deir el-Gabrawi
Asyut
Deir Rifa
el-Mustagidda
Qau

Farafra Oasis

Eastern Desert

Western Desert

UPPER EGYPT

Beit Khallaf
Abydos
Nile
Balabish
Dendara
el-Qasr wa'l-Saiyad
Deir el-Ballas
Hiw
Qift
Darb el-Bairat
Wadi Hammamat
Khizam
Deir el-Bahri
Armant
Nag el-Madamud
Tod
Thebes
Gebelein
Esna
Hierakonpolis
el-Kab
Edfu
Wadi el-Shatt el-Rigal

Wadi Qena

Wadi el-Miyah

Wadi Beiza

Red Sea

Mersa Gawasis

Kubbaniya
Qubbet el-Hawa
Aswan
Sehel Island
Shellal
Biga Island
First Cataract

Dunqul Oasis
Lake Nasser

el-Dakka
Ikkur
Quban
Sayala
Abu Seyal
Tumas
Khaefre's Quarry
Aniba
Nag el-Girgawi

Wadi Gabgaba

Wadi el-Allaqi

LOWER NUBIA

Tushka
Arminna
Faras
Serra East
Kor
Buhen
Mirgissa
Dabenarti Island
Second Cataract
Uronarti Island
Askut Island
Semna
Shalfak
Semna South
Kumma
Nile

UPPER NUBIA

temples at Hermopolis Magna in Middle Egypt, at el-Khatana in the delta, and at Qasr es-Sagha, Biahmu, Abgig and Medinet Maadi in the Faiyum, where they drained much of the lake for land reclamation.

Under the 12th-Dynasty kings, Egypt's southern frontier was pushed forward to the Second Cataract after successive campaigns against Nubia. It was protected with an imposing chain of fortresses that stretched south along the river from the largest of the garrison towns at Buhen to Semna and Kumma.

The north of Egypt, as at all periods, is poorer in surviving archaeological material than the south. Bubastis in the eastern delta was a major settlement and the site of a palace built by Amenemhat III. However, the trading center of Avaris (Tell el-Daba), occupied largely by Canaanites, was to become the most significant northern settlement during the Second Intermediate Period (c.1640–1532), which followed the collapse of the Middle Kingdom. The Hyksos, a people of Semitic origin who exploited the power vacuum created by the collapse of the Middle Kingdom to become the dominant power in the north, established their capital there ◆

New Kingdom Egypt

The expulsion of the Hyksos from northern Egypt by the 17th Dynasty kings of Thebes in around 1550 BCE marked the beginning of the New Kingdom. This was another period of internal stability for Egypt that lasted until 1070 BCE and survived several changes of ruling house (Dynasties 18 to 20). Under the Hyksos kings, the delta region had been brought more directly into contact with Near Eastern influences than ever before. Until this time Egypt had been technologically backward in comparison with the Near East; as a result of these wider contacts, a range of innovations including bronzeworking, new crops and domestic animals, the horse and chariot, and weapons such as the composite bow were introduced into Egypt. The early 18th Dynasty kings exploited new methods of warfare to pursue a much more aggressive policy toward their neighbors. Lower Nubia was reconquered and direct Egyptian control extended deeper south into Upper Nubia. At the same time, Egyptian campaigns in the Levant established a zone of control that included much of modern Israel, Jordan, and parts of Lebanon and Syria.

The wealth and power of New Kingdom monarchs is clearly exhibited in the monuments they built for the gods to whom they ascribed their victorious feats of arms – none more so than Amen, the local Theban deity who became the patron-god of the Egyptian empire. Amen's main cult center, the temple of Karnak at Thebes, became – and still remains – one of the largest religious structures ever built, as succeeding kings vied with each other to create an ever more spacious and opulent home for the god.

The Valley of the Kings

At the same time, Thebes became a royal necropolis; no attempt was made to revive the pyramid as the principal form of royal tomb, as had happened at the beginning of the Middle Kingdom. Instead, an entirely new funerary tradition was established, involving the dedication of a secret burial site behind the mountain on the west bank opposite Thebes. In this place, known today as the "Valley of the Kings", almost all the New Kingdom rulers were buried, or intended to be buried, in individual underground tombs cut into the rock and with little in the way of external superstructure. Later New Kingdom tombs, however, have elaborately carved entrance doorways, perhaps in open acknowledgment that secrecy was impossible. Today almost all these tombs are empty of their original occupants and contents, most of them plundered

BELOW The painted limestone bust of queen Nefertiti, wife of Akhenaten, which was found with a number of other pieces in the workshop of the sculptor Thutmose during German excavations at Amarna and is now in the Berlin Museum. Her crown bears the *ureaus* – the rearing cobra symbol of royalty. Many other works of art were uncovered at Amarna, but an especially important discovery was the archive of diplomatic correspondence known as the Amarna letters and written in Akkadian cuneiform on 350 clay tablets. Covering the period from c.1355–1333 – the reigns of Amenophis III (part of), his son Akhenaten, and grandson Tutankhamun (part of) – the letters throw considerable light on the administration of the New Kingdom empire.

in antiquity. In the 19th century a number of royal coffins were discovered in a tomb reached via a narrow shaft at Deir el-Bahri, but the only royal tomb known to have survived unrobbed into modern times is that of Tutankhamun. Possibly this was because it is comparatively small and was easily overlooked; it has even been suggested it may have been a non-royal tomb pressed into service at short notice.

The royal tombs were cut and decorated by one of the best-known communities of the ancient world, the workmen who occupied the village at Deir el-Medina, also on the west bank at Thebes. Located in an inhospitable spot in a desert valley, Deir el-Medina was largely abandoned once royal tomb building ceased at the end of the New Kingdom. As at Kahun, excavation of the site has uncovered a large quantity of archaeological material.

As well as a tomb in the Valley of the Kings, each ruler had his or her own memorial temple. These, too, were situated on the west bank of the Nile, but in a more accessible location near the riverbank. Only a few have survived in reasonable condition, notably those of queen Hatshepsut, Seti I, Ramesses II and Ramesses III. Nearby, the cemeteries of high-ranking officials contain vividly painted scenes of daily life on a par with those in Old Kingdom mastaba tombs.

Royal building projects

Beyond Thebes, other major population centers also enjoyed generous patronage from the New Kingdom kings, though monuments at these sites have suffered extensive damage. At Memphis, colossal statues of Ramesses II hint at the importance of what was effectively the largest city in Egypt at that time, as does the nearby necropolis at Saqqara. Ramesses II built more buildings and erected more statues of himself than any other Egyptian king. Temple reliefs celebrating his triumph over the Hittites at Qadesh in Syria (see pages 78–79) are part of a personality cult that culminated in the foundation of a new capital city in the delta called Pi-Ramesses ("domain of Ramesses"). This was located at Qantir but was stripped of its stone monuments during

RIGHT Under the New Kingdom rulers, Egyptian power extended as far south as Napata (Gebel Barkal) in Upper Nubia. Under Tuthmosis III (1479–1425) Egyptian influence in the Levant reached to the Euphrates, but was later pushed back by the Hittites.

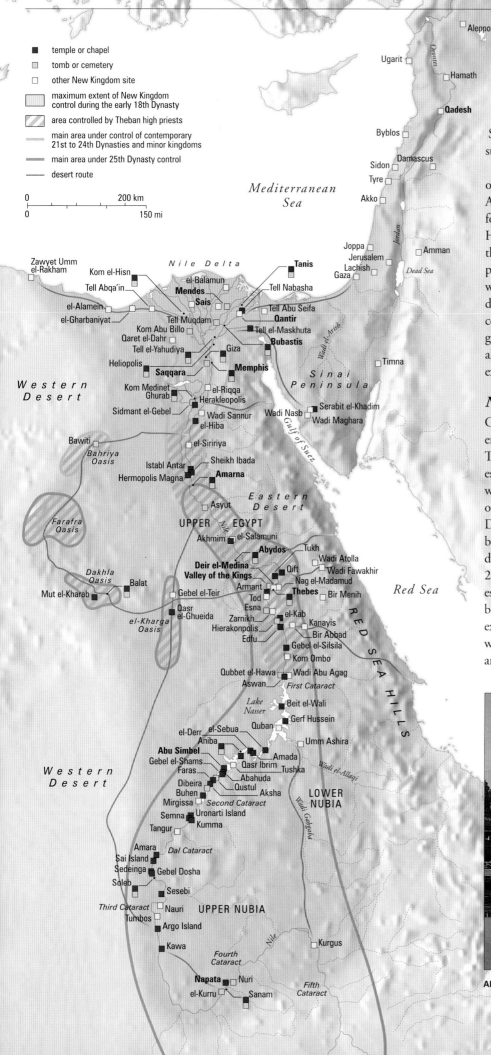

the building of nearby Tanis during Dynasties 21–22 and virtually nothing remains of it above ground. More substantial remnants of New Kingdom sacred architecture can be seen at the remarkable cenotaph-temple of Seti I at Abydos, and at various temples in Nubia, such as the rock-cut temple of Abu Simbel.

One of the most informative yet most enigmatic of New Kingdom archaeological sites is the city of Amarna (ancient Akhetaten) in Middle Egypt, founded by king Akhenaten (1353–1335 BCE). He wished to replace Egypt's traditional gods with the cult of Aten, the divine solar disk, and therefore planned his new capital away from the city of Thebes with its associations with Amen. Amarna was abandoned soon after Akhenaten's death. Since its rediscovery in the late 19th century, archaeological investigation has continued almost constantly at the site. It is almost the only ancient Egyptian city to have been extensively excavated.

New centers of power

Central royal authority collapsed in Egypt at the end of the New Kingdom as the high-priests of Thebes took over control of Upper Egypt. They established an hereditary rule that lasted until c.770 when a line of Nubian kings was recognized as rulers of Upper Egypt and founded the 25th Dynasty. During the Third Intermediate Period, Lower Egypt became divided among a number of rival ruling dynasties (Dynasties 21–24) based in the delta. The 21st and 22nd Dynasty kings (1070–712 BCE) established their power center at Tanis and were buried in great splendor in a necropolis that was excavated in the 1940s. Bubastis, Mendes and Sais were also the seats of local rulers and contain temples and tombs from this period ◆

ABOVE The sacred lake of the temple of Amen at Karnak, Thebes.

Map legend

- ■ temple or chapel
- ▨ tomb or cemetery
- ☐ other New Kingdom site
- maximum extent of New Kingdom control during the early 18th Dynasty
- area controlled by Theban high priests
- main area under control of contemporary 21st to 24th Dynasties and minor kingdoms
- main area under 25th Dynasty control
- desert route

0 — 200 km
0 — 150 mi

Map labels

Mediterranean Sea
Carchemish
Aleppo
Ugarit
Hamath
Qadesh
Byblos
Sidon
Tyre
Damascus
Akko
Joppa
Jerusalem
Lachish
Gaza
Amman
Dead Sea
Timna
Orontes
Jordan

Nile Delta
Zawyet Umm el-Rakham
Kom el-Hisn
Tell Abqa'in
el-Alamein
el-Gharbaniyat
Tanis
el-Balamun
Tell Nabasha
Mendes
Sais
Tell Muqdam
Tell Abu Seifa
Qantir
Tell el-Maskhuta
Kom Abu Billo
Qaret el-Dahr
Tell el-Yahudiya
Giza
Bubastis
Heliopolis
Saqqara
Memphis
Kom Medinet Ghurab
el-Riqqa
Herakleopolis
Sidmant el-Gebel
Wadi Sannur
el-Hiba
Serabit el-Khadim
Wadi Nasb
Wadi Maghara
Sinai Peninsula

Western Desert
Bawiti
Bahriya Oasis
el-Siririya
Istabl Antar
Sheikh Ibada
Hermopolis Magna
Amarna
Asyut
Farafra Oasis
Eastern Desert
UPPER EGYPT
Akhmim
el-Salamuni
Abydos
Tukh
Wadi Atolla
Deir el-Medina
Qift
Wadi Fawakhir
Valley of the Kings
Nag el-Madamud
Armant
Tod
Thebes
Bir Menih
Dakhla Oasis
Balat
Mut el-Kharab
Gebel el-Teir
Esna
el-Kab
Zarnikh
Kanayis
Qasr el-Ghueida
Hierakonpolis
Bir Abbad
el-Kharga Oasis
Edfu
Gebel el-Silsila
Kom Ombo
Qubbet el-Hawa
Wadi Abu Agag
Aswan
First Cataract
Red Sea
Beit el-Wali
Lake Nasser
Gerf Hussein
el-Derr
el-Sebua
Quban
Aniba
Umm Ashira
Abu Simbel
Amada
Gebel el-Shams
Qasr Ibrim
Tushka
Faras
Abahuda
Dibeira
Qustul
Aksha
Buhen
Mirgissa
Second Cataract
LOWER NUBIA
Semna
Uronarti Island
Tangur
Kumma
Amara
Dal Cataract
Sai Island
Sedeinga
Gebel Dosha
Soleb
Sesebi
Third Cataract
Nauri
UPPER NUBIA
Tumbos
Argo Island
Kawa
Fourth Cataract
Kurgus
Napata
Nuri
el-Kurru
Sanam
Fifth Cataract
RED SEA HILLS
Gulf of Suez
Wadi el-Arish
Wadi el-Allaqi
Wadi Gabgaba
Western Desert

Kingdoms of the Upper Nile

Although Egypt is the best-known ancient civilization of northeast Africa, it was not the only one. The life-giving Nile also made possible the growth of substantial cultures farther south in Nubia. The earliest, the Neolithic "A" group, were contemporary with and similar to the Naqada culture of Predynastic Egypt (see pages 140– 141). However, the unification of Egypt (c.3050 BCE) brought a halt to the process of state formation south of the First Cataract as Lower Nubia was depopulated by frequent military raids from Egypt and exploited for its mineral wealth. Only in the 2nd millennium BCE did a political state based on the city of Kerma develop on the Upper Nile.

Kerma is situated close to the third of the six cataracts – large outcrops of granite rock –that make navigation of the Upper Nile hazardous or impossible. The impetus for the development of a unified state here appears to have been the withdrawal of direct Egyptian control from between the First and Second Cataracts during the political upheavals that ended the Old Kingdom (c.2134–2040 BCE). Egyptian literary sources attribute this process to three Nubian "tribes" – Irtjet, Setjau and Wawat. The creation of an effective frontier on the Second Cataract and the take over of Lower Nubia by the Middle Kingdom rulers of Egypt does not seem to have hampered the growth of the Kerma kingdom, whose wealth lay in its rich mineral resources (particularly gold) and the trade in ivory and slaves between central Africa and the Near East. After the collapse of the Middle Kingdom, the Kerma kingdom expanded its power northward into Egypt itself.

The height of Kerma power (the "Classic Kerma" phase of c.1700-1550 BCE) is demonstrated by the growth of urban centers like that on Sai Island, but especially by the impressive monuments constructed at the city of Kerma itself. The main temple there, known as the *deffufa*, is a massive structure of mudbrick, 1,675 sq yd/1400 sq m in area. Just to the west of the city is the cemetery. In the Classic Kerma period it contained four enormous circular mounds with an average diameter of 289 ft/88 m. The size of these tumuli is an indication of royal power, further emphasized by the hundreds of sacrificial burials deposited in the central corridor of the grave at the time of the royal funeral.

The kingdom of Kush

A series of military campaigns by the New Kingdom rulers ended the power of Kerma. The city was sacked and all Nubia brought under direct Egyptian control in a manner symbolized by the colossal figures that Ramesses II erected on the front of his Nubian temple at Abu Simbel. However, the withdrawal of Egyptian rule at the end of the New Kingdom led again to the creation of a powerful kingdom on the Upper Nile by c.750 BCE. Referred to in Egyptian records as Kush (more often as "vile Kush"), its capital was at Napata, just below the Fourth Cataract. For a short time (715–664 BCE) the kings of Napata ruled in Egypt as the 25th Dynasty until expelled by the Assyrian conquest of Egypt. By c.590 BCE the Kushite capital appears to have moved south to Meroë, between the Fifth and Sixth Cataracts. Here

ABOVE This larger than life sized bronze head of the Roman emperor Augustus was discovered by archaeologists buried beneath the steps of a temple at Meroë that commemorated a successful raid into Egypt c.24 BCE. It was almost certainly brought back as part of the loot and buried beneath the steps as a triumphalist act of disrespect and scorn.

ABOVE THE CRUMBLING PYRAMIDS OF THE KUSHITE KINGS, NEAR NAPATA.

Napata: home of the Kushite kings

The most important shrine of the Kushite kingdom was the Gebel Barkal temple complex at Napata, which was dedicated to the Egyptian god Amen. The temple was founded c.1500 BCE by Tuthmosis III to mark the limit of Egypt's southern frontier in Nubia. The Nubians gradually incorporated Egyptian gods into their pantheon, giving special prominence to Amen. The Kushite kings of the 25th Dynasty restored many temples in Egypt to reinforce the legitimacy of their rule, including Amen's chief temple at Karnak itself, and many Egyptian practices appear to have been adopted into Napata at this time. The practice of human sacrifice and tumuli burials was abandoned, and instead pyramids were built for the Kushite kings long after the custom had been abandoned in Egypt. Fields of pyramids can still be seen at the royal cemeteries of el-Kurru and Nuri, close to Napata. With the transfer of the capital to Meroë the Gebel Barkal shrine declined in influence. Temples were built to commemorate local gods, including complexes at Musawwarat es-Sufra and Naga, near Meroë, dedicated to the Nubian lion god Apedemak ◆

royal palaces and other monuments were built. A Meroitic script was invented but this remains undeciphered, leaving the details of Meroë's history vague. It appears to have been at its height in the 1st century CE, but declined slowly over the next three centuries, by which time a new regional power had developed at Axum, some way to the southeast.

Axum: wealth through trade

The archaeology of Axum is comparatively new and much remains to be discovered; however, a tentative chronology (from c.1 to 630 CE) can be constructed from the coins issued by Axumite kings. The source of Axum's wealth was its outlet to the Red Sea. African luxury goods such as ivory, rhino horn, and aromatics were supplied to the Roman empire through its main port, Adulis, which also served as an entrepot for trade between India and the Mediterranean. The kings of Axum were early converts to Christianity (c.350 CE). For a time in the 6th century CE they controlled southwest Arabia until driven out by the Sassanian Persians. The city of Axum itself was abandoned c.630 CE. The most obvious indications of its past today are the towering funerary obelisks of its royal cemetery, the tallest of which was over 108 ft/33 m high ◆

LEFT Ancient Nubia (modern Sudan) was divided into Lower Nubia (from the First to the Second Cataract) and Upper Nubia (from the Second Cataract to roughly the area of Khartoum today). It was important as a source of gold and building stone and as a corridor for exotic goods such as animals, skins, ostrich eggs and feathers, ivory and ebony to Egypt and the Near East from farther south in Africa. The rise and decline of the Nubian kingdoms were closely related to the degree of control exerted by Egypt at any time.

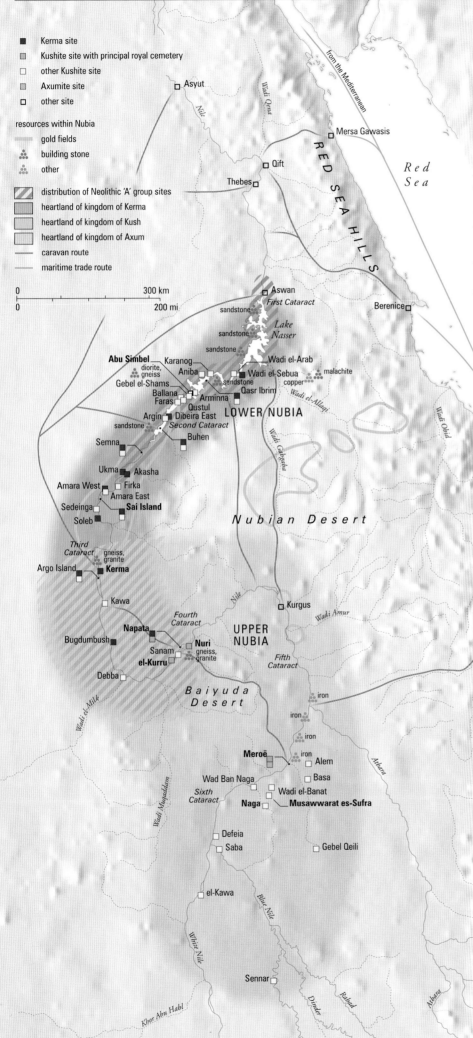

Kerma site

Kushite site with principal royal cemetery

other Kushite site

Axumite site

other site

resources within Nubia

gold fields

building stone

other

distribution of Neolithic 'A' group sites

heartland of kingdom of Kerma

heartland of kingdom of Kush

heartland of kingdom of Axum

caravan route

maritime trade route

0   300 km

0   200 mi

Iron Age Sub-Saharan Africa

Unlike many other regions of the Old World, sub-Saharan Africa moved directly from the Stone to the Iron Age without experiencing an intervening Bronze or Copper Age. Knowledge of iron smelting appears to have crossed the Sahara from the north to reach West Africa in the first millennium BCE. Early ironworking shows significant local technological innovations. The use of iron aided the spread of agriculture by improving the means of clearing land for cultivation, and is associated with the growth of large settlements and indigenous trade networks that led to early state formation. While ironworking in some instances may have traveled south of the Sahara before the expansion of Bantu-speaking farmers from the Nigeria/Cameroon border area about 2,000 years ago, their migrations over the next thousand years saw it spread into eastern and southern Africa .

Iron is known to have been in use by the people of Nok, in central Nigeria, who were producing striking terracotta sculptures between the 6th and 2nd centuries BCE. Archaeological knowledge of the ironworking peoples of West Africa is patchy and incomplete, but there are clear signs of change in the political and economic organization of the region by the first millennium CE. Excavations carried out at Igbo Ukwu, on the northern fringe of the forest belt of southwestern Nigeria, have uncovered an extraordinary cache of bronze and copper objects between the 8th and 11th centuries CE, together with the rich burial-chamber of a high-ranking individual. These finds suggest that social stratification was well established among the people of this area, with a powerful elite that controlled wealth and resources.

Trading kingdoms

At the same time, organized states were emerging among the farmers of the savanna belt south of the Sahara. An important factor in their rise was the growing trade in gold, slaves, and ivory with the Arab states of North Africa, in exchange for salt, copper, and horses. The powerful gold-trading kingdom of Ghana emerged between the Niger and Senegal rivers (some way distant from the modern West African state that bears its name) before the 8th century CE. Urbanism was beginning. Jenne-Jeno, a settlement on the inland delta of the river Niger in Mali, for example, had grown into a walled town some 82 acres/33 ha in extent and serving a population of about 27,000 people by 800 CE.

Over the next centuries a series of wealthy trading kingdoms rose and fell on the southern fringe of the Sahara. From about 1200 the empire of Mali dominated a vast area stretching to the forest region, to be succeeded by Songhay, centered at Gao on the Niger river. Farther east, Kanem and Bornu controlled the Lake Chad area.

Compelling art

Among the most remarkable of early African artworks that have come to light in archaeological excavations are near life-size figurines in terracotta or bronze (cast by the lost-wax method) from Ife in southern Nigeria. These date from early in the 2nd millennium CE, but may derive indirectly from the Nok terracottas and are thought to have been kept on altars or in house shrines for use during religious rituals. The famous "bronze" (actually brass) sculptures and plaques of the Benin kingdom, which was founded in the 14th century, provide evidence of a rich and powerful court culture.

BELOW Carved soapstone bird, 39 in/ 100 cm high, one of eight found at Great Zimbabwe. They may represent messages sent from royal ancestors.

LEFT Part of the Great Enclosure at Great Zimbabwe. This impressive structure, which dates from c.1270– 1450, is thought by some to have been used as a pre-marriage initiation school. Its outer wall contains some 900,000 stone blocks.The town's layout reflects the clear distinction that existed between the ruling class and the commoners: the king, his family, and important officials lived in stone-walled enclosures on top of a large bare granite hill known as the Hill Ruin, while commoners occupied the valley below.

LEFT There is evidence for pre-Iron Age copper metallurgy in West Africa as early as 2000 BCE, but early ironworking in this region dates only from about 600 BCE. Bantu-speaking migrants, originally from the Nigeria/Cameroon border area, spread iron as far as the coast of southeast Africa by shortly after 1 CE. From there, a second series of migrations c.1000 CE brought Late Iron Age people to southern Africa.

Southern Africa

The Iron Age farmers of southern Africa lived in settled villages and cultivated crops like sorghum, millet, ground beans, and cow peas. Ownership of cattle symbolized status and economic wealth. They worked metals, especially iron, and produced quantities of pottery. By analysing differences in pottery styles to identify separate traditions and and link them to linguistic groups, archaeologists have been able tentatively to recreate the migration routes followed by the Bantu-speaking peoples who spread the use of iron into southern Africa. The evidence is inevitably patchy though, as most archaeological investigation has taken place in the eastern half of the southern continent.

As in West Africa, trade played an important role in early state formation. Schroda, a 9th-century CE site near the confluence of the Limpopo and Shashi rivers, is the first settlement in southern Africa that has produced finds of imported goods in quantity. About the year 1000 occupation moved to the nearby K2 site, which was in turn abandoned about 1220. Mapungubwe, a short distance away to the southwest, now became the center of power. It is here that we see for the first time the spatial separation of the ruling elite from the rest of the community. Between 1220 and 1270 great wealth was accumulated by exchanging ivory and gold for imports such as ceramics, glass beads and cloth with Swahili traders on the East African coast. An extraordinary collection of gold objects, including rhinoceros figurines covered with gold foil, has been found in an elite cemetery on the hilltop.

A widespread drought brought an end to Mapungubwe's rule in about 1270 and Great Zimbabwe took over control of trade with East Africa. At its zenith in the 14th century, Great Zimbabwe was the capital of an extensive empire that stretched from northern South Africa to the Zambezi river and from eastern Botswana to western Mozambique ◆

BELOW The empire of Great Zimbabwe in the 14th century CE and the Indian Ocean stations through which it traded.

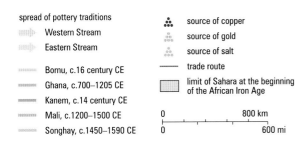

Iron Age site
- ☐ before 500 BCE
- ■ 500–200 BCE
- ▨ 200–1 BCE
- ▢ after 1 CE

▨ area of Nok culture, c.500 BCE–c.300 CE

spread of pottery traditions
- Western Stream
- Eastern Stream

- Bornu, c.16 century CE
- Ghana, c.700–1205 CE
- Kanem, c.14 century CE
- Mali, c.1200–1500 CE
- Songhay, c.1450–1590 CE

- ⁛ source of copper
- ⁞ source of gold
- ⁙ source of salt
- — trade route
- ▢ limit of Sahara at the beginning of the African Iron Age

0 ___ 800 km
0 ___ 600 mi

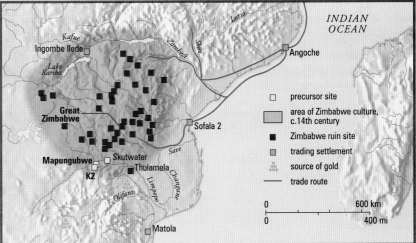

precursor site ☐
area of Zimbabwe culture, c.14th century ▨
Zimbabwe ruin site ■
trading settlement ▨
source of gold ⁛
trade route —

0 ___ 600 km
0 ___ 400 mi

THE AMERICAS

THE NEW WORLD was the scene of some of the earliest pioneering work in archaeology. As early as 1675 an exploratory tunnel was dug into the side of Teotihuacán's Pyramid of the Moon, while Thomas Jefferson, later to become third President of the United States, who dug a trench across a burial mound on his property in Virginia in 1784, is often credited with the first "scientific" excavation in history. In recent years, the origins and date of arrival of the First Americans have been the focus of major multidisciplinary research.

Some early inhabitants of the New World, for example the ancient Mesoamericans, believed that human existence stretched back tens of thousands of years. There is evidence to show that objects were often preserved from the past: some North American Iroquoian sites of the 15th and 16th centuries CE have been found to contain projectile points, stone pipes and native copper tools made thousands of years earlier; mammoth molars were discovered in a Mexican pueblo abandoned around 1400 CE; an Olmec stone mask was already 2,000 years old when placed as an offering at the Aztec Great Temple of Tenochtitlán, Mexico; the Inca emperors of Peru are said to have kept collections of centuries-old Moche pottery, probably for its pornographic interest.

Explorers and pioneers

The discovery of major civilizations in the New World came as a tremendous shock to the first European arrivals in the late 15th century. A few Spanish priests took pains to describe various aspects of Indian culture and society, and their records form an invaluable ethnographic account of prehispanic America. There were consequences for European archaeology also: the Amerindians, so alien in looks, behavior and way of life, came to be equated in culture and appearance with the ancient peoples of the Old World – indeed, reconstruction drawings of ancient Britons and Picts were directly modelled on Amerindians. Flaked and polished stone tools brought back from the Americas helped prove that comparable objects found in Europe were indeed human artifacts.

From early on, the temple ruins and burial mounds of the ancient Americans fascinated Europeans. Various theories were put forward to explain the identity of the peoples responsible for their construction. Thomas Jefferson stood apart from his contemporaries in ascribing the mounds of North America not to a mythical and vanished "Moundbuilder" race but to the ancestors of the present-day Native Americans. So carefully did he excavate the mound on his own property, he was able to recognize different layers in it, and from the varied preservation of human bones deduced that it had been reused for burial on many occasions. Jefferson was far ahead of his time in making logical deductions from carefully excavated evidence, the very basis of modern archaeology. In 1848 the amateur archaeologist and newspaper editor Ephraim Squier (1821–88) published, with Edwin Hamilton Davis, the pioneering *Ancient Monuments of the Mississippi Valley*, meticulously describing and classifying the mounds of the Ohio and Mississippi valleys. But the myth of the "Moundbuilder" race persisted until the final decades of the 19th century.

Accounts published by 19th-century explorers informed the American and European public about the archaeological sites of South and Central America. The German naturalist Baron Alexander von Humboldt made the first scientific observations of the remains of the Chimú and Inca empire on his great South American expedition (1799–1804). Frederick Catherwood's and John Lloyd Stephen's account of their travels in Central America, illustrated with Catherwood's superb drawings of ruins like Copán, Uxmal and Palenque, excited a storm of popular and scholarly interest in the Maya in 1841. Ephraim Squier's bestselling account of a journey through the Andes (1877) contained detailed descriptions of great sites such as Ollantaytambo, Sacsayhuaman and Tiwanaku.

Regional Timeline

c.30,000 y.a. Ice Age art in southwest Europe

c.9,000 y.a. Pottery comes into use in Near East

c.13,000 y.a. Clovis hunters present in North America

c.9,000–5,000 y.a. World's earliest mummies at Chinchorro (Chile)

c.33,000 y.a. Possible human occupation at Pedra Furada (Brazil) and Monte Verde (Chile)

c.10,000–8,000 y.a. Squash domestication at Guilá Naquitz (Mexico)

c.7,500–6,500 y.a. Pottery in Amazon valley

10,000 y.a.

8,000 y.a.

ABOVE The cliff dwellings of the Mesa Verde have been the focus of ongoing archaeological investigations since they were first discovered more than 100 years ago.
ABOVE LEFT A Mogollon ceramic bowl from New Mexico, 10th century CE.

Improving standards

By the end of the 19th century, North American archaeology was largely in the hands of major organizations such as the Smithsonian Institution, the Bureau of American Ethnology and Harvard's Peabody Museum. The discovery of the majestic ruins of Mesa Verde by cowboy Richard Wetherill in 1888 had given further indication of the achievements of the North American Indians and focused attention on the Southwest, where excavation and field survey of Ancestral Pueblo (Anasazi) ruins were mixed with ethnographic studies of the modern Pueblo Indians. Excavation standards were improving markedly, through the adoption of stratigraphic methods imported from Europe. One pioneer of this approach was the German-born archaeologist Max Uhle (1856–1944), whose

painstaking stratigraphic excavations of a shell-mound in San Francisco Bay were followed by ground-laying work in Peru (Pachacamac), Chile (Chinchorro) and elsewhere. The chronological framework for Andean civilization established by Uhle revolutionized South American archaeology. Initially there was some resistance to his stratigraphic technique in North America, but opposition gradually faded after Alfred Kidder (1885–1963) used the same method to establish a relative chronological sequence in his extensive digs at Pecos pueblo, near Santa Fe, New Mexico (1915–29).

During the 1920s and 1930s, key sites were excavated in New Mexico and Colorado that demonstrated conclusively that people had lived in America during the late Pleistocene. These sites, characterized by fluted stone spear points, often in association with bones of extinct bison and other large animals, were the basis for the Clovis and Folsom periods, dating back to c.13,500 and 13,000 years ago respectively. Until recently, they were considered to be the earliest occupations of the New World.

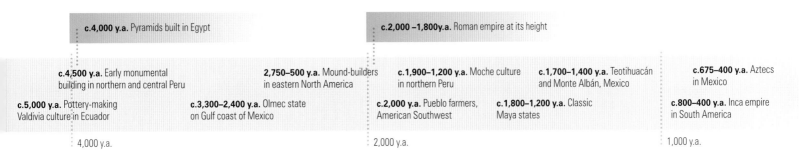

c.4,000 y.a. Pyramids built in Egypt

c.2,000 –1,800y.a. Roman empire at its height

c.4,500 y.a. Early monumental building in northern and central Peru

2,750–500 y.a. Mound-builders in eastern North America

c.1,900–1,200 y.a. Moche culture in northern Peru

c.1,700–1,400 y.a. Teotihuacán and Monte Albán, Mexico

c.675–400 y.a. Aztecs in Mexico

c.5,000 y.a. Pottery-making Valdivia culture in Ecuador

c.3,300–2,400 y.a. Olmec state on Gulf coast of Mexico

c.2,000 y.a. Pueblo farmers, American Southwest

c.1,800–1,200 y.a. Classic Maya states

c.800–400 y.a. Inca empire in South America

4,000 y.a.   2,000 y.a.   1,000 y.a.

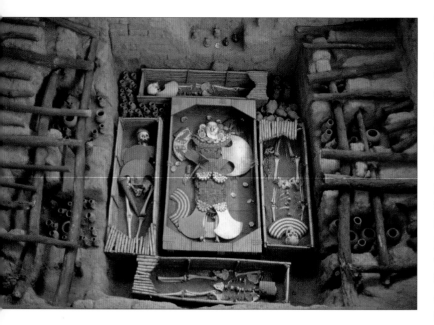

ABOVE The rich Moche burials at Sipán (Peru) came to light as recently as 1987. It may be years before archaeologists complete their studies of the tombs and their contents.

RIGHT Machu Picchu, discovered by Hiram Bingham in 1911. One of the most amazing archaeological sites in the world, it still epitomizes the Inca empire for most people.

Further discoveries in Latin America

In Central America, early archaeological investigation concentrated on the Maya civilization. Cities and monuments were systematically mapped and classified, detailed drawings made of carvings and glyphs, and work begun on the Maya calendar. The long-held view of the Maya was of a peaceful society under the control of a priestly ruling class. This theory was turned on its head when scholars began to decipher Maya inscriptions in the 1950s and 1960s, revealing the warlike basis of their society. Thanks to the work of epigraphers such as David Stuart and Linda Schele, the dynastic histories of many Maya cities are now well understood.

By the 1920s, major excavations and surveys were being done in the Valley of Mexico and at the site of Monte Albán in the Oaxaca valley. The discovery of colossal basalt heads on the Gulf coast of Mexico in the 1930s led to the identification of the Olmec civilization. In Peru, Uhle's chronological sequence continued to be refined and improved, and Peruvian archaeologist Julio Tello focused his attentions on Chavín and Wari. The first major regional survey in Latin America, of the Virú valley of Peru, was carried out in 1946 by a team from Harvard. Aerial photography played a major role in the discovery and study of the Nasca lines, among other sites.

New approaches to archaeology

Ecological studies were slower to take hold in North America than in Europe, though Theodore White's analyses of butchered animal bones from bison-kill and other North American sites in the early 1950s were pioneering examples of this approach. Environmental factors in human behavior came to the fore in the theoretical work of anthropologists Julian Steward and Leslie White, and by the 1960s American archaeology was paying close attention to the effects of the natural environment on human behavior through multidisciplinary studies focused on pollen analysis and on plant and animal remains. Among the major foci of such studies were the origins and spread of agriculture in different parts of the Americas, as exemplified by the investigations into the origins of maize carried out by Richard S. MacNeish in the Tehuacán valley in Mexico.

The development of a new theory of archaeology, often called processual archaeology, occurred in parallel with the rise of such environmental studies. Its roots lay in two key events: the invention of radiocarbon dating enabled archaeologists to turn aside from problems of chronology to address different aspects of the past; while Walter Taylor's revolutionary *A Study of Archaeology* (1948) insisted that archaeologists should go beyond simply analyzing and categorizing artifacts to try to understand the people who made them. Taylor's acerbic criticism of traditional archaeology struck a chord among young North American archaeologists in the 1960s, with the result that processual archaeology was born.

Processual archaeologists wanted to create an explicit science with testable hypotheses, and set about finding universal "laws of human behavior" that could be deduced from archaeological analysis. Alas, no such laws were ever produced, other than self-evident truisms, and attention gradually shifted to "middle-range theory", focusing on how the archaeological record is produced, how it reflects past human behavior, and why ancient people did what they did. Processual archaeology gave archaeologists greater confidence in their subject's ability to make a unique contribution to the study of human behavior – especially important in the United States, where archaeology had long been subservient to anthropology, both institutionally and intellectually. It led archaeologists to reexamine the quality and validity of their reasoning, interpretations and conclusions, and emphasized explicitness and objectivity.

Present and future concerns

A major recent development in New World archaeology has been the realization that people entered the Americas long before the Clovis hunters: finds at the open-air site of Monte Verde (Chile) are dated to 13,000 years ago, and may perhaps be as much as 33,000 years old. Other sites in South and Mesoamerica support these findings, while studies of linguistics and genetics are also contributing to the quest to discover how and when, and in how many waves, the First Americans arrived in the continent.

Cultural Resource Management (CRM) is now the dominant force in North American archaeology, as no development can take place by law on federal land without the project's impact on archaeological sites first being assessed (usually by excavation) at the developer's expense. It is also a legal requirement to publish a final report. This has brought about a huge increase in the amount of information being produced, and in the size of the publication record. Archaeologists are adjusting to these new circumstances ◆

Archaic Hunter-gatherers

During the late Pleistocene, humans spread into every part of the New World as small groups of hunters followed the migrations of megafauna like mammoth and mastodon (see pages 34–35). As the ice sheets began to shrink between 10,000 and 8,000 years ago, rapid climatic shifts between moist and arid conditions called for new survival skills. During the so-called Archaic period (c.8000–1 BCE), New World hunter–gatherers evolved localized lifestyles to cope with environments ranging from Arctic tundra, maritime coasts, plains, woodlands, and highlands to tropical forests and deserts. New tools came into use for hunting and for processing plant foods.

Because of the concentration of large herd animals on the the plains grasslands of North America, communal hunting continued as the major subsistence strategy until the 19th century (see pages 160–161). Elsewhere, the environmental changes of the early Holocene led to the exploitation of a much larger array of animal and plant species and to the evolution of new technologies such as grinding stones for processing hard nuts and seeds for storage. Subsistence strategies varied. Where resources were dependable (as in southern California where foragers exploited the annual acorn crop as a staple food), a small range of territory could be utilized, but in marginal areas like the western desert, groups often had to travel greater distances between seasonal food sources and were therefore smaller and more mobile.

The Northwest Coast (British Columbia and Washington) provided wide opportunities for hunting–foraging. Shell middens show that over time salmon fishing increased in importance and people become more sedentary, leading to the development of complex ranked societies. The Archaic lifestyle was particularly well adapted to the varied lake, river and forest environments of the Eastern Woodlands, and forager populations there were of comparable density to those supported by early farming. Even after agriculture became the dominant economy in these areas (see pages 158–159), substantial reliance was still placed on hunting and gathering, both to provide dietary supplements and to serve as "back-up systems" in times of crop failure.

RIGHT The post-glacial hunters of the New World lived for the main in small, highly mobile groups and adapted a variety of specializations to exploit the range of animal and plant species available to them locally. In favorable areas, successful foraging strategies led gradually to the development of more sedentary lifeways.

BELOW A Chinchorro mummy of a child from northern Chile. After removing the internal organs, the body cavity was filled with with clay, sticks and grass. The body was then covered with mud or clay and painted. The practice, which suggests some degree of social differentiation, died out c.3000 BCE when people began building larger, more substantial houses and burying their dead in cemeteries.

Mesoamerica

Evidence for Paleoindian occupation of Mexico and Central America is sparse, although stone tools have been discovered with mastodon remains at Ixtapan in the Valley of Mexico, and the skeletal remains of a woman found at nearby Tepexpan. A kill site in the Valsequillo region of modern Puebla has also yielded quantities of extinct animal bones in association with stone tools, and Clovis-style projectile points are known from Guatemala.

As the megafauna went extinct during the early Holocene, Paleoindian groups turned to hunting smaller animals and exploiting alternative food sources. Human occupation is likely to have been highest in coastal zones, where greater biodiversity would have provided more varied opportunities for hunter–gatherer groups. As a result of sea level changes, however, many lowland Archaic sites are now submerged, and the best documented sites are in upland areas such as the Tehuacán and Oaxaca valleys of southern central Mexico, where analysis of food remains shows increasing reliance on seasonally available wild plants over thousands of years.

Coastal foragers

Along the coast of northern Chile, small groups of hunter–gatherer–fishers were exploiting marine resources possibly by 10,000 BCE, as indicated by recent evidence from sites at Tacahuay, Jaguay, and the Ring Site, where firepits and middens of fish bone, marine bird bone and some shell show that a diet of marine foods was consumed. The abundance of these resources allowed them some degree of permanent settlement and by around 7000 BCE, at sites such as Acha II, Camarones-14 and Villa del Mar, people were living in small circular huts for some part of the year and practicing elaborate funerary ceremonies. Some of the so-called Chinchorro mummies found on this coast (which are named for the site where they were first discovered at the beginning of the 20th century) are thought to be much as 9,000 years old.

On the coast of northern Peru distinctive spear points known as Paijan were being made by hunter–gatherers between c.8000 and 5000 BCE. Their slim

Palisade
Batza Ten

Igiugig
Anangula
Ugashik Narrows

BELOW Duck decoys from Lovelock Cave, Nevada, preserved by the cave's dry atmosphere. In desert areas, shallow lakes were valuable seasonal resources for foragers.

Map labels (North America)

ogruk, Kayuk
agher Flint ion
Engigstciak
Old Crow
e Lake

Greenland
Ellesmere Island
Banks Island
Victoria Island
Baffin Island

Great Bear Lake
Mackenzie
Great Slave Lake
Peace
Fort Liard

ROCKY MOUNTAIN

Lind Coulee
Missouri
Anzick
MacHaffie
Hell Gap
Simonsen
velock Cave
Danger Cave
Lime Creek
Drake
Lindenmeier
Borax Lake
Folsom
Dalton
Modoc
Santa Rosa Island
Clovis
Hardaway
Ventana Cave
Lewisville
Lehner
Levi Rockshelter
Bonfire Shelter

Saskatchewan
Lake Winnipeg
Lake Superior
Lake Huron
Lake Michigan
Lake Ontario
Lake Erie
Debert
Bull Brook
Poverty Point

Colorado
Rio Grande
Arkansas
Ohio
Mississippi
APPALACHIAN MTS

Tamaulipas Caves
Ixtapan, Tequixquiac, **Tepexpán**
Guilá Naquitz, **Oaxaca Valley**
Valsequillo
Tehuacán Valley
Huehuetenango
Los Tapiales

Cuba
Couri
Cabaret
Loiza Cave
Hispaniola

Map labels (South America)

Guanacaste
Turrialba
Monagrillo
Cerro Iguanas
Michelena
Muaco
El Jobo
Manicuare
Puerto Hormiga
Canaima
Orinoco
Alaka

El Inga
Salango
Las Vegas
ANDES
Amazon Basin
Marañón
Amazon
Lago Grande de Villa Franca
Pedra Pintada
Mina
Paricatuba
Tapajós

Nanchoc, Pampa de Paijan
Cupisnique
La Cumbre, Quirihuac
Guitarrero Cave
Lauricocha
Pachamachay
La Paloma
Pikimachay
Chilca
Sumbay
Villa del Mar
Tacahuay
Jaguay
Ring Site
Kilometer 4, Quiani
Asana, Toquepala
Caleta Huelén
Camarones-14
Cobija
Antofagasta
Acha II, Chinchorro
Taltal

Araguaia
Pedra Furada
Brazilian Highlands
São Francisco
Paraguay
Paraná
Paranaíba

ANDES
Intihuasi Cave
Tagua Tagua
Uruguay

Los Toldos
Cueva de las Manos
Eberhard Cave
Palliaike Cave
Fell's Cave
Englefield Island
Monte Verde

Legend

□ before 10,000 BCE
■ 10,000–8000 BCE
■ 8000–5000 BCE
■ 5000–3000 BCE
□ other early site
— area of Chinchorro tradition
— area of Paijan tradition
ancient coastline, 10,000 BCE
☐ ice cap, 10,000 BCE

vegetation zones, 10,000 BCE
boreal/mountain forest
dry steppe
savanna/grassland
semi-desert/desert
temperate woodland/forest
tropical forest
tundra

0 — 2000 km
0 — 1500 mi

Body text

bases would have made them quite fragile as hunting tools and archaeologists disagree about whether they were used as implements for spear fishing, sea mammal hunting, or for hunting land animals. Research suggests that Paijan people moved seasonally between ephemeral campsites set up near marshes along the coast and slightly inland sites along river valleys, where they appear to have built small villages with houses or shelters. Analysis of midden remains shows that they ate fish, crustacea, reptiles, birds and foxes.

Camelid hunters

Inland cave sites such as Guitarrero Cave, Sumbay, and Toquepala in the central Andean region have deep midden deposits that reveal long sequences of occupation by Archaic groups who hunted wild camelids (guanaco and vicuña) and deer. Rock art found at a number of these sites depicts hunting and other scenes. Excavators of an open air site at Asana have found traces of small houses built by Archaic hunters, which they occupied for the part of each year when prey was available in greatest numbers. In the far south of the continent, rock shelters such as as Cueva de las Manos and Los Toldos in Patagonia were occupied by hunters of wild camelids and of the flightless rhea. They have left visible evidence of their presence in the form of vivid panels of rock paintings ◆

Origins of Farming

Farming in the New World had its origins in the management of a variety of wild plants by forager communities in different centers in Central and South America during the Archaic period. The process of plant domestication was a long one. Women in these societies probably had responsibility for collecting and preparing wild plants for food. Knowledge of the growing cycles of individual plants would have led to active intervention in the form of weeding, selective cropping, seed storage and nurturing to ensure abundant harvests, beginning a process of gradual hybridization whereby more productive strains were encouraged. Clues to the process of domestication come from sites as much as 12,000 years old where the wild ancestors of later domesticates are found. Wild potatoes, for example, are present at Monte Verde in southern Chile, indicating a very long history of use.

The management of the wild ancestors of many plants that were to become important domesticated crops so completely transformed them that they are known only in their hybrid forms, or cultigens. The origins of maize (corn), the most important domesticated plant of the Americas, are obscure but recent research suggests that some time before 5000 BCE *teosinte*, a wild grass with a small seedhead growing locally in southern Mexico, appears to have undergone a spontaneous mutation to produce tiny cobs. Through careful selection, maize became progressively more productive but the plant's transformation to a major staple crop was slow: its initial importance may have been for making fermented maize-beer rather than as a food source.

A large-scale study of Archaic sites in the Tehuacán valley of southern Puebla provides evidence for the gradual domestication of other plant species including beans, avocado, squash and chilis. Seeds of squash from the site of Guilá Naquitz, which are morphologically domesticated, have been dated to between 10,000 and 8,000 years ago, predating other domesticates in Mesoamerica by several millennia.

Over time, plant foods assumed an increasingly important role in the Mesoamerican diet, accompanied by a decline in hunting. As productivity increased, populations began to expand during the late Archaic Period and between 2000 and 1500 BCE a change in

RIGHT The management of wild plants by hunter–gatherer groups led very gradually to the adoption of farming in the Americas. Between 3,000 and 2500 BCE sedentary agriculture had developed independently at a number of sites in South America and central Mexico. The farming of maize, beans and squash spread later to Southwest and Southeast North America.

RIGHT Maize was cultivated throughout the New World. A Mochica vessel from Peru shows three gods emerging from a bundle of cobs.

ABOVE The Ancestral Pueblo of the North American Southwest were agriculturalists who cultivated maize and other crops on the mesa tops. Their villages are spectacular structures built into the steep sides of canyons. Shown here is Cliff Palace at Mesa Verde.

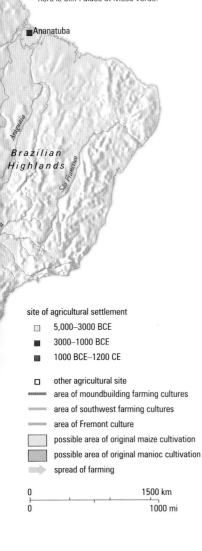

site of agricultural settlement
- ☐ 5,000–3000 BCE
- ■ 3000–1000 BCE
- ■ 1000 BCE–1200 CE
- ☐ other agricultural site
- ▦ area of moundbuilding farming cultures
- ▦ area of southwest farming cultures
- ▬ area of Fremont culture
- ☐ possible area of original maize cultivation
- ▦ possible area of original manioc cultivation
- ➡ spread of farming

0 ——————— 1500 km
0 ——————— 1000 mi

of llamas for meat and transportation and alpacas for wool by about 5,000 years ago, and pastoralism became an increasingly important way of life. Potatoes, quinoa and oca were cultivated crops.

North American farmers

For thousands of years before maize was introduced from Central America about 3,500 years ago, mobile hunter–gatherer groups in favorable environments of North America had managed the gathering and growing of native wild grasses and other annual plants, leading to the development of local cultigens. Although semi-tropical in origin, once introduced, maize was gradually hybridized to survive the harsher climates of North America and eventually its use spread as far north as North Dakota, where it was grown by the ancestors of the Mandan, Hidatsa and Arikara. Beans and squash were also introduced from sub-tropical America. They were often grown in rotation with maize, allowing the beans to replace the nitrogen that was removed from the soil by the maize. Cotton and tobacco were also quite widely cultivated. The only domesticated animal of North America (apart from the dog, a camp-follower rather than a food source) was the turkey, which was domesticated by people in the Southwest.

Farming made little impact on subsistence strategies outside of the Southwest and Southeast, where the development of complex sedentary societies followed the adoption of intensive agriculture. Maize farming was probably adopted by the peoples of the Southwest as a means of coping with an increasing population and seasonal fluctuations in wild plant resources. By at least 2,000 years ago, the cultivation of maize had spread as far north as the southwest corner of Colorado, and over the next 1,500 years pueblo-dwelling agriculturalists constructed increasingly elaborate irrigation reservoirs and canals to maximize what little rain fell (see pages 164–165). Further north and west, in central Utah, the people of the Fremont culture were farmers and foragers who appear to have moved flexibly between sedentary community life and more mobile strategies depending on the availability of food supplies.

In the east of the continent, local cultigens such as sumpweed (marsh elder) and sunflower were cultivated by small-scale horticulturalists, but it was probably not until the triad of maize, beans and squash was introduced that more complex cultures began to emerge in the Ohio and Mississippi River valleys, leading to the development of substantial towns such as Cahokia (see pages 162–163). But although these societies relied heavily on agriculture, crops were still supplemented by the hunting of animals such as deer, racoon and wild turkey, fishing and the gathering of wild nuts and berries ◆

settlement patterns took place, leading to the occupation of year-round villages. But even at this stage agricultural production remained unpredictable and there was still considerable dependence on wild plants and animals to supplement cultivated crops.

South America

The management of food plants in South America probably began between 12,000 and 10,000 years ago. Manioc (cassava), maize and the wild ancestors of other domesticated crops began to appear at sites on the Pacific coast by c.5000 BCE, or even a little earlier, and beans also made their appearance over the next millennium. Cotton, which was to become an important crop all along the coast of Peru, was used in its wild forms perhaps as early as 5000 BCE.

Between about 4000 and 2500 BCE large-scale changes took place in Andean lifestyles. The use of more specialized and complex fishing technology, including cotton nets, increased the size of fish catches and the harvesting of other marine resources, and coastal fishing communities had become sedentary by 3000 BCE. From the coast to the highlands hunter–gathering groups became more reliant on plant resources, and by 2500 BCE many plants, including cotton, beans, gourds, maize, grains, potatoes and other tubers had been transformed so completely that their remains are recognizable to archaeologists as domesticated plants. Similar changes took place farther north, in coastal Ecuador, among the people of the Valdivia culture. In northeast and central Brazil, cultivated food plants may date back 3,500 or even 4,500 years, but on the littoral and in other regions, hunting, fishing and gathering continued as before.

In the Andean highlands, the management of camelid herds for hunting led to the domestication

Bison Hunters of North America

Human occupation of the central grasslands of North America is known to be thousands of years old: by the 12th millennium BCE Paleoindians, ancestral Native Americans, were hunting large game animals like the mammoth, mastodon, camel and early forms of bison, all now extinct. Over time, they devised highly efficient hunting techniques, giving rise to the development of complex, multi-faceted cultures. Until Spanish settlers introduced the horse to the New World in the 16th century, all hunting and traveling was made on foot. The long-established way of life of the Plains Indians continued into the 19th century, when the last surviving tribes, fatally weakened by military suppression, the near extinction of the bison, and by devastating diseases such as smallpox, were forced onto reservations.

Much of the earliest evidence for prehistoric nomadic bison hunters has come from the western states of Colorado and New Mexico. In 1926, a finely worked spear point found lodged between the ribs of an extinct species of bison at an excavation near Folsom, New Mexico, was the first reliable indication of ancient human occupation. Not long after, another type of point, clearly ancestral to Folsom, was found at Clovis, also in New Mexico. It has given its name to a hunter–gatherer culture that existed around 11,500 y.a. across a wide area of North America, reaching as far north as Nova Scotia.

The people who made the Clovis spear points possessed highly advanced stone-flaking skills. They preyed on extinct forms of bison, as well as camel and mammoth. Quantities of projectile points have been recovered from kill sites where animals were slaughtered and butchered for their meat and hides, and archaeologists distinguish a number of distinct tool-making industries, evolving over time and space, which provide the basis for a chronology for the region. About 7,000 y.a. the *atlatl*, or weighted spear thrower, came into use on the Great Plains, and about 2,500 y.a. the bow and arrow was introduced, both of which enabled the hunter to project his pointed weapons more efficiently. Wild plants undoubtedly played as large a part as meat in the Paleoindian diet, and would also have been exploited for medicines, dyes, and for making baskets and other equipment, but archaeological evidence for this side of life is not easily come across.

RIGHT A Clovis point from about 11,000 y.a., associated with the hunting of very large game animals.

Map legend:
- □ Paleoindian site, c.10th–9th millennium BCE
- ▲ communal animal kill site
- △ quarry source of projectile points
- distribution of medicine wheels
- Great Plains
- range of bison before European contact, c.1500 CE

0 — 800 km
0 — 600 mi

Communal kills

Over time, kills appear to have become larger, more complex, and communally organized: vast numbers of hunters, with their families, purposefully assembled just for that one activity. The most spectacular type of communal kill was the cliff jump, in which a herd of bison was stampeded over a cliff. Other communal kills involved driving the herd into a specially constructed corral or pound, or a combination of a cliff and a pound. The hunters took advantage of natural features such as box canyons and sand dunes, laying out lines of stone cairns to channel the herd to the jump-point or pound.

One of the best documented kill sites is at Head-Smashed-In, in the foothills of the Rockies in southern Alberta, Canada. The site complex comprises a natural gathering basin, drive lanes, the actual cliff jump itself, and a campsite and butchering area at its

LEFT Clovis and Folsom spearpoints – powerful, flaked weapons used for killing very large game animals such as mammoth and mastadon– were distributed right across North America during the Late Pleistocene, and as far south as Panama. They disappear from the archaeological record during the 8th millennium BCE to be replaced by the smaller projectiles found in great numbers at communal kill sites throughout the Great Plains.

NORTH ATLANTIC OCEAN

Debert

Bull Brook

ake tario

base. Archaeologists have excavated over 30 ft/9 m of bone beds at the foot of the jump, the remains of individual kills, together with thousands of broken projectile points and other artifacts. The site, which has been used almost continuously for the last 5,700 years, remains sacred to the Blackfoot.

Large kills were often held in the autumn so that a good supply of food could be secured for the winter. Little of the slaughtered animals was wasted. Besides the meat and hide – used to make lodges, or *tipis*, and clothing – bone was turned into cooking utensils, blood and grease into glue, and sinews into cord. There is evidence to suggest that some communal kill sites were used annually, others only sporadically – possibly during wet periods when the grass grew tall and lush, increasing the size of herds. However, other communal sites seem to have been used only in times of drought. Clearly there was great variation in practice. While the chief function of organized hunts was to secure the food supply for the whole community, the immense size of some of the kills suggests that surplus resources were deliberately garnered for purposes of trade. In the historic period, communal kills provided a venue for numerous religious and social activities, and this is likely to have been so in earlier times as well.

Nomadic lifestyles

Tipi rings – circles formed by the stone weights that held down the skin walls of their portable lodges – first appear in the archaeological record about 3500 BCE. Surprisingly, perhaps, the nomadic Plains hunters developed a ceramic tradition. Their pottery was very utilitarian; decoration was often impressed on the wet surface with a net or some

other implement. It never rivalled the high technical or aesthetic quality of that produced by contemporary societies in the Southwest or Southeast.

A rich symbolic life

The rock art of the Plains, however, shows well developed artistic traditions. It is present both as petroglyphs and pictographs. However, as is the case with other rock art traditions, interpreting the meaning of these images is very difficult.

Medicine wheels are a unique phenomenon on the northern plains. These consist of stone cairns laid out in a giant circle, joined to a central cairn by lines of stones forming the spokes of a wheel. They may represent giant suns and are possibly connected to the Sun Dance lodges that were used by a number of historical Plains tribes for religious ceremonies associated with the summer solstice ◆

ABOVE At Olsen-Chubbuck in Colorado – a find dated to about 8200 BCE – the bones of around nearly 200 bison have been dug out of the bottom of a long arroyo, or ravine. They had been stampeded over the edge before being killed and butchered. It has been estimated that the herd would have provided over 50,000 lbs/22,700 kg of meat, enough to feed about 150 people for 23 days. The victims included calves only a few days old, so the drive must have taken place in late May or early June.

North American Mound Builders

During the early 1st millennium BCE some groups in the Eastern Woodlands of North America began to build sacred enclosures and burial mounds. Mound-building continued in the region more or less continuously until the European invasion. In the later period, large, flat-topped mounds, sometimes called temple mounds, formed the bases for elaborate buildings. Thousands were destroyed by Euroamerican settlement so it is difficult to estimate their original number; as many as 200,000 may once have existed.

The earliest known earthworks in North America are at Poverty Point, just west of the Mississippi River in northeastern Louisiana. The complex comprises a series of concentric ridges, divided by aisles, with associated mounds and was built between 1730 and 1350 BCE by Archaic hunter–gatherers. Artifacts found at the site include baked clay balls, which were used instead of stones for cooking, clay figurines and crude pottery. The site appears to be unique, and its function remains unclear. Some archaeologists have suggested it had a ceremonial role, but others believe that it may have been a regional center for exchange.

BELOW Both the Adena and the Hopewell cultures appear to have had their centers on the Ohio River, though the Hopewell may have originated further to the west in Illinois. Surviving artifacts give evidence of widespread trade. Hopewell craftsmen imported obsidian from Wyoming, flint from the Yellowstone area of Montana, copper from the shores of Lake Superior, and mica from the Blue Ridge Mountains.

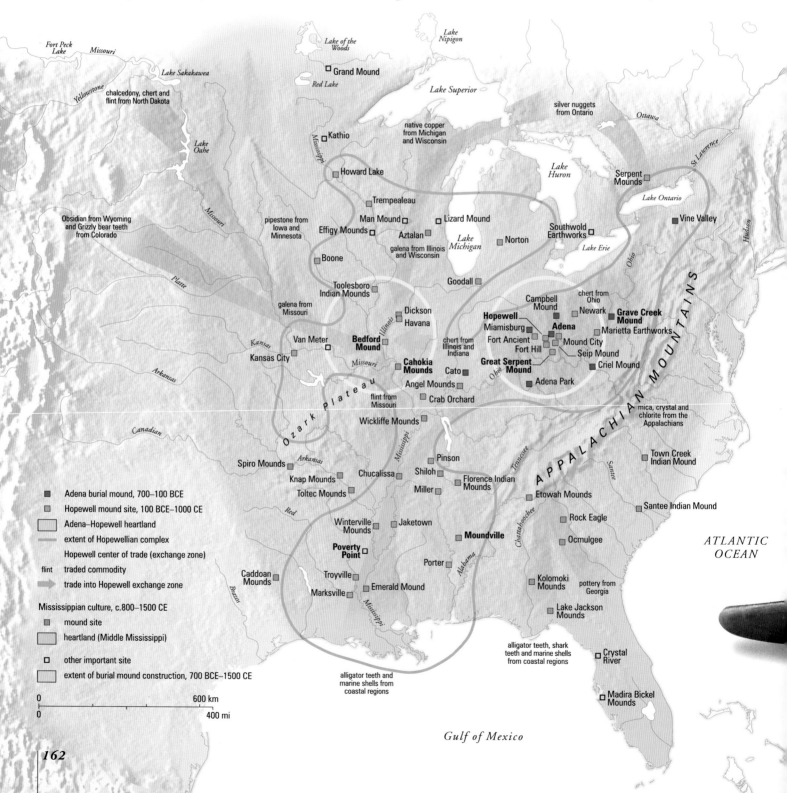

Adena culture

By about 750 BCE the people living in the Ohio River region, hunter–gatherers who also cultivated native species such as marsh elder, sunflowers and goosefoot, began to bury their dead in shallow pits beneath small conical mounds. They are known as the Adena culture, and by about 100 BCE the mounds were being constructed over elaborate wooden burial chambers. The biggest, at Grave Creek, stands 69 ft/ 21 m high, has a perimeter of 295 ft/90 m, and was originally enclosed by a moat. There is nothing to indicate permanent social hierarchies among these people, though the burials themselves are suggestive of ancestor veneration.

Hopewell culture

The Adena culture was followed by the Hopewell (c.100 BCE–500 CE), named for a site in southern Ohio excavated in the 19th century. It refers to a widespread exchange and ceremonial complex among the peoples of the Ohio and Mississippi River region. Raw materials were brought long distances to make high-value goods such as distinctive mica and copper cutouts and plaques decorated with stylized bird and animal motifs. Hopewell sites are complex affairs, sometimes comprising clusters of mounds, not all of which were burials, enclosed or linked by long earthen embankments. Some earthworks appear to have had religious or astronomical importance. One such is the Great Serpent Mound in Ohio. Variously ascribed to both the Adena and Hopewell cultures, it may in fact be later than either.

The Mississippian tradition

Four hundred years after the disappearance of the Hopewell cultural complex a new interregional culture arose in the Eastern Woodlands. The Mississippian tradition (c. 800–1500 CE) was a stratified society of local chiefdoms based on the intensive cultivation of new strains of corn. Beans and squashes were also grown, but the gathering of nuts and other wild plants remained important.

Large, flat-topped mounds, sometimes called temple mounds, are typical of the Mississippian tradition. The most spectacular site is Cahokia. It is the largest ancient American city yet excavated north of Mexico and covered an area of about 2,000 acres/ 810 hectares. Archaeologists estimate that as many as 30,000 people may have lived in the town and surrounding area. At the center was a compound of about 200 acres/81 hectares, enclosed by a log wall on three sides. Monk's Mound, which still stands more than 98 ft/30 m high, was at one end, with a plaza in front. Recent radiocarbon dating shows that the mound was built in stages over several centuries between 900 and 1150 CE, so that today it appears as a series of terraces of different heights. Visible nearby are the borrow pits from which the earth used to build it was dug. A large building, thought to have been the palatial dwelling of the community's leader, has been uncovered on top. The site contains around 100 smaller mounds, some of which were used as burial places for important people, others as platforms for wooden buildings. Moundville, Alabama, is a smaller site with 26 earthen mounds surrounding a central plaza. Its burials are especially rich in high-value artifacts ◆

ABOVE The Great Serpent Mound in Ohio was constructed along the top of a prominent ridge. The serpent's mouth, open as if to embrace an oval burial mound, can be seen in the top right of the picture; on the left is the creature's tightly coiled tail. The lack of archaeological information from the site makes it difficult to interpret but many have placed it within the Adena or Hopewell cultures. Recent research, however, dates it to about 1000 CE. The mound was saved from destruction in an early example of archaeological conservation and is now owned by the state of Ohio.

LEFT A Hopewell tobacco pipe in the shape of a beaver (1.7 in/4.5 cm high). It is carved from pipestone and decorated with freshwater pearl and bone inlays. Tobacco was placed in the a bowl in the beaver's back and smoke drawn through the hole at the front. It is typical of the finely crafted grave goods that were placed in Hopewell burial mounds. Unfortunately, very great numbers of these mounds were opened up and looted before the advent of modern archaeological techiques, and it is impossible to give a provenance or date to many Hopewell artifacts now in museums or private collections. This pipe was found by archaeologists in Bedford Mound, Illinois.

Pueblo Dwellers of the Southwest

The deserts of the American Southwest formed a distinct cultural area of ancient North America. Nomadic hunter–gatherers had occupied this harsh environment for millennia, but about 2,000 years ago their way of life underwent radical alteration, changing to one of settled farming based on corn, beans and squashes. Tobacco and cotton were also grown. They were skilled agriculturalists and used their environmental knowledge to maximize crop yields by constructing terraces to conserve rainfall and employing irrigation techniques. Because they lived in permanent settlements, they are known as "Pueblo" from the Spanish word for town or village.

The Pueblo dwellers were highly skilled craft-workers, and the dry environment of the Southwest has preserved the material remains of their culture – especially their pottery, basketry and textiles – in excellent condition. Climatic change and other pressures had caused most of their sites to be abandoned by the 14th century, but to the first Europeans who came upon them they looked as if they had only just been deserted. For this reason, the Pueblo dwellers attracted the early attention of archaeologists and ethnographers, and theirs is one of the most closely studied cultures of prehistoric North America.

Ancestral Pueblo

The Four Corners region lies on the Colorado Plateau and is the only point in the United States where four states (Colorado, Utah, Arizona and New Mexico) meet. The people who inhabited this region in ancient times are thought to be the ancestors of the present occupants, the Hopi, Zuni, Zia and Acoma. For long, archaeologists called them Anasazi, but now the term Ancestral Pueblo is more commonly used.

The Ancestral Pueblo began with the early Basketmaker peoples, who flourished about 2,000 years ago. The Basketmakers were corn farmers who still relied heavily on hunting and gathering for subsistence. At first, they did not make pottery but worked skillfully crafted basket containers from grasses, yucca fibers, twigs and bark. About 1,500 years ago they began to live in small, single-family semi-subterranean pithouses and make pots.

Around 800 CE the Ancestral Pueblo established villages on top of the mesas where they grew their crops, constructing their houses of jacal (adobe, or wattle and daub). Elsewhere they built them in the deep, stream-cut canyons that dissected the mesas, wedging them beneath steep cliff overhangs to form hive-like complexes of multi-roomed dwellings several storeys high. Their former pithouses were retained as *kivas*, underground chambers that served as social and religious gathering places for individual clans or other social groups.

As population numbers rose, outlier settlements radiated from local centers across the mesas. The Ancestral Pueblo developed extensive systems of trade. Chaco Canyon, a barren desert canyon today, was at the center of a well integrated economic-social-cultural network that extended throughout the northern Southwest. Roads and natural transportation routes like rivers linked it to outlier sites and trading contact reached as far as coastal California and Mexico to the south. Imported commodities such as turquoise and shell were worked into luxury items in workshops, and at its height in the 12th century there were 13 settlements in the canyon.

RIGHT The ancient farmers of the Southwest are divided by archaeologists into three major cultural traditions: the Ancestral Pueblo, the Hohokam and the Mogollon. While retaining distinctive characteristics, they share a number of common features and their cultural areas appear sometimes to have overlapped. Numerous smaller traditions have been defined within these broad divisions. Their trading networks extended far outside the region.

Mogollon pottery: A stylish tradition

Pueblo culture is noted for its remarkable pottery traditions. All the peoples of the regions developed distinctive styles, but the most accomplished were those produced by the Mogollon culture, belonging to the highlands of central and southern Arizona and New Mexico. Although farmers, the Mogollon relied more heavily on hunting and gathering than did the other Pueblo dwellers, and the impulse toward living in above-ground villages does not appear to have taken place here until c.1000 CE. At about the same time, a cultural florescence occurred in the

RIGHT MOGOLLON WHITE WARE PITCHER (7.8 IN/20 CM).

Mimbres valley of Arizona, characterized by the production of black-on-white and polychrome vessels, decorated with striking geometric patterns and stylized images of people and animals. Bowls were used as burial offerings and because ceremonial demanded that they were ritually killed, most have puncture holes in their bases. The clean lines of the Mimbres style make these vessels attractive to modern eyes, and they are highly desired by collectors. As a result, most Mimbres archaeological sites have been severely damaged, if not completely destroyed, by looters ◆

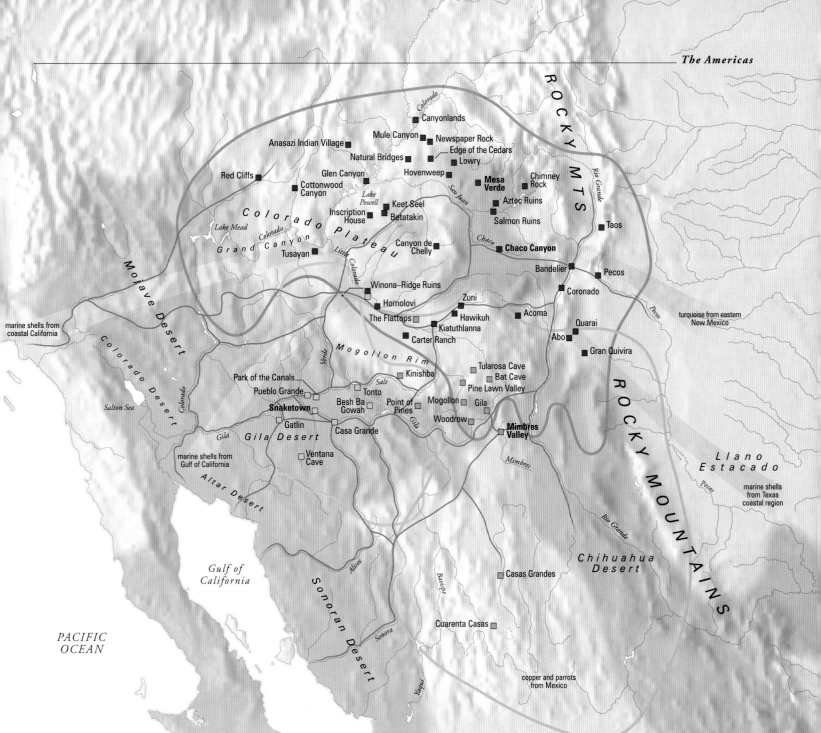

Map labels:

ROCKY MTS

Colorado

Canyonlands

Anasazi Indian Village

Mule Canyon

Newspaper Rock

Edge of the Cedars

Natural Bridges

Lowry

Red Cliffs

Glen Canyon

Hovenweep

Chimney Rock

Mesa Verde

Cottonwood Canyon

Lake Powell

Keet Seel

Aztec Ruins

Inscription House

Betatakin

Salmon Ruins

Rio Grande

Colorado Plateau

San Juan

Lake Mead

Taos

Grand Canyon

Colorado

Canyon de Chelly

Chaco

Chaco Canyon

Tusayan

Little Colorado

Bandelier

Pecos

Winona–Ridge Ruins

Coronado

Zuni

Pecos

Homolovi

turquoise from eastern New Mexico

marine shells from coastal California

The Flattops

Hawikuh

Acoma

Quarai

Mojave Desert

Verde

Mogollon Rim

Kiatuthlanna

Abo

Gran Quivira

Colorado Desert

Carter Ranch

Salton Sea

Tularosa Cave

Colorado

Kinishba

Bat Cave

Park of the Canals

Salt

Pine Lawn Valley

Pueblo Grande

Tonto

Point of Pines

Mogollon

Gila

Besh Ba Gowah

Snaketown

Woodrow

Gatlin

Casa Grande

Gila

Mimbres Valley

Gila Desert

Gila

Ventana Cave

Mimbres

Llano Estacado

Altar Desert

Pecos

marine shells from Gulf of California

marine shells from Texas coastal region

Gulf of California

Alias

Bavispe

Chihuahua Desert

ROCKY MOUNTAINS

Rio Grande

Sonoran Desert

Sonora

Casas Grandes

PACIFIC OCEAN

Cuaranta Casas

Yaqui

copper and parrots from Mexico

Legend:

- ■ Ancestral Pueblo (Anasazi) site
- □ Hohokam site
- ▪ Mogollon site
- — maximum extent of Ancestral Pueblo culture
- — maximum extent of Hohokam culture
- — maximum extent of Mogollon culture
- area of Chaco Canyon and outlier sites
- copper traded commodity
- trade into Chaco Canyon
- trade route
- desert area

0 — 300 km
0 — 200 mi

The architectural prowess of the Ancestral Pueblo culminated in the building of magnificent apartment-like complexes like those at Pueblo Bonito in Chaco Canyon, which rose five storeys high and contained 650 individual rooms and 32 *kivas*. Cliff Palace, tucked away beneath a towering cliff-face at Mesa Verde in southern Colorado, had 150 rooms and 23 *kivas*. Individual buildings were made of shaped stone, wood and plaster. Stairs were cut into the cliffside to allow the villagers to reach their fields on the mesa tops.

The cliff cities of the Four Corners region were not occupied for very long. The sites were largely abandoned early in the 14th century, probably as the result of a series of droughts that appears to have made the mesas untenable for farming. The people migrated southeast, toward the Rio Grande in northern New Mexico and Arizona.

Mesoamerican influences

Southwest of the Ancestal Pueblo, in central and southern Arizona, were the Hohokam – believed to be ancestors of the present-day Pima and Papago (O'Odham) peoples. Like the Ancestral Pueblo, their structures evolved from pithouses to above-ground villages. They appear to have had extensive contact with cultures to the south in Mexico, and large, bowl-shaped depressions found at some Hohokam sites have been interpreted as northern versions of Mesoamerican ball-game courts. Others, however, believe they were large ceremonial dance courts. One of the most famous Hohokam sites is Snaketown, south of Phoenix. Almost 0.5 sq mi/1.3 sq km in extent, it includes numerous dwelling structures, a ball court and one of the most extensive irrigation systems, consisting of check dams and irrigation ditches, yet found in North America ◆

Formative Period of Mesoamerica

State organization as conventionally characterized by social hierarchies with non-agricultural specialists and monumental architecture built by organized laborers appears to have developed much more gradually and patchily in Mesoamerica than it did in many other parts of the world. The domestication of maize and other crops was a millennia-long process (see pages 158–159), while reliance on wild plants was slow to diminish. About 1300 BCE, the hunters, fishers and small-scale agriculturalists who occupied the tropical lowlands of Mexico's southern Gulf Coast began the transition toward a complex society living in urban centers. During the Early and Middle Formative Periods, the Olmec built massive ceremonial platforms, which they decorated with monumental carved stone sculptures, and established far-flung networks of exchange with cultures throughout the region.

The humid jungles and inland waterways of the southern Gulf Coast were rich in plant and animal resources. It is here that the Olmec culture developed between c.1300 and 400 BCE at centers such as San Lorenzo and La Venta. But the Olmec heartland is relatively poor in other natural resources, particularly basalt, used for monumental sculptures and for grindstones. Cutting tools were made from fine grained obsidian and chert, imported from central Mexico, while iron ore for making polished mirrors came from Oaxaca and jade used for ceremonial axes from as far away as Costa Rica. In exchange for these materials, the Olmecs traded jungle products such as jaguar pelts and exotic feathers, which conferred prestige. Along with these material symbols, they passed on the concepts and iconography of their ruling ideology, rooted in the mythical mating of human ancestors with supernatural jaguars, thereby creating a self-sustaining network of elite consumers for their sumptuary goods.

The Valley of Oaxaca

Similar evolutionary processes were also taking place outside of the Olmec heartland, though on a less monumental scale. The Formative Period is particularly well documented at San José Mogote in the Oaxaca valley, which is located on fertile farmland. By 1200 BCE a small cluster of houses formed the nucleus of a community. As the village grew, satellite hamlets developed around the larger center. A public building constructed c.1000 BCE was probably used for ceremonial purposes, perhaps integrating the community and outlying hamlets through ritual performance. Finds of decorated ceramics and figurines,

as well as imported goods such as shell, indicate that its inhabitants were in contact with the Olmec of the Gulf Coast at this date.

In central Mexico, murals painted above a cave in Oxtotitlán depict an Olmec-style lord in a bird costume and seated on a jaguar throne. At Tlatilco, funerary remains include sculpted ceramics and figurines in Olmec style. Low relief carvings on boulders at the hillside site of Chalcatzingo depict scenes from Olmec mythology, including a seated individual, possibly a woman, in the mouth of a jaguar/earth cavern and holding a bundle, perhaps a stylized were-jaguar baby. Female figurines suggest that Olmec women may have been favored as wives to local elites, possibly as a means of solidifying trade agreements.

The appearance of Olmec "traits" in much of Mesoamerica does not indicate a widespread empire with actual political control. Nor does it imply that these diverse areas were lacking cultural complexity before the arrival of Olmec influences. What seems to have taken place is the adoption of Olmec religious ideals, as represented iconographically on pottery, figurines, and monumental art, to create a shared stylistic complex. Ideological practices of many later cultures can be traced back to Olmec origins, and are thus part of an overarching "Mesoamerican civilization", but not all cultures bought into the Olmec ideology of sacred kingship and continued on the path of political complexity. In Costa Rica, for example, carved jades indicate close ties to Olmec iconography, but local cultures were still characterized by dispersed villages with minimal social complexity. Similar choices were made in West Mexico, despite the presence of elaborate Olmecoid ceramic sculpture in tombs. The Formative Period thus presents an initial diversity of cultural practices that is eventually woven into the tapestry known as "Mesoamerica" ◆

ABOVE The dry upland valley of Oaxaca in southern Mexico provides one of the most complete data-sets for examining the rise of Mesoamerican civilization. A regional study carried out under the direction of Kent V. Flannery at various sites in the valley established a cultural sequence from Archaic Period hunter/collectors through early sedentary farmers and ultimately to a complex state centered on the hilltop site of Monte Albán.

RIGHT An Olmec head from La Venta, carved from a block of basalt. It is wearing a helmet for the ritual ball game, a "sport" that was designed to bridge the gap between the natural and supernatural realms. The monumental sculptures of the Olmec went through complex transformative changes. Beginning as rectangular altar/thrones, often with representations of human figures emerging from the jaguar mouth of the underworld, the thrones were later re-carved into colossal heads representing individuals, probably rulers. Finally, the heads were ritually "killed" by intentional defacement and were then buried within the ceremonial precinct, perhaps as lords of the underworld.

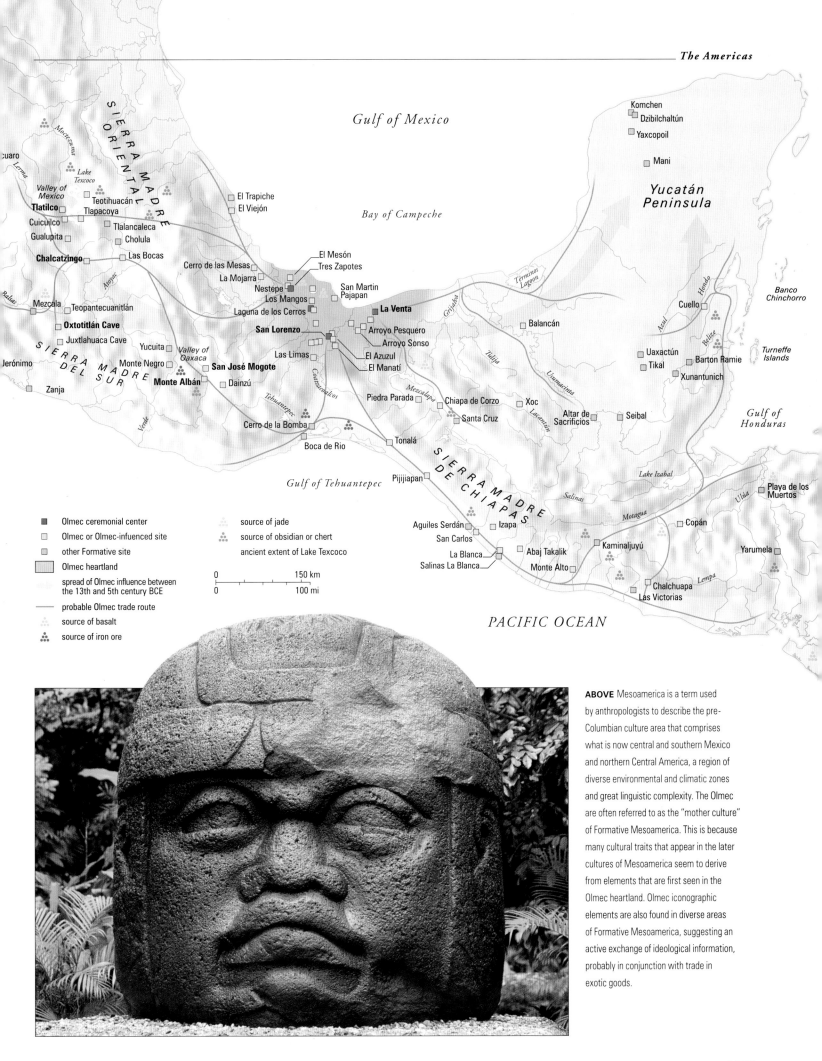

Gulf of Mexico

Komchen
Dzibilchaltún
Yaxcopoil

Bay of Campeche

Mani

Yucatán Peninsula

SIERRA MADRE ORIENTAL

Moctezuma
Lerma

cuaro

Lake Texcoco

Valley of Mexico
Tlatilco
Cuicuilco
Tlapacoya
Teotihuacán
Gualupita
Tlalancaleca
Cholula
Chalcatzingo
Las Bocas

El Trapiche
El Viejón

El Mesón
Tres Zapotes
Cerro de las Mesas
La Mojarra
Nestepe
Los Mangos
Laguna de los Cerros

San Martin
Pajapan

La Venta

San Lorenzo
Arroyo Pesquero
Arroyo Sonso
El Azuzul
El Manatí
Las Limas

Mezcala
Teopantecuanitlán
Oxtotitlán Cave
Juxtlahuaca Cave
Yucuita
Valley of Oaxaca
San José Mogote
Jerónimo
Monte Negro
Monte Albán
Zanja
Dainzú

SIERRA MADRE DEL SUR

Balas
Atoyac

Verde

Cerro de la Bomba
Boca de Rio
Tehuantepec

Coatzacoalcos

Términos Lagoon

Grijalva

Tulija

Usumacinta

Mezcalapa

Lacantún

Salinas

Banco Chinchorro

Cuello

Hondo

Azul

Belize

Uaxactún
Tikal
Barton Ramie
Xunantunich

Turneffe Islands

Piedra Parada
Chiapa de Corzo
Santa Cruz
Xoc

Altar de Sacrificios
Seibal

Gulf of Honduras

Gulf of Tehuantepec

Pijijiapan

SIERRA MADRE DE CHIAPAS

Tonalá

Aguiles Serdán
San Carlos
La Blanca
Salinas La Blanca
Izapa
Abaj Takalik
Monte Alto

Kaminaljuyú

Lake Izabal

Motagua

Uhla

Lempa

Copán

Playa de los Muertos

Yarumela

Chalchuapa
Las Victorias

PACIFIC OCEAN

■ Olmec ceremonial center
□ Olmec or Olmec-influenced site
□ other Formative site
▦ Olmec heartland
　spread of Olmec influence between the 13th and 5th century BCE
── probable Olmec trade route
⁝ source of basalt
⁝ source of iron ore

⁝ source of jade
⁝ source of obsidian or chert
　ancient extent of Lake Texcoco

0   150 km
0   100 mi

ABOVE Mesoamerica is a term used by anthropologists to describe the pre-Columbian culture area that comprises what is now central and southern Mexico and northern Central America, a region of diverse environmental and climatic zones and great linguistic complexity. The Olmec are often referred to as the "mother culture" of Formative Mesoamerica. This is because many cultural traits that appear in the later cultures of Mesoamerica seem to derive from elements that are first seen in the Olmec heartland. Olmec iconographic elements are also found in diverse areas of Formative Mesoamerica, suggesting an active exchange of ideological information, probably in conjunction with trade in exotic goods.

Classic Highland Civilizations

Between 200–700 CE, a period that is generally referred to by archaeologists as the Classic Period, Mesoamerican civilization attained new heights of cultural complexity. These developments were shared in many parts of Mesoamerica, including the central highlands of Mexico and the Maya regions of Central America. The latter are usually considered as a separate cultural entity during this period, but recent research demonstrates that the two areas were not completely isolated but were connected by subtle linkages of trade, ideology and religion (see pages 170–171). The Classic civilizations of Mexico's central highlands included urban centers like Teotihuacán, Cholula, and Monte Albán. The identifying characteristics of these state-level polities are features such as concentrated population centers, monumental architecture and standardized domestic ceramics. The appearance of similar traits, but on a smaller scale, at a number of local centers such as Yucuita and Cerro de las Minas on the fringes of the larger empires suggests that these lower-level states were engaged in emulating the political strategies of their more powerful neighbors. The Classic civilizations reached new peaks in population size and monumental building, and these states were maintained for 500 years. Then, for reasons that are still not fully understood by archaeologists, both Teotihuacán and Monte Albán rapidly declined, leading to the abandonment of their ceremonial centers.

The evolution of a Classic state has been documented at the Zapotec imperial capital of Monte Albán in the valley of Oaxaca, where regional as well as intensive site surveys (with investigators walking across fields and hill slopes to identify archaeological sites) have yielded information about the changing population size and distribution of communities across the valley landscape. This indicates that dispersed local centers had coalesced into a single regional center, Monte Albán, by 500 BCE. The capital straddles a series of high ridges at the nexus of three interrelated valley systems, and its monumental administrative architecture can be seen from all over the valley system. The carved stone images of captured and sacrificed lords that decorated the ceremonial center at Monte Albán suggest its empire was founded through military conquest.

Cosmological architecture

Other highland civilizations used less violent images to justify their rule. Teotihuacán was the largest city of the Classic Period. At its height (300–600 CE) it had a population of around 150,000. Its public architecture accentuated cosmological themes (see box).

The same is true at Cholula, which was founded at least as early as 1000 BCE, making it one of the oldest urban centers of Mesoamerica. Its ceremonial center features the largest pyramid in the Americas in terms of volume of construction material; it was aligned to face the setting sun at the summer solstice and

Teotihuacán: city of the gods

Teotihuacán (known to us today by its Aztec name, meaning "city of the gods") is located about 30 mi/50 km north of Mexico City. It is one of the most completely mapped and excavated sites of ancient Mesoamerica, offering intriguing insights into the organizing principles by which its inhabitants shaped the cultural landscape. The cosmology expressed through its site plan and monumental architecture established it as an *axis mundi*, the center of the culturally defined universe. Teotihuacán was built on a rigid grid system. At the northern end of the main axis, the so-called Avenue of the Dead, was the Pyramid of the Moon, designed to mimic the form of Cerro Gordo mountain, in whose shadow it stood. Similarly, the Pyramid of the Sun, midway along the Avenue, mirrored the profile of the hill on the horizon behind it. The San Juan river that flowed through the urban area was channeled to correspond to the grid orientation. Recent

investigations have discovered quarry tunnels beneath the pyramids from which the basalt used to build them was mined. The tunnels then served a ritual function relating to the cosmology of the underworld. A tunnel beneath the Pyramid of the Sun was created with an end chamber resembling the mythical cave from which humankind emerged, and other tunnels featured openings through which astronomical cycles could be plotted. An immense ritual space, the Ciudadela was enclosed by a rectangular platform featuring additional small pyramid platforms. Inside this enclosure is the Pyramid of the Feathered Serpent, so named for the carved representations of feathered jaguar/serpents that cover the terrace walls of the pyramid. Recent excavations around and inside the pyramid revealed more than 100 skeletons of sacrificed warriors and priests, hinting at the compound's ceremonial use ◆

RIGHT A FEATHERED SERPENT CARVING FROM TEOTIHUACÁN.

Chalchihuites

El Teul

Itztepetl

Lake Chapala

Jiquilpan

Colima

Apatzingán

Tepalcatepec

SIERRA MADRE OCCIDENTAL

SIER

ABOVE Monte Albán, the Zapotec capital that dominated the Oaxaca valley in the Classic Period.

built over a spring, perceived in Meso-american cosmology as a portal to the aqueous underworld – an interior chamber may have given access to the sacred waters. Architectural elements from an early construction stage include numerological referents to the calendar cycle; the implied claim of the priesthood to control time was a fundamental principle of Mesoamerican religion. As at Teotihuacán, the Great Pyramid was an *axis mundi* defining Cholula as the center of the universe.

Communal identities

Ceremonial art and architecture are indicators of the way the Classic highland states legitimized their existence. Individualism was minimized in favor of communal identities expressed through standardized facial characteristics and decoration. No elite tombs are known from Teotihuacán or Cholula. At Teotihuacán apartment compounds housed from five to ten families, with only minor variation to indicate status differences. The nobility of Monte Albán enjoyed greater social distance from commoners, as demonstrated by elaborate tombs beneath their palaces, and their social position was supported by ritual links to their deified ancestors. All of these societies, however, masked social distinctions behind a limited array of material culture, such as uniformly drab monochrome utilitarian pottery. Elite status was expressed through exotic imports from the Maya region, including jade beads and ear flares and brightly colored feathers.

A number of reasons have been put forward to explain the rapid decline of Teotihuacán and Monte Albán. Perhaps people became disillusioned with their gods and god-kings, or new immigrants from the north and the east disrupted the status quo. Equally inexplicably, Cholula underwent profound cultural change but continued to grow into one of the key sites that shaped the Postclassic Period (see pages 172–173). The processes by which these civilizations emerged, were sustained and ultimately declined remain the focus of continuing research ◆

ABOVE Archaeological research indicates that there were three major urban centers in Mexico's central highlands during the Classic Period – Cholula, Monte Albán and Teotihuacán – each with its own sphere of influence. Of these polities, the largest was Teotihuacán. Most of its population were farmers, growing maize, beans, squash and maguey (an agave) in fields surrounding the urban center. Craft items such as obsidian tools and weapons, pottery, ceramic figurines and jewelry (from imported semi-precious stones) manufactured in Teotihuacán were traded over great distances. Characteristic artifacts have even been found in distant Maya sites such as Tikal and Kaminaljuyú.

Map labels

Gulf of Mexico

SIERRA MADRE ORIENTAL

Pánuco
Pavón
Rio Verde
Tepetzintla
Jacala
Las Ranas
Tolimán
El Tajín
San Juan del Río
Tulancingo
Yohualinchan
Tepeji
Zinapécuaro
Teotihuacán
Calpulalpan
Xiuhtetelco
Perote
Azcapotzalco
Calixtlahuaca
Xico
Cacaxtla
Chachalacas
de Bravo
Remojadas
Huejotzingo
Cholula
Tenango
Tepeaca
Cerro de las Mesas
Los Tuxtlas
Matacapan
Huetamo
Chalcatzingo
Ixcaquixtla
Tlatlayan
Tehuacán
Tres Zapotes
Piedra Labrada
Comalcalco
Tanganhuato
Acatlán
Miguel Alemán Reservoir
Matacanela
Catemaco
Balsas
Tuxtepec
Cuicatlán
Cerro de las Minas
San Lorenzo
Silacayoapan
Yucuñudahui
Yucuita
Tilantongo
Villa Alta
Monte Albán
Yagul
Acapulco
Verde
Isthmus of Tehuantepec
Chiapa de Corzo
Tehuantepec
Tonalá
Angostura Reservoir
Atoyac
SIERRA MADRE DEL SUR
Mezcalapa
Mezcalapa
Tehuantepec
SIERRA MADRE DE CHIAPAS

PACIFIC OCEAN

Gulf of Tehuantepec

Bay of Campeche

Legend

■ major Classic site
□ other Classic site
— Cholula
▭ Monte Albán
▭ Teotihuacán
spread of Monte Albán cultural influence
spread of Teotihuacán cultural influence
ancient extent of Lake Texcoco

0   150 km
0   100 mi

Maya States of Central America

Ever since the journalist-explorers John Stephens and Frederick Catherwood first sent back reports of "lost cities" in the jungles of the Yucatán peninsula and neighboring Guatemala and Honduras, the vanished civilization of the ancient Maya has intrigued scholars and captivated the public imagination. Until quite recently, romanticized interpretations of Maya civilization focused on their close attention to astronomical and calendrical events, leading archaeologists to create a model of "classic" philosopher-princes. However, this house of cards came crashing down in the 1970s when advances in the decipherment of Maya hieroglyphs, together with iconographic "readings" of the accompanying images, revealed a much more violent character. Texts on monumental stone stelae, staircases and altars repeatedly describe inter-city conquests, often resulting in the capture and sacrifice of rival lords. Battles were enacted in accordance with astronomical cycles, particularly those relating to the planet Venus. The writing system of the Maya is now largely deciphered, providing a remarkable window on the political machinations and supernatural manipulations of the Maya elite and bringing new insights to their culture.

BOTTOM Funerary urn in the shape of a god's face mask. Maya religion was a complex mix of supernatural beings, cosmic dimensions and deified ancestors. Through ritual blood-letting (by passing a thorn or stingray spine through the tongue) and dance, shamanic rulers could open portals to the otherworld to communicate with supernatural forces. On the domestic level, too, ancestral spirits were believed to provide a means of interceding with the gods on behalf of the living.

Gulf of Mexico

Komchen
Dzibilchaltún
Izamal
Acanceh
Chichén Itzá
Oxkintok
Kabáh
Uxmal
Yaxu
Jaina
Loltún Cave
Sayil
Xcocha
Labná
Santa Rosa
Xtampak
Dzibilnocac
Edzná
Hochob

Bay of Campeche

Yucatán Peninsula

Bellote
Comalcalco
San Miguel
Becán
Xpuhil
Hormiguero
Kohunlich
Oxpemul
Río Bec
Nohmul
Calakmul
El Palmar
Cu
Uxul
Balancán
Moral
Naachtún
Río Azul
Altun Ha
El Mirador
La Honradez
Lamanai
Tortuguero
Uaxactún
Moho Ca
Palenque
San José
Holmul
Piedras Negras
Tikal
Barton Ramie
La Mar
El Cayo
Xunantunich
Toniná
Nakum
Naranjo
Yaxchilán
Yaxhá
Caracol
Po
Bonampak
Tzimin Kax
Itzán
Ixkun
(Mountain C
Chiapa de Corzo
Altar de Sacrificios
Seibal
Nimli Puni
Dos Pilas
Naj Tunich
Santa Cruz
Aguateca
Machaquila
Lubaantun
Cancuén
Pusilha
Chinkultic
Quen Santo
Castillo de San Felipe
Lake Izabal
Chamá
Motagua
Nebaj
Quiriguá
Zacualpa
Los Higos
San Agustín
El Paraiso
Izapa
Acasaguastlán
Copán
El Jobo
Río Amarillo
Abaj
Lake Atitlán
Kaminaljuyú
Takalik
Chukumuk
Salinas
El Baúl
Amatitlán
Asunción Mita
La Blanca
Pantaleón
Tiquisate
Monte Alto
Chalchuapa
Finca Arizona
Tazumal
La Nueva
Cerén

PACIFIC OCEAN

■	Late Formative period site
□	Classic Mayan site
<u>Tikal</u>	site whose dynastic history has been deciphered
	Classic Mayan states

architectural style of the Late Classic period

Puuc
Chenes
Río Bec

evidence of intensive cultivation

— raised fields
— stone-faced terraces

0   100 km
0   75 mi

The roots of Classic Maya culture can be traced back to the Olmec through the art of the Izapa culture of Pacific Guatemala, where carved stone stelae of the Late Formative Period mixed supernatural themes with representations of mortal lords. Evidence of concentrated political authority appears at sites such as Cerros and El Mirador at this time. The Maya concept of rulership, called the *k'uhul ajaw*, is associated with divine authority and claims of control over forces of nature such as rainfall, celestial movement and time.

The "long-count" calendrical system used in Maya texts locates events to a starting point in the distant past. One reading of this calendar, the Goodman-Martinez-Thompson (GMT) correlation, proposes a starting point of 3113 BCE for the present world cycle, which will terminate in 2012. Herbert Spinden and David Kelley, among others, favor other correlations with starting dates both earlier and later than the generally accepted GMT date.

Unlike the Classic states of central Mexico, the Maya were never united under a single ruler. At different times various city-states ascended to regional supremacy, only to be replaced by others. Tikal was one of the early conquest states, dominating a large kingdom in the 4th century CE (GMT correlation), but war with distant Calakmul resulted in defeat and subjugation, as described on a hieroglyphic staircase in the conquered capital. In the 6th century, however, Tikal re-emerged as a dominant polity. This pattern of cyclical rise and fall was repeated at many other Maya centers, including Copán, Quiriguá, Palenque, Cobá, Dos Pilas and Yaxchilán.

ABOVE Much of our knowledge of Maya cosmology comes from books of folded deerskin called codices, which incorporated calendrical and astronomical information with details of ritual practice, both through hieroglyphic texts and imagery. Here a hunter brings a deer for ritual sacrifice.

LEFT The Maya region presents a dynamic patchwork of competing city-states. Through marriage alliances, trade networks and conquest the political map was in constant flux as kingdoms rose and then fell. Some of the more prominent cities such as Tikal or Calakmul maintained their prominence for centuries, incorporating dozens of smaller cities in the process.

Everyday activities

Archaeological investigations of Maya settlement patterns reveal that organization of the population was predominantly based on agriculture, including the use of intensive farming techniques in the swampy lowlands surrounding the urban centers. Excavations in smaller centers and rural communities suggest that men were typically employed in farming pursuits and limited hunting of wild game, as well as craft production. Women were closely linked to tasks such as child-care, cooking and textile production. Religion at the domestic level emphasized the importance of lineage ancestors as links between mortal and supernatural realms.

The end of the Maya

Classic Maya civilization came to an end in the 9th century (GMT correlation), when the ceremonial centers were sacked and abandoned, and official histories stopped being recorded on hieroglyphic monuments. One popular explanation of this "collapse", informed by ecological theory, is that over-exploitation of the fragile tropical ecosystem by large urban populations resulted in environmental disaster. An alternative model suggests that polygamous noble families produced a top-heavy social hierarchy, and ultimately the commoner class may have risen up in revolt. Another theory interprets innovative stylistic elements in Terminal Classic art as evidence for invasion by groups from the Chontalpa region of the southern Gulf Coast. Probably no single cause was responsible, but rather a combination of factors ◆

Palenque: Maya city in the mist

Palenque, on the western edge of the Maya region, is one of the most spectacular of Maya cities. Its magnificent architecture includes the palace (with a four-story tower), the Cross group of three pyramids representing Maya creation, and the Temple of the Inscriptions, built as a burial pyramid for Hanab Pakal (603–683 CE), ruler during the period of Palenque's greatest expansion. An extensive hieroglyphic text carved on the walls of the temple documents the lineage and divine origins of the king. A stone sarcophagus placed in a burial crypt beneath the floor of the temple and surrounded with carved imagery of the underworld was found to contain the bones of an adult male. Accompanying the body was a mosaic mask and many other ritual items of jade, the precious green stone that signified eternal life ◆

ABOVE THE PALACE AND TEMPLES AT PALENQUE ARE SET ON A WOODED HILLSIDE OVERLOOKING THE USUMACINTA FLOODPLAIN.

Cobá

Tancah

ffe
ds

The Postclassic Transformation

The years following the end of the Classic Period, c.700–1100 CE, witnessed profound changes in Mesoamerican civilization. As many of the old sites were abandoned, new cities were established at sites like Chichén Itzá, El Tajín, Xochicalco, Cacaxtla and Tula. Though never abandoned, Cholula also underwent major changes with an ambitious building program that doubled the size of its Great Pyramid. A unifying characteristic of these sites was the degree to which "foreign" influences were present in public architecture and iconography, suggesting a new "internationalism", at least among the ruling elite.

One of the great enigmas of this transitional period concerns the relationship between the cities of Chichén Itzá and Tula. Although they are at the geographic extremes of Mesoamerica, they show remarkable similarities in site planning, architectural style, and decoration (see box). The traditional explanation was that Chichén Itzá was conquered by Toltecs from Tula, but this is questioned by those who now believe that the Maya city is the older of the two. An alternative view argues that both sites were part of a pan-Mesoamerican movement of eclectic internationalism that blended iconographies from various regions.

Developments at Cholula exemplify this new synthesis. During the Classic Period, Cholula had not been part of Teotihuacán's political sphere and its ceremonial precinct was architecturally distinct. But after the fall of Teotihuacán, the Great Pyramid was enlarged and its new facades built in a style that had been characteristic of Teotihuacán, as if to declare that Cholula had inherited the cosmological significance of its abandoned neighbor. Additional architectural elements included features from Monte Albán, Chichén Itzá and El Tajín.

International movements

This internationalism was appropriate to Cholula's status as the center of the Quetzalcoatl ("Feathered Serpent") religious cult that swept through Mesoamerica at this time, especially among the nobility, who visited the shrine to receive legitimation of their authority. A brilliantly colored pottery decorated with religious themes originated in Cholula and became a popular status symbol of elite consumption in diverse parts of Mesoamerica during the Postclassic period. Other sites in central Mexico reflect similar developments. Magnificent polychrome murals from Cacaxtla depict ethnic conflict between central Mexican and Maya warriors based on costume and facial characteristics, resulting in the foundation of a mixed ethnic dynasty. Another mural shows the Maya merchant god, suggesting long-distance trade contacts between the regions, while at Xochicalco a Maya-style lord is

ABOVE Tripod vase from Xochicalco, made of alabaster and finished to a translucent thinness. Painted on the wall of the vessel is a descending bird with green plumage, probably a quetzal bird from the tropical Maya lowlands. The vase was part of a burial offering, and the quetzal image plus the circular glyph beneath it may be naming elements of the deceased.

Map labels:

Chalchihuites
San Pedro
SIERRA MADRE OCCIDENTAL
La Quemada
Buenavista
SIERRA MADRE ORIENTAL
Las Flores
Pánuco
Tamuín
Teul
Río Grande de Santiago
Bolaños
Santa María
Ixtlán
Léon
Moctezuma
Teayo
El Tajín
Etzatlán
Itztepetl
San Miguel de Allende
Las Higueras
Ameca
Chiquihuítillo
Tula
El Pital
Lake Chapala
Lerma
Xilotepec
Tulancingo
Cojumatlán
Lake Cuitzeo
Chiapa
Tepeji de Ocampo
Zémpoala
Cantona
Zacapu
Atlacomulco
see inset map
Isla Sacrificí
Tzintzuntzán
Xocotitlán
Ixtlahuacan
Xochitecatl
Tepalcatepec
Cuahuacan
Cacaxtla
Apatzingán
Valle de Bravo
Tepoztlán
Cholula
El Zap
Calixtlahuaca
Infiernillo Reservoir
Teotenango
Xochicalco
Huetamo
Malinalco
Mexiquito
Miguel Alemán Reservoir
SIERRA MADRE DEL SUR
Teloloapan
Teotitlán
Zacatollán
Balsas
Ayoyac
Petatlán
Tetzmoliuhuacan
Monte Albán
Ayoyac
Lambit
Tututepec

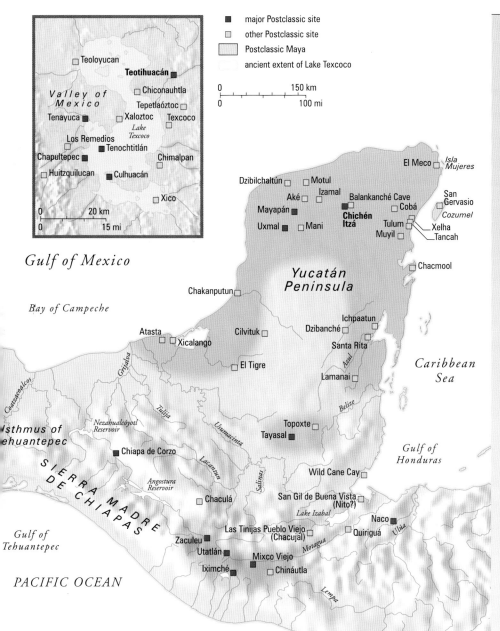

major Postclassic site
other Postclassic site
Postclassic Maya
ancient extent of Lake Texcoco

Tula and Chichén Itzá: "twin cities"

Chichén Itzá, in semitropical Yucatán, and Tula, located in the arid north of Mesoamerica, have puzzled scholars for decades, for despite being over a thousand kilometers apart, their two ceremonial centers seem almost to have been built from the same blueprint. At Chichén Itzá, the architecture combines the intricately ornate facades of Maya Puuc style with more geometric structures that have been called Mexican in style. Feathered Serpents carved in low relief are prominent characteristics of "Mexican" buildings like the Great Ballcourt and the Temple of the Warriors. Other relief facades depict alternating eagles and jaguars, marching warriors and a narrative scene that may represent the mythical origins of the ruling elite. The layout and architecture of Tula's ceremonial center are remarkably similar. Structure B, with its multi-tiered construction and carved pillars in the shape of warriors and feathered serpents, parallels Chichén's Temple of the Warriors. Reclining human figures carved in three dimensions, known as chac-mools, form another strong parallel between the sites. In contrast, however, there is little resemblance between domestic remains such as utilitarian pottery at the two sites, indicating that the populations were culturally distinct. Were these great cities part of a shared ideology of internationalism that revolved around the Feathered Serpent cult? The debate is not yet decided ◆

ABOVE WARRIOR COLUMNS IN TULA'S CEREMONIAL CENTER.

ABOVE During the Postclassic transformation, the monolithic empires of the central highlands gave way to a political landscape of many independent city-states that rarely encompassed vast stretches of territory. Instead of political control, the Postclassic is characterized more by the ideological expansion of the cult of Quetzalcoatl, whereby kingdoms throughout Mesoamerica claimed legitimation through the supernatural power of the Feathered Serpent. Postclassic economics were similarly influenced by this force, as long-distance *pochteca* merchants under the protection of their patron deity Yiacatecuhtli (an avatar of Quetzalcoatl) traded exotic goods such as quetzal feathers, cacao and precious stones used to display prestige.

depicted in the coil of a gigantic Feathered Serpent. Yet there is little to suggest that Maya people were a significant component of the population. The idea of internationalism seems to have outweighed actual migration.

El Tajín, on the Gulf Coast, would have been a likely midway point between the Maya and highland cultures. An elaborate architectural program featuring low-relief carving is clearly related to that of Chichén Itzá. The walls of the main ballcourt, for example, vividly depict the symbolic significance of the ballgame as a ritual of sacrifice and renewal. But it is important to recognize that El Tajín represents its own unique style, blending foreign ideas with local style to create its own identity. Here, as elsewhere, the Postclassic Period represents a transformation from the relatively isolated styles of the Classic Period to more dynamic mosaics of multiple influences ◆

The Aztecs of Central Mexico

The Aztecs were latecomers to the Mesoamerican cultural area. Originating in the northern desert of Mexico in a mythical homeland known as Aztlan, they migrated south as one of many seminomadic tribes known collectively as the Chichimecs. According to their origin myth, they settled on an island in the middle of Lake Texcoco where their patron deity Huitzilopochtli had predicted they would see an eagle perched atop a cactus with a snake in its mouth. Here they founded their capital city of Tenochtitlán in 1325. When conquered by the Spanish in 1519, it had a population of approximately 1 million.

The Aztecs began their occupation of central Mexico in a most inauspicious manner, as impoverished mercenaries for more powerful city-states such as Azcatpotzalco. But according to their chronicles, they had an astute sense of history and propaganda as Aztec nobles arranged marriages with women of Toltec bloodlines from the city of Culhuacán in an effort to infuse their own dynasties with imperial legitimacy. By the early 1400s the strategy had paid off. The Aztecs of Tenochtitlán were able to forge an alliance with the surrounding cities of Texcoco and Tacuba to overthrow the domination of Azcapotzalco, and this "Triple Alliance" became the basis for subsequent military conquests as the Aztec empire began a meteoric expansion. On the eve of the Spanish conquest, the vast territory under direct Aztec control included all of the central highlands and Gulf Coast. Tribute in the form of exotic goods came from as far as the Pacific coast of Central America.

Aztec religion

Religion was the organizing principle of Aztec society. A complex pantheon of gods and goddesses controlled natural forces such as the sun, wind and rain. The patron deity was Huitzilopochtli, associated with warfare and the sun. Other important deities included Tlaloc (rainstorms), Cihuacoatl (earth/fertility), Quetzalcoatl (wind), and Xochiquetzal (sexuality and the arts). The written and pictorial accounts of 16th-century Spanish priests provide detailed information on the deities and the rituals associated with their worship. The sacred calendar divided the year into thirteen 20-day "months" presided over by specific deities, during which elaborate ceremonies were practiced. One of the fundamental rituals, and the one for which the Aztecs are best known, was human heart sacrifice, when human hearts were ripped from the chest of living victims and offered as nourishment for the sun. A driving force behind Aztec militarism was the need to capture victims for sacrifice. In the case of the neighboring kingdoms of Tlaxcala and Cholula, this took the form of ritualized warfare.

City of the chinampas

The Aztec capital of Tenochtitlán was of unprecedented size in Mesoamerica. A series of causeways connected the island in Lake Texcoco to the mainland, where "suburban" population centers spread out over a wide area. Additional living space was located on the *chinampa* islands, created by dredging the bottom of the shallow lake to create dry platforms between deeper canals. The *chinampas* were a technological modification of the lake environment that allowed intensive production of fruit and vegetables to supply the large urban population. Multiple crops of maize greatly enhanced the carrying capacity of the land. Goods were transported by water to markets in and around the city. Canoe-loads of produce, items of trade, fresh water, and even human waste for fertilizer made Tenochtitlán a bustling commercial center.

The Great Temple and ceremonial center were at the heart of the city. Outside of the ceremonial center, the city was divided into quadrants containing specific neighborhoods called *calpulli* that were the basis of tribute collection and military service. Temple and secular schools trained youths in ritual practices, military techniques and craft specializations. Girls could also enter temple schools, but domestic arts were generally learned at home.

BELOW A pectoral ornament in the form of a double-headed serpent, 17 in/42 cm long, which probably formed part of the treasure sent by the Aztec king Moctezoma II to the Spanish conquistador Hernán Cortès. One of the symbols of Tlaloc, it would have formed part of the apparel of a high priest. When the force of Spanish mercenaries led by Cortès arrived in central Mexico in 1519, the Aztec civilization was at its fullest. Spurred on by dreams of gold and glory, the Spanish received support from recently conquered subjects of the Aztec empire looking to throw off the tribute demands of their overlords. The deeply religious Moctezoma, who had received omens of foreboding regarding the newly arrived foreigners, sent them rich offerings of treasure before allowing them to enter Tenochtitlán unopposed. These overtures did nothing to avert disaster. Although the Spanish suffered their worst defeat of the campaign and were forced to flee the city, Moctezoma was taken hostage and died in captivity. After regrouping in the allied city of Texcoco, the Spanish laid siege to Tenochtitlán even as the first waves of smallpox were ravaging the Aztecs behind the city walls. Within two years of their arrival, the Spanish had conquered the most powerful empire in Mesoamerican history.

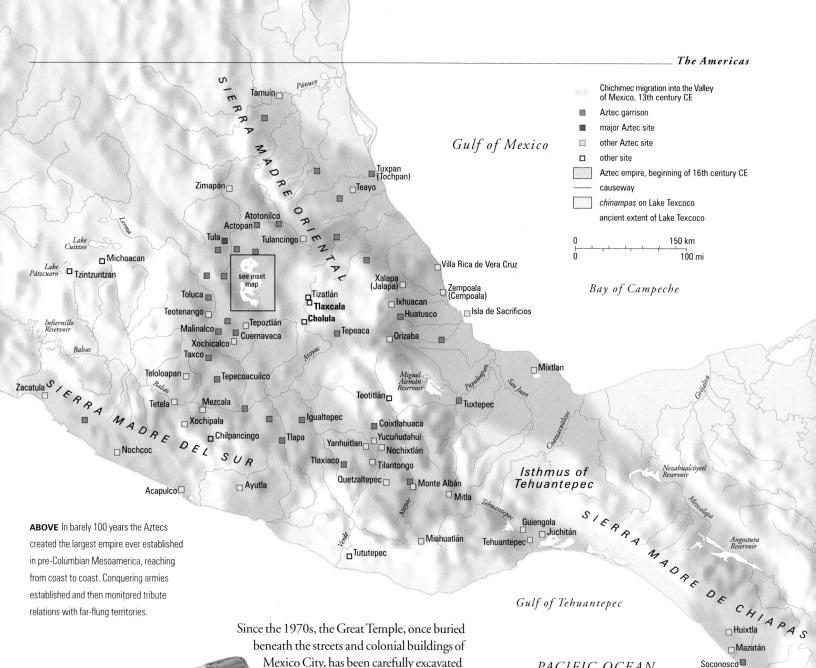

Gulf of Mexico

Bay of Campeche

Chichimec migration into the Valley of Mexico, 13th century CE
■ Aztec garrison
■ major Aztec site
□ other Aztec site
□ other site
Aztec empire, beginning of 16th century CE
— causeway
chinampas on Lake Texcoco
ancient extent of Lake Texcoco

| 0 | 150 km |
| 0 | 100 mi |

SIERRA MADRE ORIENTAL

SIERRA MADRE DEL SUR

SIERRA MADRE DE CHIAPAS

Isthmus of Tehuantepec

PACIFIC OCEAN

Gulf of Tehuantepec

ABOVE In barely 100 years the Aztecs created the largest empire ever established in pre-Columbian Mesoamerica, reaching from coast to coast. Conquering armies established and then monitored tribute relations with far-flung territories.

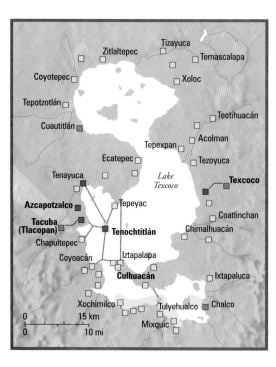

Since the 1970s, the Great Temple, once buried beneath the streets and colonial buildings of Mexico City, has been carefully excavated to reveal seven stages of construction dating back to the foundations of the Aztec capital. Associated structures include small shrines, a *tzompantli* skull rack platform and the ceremonial precinct for a warrior guild. Over 100 offerings representing the sea, land and heavens, and from earlier time periods, including the Olmec, show that the Great Temple was constructed as an *axis mundi* of international proportions.

The Aztecs provide an important key to understanding Mesoamerican civilization because their culture was abundantly described by colonial-period chroniclers such as Fray Bernardino de Sahagún, whose Florentine Codex, using the testimony of indigenous informants, includes minute details of Aztec life. These ethnohistoric sources are not without bias, as different scribes shifted the focus of their account to suit their particular agenda. Nevertheless, they provide a rich source for interpreting Late Postclassic society and, by extrapolation back in time, for modeling earlier Mesoamerican societies ◆

Pre-civilizations of South America

Large adobe-brick mounds at Aspero, El Paraíso, Huaca Prieta and a number of other sites along the coast of northern and central Peru are evidence for the first complex societies in the Andes. It was long assumed by archaeologists that these impressive structures had been built by developed farming peoples, but research in the 1960s and 1970s revealed the absence of pottery at any of the sites; they also contained very few domesticated plants. It became clear that the people who built them were primarily fishers, and it was only after their societies had became well established that they began making pottery and cultivating food crops. Similar changes were taking place among other small groups in a number of different areas. At first they developed in isolation from each other, but soon larger regional cultural traditions emerged, giving rise to the earliest civilizations of South America in the 1st millennium BCE.

The earliest adobe mound sites of Peru belong to the period that archaeologists refer to as the Cotton Preceramic (2500–1800 BCE). It is clear that important economic, technological, and social changes were taking place at this time and there is evidence for the performance of ever more complex activities by large groups of people. At Aspero, for example, a series of 13 earth and rubble mounds of varying sizes were built, with adobe walls forming rooms and small courts on their summits. In and around the mounds, archaeologists have uncovered caches of small unbaked clay figurines, engraved gourds, textiles woven from cultivated cotton, and human burials.

Monumental building appeared around this time in the Andean highlands as well, at sites such as Kotosh, Huaricoto, and La Galgada. At Kotosh, approximately 6500 ft/2000 m above sea level, a series of structures were built and then ritually buried. They are about 30 ft/9 m square and adorned with adobe friezes, and have been identified as temples. The inhabitants of these Late Preceramic highland sites seem to have subsisted on a combination of horticulture, hunting and trade, with perhaps some herding.

The earliest known pottery tradition of South America is that of Valdivia, on the coast of Ecuador, which developed around 3000 BCE among settled horticulturalists who cultivated maize, beans, root

BELOW Pottery figure, seated with legs crossed and wearing helmet headgear, belonging to the Chorrera culture of coastal Ecuador (1800–500 BCE). Pottery is often considered to be one of the hallmarks of societies moving toward civilization. Pottery vessels can be made in uniform sizes, which are useful for measuring uniform quantities of goods. Pottery is also an important medium for artistic and iconographic expression, and many early civilizations manufactured distinctive and highly decorative pottery vessels, as well as figurines and other ceramic objects. The Chorrera ceramic tradition contains vessels forms such as the stirrup spout as well as various decorative elements that are similar to contemporary ceramics in northern Peru, suggesting the possibility of cultural exchange between these groups.

crops, and cotton and lived in horseshoe-shaped villages. Their characteristic pottery includes figurines, bowls, and wide-mouthed jars. Pottery did not become important along the coast of Peru until about 1,000 years later. It was possibly introduced through trading contact with the north, and then spread quickly throughout the central Andean region. The adoption of pottery was one of a number of technological changes taking place at this time that transformed the economic and social landscape of coastal Peru. The diet of marine fish and shellfish had formerly been supplemented with limited crop cultivation, but after the introduction of irrigation techniques the importance of agriculture rapidly increased and settlements began to move away from the shore and occupy strategic sites along river valleys. As monumental architecture took on new forms, large U-shaped structures with sunken circular courts began to be built. One of the earliest was at El Paraíso, followed by similar structures at Cardal, La Galgada, La Florida, and San Jacinto.

Local cultural traditions

A series of local cultural traditions, distinguished by the particular forms of ritual architecture and iconographical styles, emerged on the coast and in the highlands of the central Andes during the Early Ceramic period (2200–1100 BCE). The Cupisnique tradition, which flourished along the northern coast of Peru, is noted for the construction of platform mounds decorated with polychrome murals, and for the manufacture of modeled pottery vessels with incised designs. The complex U-shaped structure at Caballo Muerto in the Moche valley of northern Peru, dating from 1300 BCE, is decorated with low-relief clay sculptures that foreshadow those of the later Chavín culture (see pages 178–179). One of the most striking Early Ceramic iconographies is found at Cerro Sechín in the Casma valley of central Peru. Its bold reliefs display severed heads with closed eyes, flowing hair and blood streaming from the neck—probably depictions of executed war captives. In the northern highlands, Kuntur Wasi and related sites feature terraces, stairways, platforms, and sunken courts, while a distinct south-central Andean tradition of stone architecture with sunken courts was developing at Chiripa and other early urban sites on the altiplano in the region of Lake Titicaca, nearly 13,000 ft/4,000 m above sea level.

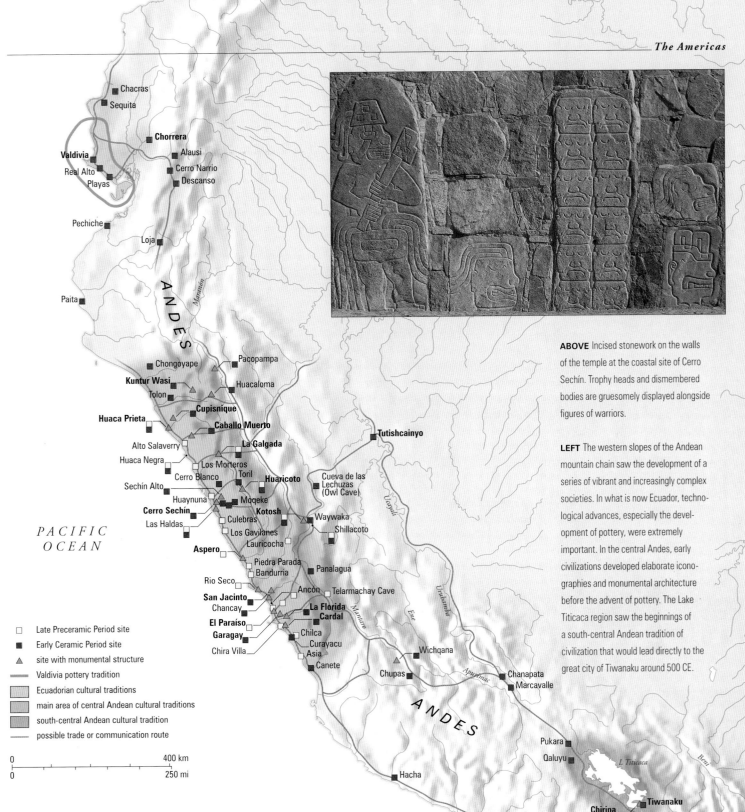

Map labels:

Chacras
Sequita
Chorrera
Alausi
Valdivia
Real Alto
Playas
Cerro Narrio
Descanso
Pechiche
Loja
Paita

A N D E S

Marañón

Chongoyape
Pacopampa
Kuntur Wasi
Huacaloma
Tolon
Cupisnique
Huaca Prieta
Caballo Muerto
Alto Salaverry
La Galgada
Tutishcainyo
Huaca Negra
Los Morteros
Toril
Cerro Blanco
Huaricoto
Cueva de las Lechuzas (Owl Cave)
Sechín Alto
Huaynuna
Moqeke
Kotosh
Cerro Sechín
Culebras
Waywaka
Las Haldas
Los Gavilanes
Shillacoto
Lauricocha
Aspero
Piedra Parada
Bandurria
Panalagua
Rio Seco
Ancón
Telarmachay Cave
San Jacinto
Chancay
La Florida
Cardal
El Paraíso
Chilca
Garagay
Curayacu
Chira Villa
Asia
Canete
Wichqana
Chupas
Chanapata
Marcavalle

Ucayali

Ene

Urubamba

Mantaro

Apurímac

A N D E S

Pukara
Qaluyu
L. Titicaca
Hacha
Beni
Chiripa
Tiwanaku
Warakani
Wankarani
Desaguadero
Ilo

PACIFIC OCEAN

Legend:
□ Late Preceramic Period site
■ Early Ceramic Period site
▲ site with monumental structure
— Valdivia pottery tradition
▨ Ecuadorian cultural traditions
▨ main area of central Andean cultural traditions
▨ south-central Andean cultural tradition
— possible trade or communication route

0 ———— 400 km
0 ———— 250 mi

ABOVE Incised stonework on the walls of the temple at the coastal site of Cerro Sechín. Trophy heads and dismembered bodies are gruesomely displayed alongside figures of warriors.

LEFT The western slopes of the Andean mountain chain saw the development of a series of vibrant and increasingly complex societies. In what is now Ecuador, technological advances, especially the development of pottery, were extremely important. In the central Andes, early civilizations developed elaborate iconographies and monumental architecture before the advent of pottery. The Lake Titicaca region saw the beginnings of a south-central Andean tradition of civilization that would lead directly to the great city of Tiwanaku around 500 CE.

The Upper Amazon region

Outside of the central Andean area, the important technological and social changes that were a distinguishing mark of the Late Preceramic and Early Ceramic periods appear to have been adopted in some areas but not in others. Pottery had appeared in Amazonia long before it became a feature of Andean societies; some finds of ceramics in the Orinoco region and at the mouth of the Amazon River have been dated to around 3600–3100 BCE. A tropical forest culture based on root-crop agriculture, particularly of manioc, developed in the Upper Amazon. Around 2000 BCE, a type of incised pottery was being made at Tutishcainyo, and its distribution along the tributaries of the Upper Amazon into the Andean foothills and highlands, and even into the Pacific coastal region from about 1600 BCE suggests there was widespread trade via the Ucayali and Urubamba rivers. This was to remain a significant enterprise until the arrival of the Spanish. The exotic goods brought by traders from the Amazon were highly valued by Andean societies: they included tropical birds, feathers, and hallucinogenic plants that were used by religious and ritual specialists ◆

Andean States and Empires

In the 1st millennium BCE recognizable civilizations whose influence extended beyond local boundaries began to emerge in the central Andes. The first to appear, around 800 BCE, was Chavín, centered on a small valley on the eastern slopes of the Andes. Subsequently, in the coastal regions of north and south Peru, other regional societies developed – most notably the Moche, Paracas, and Nasca. All have left substantial archaeological evidence of their distinctive cultural and artisanal traditions. The Moche in particular were among the most skilled craftworkers of Precolumbian America, producing sophisticated ceramics, textiles, and metalwork. These early coastal societies were eclipsed by two remarkable states that rose to prominence in the period 400–600 CE: Tiwanaku, in the area around Lake Titicaca in the south and Wari, based in the Ayacucho region of the central Andes. Both appear to have extended their power and influence over vast territories though military conquest. They established complex polities and economic networks, based on intensive agriculture and wide-ranging trade, that justify their description as South America's first empires. Their joint influence on later Andean societies is unquestionable. The reasons for their decline are unknown, but Wari appears to have collapsed by 900 CE and Tiwanaku by 1100 CE. They were supplanted by a series of warlike chiefdoms and states with smaller, regional power bases. The most important of these appears to have been the kingdom of Chimor (Chimú). All would be absorbed into the Inca empire during the 15th century.

LEFT Detail from a Paracas textile showing a mythical creature with protruding tongue and cat's whiskers, known as the "oculate being".

The town of Chavín de Huantar, the center of the Chavín state, nearly 10,500 ft/3,200 m above sea-level, is situated at a crossroads where the north–south routes through the mountains meet the east–west routes leading to the coast and Amazonia. Its U-shaped temple and sunken circular court are in the tradition of earlier Peruvian ritual sites, but the site contains in addition an extraordinary series of underground galleries and passages, completed around 300 BCE. Stone stelae inside the galleries are decorated with carvings showing mythical creatures that combine feline, serpent, avian raptor, or human features. Such motifs, deriving in part from earlier Peruvian cultures such as Cerro Sechín, are characteristic of the Chavín style, which was the first to spread throughout the central Andes.

Farther north, the Moche (or Mochica) were a powerful regional society from about the 1st to the 8th century CE. The Moche established ceremonial centers with platform mounds in each river valley. At some 130ft/40 m high by 1,150 ft/350 m long, the Pyramid of the Sun is the largest such mound in the Americas. The rulers of the valley centers presided over an elaborate ritual and religious life and a productive economy based on agriculture and fishing. Wealth also came from exploiting gold and other metal resources. Excavations at Sipán and other sites have uncovered the burials of Moche rulers who were found wearing sumptuous garments decorated with gold and silver beadwork; they were accompanied by the bodies of human retainers. The huge array of grave goods found in such burials includes highly crafted metalwork, precious stones, textiles, and pottery, much of it painted with scenes of ritual activities, warfare, and sacrifice. Exotic items such as feathers from the Amazonian jungle indicate that the Moche had access to an extensive trading network.

Chan Chan: city of the Chimú

The site of ancient Chan Chan lies on the northern Peruvian coast not far from the modern city of Trujillo. It was the largest and most important city of Chimor, a powerful kingdom that controlled a territory extending more than 620 mi/1,000 km along the Pacific littoral during the early centuries of the 2nd millennium CE. The dry desert climate has preserved Chan Chan's adobe (sun-dried clay) structures and the city, whose central core covered 2.3 sq mi/6 sq km, has been extensively excavated. At its heart were ten compounds, or *ciudadelas* ("little cities"), enclaves for the ruling elite, which contained burial platforms, residences, administrative buildings, large wells and storerooms. Each *ciudadela* appears to have been occupied by an individual Chimú ruler and his entourage. On his death, the walls of his compound were sealed shut, to become a mausoleum. Outside of Chan Chan's elite central core were the residential quarters that housed craftspeople, farmers and fishermen, as well as the herders who brought exotic goods from the highlands on llama caravans. Chimor's society was agriculturally based and relied on sophisticated engineering techniques to reclaim land from the desert, including a 40 mi/65 km-long canal ◆

ABOVE THE DECORATED ADOBE WALLS OF ONE OF CHAN CHAN'S ELITE COMPOUNDS

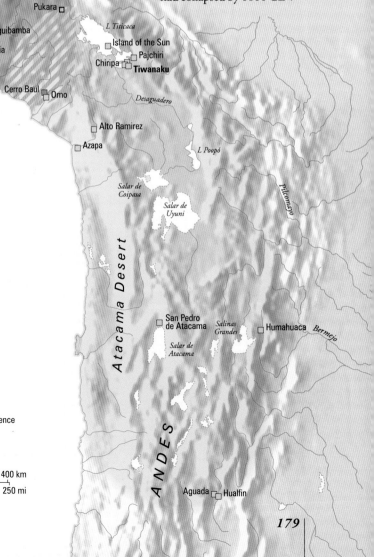

Analysis of the patina and of the styles and locations of the figures shows that, while most were created by the Nasca people, some predate them and the tradition continued afterwards.

Highland empires

In the mid-1st millennium CE the central Andean highlands came to be dominated by the state of Tiwanaku (Tiahuanaco), which ultimately gained control of an area of about 135,150 sq mi/350,000 sq km. The densely populated city of Tiwanaku had a huge stone-faced platform, the Akapana, and several other imposing buildings decorated with giant monolithic sculptures of human figures. The country around was intensively cultivated by means of raised fields and terraces. North of Lake Titicaca, another remarkable empire, the Wari (Huari), emerged as an expansive state around 600 BCE. It extended its control over a vast region of the Peruvian highlands by military force, and influenced a far greater area through trade and, more directly, by pacts with local elites. Although the economy, art, and iconography of Tiwanaku and Wari appear largely similar, archaeologists are unclear about the nature of the relationship between them. Both Tiwanaku and Wari had collapsed by 1100 CE ◆

RIGHT Well before the beginning of the Common Era, a number of coastal and highland civilizations flourished throughout the Andes, developing a unique tradition of art, architecture, economy and religion, the influence of which is still present today.

Paracas and Nasca

Along Peru's south coast between c.400 BCE and 300 CE, the Paracas people farmed the river valleys south of Lima and built several large settlements on artificial mounds. Important individuals were buried in elaborate multiple graves on the nearby windswept Paracas peninsula. The dry conditions here have preserved their mummified bodies as well as the textiles in which they were wrapped. Embroidered with complex designs of bipedal creatures wearing ritual costumes and masks, they are some of the most impressive examples of ancient cloth ever seen.

The Paracas culture was succeeded by the Nasca (100 BCE–700 CE), known for its elaborate polychrome pottery. In order to settle the dry middle valley of the southern deserts, the Nasca created a series of underground aqueducts to bring water from a subterranean river to the surface, from where it was led through irrigation channels to the fields. This ingenious system is still in use today.

The Nasca people also created thousands of straight lines and geometric patterns extending for miles across the desert. The most striking depict huge animal figures. Seen most easily from the air, the Nasca lines were unknown until the 1930s, when airplanes began to fly over the desert. Archaeologists have been investigating their origin and use ever since.

site showing Chavín influence
Moche site
Paracas site
Nasca site
Tiwanaku site
Wari site
Chimor site
other site
limit of Chavín influence
limit of Moche civilization
limit of Paracas and Nasca influence
area under Tiwanaku influence
area under Wari influence

0   400 km
0   250 mi

The Inca Empire

The Inca empire – the largest ancient state of the New World, extending over much of what is now Peru, Bolivia, Ecuador, and Chile – had its origins in the area around Cuzco in the highlands of southern Peru. By about 1200 CE, the Inca chiefdom had emerged as the dominant power in the region, conquering and absorbing the other warring chiefdoms that had sprung up after the collapse of the Wari empire c.900 CE. The Incas formed strong alliances with their onetime enemies in the area of Cuzco, and enlisted their help to build their powerful empire, which was known as Tawatinsuyu, the "Land of the Four Quarters". They conquered hundreds of different peoples of widely divergent languages, traditions and customs who inhabited a number of contrasting environments: coastal deserts, high mountain altitudes, fertile river valleys, windswept plains, forest and jungle. In the late 15th century the Inca extended their rule over the powerful kingdom of Chimor, in the first true conquest of the north Pacific coastal region by an outside power. Barely half a century later, in 1532, the Inca empire itself was conquered by an invading army of Spanish conquistadors.

RIGHT Gold was highly valued by the Inca, who thought of it as "the sweat of the sun". This gold mask, with turquoise inlays, is of Chimú manufacture. Several chronicles written shortly after the Spanish conquest describe the Inca subjugation of Chimor and provide information about various aspects of Chimú society. There is evidence that after conquering the Chimú, the Inca deliberately broke up their powerful empire, for instance by transporting artisans from Chan Chan (see page 178) to Cuzco. They also built a new regional center in the Chicama Valley, Chiquitoy, to replace Chan Chan. Chimú fishermen, farmers, craftspeople and state functionaries were brought into the Inca state. But despite the superimposition of Inca administration and state religion, many local traditions continued. The Inca even adopted some of the Chimú mechanisms of administration and local control that had made the once great coastal empire so successful.

Cuzco: center of the world

The Inca considered the sacred city of Cuzco to be the very center of the world: its name means "navel" in the Quechua language. At its heart was an open plaza used for the public performance of rituals and celebrations of victory. The Four Quarters of the empire began here, and all the major roads radiated out from it. Here, too, were the Inca's principal religious buildings: the Coricancha, or Temple of the Sun, where the tokens of the major Incan deities were displayed, and the palaces of the Inca emperors, living and dead. Important administrative buildings ringed this sacred core, for Cuzco was also a political capital, housing the governors of the Four Quarters. Only the Inca royal families and those in state or religious service were allowed to reside there. Cuzco was a carefully planned city. It has been suggested that its streets and walls were laid out in the shape of a puma, the head of which was formed by the fortress of Sacsahuaman. Evidence of Inca construction can still be seen in the walls of many buildings in the central part of modern Cuzco ◆

ABOVE THE ELABORATE STONE WALLS OF SACSAHUAMAN FORTRESS, OVERLOOKING CUZCO.

The Inca were military conquerors who governed their captured lands with an iron hand, molding region after region to fit with their expectations of intensive agricultural and labor production. Lands were shared between the state, the gods, and the local community. Taxes were paid by both men and women in the form of a labor draft and as goods. The labor draft, known as *mit'a*, included crop cultivation (potatoes and maize), animal herding, military service, craftwork, construction and mining. Goods paid as taxes included textiles and animals.

Centralized control

Historical documents from the early years of the Spanish occupation provide detailed accounts of the Inca's imperial strategies. Newly conquered territories were incorporated into the provinces that comprised the Four Quarters, or major regions, of the empire: Chinchasuyu, Cuntisuyu, Antisuyu, and Collasuyu. If the local rulers capitulated completely, they were allowed to remain as provincial governors, and were sometimes even enriched with new privileges. Less cooperative rulers were removed and replaced either by more compliant members of local groups or by imported governors of proven loyalty to the Inca. The sons of local governors were taken to Cuzco, the Inca capital (see box), where they were educated in Inca ways and taught Quechua, the language spoken by the Incas, in which all official business was conducted throughout the empire.

LEFT The Inca empire covered enormous expanses of coastal desert, steep mountains, wide valley, high plains, forests and jungle lands. A network of roads was constructed across this varied landscape, as the Inca joined ancient cities together within their new empire and built new towns wherever they needed them. By the time the Spanish arrived in 1532, the Inca landscape included thousands of cities, towns, and hamlets connected by a system of roads and paths, and all administered from the Inca capital of Cuzco.

Map legend:

- ■ Inca capital
- ■ known Inca provincial capital
- □ other Inca site
- Inca heartland, 13th century
- Inca empire at maximum extent, early 16th century
- — Inca road
- — boundary of empire quarter

The Inca exploited ethnic and cultural differences to their own advantage, counting on the distrust between local groups to keep them from revolt. If a region proved particularly rebellious, the population was resettled elsewhere to live side by side with peoples who spoke different languages and wore different dress. Loyal groups, meanwhile, would be moved into the new territory.

For the Andean peoples, the environment was a spiritual landscape of sacred sites or shrines (*huaca*) such as mountains, streams, or individual rocks. Inca religion and ritual were concentrated on Cuzco, where the Temple of the Sun was situated. Although the Inca allowed the peoples of their empire to venerate their own particular gods, they frequently relocated their main shrines to Cuzco, thereby compelling worshipers to make lengthy pilgrimages.

Inca achievements

Inca engineering remade the Andean landscape. In order to increase agricultural production, the Inca built vast networks of canals to irrigate new land. They brought new architectural skills and aesthetic sensibilities to the construction of agricultural terraces, which had been utilized by the highland farmers of the Andes for 2,000 years. Towering flights of stone-faced terraces completely reshaped the valleys around Cuzco and other major Inca settlements.

Inca architecture featured huge, individually cut stone blocks that were fitted together without mortar.

Using human labor, levers, rollers, and pulleys, the huge stones were moved into place. The resulting buildings were so strong that many have survived earthquakes that have destroyed Spanish colonial buildings in Cuzco and elsewhere. Nowhere is the artistry of Inca construction better observed than at the remote mountain stronghold of Machu Picchu, which escaped detection by the Spanish and was not rediscovered until 1911.

The Inca built an extensive network of roads the length and breadth of the empire, with many interconnecting routes and paths – an estimated total of 24,855 mi/40,000 km. Most of the roads were narrow: the llama, the pack animal of the Andes, which carries only small loads, does not require much passing space. However, at strategic intervals along the major routes the roads widened to accommodate *tambos* – wayside hostels and storage depots. Relays of official runners known as *chaski* were kept ready to convey important messages across the empire. Human couriers also carried packages and heavy loads along the roads

When the Spanish, with their horses and weapons, arrived in Peru in 1532, the Inca empire was in turmoil. The emperor Huayna Capa had died some five years before and a long civil war had only just ended. Many local ethnic groups joined the Spanish. This explains the ease with which the Inca were defeated ◆

AUSTRALIA & THE PACIFIC

EUROPEAN EXPLORATION of Australia and the Pacific, which began in the late 18th century, challenged contemporary ideas about the natural and social world. But while speculation about the origins of the region's indigenous peoples fed scientific and religious debate about human and social evolution, archaeological enquiry was limited by the prevailing view of indigenous societies as unchanging since the "Stone Age". Only with the development of radiocarbon dating in the 1950s did these attitudes begin to alter.

In Australia especially, the Aborigines were regarded as "living fossils" who were a useful source of ethnographic information to interpret ancient remains elsewhere, but whose culture was primitive and backward. Although investigations by amateur collectors demonstrated changing sequences of stone tool assemblages, these were thought to result purely from the availability of raw materials rather than from social or cultural development.

In the 1950s Australia was believed to have been occupied for perhaps 10,000 years at most. Since then, radiocarbon dating and the introduction of a rigorous professional approach to archaeological fieldwork by John Mulvaney and others have transformed prevailing ideas. Mulvaney obtained the first older dates at Kenniff Cave, Queensland, in 1962; by the end of the decade human occupation had been pushed back to about 30,000 years, and over the next ten years dates of up to 40,000 years were accepted for several older sites in both Australia and New Guinea (part of the Greater Australian continent during periods of lower sea level). As a result of new dating techniques in the 1990s, dates of 60,000 years and beyond are now claimed for several sites.

This startling increase in antiquity has had important implications for world prehistory. Since Greater Australia was not linked by land to Southeast Asia, the first colonists must have come by sea. It is now clear that early modern humans must have had considerable seafaring skills (recent claims for an even more ancient occupation on the Indonesian island of Flores suggest that these skills may be even older). The discovery of 20,000-year-old ground-stone axes in northern Australia also challenged European-centered views of prehistory, which held that grinding and polishing stone-working techniques were Old World Neolithic innovations. Evidence of underground flint mining of about the same age was also a surprise. Other fields of archaeological research have investigated the complexity and richness of traditional Aboriginal society. It is now clear that Aboriginal art is probably as ancient as the first colonization of the continent and may well be the world's oldest and longest art tradition. Understanding how Aborigines actively managed their environment, especially as "fire-stick farmers", has helped to overturn ideas that hunter–gatherer life was a miserable struggle for existence.

Island archaeology

In New Guinea, too, research during the 1960s and 1970s pushed back the antiquity of occupation. More recently, sites dating back 30,000 years and more have been found in island Melanesia as far as the Solomons. The discovery of 10,000-year-old drainage systems at Kuk in the New Guinea Highlands has established the area as an independent center of plant domestication.

Radiocarbon dating also opened up the possibilities of archaeological research in the Pacific. During the 1950s the first dates were obtained for the human occupation of Easter Island, and unexpectedly early dates were obtained from a rock shelter in Hawaii. The process of colonization of this vast area of ocean with its sparse islands has proved an enduring and important theme. The origins of the extraordinary diversity of Pacific societies, ranging from the complex chiefdoms of Hawaii to the egalitarian trading communities of Melanesia, have also interested archaeologists. In New Zealand, radiocarbon dating and DNA analysis are throwing new light on the character of early Maori settlement.

Regional Timeline

c.90,000 y.a. Modern humans begin to move out of Africa

c.40,000–30,000 y.a. Colonization of Melanesia

c.13,000 y.a. Ice Age cemetery at Kow Swamp (Victoria)

c.60,000–50,000 y.a. First humans present in Australia

c.26,000 y.a. Ritual cremation at Lake Mungo (New South Wales)

c.9,000 –5,500y.a. Early agriculture at Kuk (New Guinea)

50,000 y.a.

10,000 y.a.

Who owns the sites?

In the post-colonial period, archaeology has contributed to a developing national identity in many of the emerging states of the region, such as Papua New Guinea. In the settler societies of New Zealand and Australia, however, where indigenous peoples have become increasingly assertive in their struggle for political recognition and land rights, archaeologists have come under increasing criticism.

The arrival of Europeans was a disaster for indigenous peoples, causing enormous loss of life and the wholesale destruction of their traditional societies. Indigenous people consider archaeologists to have contributed to their dispossession by portraying them as primitive and doomed to extinction. They reject as just another pretext for cultural domination the idea that archaeological sites are the common heritage of humanity, and assert their right to own and control their own culture. Many also believe that scientific accounts

ABOVE The "Walls of China", eroded dunes on the edge of Lake Mungo. The discovery of human burials here in the 1960s and 1970s revolutionized Australian archaeology.
FAR LEFT A shell hook, used for fishing in the coastal waters of Southeast Australia.

of the past undermine traditional beliefs. Debates over the excavation and study of human remains have been particularly bitter.

The controversy over archaeological material is one aspect of radical change that is taking place in the relations between indigenous people and the wider community. Resulting from this process, in both Australia and New Zealand state and national governments have taken measures to involve indigenous people in the management of sites and the regulation of research. Recruiting and training indigenous staff have become priorities for heritage organizations, and archaeological research now increasingly involves collaboration between archaeologists and indigenous people ◆

c.4,900 y.a. Construction of Stonehenge

c.1,000 y.a. Viking navigators reach North America

c. 5,000–4,000 y.a. Microlith tools come into use in Australia

c.1,800–1,400 y.a. Settlement of Hawaiian islands

c.1,000–700 y.a. Settlement of New Zealand

c.400 y.a. *Moai* building ceases on Easter Island

c.5,500–4,500 y.a. Lapita peoples colonize western Polynesia

c.1,600–1,000 y.a. Settlement of Easter Island

c.500 y.a. Construction of *pa* in New Zealand

c.200 y.a. Arrival of first European settlers

5,000 y.a.

1,000 y.a.

100 y.a.

Ice Age Peoples of Australia

During the last Ice Age of the Pleistocene, sea levels were considerably lower than they are today, and Australia, New Guinea and Tasmania formed a single landmass known as Greater Australia, or Sahul. Anatomically modern humans are known to have navigated the water barriers that separated this continent from Asia by at least 40,000 years ago (see page 188). Radiocarbon-dated sites of 40,000–35,000 years ago are widely distributed across the entire continent from New Guinea to Tasmania, but some archaeologists believe that human occupation began considerably earlier than this. Thermoluminescence (TL) dates of 60–50,000 years ago claimed for two sites in northern Australia remain controversial, however, and a date of 60,000 years ago recently proposed for an early burial at Lake Mungo (see box) has yet to be confirmed. By c.30,000 years ago, all the continent's major environmental zones appear to have been successfully colonized.

The archaeology of ancient Australia contains a number of enigmas – not the least of which is uncertainty over the dating of its earliest occupation by anatomically modern humans. Not everyone accepts the TL dates of 60–50,000 years ago claimed for two rockshelter sites at Nauwalabila and Malakunanja in northern Australia; moreover, the association of these dates (obtained from sand sediments) with the oldest artifacts at these sites has been called into question. Controversy also surrounds the citing of vegetation changes or increased amounts of charcoal as circumstantial evidence of human intervention for these early periods, but recent work at Lake Mungo may push the date back to more than 60,000 years ago.

Diverse societies

By c.30,000 years ago humans were living in environments as diverse as the tropical north of Australia and New Guinea and the glaciated highlands of southwest Tasmania. Sites at Puritjarra and Kulpi Mara show that even the arid core of the continent was occupied 30,000 years ago or soon after. The economic strategies of the earliest Australians appear as diverse as their environments. The early inhabitants of the Willandra Lakes seem to have enjoyed a highly varied diet (see box). By contrast, hunting in southwest Tasmania was much more specialized and mainly involved the red-necked wallaby.

When the first humans reached Australia giant marsupials still occupied the continent. Whether human hunting or climatic change was responsible for their extinction remains undecided. Evidence of any association between humans and megafauna has been scarce. The most detailed information comes from a 30,000-year-old campsite at Cuddie Springs, New South Wales, where stone tools have been found alongside bones of *Diprotodon*, a rhinoceros-sized wombat, and giant kangaroos. Grindstone fragments with microscopic starch residues from the site are the oldest direct evidence for plant processing yet found.

The Pleistocene toolkit included a range of stone tools for scraping, cutting and chopping. Usually, local stone was used, but in southwest Tasmania artifacts made of Darwin glass, a natural glass formed as a result of a meteorite impact, were transported to sites up to 62 mi/100 km away. Bone points have been found in southwestern Australia and Tasmania. Studies of use wear on the Tasmanian points suggest that some were used as spear tips and others as awls, perhaps for making skin cloaks. Axes with ground cutting edges, usually associated with farming communities in most parts of the world, are a surprising feature of the Ice Age toolkit in Australia; they are widespread in the tropical north and in New Guinea.

cave or rockshelter

☐ before 30,000 years ago

■ 30,000–15,000 years ago

▨ 15,000–10,000 years ago

open camp site

△ before 30,000 years ago

▲ 30,000–15,000 years ago

▲ 15,000–10,000 years ago

△ site of Panaramitee engraving

⇛ hypothetical route of colonization

☐ ancient coastline, c.18,000 years ago

vegetation, 18,000 years ago

☐ arid grassland and shrub

▨ semi-arid grassland and shrub

▨ woodlands

▨ forest

| 0 | | 600 km |
| 0 | | 400 mi |

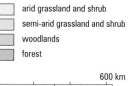

LEFT Pecked petroglyphs showing characteristic Panaramitee motifs of animal tracks and circles. Panaramitee designs are found at many Pleistocene sites and also occur in recent Aboriginal art, making it a very ancient tradition indeed.

Lake Mungo: an early occupation site

Lake Mungo, a site in the Willandra Lakes region of New South Wales, holds an important place in the history of Australian archaeology. In 1968, the cremated remains of a young woman dating to about 25,000 years ago were found there. This remarkable find is the oldest evidence of cremation in the world. A few years later, in 1974, the complete skeleton of an adult male was discovered nearby. He had been ritually buried and his body sprinkled with red ocher. At the time, he was believed to be about 30,000 years old, but new methods of dating have recently suggested a date of perhaps 60,000 years: if accepted, this will confirm a very early date for the colonization of Australia. The Lake Mungo burials provide evidence of a complex ceremonial life during the Pleistocene. Investigation of the many midden sites (prehistoric refuse heaps) in the area shows that until the Willandra Lakes dried up 15,000 years ago people hunted a range of large and small animals, collected frogs, freshwater mussels and crayfish, and fished in the lakes, probably with nets. They used stone tools to scrape meat from bone and to clean plant tubers. The recent return of human skeletal remains to local Aboriginal communities was a landmark in relations between archaeologists and Indigenous Australians ◆

Ice Age art

Although most rock art is difficult to date, it was certainly a feature of life in Ice Age Australia. Pieces of ocher found in the oldest levels of several sites and engravings buried under Pleistocene occupation deposits in a few sites indicate that painting and engraving are at least 20,000 years old. Ages of 40,000 years ago obtained for engravings from the Olary region of Southern Australia are more controversial, however. The oldest art in Australia takes a number of different forms. Meandering lines and geometric figures are incised in soft limestone caves at Koonalda and other sites in the Mount Gambier area of Southern Australia. Pecked designs of geometric motifs and animal tracks belonging to the Panaramitee style are found on exposed rock surfaces in many areas. Bone beads from Devil's Lair and a shell necklace from Mandu Mandu Creek show that personal adornment was also a feature of life in Ice Age Australia ◆

ABOVE Ice Age sites are found in highly contrasting environments from Tasmania to the continent's arid center. The wide distribution of early sites indicates that the first colonists must have spread very rapidly across the continent. The demonstration of more than 40,000 years of human occupation of Australia is one of the most remarkable stories of modern archaeology. Until 1962, when the Australian archaeologist John Mulvaney obtained the first Pleistocene date from a site at Kenniff Cave, Queensland, human settlement was thought to be only 10,000 years old.

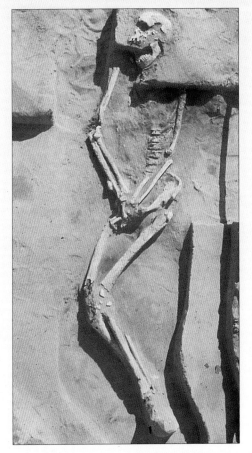

ABOVE THE COMPLETE MALE SKELETON FOUND AT LAKE MUNGO.

Australia: Later Hunter–gatherers

Australia is unique in that it was occupied exclusively by hunter–gatherers until European settlers arrived in the late 18th century. Examination of the ethnographic and historical information from the last two centuries and better understanding of the archaeological record shows that, far from being uniform and unchanging, its society was extraordinarily diverse and dynamic. Some 500 different tribal groups, speaking at least 250 languages, practiced a range of highly successful adaptations to different environments. There was a richly creative spiritual life that drew its inspiration from the natural environment. Study of the dynamic, innovative nature of Aboriginal society over the last 10,000 years provides a unique perspective on the enormous diversity of hunter–gathering life in time and space.

BELOW Human figures painted in the elaborate x-ray style from Nourlangie Rock, Arnhem Land (now part of the Kakadu National Park), Northern Territory. The diversity of Aboriginal society is reflected in the stylistic diversity of its rock art. While the oldest Australian art seems to have been primarily abstract and geometric, more recent art is often figurative with images of people, animals and plants. The tradition of rock art survived until very recently in some areas and paintings were regularly retouched and repainted over hundreds of years. The continuation of traditional themes in new media in contemporary Aboriginal art provides a unique insight into meaning and shows that most artistic expression is intimately bound up with Aboriginal spiritual life.

Rising sea levels at the end of the last Ice Age severed the land connections between mainland Australia and Tasmania and New Guinea. Substantial areas of the populated coastal plains were flooded. By c.6,000 years ago climatic conditions were broadly as they are today. A number of new elements begin to appear in Australian sites, which may be seen as part of a process leading to greater social complexity, though others consider them to have come about in response to environmental change and an increase in population. In many areas, people seem to have become less mobile. The appearance of cemeteries along the Murray River from c.10,000 years ago can be seen as evidence of a more settled life within defined territories. Earth mounds, found in parts of the Southeast from about 4,000 years ago, may also indicate a more settled life.

New stone tool types came into use. In the southern half of the continent small backed stone implements were widespread. As one edge of these tools was deliberately blunted, probably for fitting to a haft, they are likely to have been spear barbs. Points, found in a variety of forms, were much more common over the central third of the continent. In the Kimberley area of the northwest, they were elaborately pressure flaked and might even be made of glass or porcelain in historic times. Such points were widely traded. Flaked adzes, used for woodworking, also became more common and more specialized in form. Ground stone hatchets are found throughout most of Australia.

The dingo, the Australian wild dog, appears to have entered the continent about 4,000 to 3,500 years ago (probably a native of Southeast Asia, it may have been introduced to northern Australia by fishermen from Indonesia). At about the same time, probably as a direct result, the thylacine and Tasmanian devil, native marsupial carnivores, became extinct on the mainland, although they survived until modern times in Tasmania. Dingoes have an important place in Aboriginal mythology. The presence of dingo burials in archaeological sites suggests they had high value and status.

Australia's Aboriginal hunter–gatherers are sometimes termed "fire-stick farmers" owing to their use of fire as a land management tool to regenerate grasslands and attract game back into areas of fresh growth. Complex fish trapping systems were developed in many areas. At Lake Condah, southwest Victoria, the visible remains of stone traps, channels and weirs used for trapping eels date to at least 4,000 years ago, but the systems may have been in use for far longer. Food processing also became more elaborate; for example, laborious methods were developed for removing toxins from the kernels of cycads, primitive palm-like plants that have high calorific value but are highly poisonous. These involved fermenting the kernels in pits for several months, or leaching out the poison with water.

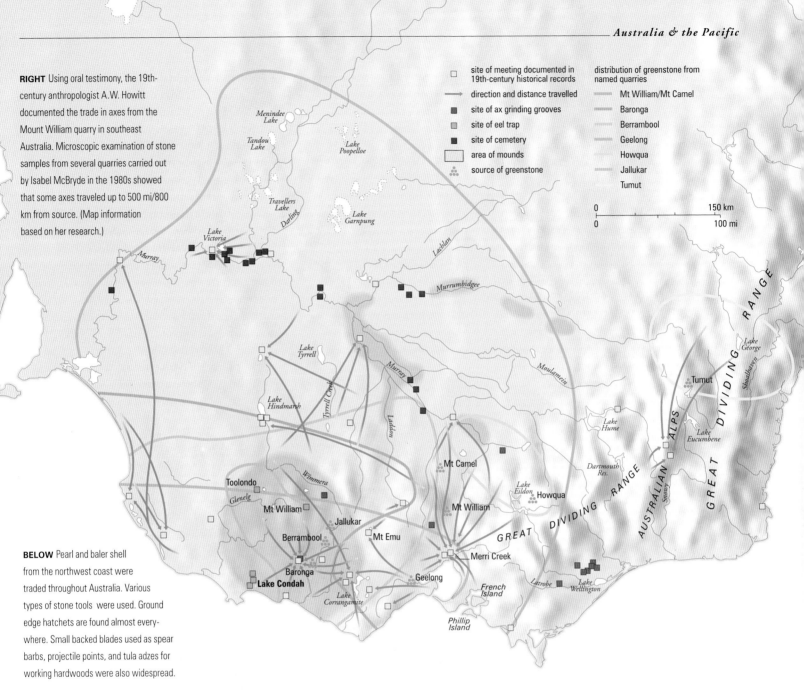

RIGHT Using oral testimony, the 19th-century anthropologist A.W. Howitt documented the trade in axes from the Mount William quarry in southeast Australia. Microscopic examination of stone samples from several quarries carried out by Isabel McBryde in the 1980s showed that some axes traveled up to 500 mi/800 km from source. (Map information based on her research.)

site of meeting documented in 19th-century historical records
direction and distance travelled
site of ax grinding grooves
site of eel trap
site of cemetery
area of mounds
source of greenstone

distribution of greenstone from named quarries
Mt William/Mt Camel
Baronga
Berrambool
Geelong
Howqua
Jallukar
Tumut

0   150 km
0   100 mi

BELOW Pearl and baler shell from the northwest coast were traded throughout Australia. Various types of stone tools were used. Ground edge hatchets are found almost everywhere. Small backed blades used as spear barbs, projectile points, and tula adzes for working hardwoods were also widespread.

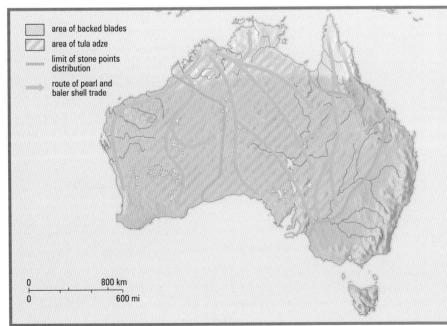

area of backed blades
area of tula adze
limit of stone points distribution
route of pearl and baler shell trade

0   800 km
0   600 mi

Exchange networks

Exchange was an important feature of Aboriginal life; reciprocal gift-giving at established meeting places commonly fulfilled important social and ritual purposes. Some items such as pearl shell from the northwest of Australia and pituri (native tobacco), a narcotic plant that grows in Queensland and Central Australia, are known from historical records to have traveled very long distances. Many other goods such as foodstuffs, ocher, and spinifex gum (used for fixing axes and spear barbs to wooden handles) were exchanged, but most traded items do not normally survive in archaeological sites. However, stone for making tools was often traded over very large areas and much work has been carried out into the distribution of greenstone from a number of quarry sites in southeast Australia. The stone was shaped at the quarry into rough "blanks", but the finishing work, including grinding the blade, took place elsewhere ◆

Early Settlement of Melanesia

Melanesia, one of the three major cultural regions of the Pacific Ocean (the others are Polynesia and Micronesia) consists of New Guinea, the Solomon Islands, Vanuatu, New Caledonia and Fiji. During the Pleistocene, western Melanesia belonged to the continent of Greater Australia, or Sahul, and was linked to Southeast Asia by the island chain of Indonesia. This narrow "voyaging corridor" was the probable route by which modern humans entered Greater Australia. Even when sea levels were at their lowest, the journeys between these islands could have been made only by boat. Nevertheless, these water barriers had been successfully crossed by c.40,000 years ago. Winds and currents are generally predictable in the region and few crossings would have been made out of sight of land.

BELOW The earliest sites of Melanesia, on the north coast of Papua New Guinea, are comparable in age to those on the Australian mainland. Occupation of coastal sites on several islands of the Bismarck Archipelago also took place during the Pleistocene. These islands did not form part of the Greater Australian continent, and their rapid colonization is testimony to the maritime nature of the early settlement of Melanesia. By about 25,000 years ago inland sites in the New Guinea Highlands had also been occupied, involving a different range of environmental adaptations. It is highly probable that many early coastal sites were flooded by rising sea levels at the end of the Ice Age.

Although archaeologists realized that the colonization of Greater Australia during the Pleistocene implied that modern humans must have possessed adequate watercraft, until quite recently most people believed that landfalls on the coast of Australia were rare and probably accidental. However, in the late 1980s a new picture began to emerge when several occupation sites dating to between 40,000 and 30,000 years ago were discovered in western Melanesia. The first of these was on the Huon Peninsula on the north coast of Papua New Guinea where a series of terraces (the remains of ancient coral reefs) have been uplifted well above modern sea level by earthquakes and volcanic activity. In 1985, flaked stone axes and stone tools were found here in a layer of volcanic ash dating to about 40,000 years ago. Also on New Guinea's north coast, Lachitu rockshelter has evidence of occupation dating back 35,000 years. Matenkupkum and Buang Merabek,

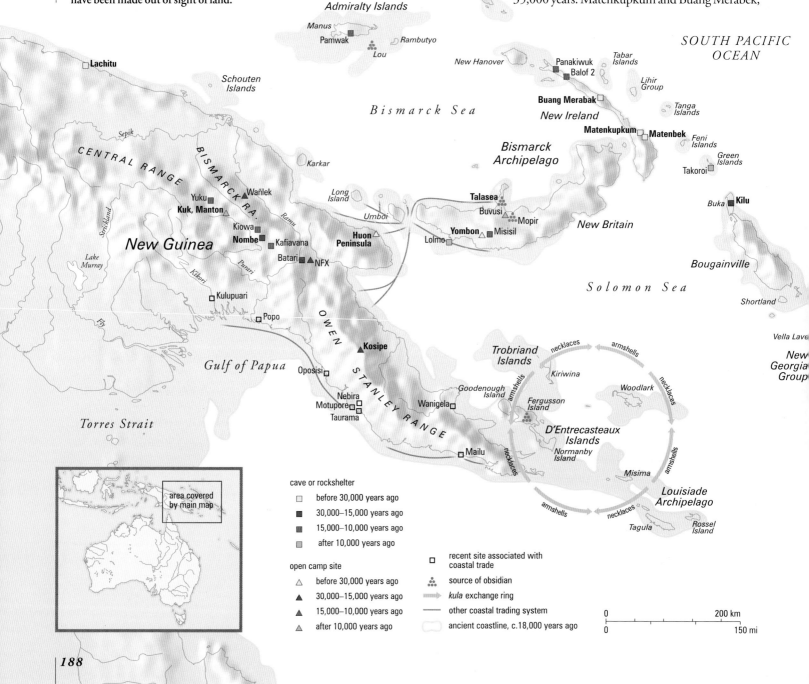

cave or rockshelter
□ before 30,000 years ago
■ 30,000–15,000 years ago
■ 15,000–10,000 years ago
■ after 10,000 years ago

open camp site
△ before 30,000 years ago
▲ 30,000–15,000 years ago
▲ 15,000–10,000 years ago
△ after 10,000 years ago

□ recent site associated with coastal trade
⁙ source of obsidian
⇨ *kula* exchange ring
— other coastal trading system
▱ ancient coastline, c.18,000 years ago

0   200 km
0   150 mi

rockshelter sites on New Ireland, were occupied more than 30,000 years ago, while a site at Kilu on Buka, the most northern of the Solomon Islands, is dated to 29,000 years ago. This new evidence suggests that the islands of western Melanesia were colonized by a rapid dispersal of people some 40,000–30,000 years ago, and that these early settlers were competent in coastal sailing and island hopping. Few crossings called for venturing out of sight of land, but clearly people were capable of doing so if necessary.

Adaptation and diversification

Not surprisingly, the early inhabitants of coastal sites in New Guinea and the Bismarcks appear to have subsisted by exploiting reef species of fish and shellfish. However, the inland site of Yombon in west New Britain shows that people were also established in the lowland rain forest from about 35,000 years ago, while Nombe and Kosipe in the Highlands of New Guinea were settled by at least 25,000 years ago. The evidence from these sites shows that a wide range of animals was hunted. There is also some evidence from pollen analysis of forest clearance at a very early date. The waisted axes and adzes found at several sites would have been suitable for working away at the margins of the forest, and it is possible that very limited horticulture was practiced, foreshadowing the very early and independent development of agriculture in the New Guinea Highlands from about 10,000 years ago. This may have come about in response to environmental change at the end of the Ice Age, which saw a greater movement of people into the Highlands as sea levels rose. Traces of gutters, hollows and mounds found at a site at Kuk in the Mount Hagen region, dating to between 9,000 and 5,500 years ago, have been interpreted as evidence of a ditch and drainage system for growing taro, a starchy rootcrop introduced from Southeast Asia.

Geoff Irwin, who has made a study of traditional sailing methods in the region, believes that it was the continuing development of navigation skills and maritime technology by the early inhabitants of maritime Melanesia that ultimately made possible the settlement of the remote Pacific. The distribution of obsidian illustrates the extent to which regular voyaging

was carried on between the islands. Obsidian, volcanic glass that can be flaked to give a razor-sharp edge, was highly prized for toolmaking. Spectrographic analysis can establish the source of individual samples of obsidian. Talasea in New Britain was an important source for thousands of years and obsidian from here was traded throughout the Pacific as far as Fiji. As early as 20,000 years ago, Talasea obsidian had made its way to Matenbek on New Ireland, a voyage of 220 mi/350 km.

There is some evidence to suggest that marsupials like the phalanger and thylogale had been introduced to New Ireland by humans toward the end of the last Ice Age. This may have been an accidental result of human colonization, but it could also have been a deliberate attempt to import new food resources to islands with relatively sparse animal populations.

Complex trading systems

Within Melanesia voyaging remained important and is best shown by the complex trading systems that developed in coastal New Guinea and neighboring islands. The most famous of these is probably the ceremonial *kula* ring of the Trobriand and D'Entrecasteaux islands, but there are many others. The Siassi, for example, were specialist middlemen operating trade networks between New Guinea and the Bismarck archipelago. Other networks linked south coast Papuan communities from Milne Bay to the Papuan Gulf. A range of goods was exchanged including shell valuables, pottery, and various foodstuffs ◆

ABOVE A highland village near Kosipe in the Owen Stanley Range of Papua New Guinea. Human settlement of the area began about 25,000 years ago. Evidence for agriculture in the New Guinea Highlands is among the oldest in the world. Features such as ditches and hollows have been interpreted as evidence for wetland cultivation of crops like taro. Pollen analysis from a number of sites documents forest clearing and erosion, suggesting that dryland agriculture was also practiced.

LEFT A bird-shaped stone pestle from Western Province, Papua New Guinea, 12 in/30 cm high, now in the Australian Museum. Stone pestles and mortars, decorated club heads and stone sculptures have been found throughout New Guinea, but are particularly common in the Highlands. A few dated examples suggest that these objects go back at least 3,500 years. Their function is unknown. Stone mortars and pestles were no longer being made over most most of New Guinea by the time of European contact in the 19th century, although they had a role in magic ritual. Mortars and pestles in use in New Guinea today are normally made of hardwood.

Colonizing the Pacific

The Pacific Ocean covers about one-third of the Earth's surface and contains more than 20,000 islands. Anthropologists in the 19th century divided it into three cultural zones: the island chains of Melanesia on the western edge; the scattered island clusters of Micronesia in the north; and the great triangle of Polynesia, extending eastward from Tonga and Samoa to Hawaii in the north and New Zealand and Easter Island in the south. The western islands, occupied from about 30,000 years ago, are the peaks of submerged mountain ranges. They contain a range of soils, vegetation and fauna. The oceanic islands include high volcanic islands, low islands of coral or limestone, and atolls – coral reefs surrounding a lagoon. They are widely scattered and have fewer resources. The settlement of this vast area involved remarkable feats of voyaging. How it was achieved has been much debated, but archaeologists now believe that colonization of the remote Pacific (Oceania) began around 3,500 years ago and was very rapid.

ABOVE Lapita people had reached Fiji, Tonga and Samoa by c.1300. From here, over the next 2,500 years, Polynesian culture spread through the eastern Pacific in a series of colonizing voyages.

Nan Madol: a burial site in Micronesia

The settlement of Micronesia is complex and poorly understood. The archaeological evidence is scanty, but the linguistic evidence suggests that the region may have been colonized both from island Southeast Asia and from Melanesia. The languages of Palau and the Marianas have affinities with the western Austronesian languages of Indonesia and the Philippines, while those of most other Micronesian islands are more closely related to those of the Solomon Islands and Vanuatu. Some archaeologists believe that a type of decorated pottery found in the Marianas, known as Marianas Red, is related to the pottery traditions of the Philippines. Pottery on the high island of Pohnpei in the Carolines could have developed from late Lapita styles, and although no actual Lapita ware has been found in Micronesia, it is likely that the initial settlers were Lapita people. Elaborate burial enclosures on Pohnpei, consisting of platforms and tombs within massive outer walls, are thought to have been built from the 9th century BCE and abandoned before the European settlement. They are clearly linked to status. Those at Nan Madol are the most impressive. Built on about 100 artificial islets within a shallow lagoon, the site is known as "the Venice of the Pacific" ◆

ABOVE THE MASSIVE OUTER WALL, BUILT OF BASALT BLOCKS, AT NAN MADOL.

An important key to unraveling the story of the settlement of the Pacific is a type of decorated ware known as Lapita. Since it was first recognized in New Caledonia in the 1950s, examples of the ware have been found at sites throughout the Melanesian islands and as far east as Fiji, Tonga and Samoa. The earliest examples date to c.3,500 years ago and it appears to have been in use for about 1,000 years.

Some archaeologists argue that Lapita was a local development that began in the Bismarck Archipelago and spread from there. Others believe it was introduced to western Melanesia from Southeast Asia. Certainly, the spread of Lapita culture seems to be linked with the expansion of Austronesian languages through the region. Austronesian languages are spoken in Malaya, the Philippines, Indonesia, Taiwan, Vietnam and Cambodia. They are found in Melanesia and Micronesia, and include all the languages of Polynesia. Austronesian-speakers are believed to have migrated from Southeast Asia into the western Pacific between 6,000 and 5,000 years ago, bringing with them new food plants and animals such as pigs.

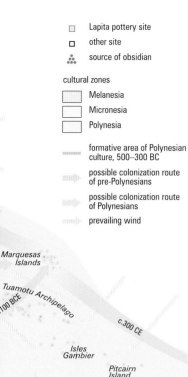

Lapita pottery site
other site
source of obsidian

cultural zones
Melanesia
Micronesia
Polynesia

formative area of Polynesian culture, 500–300 BC

possible colonization route of pre-Polynesians

possible colonization route of Polynesians

prevailing wind

Marquesas Islands

Tuamotu Archipelago
c.100 BCE

c.300 CE

Isles Gambier

Pitcairn Island

Easter Island

The Lapita people

As Lapita people moved eastward through the island chains of the western Pacific, they settled along the coasts; some of their settlements may have been built on piles over the water. They brought domestic pigs, dogs and chickens with them and cultivated taro, yams and tree crops, but marine resources were clearly also very important. Lapita sites often contain shell ornaments, fishhooks, files, bone awls, tattooing needles, and shell and stone adzes. There is evidence for long distance exchange. Obsidian from Manus, the largest of the Admiralty Islands, is found in Vanuatu, while obsidian from New Britain is found in places as far apart as Borneo and Fiji.

Although plain wares were also made, most Lapita pottery is highly decorated with stamped designs. Detailed study shows that particular motifs are very widely distributed over the entire Lapita cultural complex. In the course of time, Lapita pottery became less sophisticated, and complex designs were simplified or abandoned. Ceramics skills died out altogether in Polynesia about 2,000 years ago. But archaeologists have no doubt that Polynesians were the descendants of the Lapita people and that the Fiji-Tonga-Samoa triangle was the formative area of Polynesian culture.

The Polynesian voyages

The dispersal of the Polynesians into the remote Pacific seems to have begun some 2,000 years ago with the settlement of the Marquesas, and later spread

ABOVE A modern replica of a Polynesian double-hulled sailing canoe. One such replica, the *Hokule'a,* sailed from Hawaii to Tahiti in 1976, demonstrating the skills of traditional Pacific seafarers.

from there to the Society and Cook Islands, Hawaii, and Easter Island (see pages 192–193). New Zealand and the Chatham Islands, the last places to be reached, were settled between 1000 and 1300 CE. Some remote islands such as Pitcairn appear to have been occupied and later abandoned. The sweet potato, an Andean native, was cultivated in the eastern Polynesian islands, which suggests that voyagers may even have reached the coast of South America.

It used to be thought that colonization occurred as the result of accidental drifting: once an island was reached, there was no prospect of return. However, computer simulations of canoe journeys using information on winds and currents indicate that some islands are unlikely to have been reached without following a deliberate course. Traditional Pacific seafarers today use complex systems of spatial visualization based on the stars, patterns of ocean swells, and other natural phenomena such as the flight of birds and cloud movements to determine direction and keep track of the position of the canoe. Simple maps made of sticks and shells or pebbles are used to record and pass on navigational knowledge. Using such seafaring skills, return voyages of exploration were certainly feasible. The large double-hulled Polynesian canoe had space to carry the crops, animals and other equipment, and colonizing groups were large enough to make sure that new settlements survived. We can only guess at some of the reasons for undertaking such perilous voyaging ventures: overpopulation, environmental degradation, competition for resources, inter-tribal rivalry. But perhaps it was simply that seafaring and the urge to voyage and explore lay at the very heart of the Polynesian cultural tradition ◆

BELOW Reconstructed Lapita pot from New Caledonia impressed with a linear pattern and decorated with a red slip around the neck (diameter 17.7 in/45 cm).

Easter Island

Easter Island, which lies in the South Pacific some 2,340 mi/ 3,765 km from South America, is one of the most remote places on Earth. Yet, amazingly, this tiny speck of volcanic rock, only 64 sq mi/166 sq km in extent, was colonized by Polynesian seafarers, most probably from the Marquesas far away to the north-west, at some point between c. 400 and 1000 CE. There is likely to have been only one major influx of settlers. Isolated from the rest of the world, they evolved a unique Stone Age culture.

The original colonizers were probably a few dozen men, women and children who arrived in one or more large double-hulled canoes, carrying the normal collection of animals and plants that Polynesian venturers took on their long sea-journeys to new lands. Breadfruit could not grow here because of the cool, subtropical climate, but bananas and sweet potato flourished. Pigs and dogs did not survive – at least their bones have never been found here – but chickens and Polynesian rats did, to become vital sources of protein. Recent excavations have shown that Easter Island was originally rich in indigenous land and sea birds, but they were swiftly wiped out.

Ancestral guardians

The islanders lived in small villages of oval houses shaped like upturned boats, and grew crops in fields and gardens protected from the constant winds and salt spray. Soon after their arrival they began to erect *ahu*, ceremonial stone platforms, around the perimeter of the island. After c.1000 CE the *ahu* became bigger and more numerous. Eventually statues known as *moai*, thought to be of ancestor figures and carved from soft volcanic tuff, were set up on some of them. Less than half the island's *ahu* have statues.

All the statues are cut off at the abdomen and have elongated heads. Their arms are held tightly at the sides and the elongated fingers meet at the stylized loincloth. The ears are sometimes lengthened and perforated. At least 800 statues were sculpted, ranging in height from 6.5 ft/2 m to 33 ft/10 m and weighing up to 82 tons. They were carved at the quarry. Thousands of basalt picks used for the purpose have been found here, together with hundreds of unfinished statues in every stage of production.

More than 230 finished statues were transported to the *ahu*. It used to be thought that they were dragged horizontally, but experiments have shown that upright transportation on a wooden sledge is a fast and efficient method. They were then set up on

BELOW Part of the row of *moai* statues at Ahu Tongariki, one of which wears a scoria topknot. This platform carries no less than 15 statues of different sizes, and was the biggest and most impressive on the island. Its statues had been toppled, like all others, by the mid-19th century. In 1960, a tsunami (tidal wave) did tremendous damage to the platform and scattered its fallen statues. A Japanese crane company undertook the task of restoring the site and re-erecting all its statues in the 1990s, thus giving back to the island one of its most impressive monuments. The elaborately carved, elongated ears on the statues can be clearly seen in this photograph. The *moai* are all variations on a single theme. They generally face inward, forming a protective barrier between the villages and the ocean, the outside world.

RIGHT The materials used for Easter Island's great statues came from different quarry areas. The soft volcanic tuff for most of the *moai* was from the crater of Rano Raraku, the red scoria for the cylindrical "topknots" from Puna Pau, while obsidian, used for the pupils of the white coral eyes as well as for daggers and spearpoints, came primarily from two sites – close to the crater of Rano Kao and from the offshore island of Motu Iti. The finest *moai* of all, known as *Hoa Hakananai'a* (Friend Which Has Been Stolen), was unearthed in a house at the ceremonial clifftop village of Orongo. It is carved in basalt and decorated with fine bas-reliefs. Statue carving on Easter Island sprang from the same tradition that produced ancestor figures on the Marquesas and other Polynesian islands. The practice most probably started c.1000 CE and lasted until c.1600, when lack of trees (for rollers, levers and cordage) put an end to this exercise in prestige and display.

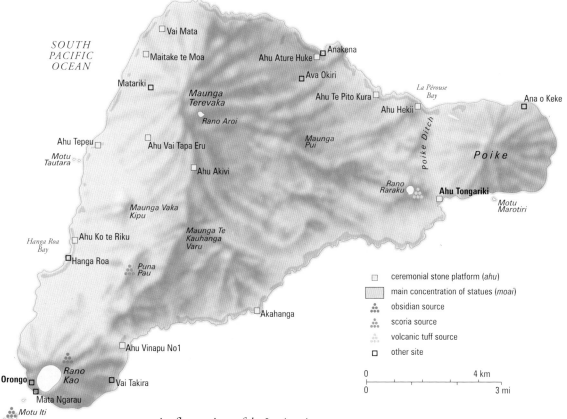

SOUTH PACIFIC OCEAN

Vai Mata

Maitake te Moa

Matariki

Maunga Terevaka

Rano Aroi

Ahu Tepeu

Motu Tautara

Ahu Vai Tapa Eru

Ahu Akivi

Maunga Vaka Kipu

Maunga Te Kauhanga Varu

Hanga Roa Bay

Ahu Ko te Riku

Hanga Roa

Puna Pau

Ahu Vinapu No1

Orongo

Rano Kao

Vai Takira

Mata Ngarau

Motu Iti

Motu Nui

Ahu Ature Huke

Anakena

Ava Okiri

Ahu Te Pito Kura

Ahu Hekii

La Pérouse Bay

Ana o Keke

Maunga Pui

Poike Ditch

Poike

Rano Raraku

Ahu Tongariki

Motu Marotiri

Akahanga

☐ ceremonial stone platform (*ahu*)

▨ main concentration of statues (*moai*)

⁂ obsidian source

⁂ scoria source

⁂ volcanic tuff source

☐ other site

0 — 4 km
0 — 3 mi

the platforms – as many as 15 in a row – always with their backs to the sea, protectively facing the villages. Some of the *moai* have heavy cylindrical "topknots" of red scoria, a coarse lava. Eyes made of white coral with pupils of obsidian (black volcanic glass) were inserted into the sockets for certain ceremonies.

Deforestation and decline

As far as can be ascertained from the archaeological record, the islanders lived quite peaceably for up to a thousand years before violence suddenly became endemic among them, and they began to manufacture huge quantities of *mataa*, spearpoints and daggers of obsidian. The most probable reason for this metamorphosis was revealed by analysis of pollen grains from cores extracted from the freshwater lakes in the island's craters. This showed that the now treeless island had been covered by a rainforest of the world's biggest palmtrees, as well as other trees and shrubs, until at least 1,200 years ago. Over the centuries of the island's occupation, this cover had been steadily removed, doubtless to create fields, and also to provide timber for fuel (for fires, cooking and cremation) as well as to make the apparatus for moving the statues. Deforestation in turn caused soil erosion, which damaged crop productivity, while the lack of wood for canoes eventually prevented the catching of deep-sea fish. Some have argued that climatic factors such as a drought or the "Little Ice Age" may have played a role, but as the indigenous vegetation had survived for 30,000 years throughout the

major fluctuations of the Ice Age, it seems clear that humans were primarily responsible for the reckless destruction of their island environment.

The population of the island had risen steadily to many thousands, and as crop production and fishing declined, severe food shortages must have occurred, producing the conditions for widespread inter-village raids and warfare. Statues in rival villages began to be toppled, and the old ancestor cult of the *moai* died out, to be replaced eventually by the birdman cult: each year the warrior elite from the island's clans competed to elect the "birdman" who would rule the island for the next year. Population numbers fell as a result of unchecked environmental degradation and escalating violence, and by the time the first Europeans arrived, on Easter Day, 1722, the islanders numbered around two thousand only ◆

BELOW Rocks carved with birdman figures on a cliff at Orongo, the ceremonial center of the birdman cult, which developed late in the island's history. On a certain day in September each year, a group of young men, each representing a warrior from the island's competing clans who wished to become birdman, would scramble down the sheer cliff at Orongo, swim out through the strong currents and shark-infested waters to the biggest offshore islet of Motu Nui, and search the nesting grounds of the Sooty tern for an egg. Whoever returned first to Orongo with an egg decided which clan would provide the birdman for the year. This meant his clan could raid and plunder the other island groups with impunity.

Maori Settlement of New Zealand

New Zealand, the largest of the islands of the Pacific, was the last major landmass to be colonized by humans, probably by the mid 13th century CE. A trail of archaeological, linguistic and genetic evidence traces the origins of the Maori, the indigenous people of New Zealand, all the way back to the western Pacific (see pages 190–191). The Maori's Polynesian ancestors were skilled navigators who discovered islands by sailing into the easterly trade winds. New Zealand, to the south of tropical Polynesia, lay in a quite different direction, which may account for the lateness of its discovery. Maori traditions describe the arrival of a fleet of canoes whose captains were remembered in oral tradition and whose names live on in the *whakapapa* (geneologies) of different tribes. According to one famous legend, the discovery of North Island was made by Kupe, who called it Aotearoa ("land of the long white cloud").

FAR RIGHT New Zealand is a continental-sized landmass, larger in area than the rest of Polynesia put together. Its climate ranges from sub-tropical in the far north to temperate and cold in the south and its environments include active volcanoes, high alpine fold mountains, inland plains and a highly dissected coastline. The South Island was the focus of early settlement during the first (Archaic) phase of prehistory from the 13th century. For the first settlers, New Zealand must have appeared tremendously attractive in terms of its abundant natural resources. Its podocarp forests and extensive tussock interior were inhabited by moa and other birds that were flightless and easy prey to hunters, while coastal margins supported large populations of seals, fish and shellfish. Unrestricted hunting in the first 300 years of settlement resulted in the extinction of many avifaunal populations.

Determining the date of New Zealand's colonization has proved controversial. Critical appraisal of the radiocarbon evidence suggests that the first settlers probably arrived in the late 12th/13th centuries CE. This is confirmed by studies of pollen sites, which show an increase in shrub species and a reduction in large trees at a time that is consistent with the firing of forest cover. Some prehistorians, however, argue for an earlier arrival, citing evidence of burning in natural sites. More controversially, a recent study has given a series of 2,000-year-old radiocarbon dates for bones of the Polynesian rat, a species that was introduced by humans. However, all the bones in the study were obtained from natural cave sites. Similar rat bones at securely dated human sites do not concur with dates of other reliable materials, so it is unwise to draw any firm conclusion from the evidence so far presented. Studies of mitochondrial DNA of rat bones from archaeological sites suggests there was more than one founding population, implying that multiple visits were made from Polynesia, but as yet there is no corroborating evidence for this.

Maungakiekie: a terraced pa

Maungakiekie (also known as One Tree Hill) is one of the many impressive *pa* that dot the mostly extinct volcanic cones on the isthmus upon which Auckland City now stands. The site is typical of the readily defended ridges and hills that were selected by the Maori for *pa*, both in the Tamaki volcanic field of Auckland and throughout the rest of New Zealand. Maungakiekie was constructed within three volcanic cones that are composed of soft scoria. The remains of defensive ditches and banks, modified terraces for houses (*whare*) and storage pits for horticultural crops are quite visible over most of the hill slopes. The site covers an area of 114 acres/46 hectares, making it one of the two largest *pa* in Auckland City. Archaeological excavation has shown that the site was occupied repeatedly over many centuries, and radiocarbon determinations suggest that the construction of Maungakiekie's defensive features date from the 16th century, a time of intense warfare. The fertile soils of the Tamaki volcanic fields made this an area of prime horticultural land before the arrival of Europeans, but modern city suburbs now nestle at the foot of the hill where the Maori gardens once extended. Although about 20 percent of the site has been destroyed or damaged by road construction, Maungakiekie remains one of the most fully explored examples of a volcanic *pa* complex ◆

The early moa hunters

Recent analyses of DNA from modern Maori imply that the founding population was small and must have comprised a group including about 70 women. The first colonizers do not appear to have brought pigs and chickens, the staple meat of the Polynesians, with them (though they did introduce dogs as well as rats) but instead found an abundance of animal species: coastal and forest-dwelling birds, large sea mammals, particularly seals, and shellfish. Most early archaeological sites are located at the mouths of rivers and appear to have been occupied for less than 50 years. Excavations reveal a hunter–gatherer economy centered on the moa, the flightless bird of New Zealand, of which there were 11 species. The largest, *Dinornis giganteus*, stood over 6.5 ft/ 2 m high. Lacking natural predators, the giant moa had lost any instinct to flee and was probably hunted to extinction within 300 years of human settlement.

One of the most important early sites in New Zealand is Wairau Bar, excavated between 1950 and 1964. Over 40 human burials (*koiwi*) were uncovered, along with an array of material culture, including a range of adzes of typical eastern Polynesian style, complete moa eggs, worked moa bones, sperm whale tooth necklaces, imitation whaletooth pendants, and sharksteeth ornaments . The term "moa hunter" was coined to describe the culture found at Wairau Bar. Recent radiocarbon dating of moa eggshell from 10 of the graves suggests that the site was occupied from the late 13th century CE for only a few decades at most.

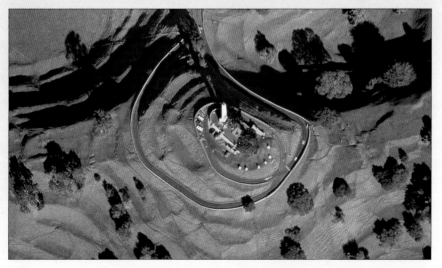

ABOVE AERIAL VIEW OF MAUNGAKIEKIE, A TERRACED PA BUILT AROUND AN EXTINCT VOLCANIC CONE.

Bar

Owens Fe
Wak
Lake Te Anau
Takahe Valley
Breaksea Sou
Doubtful Sound
Chalky Inlet
Pa
Wakapatu
Tiwai

Legend

- traditional canoe landing site
- □ Archaic site, before c.1400 CE
- ■ site of major *Pa*
- ▪ site of other *Pa*
- ▪ other Classic site, after c.1400 CE
- ▨ area of moa hunting
- ⋮ area of seal hunting
- limit of sweet potato cultivation

important stone source
- argillite
- basalt
- chert
- jade
- obsidian
- silcrete

RIGHT A greenstone *(pounamu) hei matau* ornament made in the style of a fishhook, from Pahia, South Island (length 3.3 in/8.6 cm).

Tools and horticulture

Continental New Zealand contains a much wider range of rock types than island Polynesia. The first settlers were quick to exploit the tool-making capabilities of these new materials. At first tools were manufactured in typical East Polynesian style, but pretty soon the settlers began experimenting with new tool types such as adzes made from argillites (compacted clays). Long-distance trade in stone resources appears to have started early. Obsidian from Mayor Island in the north was particularly highly prized. This distinctive black-green obsidian is found in almost every site in New Zealand, and if return visits were made to Polynesia, it is surprising that no Mayor Island obsidian has been found there. Greenstone (nephrite) was not widely used until the 16th century.

Although Polynesian food crops such as kumara (sweet potato) and taro were introduced, New Zealand was at the very limit of their climatic range and they could not be cultivated south of Banks Peninsula. Kumara tubers had to be stored in underground pits in preparation for planting the next season: a few pits have been found from the Archaic period but most belong to the Classic period (post 1450 CE). Ditches were built and gravel added to soils to improve drainage. But until the potato was introduced in the 19th century, horticulture appears always to have been marginal in some areas.

Classic Maori culture

Around 1500 CE, there was a transformation in Maori society. This is marked archaeologically by the construction of *pa* (hill forts) and a move from open to defensive settlements. Literally thousands of *pa* sites have been identified, and population growth leading to competition for resources and increased warfare is the most likely explanation for their development. The majority of *pa* are in the North Island and it is tempting to consider access to horticultural land as a critical variable. Others have argued that they reflect a monumental architectural tradition related to the status (*mana*) of chiefs. The development of the Classic Maori cultural tradition, embodied in the stylistic wood carving and tattooing that continue in modern Maori culture, paralleled this increasingly turbulent social situation. The journals of Tasman, Cook and other early European visitors provide a valuable ethnographic resource for documenting the ways of life of the Maori before European settlement in the mid 19th century ◆

GLOSSARY

Achaemenids a branch of the Persian tribes that moved into western Iran early in the 1st millennium BCE and settled in Fars. From there, the ruling house expanded during the 6th century BCE to create a world empire that stretched from Central Asia and northern India to Thrace and Egypt. Notable Achaemenid rulers include Cyrus, Darius and Xerxes.

agora a focal point for civic life in the Greek city, equivalent to the forum in a Roman city. The agora was usually surrounded by buildings linked to the government of the state, and might also include markets and spaces for athletic events and festivals.

Akkadian denotes a group of SEMITIC languages in MESOPOTAMIA, first known in CUNEIFORM texts of the mid 3rd millennium BCE in the northern part of the Mesopotamian flood-plain, the ancient Akkad, and which includes the later Babylonian and Assyrian languages. In the political history of Mesopotamia, it also refers to the dynasty of Sargon (c.2330–2150 BCE), which had its capital at Agade in Akkad, and to the material culture of this period.

amphora a large jar, typically two-handled, used to store oil, wine or other such liquids.

AMS accelerator mass spectrometry, a fast but expensive RADIOCARBON-DATING method that can determine the actual numbers of 14C atoms present in a tiny sample, rather than the relatively small numbers of 14C atoms that decay radioactively during the measurement time of the conventional counting method. Both methods have approximately the same dating age limit of about 50,000 y.a.

Aramaean a series of small IRON AGE states in Syria that were eventually absorbed into the Assyrian empire. During the 1st millennium BCE the Aramaic language, which used an alphabetic script, became the administrative language of the Near East in succession to AKKADIAN, being adopted by the Assyrian, Babylonian and ACHAEMENID empires.

archaeology the study of the human past through its material remains.

Archaic (1) in North American archaeology, cultures that have a broad-spectrum hunting and gathering base, GROUND STONE tools, and increasing SEDENTISM. (2) in Greek art, it relates to the period of the emerging city-states from the mid 8th century BCE. Traditionally, the Persian attack on Greece in 480 BCE marks the end of the Greek Archaic.

Archaic *Homo* a loose term for HOMINID fossils dating to the period between c.800,000 and 200,000 y.a. They were powerfully built creatures who had brain sizes gradually increasing to approach that of the modern average, but with backward-sloping foreheads behind large brow ridges, as well as large faces with big teeth positioned in front of rather than directly below the braincase. They are usually regarded as the ancestor of both modern *H. SAPIENS* and the extinct *H. sapiens neanderthalensis* or *H. neanderthalensis* (see NEANDERTALS).

Ardipithecus a genus of early HOMINID, known from 4.4 million-year-old fossils of the species *Ardipithecus ramidus*, from Aramis in Ethiopia, thought to represent the earliest hominid yet found. It may have used a form of BIPEDAL locomotion.

argon-argon dating an isotopic dating method in which the isotopic composition of argon in rocks is measured. Material can be dated in the age range of 10,000 y.a. to greater than 1 m.y.a, with varying degrees of precision. The method is used to date the timing of mineralization and volcanic activity, as well as establishing stratigraphic relationships within the QUATERNARY geochronology.

artifact any movable object that has been used, modified or manufactured by humans.

assemblage a collection of ARTIFACTS that can be considered a single analytical unit. The size of an individual assemblage varies considerably. For example, an assemblage may represent artifacts used in a particular activity or the remains of a particular CULTURE found at a site.

Assyria see MESOPOTAMIA

australopithecine a small-brained, bipedal, fossil HOMINID, known from sites in a belt stretching from East to southern Africa, as well as a single site in Chad. Some species of australopithecine are considered ancestral to humans. The best represented is *A. afarensis*, known from 4–3 million year old deposits in East Africa. *A. afarensis* and *A. africanus* are sometimes called "gracile" because they were small and lightly built. More massive "robust" australopithecines appear later in time than the gracile species.

Babylonia see MESOPOTAMIA

barrow a mound, usually of earth, covering burials which are either dug into the original ground surface or placed within the body of the mound itself. The term was much used in the 18th and 19th centuries, when "barrow-digging" in Britain became an amateur pastime among the educated or the simply curious.

bas-relief low-relief carving, where the design only projects slightly from the background, like on a coin.

Beringia a land mass located in the present-day Bering and Chukchi Seas, formed by the drop in sea level as a result of the formation of continental glaciers at the end of the PLEISTOCENE. This allowed humans to enter the New World by a route called the Bering land bridge.

biface (or **handax**) a stone tool worked on opposite faces to form a cutting edge. Biface technology developed from African PEBBLETOOL INDUSTRIES, spreading to Europe, India and southwest Asia in the Lower and part of the Middle PALEOLITHIC periods. Bifaces range in shape from triangular or pearshaped to oval, and in length from approximately 3 to 7.8 in/8 to 20 cm. They are believed to be multipurpose tools.

bipedalism the ability to travel over ground on two feet in a more or less upright posture.

blade a long parallel-sided stone FLAKE removed by percussive action from a larger CORE; used either as a tool itself or as the blank from which a tool such as a BURIN would be struck.

breccia a rock consisting of sharp fragments embedded in a fine-grained matrix such as sand or limestone.

Bronze Age in Old World archaeology, the period of prehistory in which bronze was the primary material for tools and weapons. In Europe, the Bronze Age spans the period from c.2200–c.800 BCE. In East Asia, the period of bronze use on the China mainland coincided with the SHANG and ZHOU dynasties (2nd–1st millennia BCE).

burin a characteristic Upper PALEO-LITHIC blade tool with a sharp trans-verse chisel-like working edge formed by the removal of a sliver of stone. They were traditionally regarded as engraving tools used to work bone, ivory, antler, soft stone and wood, but recent USEWEAR ANALYSIS suggests that burins may be multipurpose.

Canaanites an ethnic group identified with the sophisticated urban civilization of the Levant during the BRONZE AGE.

chamber tomb a stone-built tomb, often MEGALITHIC in construction, generally used for communal burials over a long period. Chamber tombs are found in many parts of the world and in many different forms.

chiefdom a society based on ranking, generally one in which lineages (groups claiming descent from a common ancestor) are graded by how closely they are related to the chief.

chronology any system of dating. Relative chronology uses STRATIGRAPHY and TYPOLOGY to establish a sequence of events for a particular site or region. Absolute chronology has recourse to a specific time scale, determined by scientific methods such as RADIOCARBON DATING or by a fixed calendrical system.

Clovis the earliest type of stone tool of the PALEOINDIAN period in North America, a projectile point characterized by symmetry, careful flaking and the removal of a small groove or flute from the base of each face. The Clovis tradition may have begun as early as 13,500 BCE.

Copper Age a period (primarily in the 5th, 4th and 3rd millennia BCE) in many parts of the Near East and Europe (especially southeastern Europe), when copper metallurgy was in the process of being adopted by cultures that were otherwise essentially NEOLITHIC in character.

core (also **blank** or **nucleus**) a piece of stone from which flakes are removed by striking it with another stone (a process known as knapping). The core may itself be shaped to create a core tool such as a BIFACE or chopper, or may simply be the raw material for the manufacture of flakes, which are then further retouched to make FLAKE tools.

culture in archaeology, the constellation of specific artifactual elements (MATERIAL CULTURE) thought to represent a particular people.

cuneiform the characteristic wedge-shaped writing of western Asia, used for over 3,000 years, which was produced by impressing sharpened reeds into clay tablets. The writing system emerged during the 4th millennium BCE in southern MESOPOTAMIA and continued in use until the end of the 1st millennium BCE. It was used to represent many different languages.

dendrochronology a dating method based on tree-ring sequences used to date timbers from archaeological structures and sites. The annual growth ring of a tree is thinner in dry years and thicker in moist years, and trees of the same species and similar age in an area affected by similar climatic conditions will exhibit similar sequences of ring widths. By finding older and younger trees that overlap in age, a relative CHRONOLOGY can be constructed to which the tree-ring pattern of timber finds can be compared. Absolute ages can be obtained where the known tree-ring sequence for a particular species extends to the present. The longest (oldest) sequence to date, based on the Bristlecone Pine for western America, extends back 9,000 years.

diffusionism the theory, now widely discredited, that all the major attributes of civilization, from MEGALITHS to metal-working, spread from the Near East and Egypt to Europe.

Dryas a series of cold climatic phases in northern Eurasia, named after a tundra plant, when the climate returned to almost full glacial conditions. Dryas I lasted from c.16,000–14,000 y.a., Dryas II (Older Dryas) from c.12,300–11,800 y.a. and Dryas III (Younger Dryas) from c.11,000– 10,000 y.a.

einkorn a wild (*Triticum boeoticum*) and domestic (*T. monococcum*) form of wheat that appears at some early farming sites in the Near East.

emmer a wild (*Triticum dicoccoides*) and domestic (*T. dicoccum*) form of wheat that is found more commonly than einkorn on early farming sites in the Near East and spread in its domestic form throughout Europe.

environmental archaeology a subfield of archaeology where the aim is to identify processes, factors and conditions of past biological and physical environmental systems and establish how they relate to cultural systems.

excavation the systematic recovery of archaeological data through the exposure of buried sites and artifacts. Excavation can be either partial, in which case only a sample of the site is investigated, or total. An important goal of excavation is a full understanding of a site's STRATIGRAPHY. Excavation is destructive to any site, so the fullest possible amount of material and information must be recovered from any "dig" and a full record kept of all the techniques employed in the excavation to enable future archaeologists to evaluate the results of the work accurately. It is also expensive. For both these reasons, it should be used only as a last resort.

faience a material used in ancient Egypt, the Near East and the Aegean for glazed figurines and jewelry. It consists of a body of quartz sand, soda and lime, covered by a soda-lime glaze that is usually green or greenish-blue but can be polychrome.

flake a piece of stone detached from a core by striking it with another stone.

fossil the remains, impression or trace of any living organism from a past geological age found preserved in rock or sediment.

glacial a cold climatic episode characterized in northern latitudes by the presence and spread of widespread glacial ice and cold climate processes, deposits, flora and fauna (compare **interglacial**).

ground-edge tool a stone tool with a sharp cutting edge at one end produced by grinding rather than flaking.

Han a historical period or dynasty in China (206 BCE–220 CE), with the Wangman interregnum (9-25 CE) separating the Early (Western) and Late (Eastern) Han periods. It was the first centralized state in China following unification by Qin in 221 BCE.

handax see biface.

Hellenistic a period of time dating from the death of Alexander the Great (323 BCE) to the establishment of the Roman empire in the 1st century BCE. The Hellenistic world consisted of the kingdoms carved out from the former Persian empire as well as the Greek mainland. The term Hellenistic art can be applied to post-classical material outside this geographical area, such as in Etruria or southern Italy.

hieroglyphic from the Greek meaning "sacred carved writing", a pictorial script used by the ancient Egyptians from the beginning of the 3rd millennium BCE until the end of the 4th century CE for religious purposes and on public monuments. It survived in these contexts even after it had been superseded in more vernacular contexts by the cursive hieratic and demotic scripts that evolved from it. More loosely, the term is also used for other scripts based on pictograms, especially the Maya (also called glyphs).

Holocene following the PLEISTOCENE epoch, the latest and present epoch of the QUATERNARY period. Its lower boundary is generally assigned an age of 8000 BCE.

hominid a member of the family of Hominidae, BIPEDAL primates with relatively large brains, including AUSTRALOPITHECINES and humans.

Homo erectus a name (meaning "upright man") assigned to HOMINID FOSSILS with a muscular, stocky build and heavy face with thick brow ridge . The earliest example was found in Java in 1891, the first early human fossil recognized outside Europe. *H. erectus* was considered to have been the first hominid to spread out of Africa about 1 million years ago and to have been a direct ancestor of *H. SAPIENS*, but many African fossils previously ascribed to *H. erectus* are now being reclassified as *H. ERGASTER*, and it is possible that the East Asian *H.erectus* was a specialized local development.

Homo ergaster an early African *Homo* species (the "workman") known from 1.8–1.5 million-year-old FOSSILS. *H. ergaster* is associated with stone ARTIFACTS, had a larger brain, reduced teeth and jaws, as well as a build and locomotion more like those of later *Homo*, and is considered an ancestor to later species of *Homo*.

Homo habilis a HOMINID ("handy man") thought until recently to be the oldest species of *Homo*. First described from Olduvai Gorge in Tanzania in 1964, it was the first early *Homo* identified in Africa. FOSSILS assigned to this species date to the period between 1.9 and 1.6 million years ago and are known from sites in East and South Africa. *H. habilis* had a small and light apelike build, but with a larger brain than gracile AUSTRALOPITHECINES.

Homo heidelbergensis a distinct human species that lived between 800,000–200,000 years ago. Known from Europe, Africa, and possibly China, it is sometimes regarded as the ancestor of the NEANDERTALS (*H. neanderthalensis)* and modern *H. SAPIENS*.

Homo sapiens "wise man", our own species. The oldest known anatomically modern *H. sapiens* or *H. sapiens sapiens* FOSSILS come from sites in Africa and the Near East, where they date to between 130,000 and 80,000 y.a. (See also ARCHAIC HOMO and NEANDERTALS)

hunter–gatherers members of small-scale mobile or semi-sedentary societies whose subsistence is based mainly on the hunting of wild animals and the gathering of wild plants.

Ice Age a general term for periods characterized by the expansion of continental and alpine glaciers. It is often used to refer to the last GLACIAL of the QUATERNARY.

Indo-European a large language group that includes most modern European languages (e.g. Romance, Germanic, Slavic, Baltic, Greek, Albanian) except Basque, Finnish and Hungarian, modern Indo-Iranian (e.g. Persian, Hindi) and other tongues (e.g. Armenian), and numerous dead languages (e.g. Hittite). Many attempts have been made to explain this pattern of languages as a result of migrations or invasions in prehistoric and early historic times. The most widely accepted solution places the Proto-Indo-European homeland in the southern Russian steppes in the broad zone north of the Black and Caspian Seas during the 5th millennium BCE.

industry an ASSEMBLAGE of ARTIFACTS including the same tool types so consistently as to suggest it is the product of a single society.

interglacial a relatively warm climatic episode, between glacial episodes, characterized by little or no glacial ice, warm climate processes, deposits, flora and fauna, and increased soil-forming processes in some areas. In reference to the QUATERNARY, interglacials were considerably briefer than glacials.

Iron Age a period of Old World antiquity when iron superseded the use of bronze for tools and weapons. In Europe, the earliest iron appears around 1100 BCE, but the transition from the BRONZE AGE to the Iron Age is conventionally placed in the early part of the 1st millennium BCE. In western Europe, the Iron Age is held to end with the Roman empire, while beyond the Roman frontier it continues until the so-called migration period in the 4th to 6th centuries CE. In East Asia, iron came into use in China c.500 BCE. Iron smelting apparently spread from western Asia to north Africa by the 8th century BCE.

Jomon the postglacial period of hunting and gathering in Japan (10,000–300 BCE), which coincides with the existence of Jomon pottery. It is characterized by marine resource utilization and SEDENTISM.

Linearbandkeramik (LBK) see LINEAR POTTERY CULTURE.

Linear Pottery culture the earliest NEOLITHIC culture of central Europe, distributed broadly from the western Ukraine to eastern France (c.5600–5000 BCE), which takes its name from the incised lines on its fine pottery. These begin with simple meander and spiral patterns and develop into complex designs, often including punctates (small depressions or pits) and stroked ornamentation.

loess windborne (eolian) deposits of silt laid down in a thick stratum during periglacial conditions. In central and eastern Europe, loess soil was favored by the earliest farming communities, especially the LINEAR POTTERY CULTURE.

lost wax (cire perdue) a method of casting awkwardly shaped objects in metal. A wax model of the object is coated in clay and baked, and the melted wax allowed to escape. Liquid metal, poured into the resulting cavity in the mold, assumes the model's shape, and is released when hard by breaking the clay surround: each mold can be used only once. Its earliest use is in the 4th millennium BCE in the Near East. It was used primarily for bronze in the Old World (especially in Southeast Asia), and for gold in South America and Mesoamerica.

material culture the buildings, tools and other ARTIFACTS that make up the material remains of former societies.

megalithic a monument constructed of large stones such as a CHAMBER TOMB or stone circle (from the Greek *megas* "large" and *lithos* "stone").

Mesolithic literally the "Middle Stone Age", a period of transition in the early HOLOCENE between the Upper PALAEOLITHIC HUNTER–GATHERER existence of the last ICE AGE and the development of farming and pottery production during the postglacial NEOLITHIC. The Mesolithic was a response to changing climatic conditions following the retreat of the glacial ice c.8500 BCE. Mesolithic toolkits reflect the need to adapt to the changing environment and are characterized by the presence of MICROLITHS and stone axes or adzes used in woodworking.

Mesopotamia from the Greek "(the land) between the rivers", the region of western Asia defined by the Euphrates and Tigris rivers together with their tributaries. It is further divided between the northern upland zone (corresponding roughly to Assyria) and the southern alluvial zone (Sumer and Akkad; later Babylonia). These two zones form the central focus of western Asian civilizations from the emergence of complex societies during the 4th millennium BCE to the end of the Mesopotamian tradition in the late 1st millennium BCE.

microlith a small Later Upper PALEOLITHIC or MESOLITHIC stone ARTIFACT varying from about 0.4 to 2 in/1 to 5 cm in length and used as the tip of a bone or wooden implement or as an arrowpoint.

mitochondrial DNA or mtDNA genetic instructions inherited through the maternal line. Deoxyribonucleic acid (DNA) is a molecule that carries genetic instructions from parents to offspring, and is mostly found in the nucleus of cells. In sexually reproducing species, each individual inherits approximately equal amounts of nuclear DNA from both parents. A small quantity of DNA is also found in another structure within cells, known as the mitochondrion, which generates energy for the cell. Mitochondrial DNA is inherited only from the mother. Studies of mtDNA in modern human populations indicate that the greatest genetic diversity (hence antiquity) occurs in Africans and that other populations diverged more recently.

native copper copper that occurs naturally in nuggets and can be easily worked by cutting and hammering.

Neandertals (also Neanderthals) ARCHAIC HUMANS who inhabited Europe, Central Asia, and the Near East during the Late PLEISTOCENE. They are generally classified as a separate species of *Homo* (*H. neandertalensis*). The earliest Neandertal remains date to the late Middle Pleistocene (roughly 200,000 y.a.). The most recent remains have been dated by radiocarbon to c.30 000 y.a. in Spain and Croatia. The Neandertals are widely believed to have been replaced by modern humans (*H. SAPIENS*) 40,000–30 000 y.a., but may have interbred with the latter in some areas.

Neolithic the period of antiquity in which people began to use ground stone tools, cultivate plants and keep domestic livestock (in contrast to the PALEOLITHIC). In a number of parts of the world including western Europe, the appearance of pottery is also considered a hallmark of the Neolithic. The dating of the Neolithic is quite variable, beginning in the Near East in the 9th millennium BCE and lasting into the 2nd millennium BCE in the more northerly parts of Europe.

obsidian a naturally occurring volcanic glass, easily chipped to form extremely sharp (though brittle) edges; this makes it a desirable raw material for tools. In western Asia, important obsidian sources occur in central and eastern Anatolia, the neighbouring Transcaucasus and southwest Arabia. Obsidian was an important trade item in Mesoamerica, and many of the basic tools of prehistoric households there were made of this material. It was also an important resource in the Pacific Islands, and was widely exchanged.

Oldowan an early PALEOLITHIC stone tool INDUSTRY represented at Olduvai Gorge and other African sites, dating from about 2.5–1.4 m.y.a. and later, characterized by the production of small FLAKES removed from alternate faces along the edge of a pebble. Traditionally ascribed to *HOMO HABILIS*, Oldowan tools were probably also made by other early *Homo* species such as *H. rudolfensis*, and possibly also AUSTRALOPITHECINES.

paleoanthropology a multidisciplinary approach to the study of human evolution.

paleobotany the study of plant remains recovered from prehistoric soil deposits, from which it is possible to obtain information about (for example) prehistoric climate, utilization of plant resources, diet, and the transition from wild plant collecting to plant domestication and farming.

Paleoindians the inhabitants of the Americas in the Late PLEISTOCENE who lived by hunting megafauna such as mammoths and forms of bison and are associated with CLOVIS weapons.

Paleolithic literally the "Old Stone Age", the technological division of prehistory extending from the first appearance of tool-using humans to the retreat of the glacial ice in the northern hemisphere at c.8500 BCE and the emergence of the MESOLITHIC. Paleolithic people lived as HUNTER–GATHERERS without agriculture and without formal pottery production. The Paleolithic is traditionally subdivided into three successive phases based mainly on ARTIFACT TYPOLOGY: the Lower Paleolithic is the period of early HOMINID PEBBLETOOL and CORE tool manufacture. More technologically advanced tools appear in the Middle Paleolithic, with a developing aesthetic and religious awareness. Fully modern humans, *HOMO SAPIENS SAPIENS*, emerge in the Upper Paleolithic, a period of delicate stone and bone tool manufacture and the development of art. In East Asia, the Paleolithic period divides into Early (1,000,000–75,000 y.a.), Middle (c.75,000–42,000 y.a.), and Late (42,000–12,000 y.a.).

Panaramitee a rock art tradition that is widely distributed in Australia but is best known from the arid center, which is characterized by pecked figures depicting a limited range of motifs, mostly bird and animal tracks, and circles. Like all rock art, is difficult to date, but some of it definitely goes back to the ICE AGE.

parietal art literally "art on walls"; the term is used of prehistoric works of art on any non-movable surface, including blocks, ceilings and floors.

Parthians the inhabitants of Khorasan in northeastern Iran, who formed an empire that incorporated Iran and most of MESOPOTAMIA during the 2nd century BCE. Best known historically for their intermittent wars with the Romans, their empire was overthrown early in the 3rd century CE by the SASSANIANS.

Pazyryk a complex of IRON AGE tumuli in the Altai Mountains of southwestern Siberia, dating to the 5th to 3rd centuries BCE, many of which are the graves of high-status individuals among the nomadic pastoralists of this region and are characterized by the exceptional preservation of their contents.

pebbletool a chopping tool made by striking flakes from a pebble or cobble to produce a working edge; the earliest examples are 2.5 million years old.

Phoenicians a SEMITIC people, the cultural heirs of the CANAANITEs, who flourished as traders from their ports of Byblos, Sidon and Tyre during the 1st millennium BCE.

Pleistocene a geochronological division, the earliest epoch of the QUATERNARY period, corresponding with the last ICE AGE. The Early Pleistocene begins c.1.8 m.y.a, the Middle c.780,000 y.a., and the Late c.127,000 y.a. It is regarded as ending c.10 000 y.a. and is followed by the HOLOCENE.

polity a term used to describe small-scale but politically autonomous early states.

pollen analysis or **palynology** the study of FOSSIL and living pollen and spores including their production, dispersal and applications. The resilient exine (outer coating) of the pollen and spores of plants, mosses and ferns is preserved in anaerobic environments such as lakes and bogs, and some acidic and dry soils, such as in caves. By identifying and counting the pollen and spores in a soil sample it is possible to reconstruct past environments, identify natural and human-induced vegetation changes, and develop relative CHRONOLOGIES.

potassium-argon (K-A) dating a method of dating rocks based on the ratio between the 40K isotope, which has a known rate of radioactive decay, and the stable 40Ar isotope. The method is used primarily to date lava flows and tuffs. These deposits have no 40Ar when originally formed because the heat at time of emplacement has driven it away. The age is based on the known half-life of 40K, the constant proportion of 39K and 40K in rocks, and the 40K/40Ar ratio with both isotopes being measured in the sample. The method is routinely applied to volcanic rocks from about 100,000 to 30 million y.a., and is one of the most widely used methods of dating early HOMINID sites in Africa.

processual archaeology a theoretical approach, formulated in the 1960s, that stresses the dynamic relationship between social and economic aspects of culture and the environment as the basis for understanding the processes of culture change.

Quaternary the latest period of the geological time-scale, starting about 1.8 m.y.a.

radiocarbon dating a dating technique for determining the age of late QUATERNARY carbon-bearing materials, including wood and plant remains, bone, peat and calcium carbonate shell. The method is based on the radioactive decay of the 14C isotope in the sample to nitrogen, with the release of particles that is initiated when an organism dies and ceases to exchange 14C with the atmosphere. After death the 14C content is a function of time and is determined by counting particles for a period of time. The method yields reliable ages back to c.50,000 y.a. and in extreme conditions to c.75,000 y.a.

Sahul the continental shelf that comprises Australia, Tasmania and New Guinea, which has been exposed as dry land at times of low sea level to form a single land mass with a common prehistory.

Sassanians a Persian dynasty that overthrew the PARTHIANS in 224 CE after a revolt against Parthian rule and controlled much of western Asia until the Arab Islamic invasion in 651. At its largest, the empire extended from Transcaucasia and western Central Asia in the north to the Indus and southern Arabia in the east and south, and to the frontier with the Romans and Byzantines in the west.

Scythians horse-riding nomads of the steppes of southern Russia and Ukraine during the 1st millennium BCE, who were in contact with the Greeks through their trading colonies on the Black Sea.

sedentism a way of life based upon permanent villages, as opposed to one of mobile foraging. In western Asia, sedentism is generally associated with the adoption of farming but this is not the case in other parts of the world such as coastal Peru and East Asia where there was a natural abundance of marine and plant resources to support settled village living.

Semitic a group of languages originating in western Asia, which includes ancient Akkadian, Canaanite, Aramaic, and Phoenician as well as modern Hebrew and Arabic.

Shang the second of the Chinese dynasties, dating to the 16th–11th centuries BCE. It originated as the name of a BRONZE AGE people, who are now said to have ruled the Shang state known by a characteristic set of bronze weapons, ritual vessels, and oracle bone inscriptions.

state the most complex form of social organization, characterized by a strong, centralized government, socio-economic class divisions and a market economy. Populations are normally very large, and have cities and monumental architecture.

stela or **stele** an upright stone slab, often inscribed or carved in relief, and sometimes painted. In Egypt, a stela is generally an upright slab (of stone or other durable material), usually with a rounded or flat top, upon which texts and illustrations intended to be of a permanent nature were inscribed. In Mesoamerica, stelae take the form of carved stone shafts usually found with temples. Decipherment has shown they are historical monuments recording the exploits and genealogy of rulers.

stratigraphy the study of the formation, composition, sequence and correlation of stratified sediment, soils and rocks. Stratigraphy is the principal means by which the context of archaeological deposits is evaluated, CHRONOLOGIES are constructed and events are sequenced. It is governed by a number of stratigraphic principles developed to help order materials and events in time and space: for example, the law of superposition, where older beds or strata are overlain and buried by progressively younger beds or strata. The stratigraphy of an archaeological site is invaluable for interpreting the sequence of deposition of the site, and thereby the relative ages of ARTIFACTS, features and other phenomena.

Sumerians people speaking and writing Sumerian, a language spoken in southern MESOPOTAMIA, which is unrelated to any other known language; considerable controversy surrounds the question of its origins. The tradition of social and political organization, art, literature and religious observation created by the Sumerians, along with AKKADIAN-speaking elements in southern Mesopotamia in the late 4th and 3rd millennia BCE greatly influenced neighboring cultures and provided many of the central features that defined the Mesopotamian world until the end of its existence.

teosinte a wild grass indigenous to the Mexican Highlands, thought to be the ancestor of maize.

thermoluminescence dating a technique developed for dating fired archaeological material. Sediments and the materials buried in them are exposed to ionizing radiation from the decay of radioactive isotopes. This causes energy in the form of displaced electrons to be stored in electron traps within mineral crystal lattices. Trapped electrons accumulate through time. When stimulated, they release energy in the form of light (luminescence). The intensity of the signal is a measure of the accumulated radiation exposure, or equivalent dose; the longer the exposure or the stronger the radiation level, or dose rate, the greater the emitted luminescence of a sample. When, for example, pottery is fired, any stored energy in the mineral grain inclusions is released and the thermoluminescent clock is reset. Upon burial, the mineral inclusions begin to store energy anew, and the length of time the object has been in the ground can be calculated by measuring their luminescence.

typology the classification of a contemporary series of ARTIFACTS by dividing them into types and subtypes based upon a consideration of a number of attributes including shape, function, technique of manufacture and so forth. Typologies are often constructed to help in the formation of CHRONOLOGIES and CULTURE history.

usewear (microwear) analysis microscopic study of the pattern of wear or damage on the edge of stone tools, which provides valuable information on the way in which the tool was used (for chopping, cutting, scraping or grinding, etc.).

Zhou the name of a BRONZE AGE ethnic group that overthrew the SHANG c.1027 BCE and established the Zhou dynasty in China. Its period of rule is divided into Western or Royal Zhou (1027–771 BCE) and historic Eastern Zhou (770–221 BCE), and further divided into the Spring and Autumn (770–476 BCE) and Warring States (475–221 BCE) periods. Major advances during the Zhou period were the discovery and development of ironworking, construction of the Great Wall, coinage, and the institution of county-level administration, but it is characterized by endemic warfare between small competing states. The Zhou state of Qin eventually conquered its rivals and united the various states in 220 BCE.

FURTHER READING

GENERAL

Aitken, M. J. *Science-based Dating in Archaeology*. London: Longman, 1990.

Bahn, P. G. (ed.) *The Cambridge Illustrated History of Archaeology*. Cambridge, UK: Cambridge University Press,1996.

Binford, L. *Working at Archaeology*. Orlando, Florida: Academic Press, 1983.

Clark, A. *Seeing Beneath the Soil: Prospecting Methods in Archaeology*. London: Routledge, 1996.

Hester, T. N. et al. *Field Methods in Archaeology*. Palo Alto: Mayfield,1997.

Hodder, I. *The Archaeological Process*. Oxford: Blackwell, 1999.

Renfrew, C. & Bahn, P. *Archaeology: Theories, Methods and Practice* (3rd edn.). New York: Harry N. Abrams/London: Thames & Hudson, 2000.

Trigger, B. *A History of Archaeological Thought*. Cambridge, UK: Cambridge University Press, 1989.

Willey, G. & Sabloff, J. *A History of American Archaeology* . San Francisco: W.H. Freeman/London: Thames & Hudson, 1993.

THE FIRST HUMANS

Atlas of Primitive Man in China. Beijing: Science Press, 1980.

Bahn, P. G. & Vertut, J. *Journey Through the Ice Age*. Berkeley: University of California Press/London: Weidenfeld & Nicolson, 1997.

Chard, C. S. *Northeast Asia in Prehistory*. Madison: University of Wisconsin Press, 1974.

Derevanko, A. P. et al (eds.) *The Paleolithic of Siberia: New Discoveries and Interpretations*. Urbana: University of Illinois Press, 1998.

Fagan, B. *The Journey from Eden: The Peopling of Our World*. New York: Harry N. Abrams/London: Thames & Hudson, 1990

Gamble, C. *The Palaeolithic Settlement of Europe*. Cambridge, UK: Cambridge University Press, 1986.

Gamble, C. *Timewalkers: The Prehistory of Global Colonization*. Cambridge, Mass: Harvard University Press, 1993.

Jia, L. *Early Man in China*. Beijing: Foreign Language Press, 1980.

Johanson, D. & Edgar, B. *From Lucy to Language*. New York: Simon & Schuster, 1996.

Klein, R.G. *The Human Career* (2nd edn.). Chicago: University of Chicago Press, 1999.

Otte, M. *Le Paléolithique Inférieur et Moyen en Europe*. Paris: Armand Colin, 1996.

Roebroeks, W. & van Kolfschoten, T. (eds.) *The Earliest Occupation of Europe*. Leiden, Netherlands: University of Leiden, 1995.

Shreeve, J. *The Neandertal Enigma: Solving the Mystery of Modern Human Origins*. New York: William Morrow & Co., 1995.

Soffer, O. *The Upper Paleolithic of the Central Russian Plain*. San Diego, California: Academic Press, 1985.

Soffer, O. & Gamble, C. (eds.) *The World at 18,000 BP, vols 1 & 2*. London: Unwin & Hyman, 1990.

Soffer, O. & Praslov, N. (eds.) *From Kostenki to Clovis: Upper Paleolithic – Paleo-Indian Adaptations*. New York: Plenum Press, 1993.

Tattersall, I. "Out of Africa again ... and again?", *Scientific American* 276 (4), pp.46-53, 1997.

Trinkhaus, E. & Shipman, P. *The Neandertals: Of Skeletons, Scientists, and Scandal*. New York: Vintage Books, 1994.

West, F. H. (ed.) *American Beginnings: The Prehistory and Paleoecology of Beringia*. Chicago: University of Chicago Press, 1996.

Wu, R. & Olsen, J. W. (eds.) *Palaeoanthropology and Palaeolithic Archaeology in the People's Republic of China*. Orlando, Florida: Academic Press, 1985.

POSTGLACIAL REVOLUTIONS

Bogucki, P. *The Origins of Human Society*. Oxford: Blackwell, 1999.

Harris, D. (ed.) *The Origins and Spread of Agriculture and Pastoralism in Eurasia*. Washington, DC: Smithsonian Institution Press, 1996.

Maisels, C. K. *The Emergence of Civilization: From Hunting and Gathering to Agriculture, Cities, and the State in the Near East*. London: Routledge, 1990.

Price, T. & Gebauer, A. (eds.) *Last Hunters, First Farmers: New Perspectives on the Prehistoric Transition to Agriculture*. Santa Fe, New Mexico: School of American Research, 1995.

Redman, C. *The Rise of Civilization: From Early Farmers to Urban Society in the Ancient Near East*. San Francisco: W.H. Freeman, 1978.

Robinson, A. *The Story of Writing*. London & New York: Thames & Hudson, 1995.

Stein, G. & Rothman, M. (eds.) *Chiefdoms and Early States in the Near East*. Madison, Wisconsin: Prehistory Press, 1994.

EUROPE AND WESTERN ASIA
Europe

Andronikos, M. Vergina: *The Royal Tombs*. Athens: Ekdotike Athenon, 1984.

Audouze, F. & Bchsenschtz, O. *Towns, Villages and Countryside of Celtic Europe*. Indianapolis: Indiana University Press/London: Batsford, 1992.

Balfour, M. *Megalithic Mysteries*. London: Parkgate Books, 1992.

Barber, R. *The Cyclades in the Bronze Age*. London: Duckworth, 1987.

Biers, W. R. *The Archaeology of Greece: An Introduction* (2nd edn.). Ithaca & London: Cornell University Press, 1996.

Boardman, J. *The Greeks Overseas: Their Early Colonies and Trade*. London & New York: Thames & Hudson, 1980.

Boardman, J. (ed.) *The Oxford History of Classical Art*. Oxford & New York: Oxford University Press, 1993.

Boardman, J. *The Diffusion of Classical Art in Antiquity*. Princeton, NJ: Princeton University Press/London: Thames & Hudson, 1994.

Bogucki, P. *Forest Farmers and Stockherders*. Cambridge, UK: Cambridge University Press, 1988.

Bonsall, C. (ed.) *The Mesolithic in Europe*. Edinburgh: John Donald, 1989.

Bradley, R. *The Significance of Monuments*. London: Routledge, 1998.

Breeze, D. & Dobson, B. *Hadrian's Wall* (3rd ed.) London: Penguin, 1987.

Brendel, O. J. *Etruscan Art*. Pelican History of Art, reprinted New Haven & London: Yale University Press, 1995.

Burl, A. *Great Stone Circles*. New Haven & London: Yale University Press, 1999.

Cadogan, G. *Palaces of Minoan Crete*. London: Routledge, 1991.

Camp, J. M. *The Athenian Agora: Excavations in the Heart of Classical Athens*. London & New York: Thames & Hudson, 1986.

Chadwick, J. *The Mycenaean World*. Cambridge, UK: Cambridge University Press, 1976.

Coles, J. M. & Harding, A. F. *The Bronze Age in Europe*. London: Methuen, 1979.

Collis, J. *The European Iron Age* (new edn.). London: Routledge, 1997.

Cornell, T. & Matthews, J. *Atlas of the Roman World:*. New York: Facts on File Inc./Oxford: Phaidon, 1982.

Cunliffe, B. (ed.) *The Oxford Illustrated Prehistory of Europe*. Oxford & New York: Oxford University Press, 1994.

Darvill, T.C. *Prehistoric Britain* (new edn.). London: Routledge, 1997.

Dickinson, O. T. P. K. *The Aegean Bronze Age*. Cambridge, UK: Cambridge University Press, 1994.

Dolukhanov, P. *The Early Slavs*. New York: Addison Wesley/London: Longman, 1996.

Ehrich, R. *Chronologies in Old World Archaeology*. Chicago: University of Chicago Press, 1992.

Favro, D. *The Urban Image of Augustan Rome*. Cambridge UK: Cambridge University Press, 1996.

Fitton, J. L. *The Discovery of the Greek Bronze Age*. Cambridge, Mass: Harvard University Press/London: British Museum Press, 1995.

Goodman, M. *The Roman World 44 BC–AD 180*. London: Routledge, 1997.

Graham, J. W. *The Palaces of Crete*. Princeton, NJ: Princeton University Press, 1987.

Hodder, I. *The Domestication of Europe*. Oxford: Blackwell, 1990.

Hood, M. S. F. *The Arts in Prehistoric Greece*. Pelican History of Art, reprinted New Haven & London: Yale University Press, 1992.

James, S. *The World of the Celts*. New York: Harry N. Abrams/London: Thames & Hudson,1993.

Joussaume, R. *Dolmens for the Dead*. London: Batsford, 1987.

Levi, P. *Atlas of the Greek World*. New York: Facts on File Inc./Oxford: Phaidon, 1982.

Macnamara, E. *The Etruscans.* Cambridge, Mass: Harvard University Press/London: British Museum Press, 1990.

Midgley, M. S. *TRB Culture: the First Farmers of the North European Plain.* Edinburgh: Edinburgh University Press, 1992.

Millar, F. *The Roman Empire and its Neighbours* London: Duckworth, 1981.

Mohen, J. P. *Megaliths: Stones of Mystery.* New York: Harry N. Abrams, 1999.

Moscati, S., (ed.) *The Celts.* New York: Harry N. Abrams/London: Thames & Hudson, 1991.

Myers, J. W. et al. *Aerial Atlas of Ancient Crete.* Berkeley: University of California Press, 1992.

Pollitt, J. J. *Art in the Hellenistic Age.* Cambridge, UK: Cambridge University Press, 1986.

Price, T. D. (ed.) *Europe's First Farmers.* Cambridge, UK: Cambridge University Press, 2000.

Scarre, C. *Exploring Prehistoric Europe.* Oxford & New York: Oxford University Press, 1998.

Sherratt, A. *Economy and Society in Prehistoric Europe. Changing Perspectives.* Princeton, NJ: Princeton University Press, 1997.

Smith, R. R. R. *Hellenistic Sculpture.* New York: Harry N. Abrams/London: Thames & Hudson, 1991.

Snodgrass, A. M. *Archaic Greece: The Age of Experiment.* London: Dent, 1980/Berkeley: University of California Press, 1981.

Spivey, N. *Etruscan Art.* London & New York: Thames & Hudson, 1997.

Srejovic, D. *Lepenski Vir.* London & New York: Thames and Hudson, 1969.

Strong, D. et al. *Roman Art.* Pelican History of Art, reprinted New Haven & London: Yale University Press, 1992

Taylour, W. D. *The Mycenaeans* (rev. edn.). New York: W. W. Norton, 1990.

Travlos, J. *Pictorial Dictionary of Ancient Athens.* New York: Hacker Art Books,1980.

Warren, P. M. *The Aegean Civilisations.* Oxford: Phaidon, 1989.

Wells, P. S. *Farms, Villages, and Cities: Commerce and Urban Origins in Late Prehistoric Europe.* Ithaca, NY: Cornell University Press, 1984.

Whittle, A. *Europe in the Neolithic.* Cambridge, UK: Cambridge University Press, 1996.

Zanker, P. *The Power of Images in the Age of Augustus.* Ann Arbor, Michigan: University of Michigan Press, 1988.

Near East

Doe, B. *South Arabia.* London & New York: Thames & Hudson, 1971.

Doe, B. *Monuments of South Arabia.* Cambridge: Oleander Press, 1983.

Kuhrt, A. *The Ancient Near East, c. 3000-330 BC.* London & New York, Routledge, 1997.

Lloyd, S. *Archaeology of Mesopotamia, From the Old Stone Age to the Persian Conquest* (revised edn.). London & New York: Thames & Hudson, 1984.

Macqueen, J. *The Hittites and Their Contemporaries in Asia Minor* (revised edn.). London & New York: Thames & Hudson, 1996.

Matthiae, P. *Ebla: An Empire Rediscovered.* Garden City, NY: Doubleday, 1981.

Mazar, A. *Archaeology of the Land of the Bible 10,000–586 BCE* (reprint edn.). Garden City, NY: Doubleday, 1992.

Mellaart, J. *The Archaeology of Ancient Turkey.* Totowa, NJ: Rowman & Littlefield, 1978.

Mellaart, J. *The Neolithic of the Near East.* London & New York: Thames & Hudson, 1975.

Meyers, E. M. (ed.) *The Oxford Encyclopedia of Archaeology in the Near East* (5 vols). Oxford & New York: Oxford University Press, 1997.

Mitchell, S. *Anatolia: Land, Men and Gods: (1) The Celts in Anatolia and the Impact of Roman Rule.* Oxford & New York: Oxford University Press, 1993.

Moscati, S. *The Phoenicians.* Milan: Bompiani, 1988.

Nissen, H. *The Early History of the Ancient Near East 9000-2000 BC.* Chicago: University of Chicago Press, 1988.

Oates, J. *Babylon.* London & New York: Thames & Hudson, 1986.

Postgate, N. *Early Mesopotamia. Society and Economy at the Dawn of History.* (reprint edn.). New York & London: Routledge, 1994.

Potts, D. *The Arabian Gulf in Antiquity.* Oxford: Clarendon Press,1991.

Roaf, M. *Cultural Atlas of Mesopotamia and the Ancient Near East.*

New York: Facts on File, 1990.

Roux, G. *Ancient Iraq* (3rd edn.). New York & London: Penguin Books, 1993.

Saggs, H. *The Might that Was Assyria.* New York: St Martins Press, 1990.

Sasson, J. et al. (eds.) *Civilizations of the Ancient Near East.* New York: Charles Scribners Sons, 1995.

Stern, E. (ed.) *The New Encyclopedia of Archaeological Excavations in the Holy Land.* New York: Simon & Schuster, 1993.

van de Mieroop, M. *The Ancient Mesopotamian City.* New York: Oxford University Press, 1997.

Weiss, H. (ed.) *Ebla to Damascus. Art and Archaeology of Ancient Syria.* Washington DC: Smithsonian Institution, 1985.

Yadin, Y. *Masada: Herod's Fortress and the Zealots' Last Stand.* New York: Random House/London: Phoenix, 1997.

CENTRAL, SOUTH AND EAST ASIA

Aikens, C. M. & Higuchi, T. *Prehistory of Japan.* New York & London: Academic Press, 1982.

Allchin, B. & Allchin, R. *The Rise of Civilization in India and Pakistan.* Cambridge, UK: Cambridge University Press, 1992.

Allchin, R. *The Archaeology of Early Historic South Asia.* Cambridge, UK: Cambridge University Press, 1995.

Barnes, G. L. *China, Korea and Japan: The Rise of Civilization in East Asia.* London & New York: Thames & Hudson, 1993.

Chakrabarti, D. K. *Archaeology of Ancient Indian Cities.* Delhi: Oxford University Press, 1995.

Chang, K. C. *The Archaeology of Ancient China.* New Haven: Yale University Press, 1986.

Cook, J. *The Persian Empire.* New York; Schocken Books, 1983.

Cottrell, A. *The First Emperor of China.* London: Macmillan, 1981.

Debaine-Francfort, C. *The Search for Ancient China.* New York: Harry N. Abrams/London:Thames & Hudson, 1999.

Frye, R. *Heritage of Central Asia from Antiquity to the Turkish Expansion.* Princeton, NJ: Markus Weiner Publishers, 1996.

Ghosh, A (ed.) *Encylopaedia of Indian Archaeology.* Leiden, Netherlands: E. J. Brill, 1991.

Higham, C. F. W. *The Bronze Age of Southeast Asia.* Cambridge, UK: Cambridge University Press, 1996.

Higham, C. F. W. "Archaeology, linguistics and the expansion of the East and Southeast Asian Neolithic" in *Archaeology and Language* (Blench, R. M. & Spriggs, M. eds.) London: Routledge, 1998.

Higham, C. F. W. & Glover, I. C. "New evidence for early rice cultivation in South, Southeast and East Asia" in Harris, D. R. ed. *The Origins and Spread of Agriculture and Pastoralism in Eurasia* (op. cit.).

Higham, C. F. W. & Thosarat, R. *Prehistoric Thailand. From First Settlement to Sukhothai.* Bangkok: River Books, 1998.

Imamura, K. *Prehistoric Japan.* Honolulu: University Press of Hawaii 1995.

Kenoyer, J. M. *Ancient Cities of the Indus Valley Civilization.* Karachi: Oxford University Press, 1998.

Kim, J-H. *The Prehistory of Korea.* Honolulu: University Press of Hawaii, 1978.

Kohl, P. *The Bronze Age Civilisation of Central Asia: Recent Soviet Discoveries.* New York: Sharpe, 1981.

Nelson, S. M. *The Archaeology of Korea.* Cambridge, UK: Cambridge University Press, 1993.

Nelson, S. M. (ed.) *The Archaeology of Northeast China, Beyond the Great Wall.* London: Routledge, 1995.

Possehl, G. (ed.) *Harappan Civilization.* Delhi: Oxford University Press, 1993.

Rawson, J. *Ancient China: Art and Archaeology.* London: British Museum Press, 1980.

Rawson, J. (ed.) *Mysteries of Ancient China. New Discoveries from the Early Dynasties.* New York: Braziller/London: British Museum Press, 1996.

Rudenko, S. I. *Frozen Tombs of Siberia. The Pazyryk Burials of Iron Age Horsemen.* Berkeley: University of California Press, 1970.

Sherwin-White, S. & Kuhrt, A. *From Samarkhand to Sardis. A New Approach to the Seleucid Empire.* Berkeley: University of California Press/London: Duckworth, 1993.

AFRICA

Adams, W. Y. *Nubia: Corridor to Africa.* London: Allen Lane, 1977.

Baines, J. & Malek, J. *Atlas of Ancient Egypt* (revised edn.). New York: Checkmark Books, 2000.

Connah, G. *African Civilisations.* Cambridge, UK: University of Cambridge Press, 1987.

Deacon, H. J. & Deacon, J. *Human Beginnings in South Africa. Uncovering the Secrets of the Stone Age.* Cape Town: David Philip, 1999.

Edwards, I. E. S. *The Pyramids of Egypt.* New York & London: Penguin, 1991.

Fagan, B. *The Rape of the Nile. Tomb Robbers, Tourists and Archaeologists in Egypt.* New York: Scribner, 1975.

Grimal, N. *A History of Ancient Egypt.* Oxford: Blackwell, 1992.

Huffman, T. N. *Snakes and Crocodiles. Power and Symbolism in Ancient Zimbabwe.* Johannesburg: Witwatersrand University Press, 1996.

Kemp. B. J. *Ancient Egypt: Anatomy of a Civilisation.* London: Routledge, 1989.

Lewis-Williams, J. D. *The Rock Art of Southern Africa.* Cambridge, UK: Cambridge University Press, 1983.

Midant-Reynes, B. *The Prehistory of Egypt.* Oxford: Blackwell, 1999.

Phillipson, D. W. *African Archaeology.* Cambridge, UK: Cambridge University Press, 1995.

Redford, D. *Egypt, Canaan and Israel in Ancient Times.* Princeton, NJ: Princeton University Press, 1992.

Reeves, C. N. & Wilkinson, R. H. *The Complete Valley of the Kings.* London & New York: Thames & Hudson, 1996.

Robertshaw, P. (ed.) *A History of African Archaeology.* Portsmouth, New Hampshire: Heinemann/London: James Currey, 1990.

Shaw, T. et al (eds.) *The Archaeology of Africa. Food, Metals and Towns.* London & New York, Routledge, 1995.

Solomon, A. "Rock art in southern Africa" in *Scientific American* 275 (5), pages 86–93, 1996.

Spencer, A. J. *Death in Ancient Egypt.* London: Penguin Books, 1982.

Welsby, D. *The Kingdom of Kush.* Princeton, NJ: Markus Wiener Publishers/London: British Museum Press, 1996.

THE AMERICAS

Baudez, C. & Picasso, S. *Lost Cities of the Maya.* New York: Harry N. Abrams/London: Thames & Hudson, 1992.

Bernand, C. *The Incas. People of the Sun.* New York: Harry N. Abrams/London: Thames & Hudson, 1994.

Bruhns, K. O. *Ancient South America.* Cambridge, UK: Cambridge University Press, 1994.

Burger, R. L. *Chavín and the Origins of Andean Civilization.* New York & London: Thames & Hudson, 1992.

Cordell, L. S. *Archaeology of the Southwest* (2nd edn.). San Diego, CA: Academic Press,1997.

Donnan, C. B. (ed.) *Early Ceremonial Architecture in the Andes.* Washington DC: Dumbarton Oaks Research Library and Collection, 1985.

Fagan, B. M. *Kingdoms of Gold, Kingdoms of Jade, The Americas before Columbus.* London & New York: Thames & Hudson, 1992.

Fagan, B. M. *Ancient North America* (2nd edn.). London & New York: Thames & Hudson, 1995.

Fash, W. L. *Scribes, Warriors and Kings. The City of Copán and the Ancient Maya.* London & New York: Thames & Hudson, 1991.

Frison, G. *Prehistoric Hunters of the High Plains.* Orlando: Academic Press, 1978.

Gruzinski, S. *The Aztecs: Rise and Fall of an Empire.* New York: Harry N. Abrams/London: Thames & Hudson, 1992.

Hagen, A. von & Morris, C. *The Cities of the Ancient Andes.* London & New York:Thames & Hudson, 1998.

Hammond, N. *Ancient Maya Civilization.* New Brunswick, NJ: Rutgers University Press/Cambridge, UK: Cambridge University Press, 1982.

Jennings, J. (ed.) *Ancient North Americans.* San Francisco: W. H. Freeman, 1983.

Jennings, J. D. *Prehistory of North America.* Palo Alto, CA: Mayfield,1989.

Keatinge, R. W. (ed.) *Peruvian Prehistory: An Overview of Pre-Inca and Inca Society.* Cambridge, UK: Cambridge University Press, 1988.

Lavallé, D. *The First South Americans: From Origin to High Culture.* Salt Lake City: University of Utah Press, 2000.

Marcus, J. & Flannery, K. *Zapotec Civilization.* London & New York: Thames & Hudson, 1996.

McEwan, C. et al. *Patagonia.* Princeton, NJ: Princeton University Press, 1997.

McGhee, R. *Ancient Canada.* Ottawa: Canadian Museum of Civilization, 1989.

Moseley, M. E. *The Incas and their Ancestors.* London & New York: Thames & Hudson, 1992.

Plog, S. *Ancient Peoples of the American Southwest.* London & New York: Thames & Hudson, 1997.

Sabloff, J. A. *The Cities of Ancient Mexico. Reconstructing a Lost World.* New York: Harry N. Abrams/London: Thames & Hudson, 1989.

Sabloff, J. A. *The New Archaeology and the Ancient Maya.* New York: Scientific American Library, 1990.

Schele, L. & Freidel, D. *A Forest of Kings. The Untold Story of the Ancient Maya.* New York: William Morrow, 1990.

Silverberg, R. *The Moundbuilders.* Columbus: Ohio University Press, 1986.

Thomas, D. H. *Exploring Ancient Native America.* London: Routledge, 1999.

Townsend, R. F. *The Aztecs.* New York& London: Thames & Hudson, 1992.

Wood, W. R. (ed.) *Archaeology of the Great Plains.* Lawrence, Kansas: University Press of Kansas, 1998.

AUSTRALIA AND THE PACIFIC

Allen, J. & Gosden, C. (eds.) *Report of the Lapita Homeland Project.* Canberra: Research School of Pacific Studies, Australian National University, 1991.

Anderson, A. J. *Prodigious Birds. Moas and Moa-hunting in Preshistoric New Zealand.* Cambridge, UK: Cambridge University Press, 1989.

Bahn, P. & Flenley, J. *Easter Island, Earth Island.* London & New YOrk: Thames & Hudson, 1992.

Bellwood, P. *Man's Conquest of the Pacific: The Prehistory of Southeast Asia and Oceania.* Auckland: Collins, 1978.

Davidson, J. *The Prehistory of New Zealand.* Auckland: Longman Paul, 1984.

Flood, J. *Archaeology of the Dreamtime* (3rd edn.). Sydney: Angus & Robertson, 1995.

Flood, J. *Rock Art of the Dreamtime.* Sydney: Angus & Robertson, 1997.

Frankel, D. *Remains to be Seen: Archaeological Insights into Australian Prehistory.* Melbourne: Longman Cheshire, 1991.

Goodenough, W. (ed.) *Prehistoric settlement of the Pacific.* Transactions of the American Philosophical Society 86 (5), 1996.

Irwin, G. *The Prehistoric Exploration and Colonisation of the Pacific.* Cambridge, UK: Cambridge University Press, 1992.

Jennings, J. D. (ed.) *The Prehistory of Polynesia.* Cambridge, Mass: Harvard University Press, 1979.

Kirch, P.V. *Feathered Gods and Fish-hooks.* Honolulu: University of Hawaii Press, 1985.

Lourandos, H. *Continent of Hunter-gatherers: New perspectives in Australian Prehistory.* Cambridge, UK: Cambridge University Press, 1997.

Mulvaney, D. J. & Kamminga, J. *Prehistory of Australia.* St Leonards: Allen & Unwin, 1999.

Orliac, C. & Orliac, M. *Easter Island: Mystery of the Stone Giants.* New York: Harry N. Abrams/London: Thames & Hudson, 1995.

Smith, M.A. et al. *Sahul in Review: Pleistocene Archaeology in Australia, New Guinea and Island Melanesia.* Canberra: Australian National University, 1993.

Spriggs, M. *The Island Melanesians.* Oxford: Blackwell, 1997.

Spriggs, M. et al (eds.) *A Community of Culture: The People and Prehistory of the Pacific.* Canberra: Australian National University, 1993.

Trotter, M. & McCulloch, B. *Unearthing New Zealand.* Wellington: Government Printer of New Zealand, 1989.

Wilson, J. (ed.) *In the Beginning: The Archaeology of the Maori.* New Zealand: NZ Historic Places Trust, 1987.

Acknowledgments

AAA   Ancient Art and Architecture Collection
AKG   Archiv für Kunst und Geschichte
AM   Ashmolean Museum, Oxford
BAL   Bridgeman Art Library
BM   British Museum, London
C   Corbis
EHPL   English Heritage Photographic Library

IAA   Israel Antiquities Authority
MMA   Maxwell Museum of Anthropology, Albuquerque
NHM   Natural History Museum, London
RHPL   Robert Harding Picture Library
SPL   Science Photo Library
TAA   The Art Archive
WFA   Werner Forman Archive

1 WFA/National Museum, Copenhagen; 3 National Museum of India, New Delhi/BAL; 4 Charles Higham; 5 WFA/Private Collection; 6 © BM/TAA; 7 National Museum, Belgrade/TAA; 9 AKG/Erich Lessing; 10t James King-Holmes/SPL; 10c York Archaeological Trust; 10b Volker Steger/SPL; 11 Keith Kent/SPL; 12 Ron Wagter; 13 Margaret S. Watters; 14–15 Jean Vertut; 16 C/Buddy Mays; 17,18 John Reader/SPL; 20t Peter Davey/Bruce Coleman Collection; 20b NHM; 21 C.K. Brain; 22 F. Jack Jackson/RHPL; 22–23 John Reader/SPL; 24t Jane Taylor/Sonia Halliday Photographs; 24b Javier Trueba/Madrid Scientific Films; 25 NHM; 26 John Reader/SPL; 28 Institute of Human Origins/Donald C. Johanson; 29 Anthropological Institute, Turin/TAA; 30 C.M. Dixon; 30–31 NHM; 32 C.M. Dixon; 32–33 French Ministry of Culture and Communication, Regional Direction for Cultural Affairs – Rhône-Alpes, Regional Department of Archaeology; 33 Jean Vertut; 34 Robert Frerck/Odyssey/Chicago/RHPL; 35 J.M. Adovasio/Mercyhurst Archaeological Institute; 36–37 © BM/BAL; 38 AKG/Erich Lessing; 38–39 P. Colombel; 40 Aleppo Museum, Syria/TAA; 41t Michael Holford; 41b Photobank Photo Library; 42 WFA; 43 IAA/© The Israel Museum, Jerusalem; 44–45 © BM/BAL/AAA; 45 C/Randy Faris; 46 AM/BAL; 47t AKG; 47b Art Exhibitions, China; 48–49 EHPL; 50 Scala, Florence; 51 National Monuments Record/© English Heritage; 52 © Silkeborg Museum, Denmark; 53 C/Nik Wheeler; 54 The National Museum of Denmark; 56t IAA/© The Israel Museum, Jerusalem; 56b Z. Radovan, Jerusalem; 58t Photostock-Studio Kontos; 58b H. Lilienthal/Rheinisches Landesmuseum, Bonn; 59 Archeologický Ústav; 60 C/Nik Wheeler; 61 Louvre, Paris/BAL; 62t WFA/National Archaeological Museum, Madrid; 62b Michael Jenner/RHPL; 64t EHPL; 64b TAA; 65 B. Gibbons/Eye Ubiquitous; 66 Paul Hanny/Gamma/Frank Spooner Pictures; 66–67 AM/BAL; 67 AAA; 68 B. Norman/AAA; 69 Louvre, Paris/BAL; 70t WFA; 70b C/Nik Wheeler; 71 AM/BAL; 72 Scala, Florence; 73 Louvre, Paris/BAL; 74, 75 C.M. Dixon; 76 RHPL; 77 C.M. Dixon; 78t Jane Taylor/Sonia Halliday Photographs; 78b © BM/RHPL; 80 AKG/Erich Lessing; 81 Courtesy of the Institute of Nautical Archaeology; 82 IAA/© The Israel Museum, Jerusalem; 83 AKG/Erich Lessing; 84 WFA/Iraq Museum, Baghdad; 85 Louvre, Paris/BAL; 86 Louvre, Paris/Giraudon/BAL; 88 WFA; 89 © BM; 90 © BM/BAL; 92 Louvre, Paris/BAL; 93 AKG/Robert O'Dea; 94t EHPL/Skyscan Balloon Photography; 94b Landesdenkmalamt Baden-Württemberg; 96 Roy Rainford/RHPL; 97 © G. Dagli Orti, Paris; 98t Michael Short/RHPL; 98b Stephane Compoint/Sygma; 100t Philip Craven/RHPL; 100b Alfredo Foglia; 102 © BM; 103 Rheinisches Landesmuseum, Bonn; 104t The Stock Market; 104b © BM; 106 Art Exhibitions, China; 107 Adam Woolfitt/RHPL; 108 Rex Features Limited; 109 The British Library; 110 AM; 112t C/Michael S. Yamashita;

112b Photobank Photo Library; 113 Charles Higham; 114t RHPL; 114b National Museum of India, New Delhi/BAL; 116 Tom Ang/RHPL; 116–117 Arthur M. Sackler Museum, Harvard University Art Museums, USA/BAL/Bequest of Grenville L. Winthrop; 118 Photobank Photo Library; 119 Charles Higham; 120 RHPL; 122 C/Robert Holmes; 123 C/Kimbell Art Museum; 124 Charles Higham; 125 © BM; 126 C/Adam Woolfitt; 128 C/Charles O'Rear; 129 Archaeological Institute of the National Academy of Science, Kiev/TAA; 130 Louvre, Paris/BAL; 131 Powerstock/Zefa Photo Library; 133t Adam Woolfitt/RHPL; 133bl AM; 133br AAA; 134t WFA; 134b © Photo RMN/Richard Lambert; 136 RHPL; 137 John Reader/SPL; 138 Mary Jelliffe/Hutchison Library; 140 WFA/Egyptian Museum, Cairo; 141t Axiom/Chris Caldicott; 141b WFA/AM; 142 GettyOne Stone; 143 Photo Archive/Jürgen Liepe; 144 C/G. Dagli Orti; 144–145 Photo Archive/Jürgen Liepe; 146 Bode Museum, Berlin/BAL; 147 Ellen Rooney/RHPL; 148t © BM; 148b C/Jonathan Blair; 150l RHPL; 150r Private Collection/Heini Schneebeli/BAL; 152 WFA/MMA; 153 Courtesy of National Park Service; 154 C/Kevin Schafer; 155 Christopher Rennie/RHPL; 156 Enrico Ferorelli/Colorific; 157 Smithsonian Institution, National Museum of the American Indian/David Heald; 158 © BM/BAL; 159 WFA; 160 © BM; 161 University of Colorado Museum, Joe Ben Wheat Photo; 162–163 Thomas Gilcrease Institute of American History and Art, Tulsa; 163 C/Richard A. Cooke; 164 WFA/MMA; 166 South American Pictures/Tony Morrison; 167 C/Danny Lehman; 168–169 Teotihuacan, Valley of Mexico/Sean Sprague/Mexicolore/BAL; 169 Axiom/Chris Caldicott; 170 South American Pictures/Tony Morrison; 171t Mireille Vautier; 171b Robert Frerck/RHPL; 172 Mireille Vautier; 173 GettyOne Stone/Robert Frerck; 174–175 WFA/© BM; 176 Museo Banco Central de Quito/TAA; 177 Walter Rawlings/RHPL; 178t WFA/David Bernstein Fine Art, New York; 178b RHPL; 180t, 180b Robert Frerck/RHPL; 182 Anthony Farr/Nature Focus; 183 A.N.T. Photo Library/Natural History Photographic Agency; 184, 185 J. Flood; 186 GettyOne Stone/Penny Tweedie; 189t I. Griffiths/RHPL; 189b Ric Bolzan/Nature Focus; 190 C/Douglas Peebles; 191t Peter Crawford; 191b Carl Bento/Nature Focus; 192 A.N.T. Photo Library/Natural History Photographic Agency; 193 N.J. Saunders; 194 K. Jones; 195 Otago Museum, Dunedin, New Zealand.

Illustrations on pages 18 and 27 by Karen Hiscock.

Every effort has been made to trace copyright holders of the pictures used in this book. Anyone having claims to ownership not identified above is invited to contact Andromeda Oxford Limited.

Contributors

Paul BAHN, Hull, England.
Caroline BIRD, Greenmount, Australia.
Peter BOGUCKI, School of Engineering and Applied Science, Princeton University, New Jersey.
Philip DUKE, Department of Anthropology, Fort Lewis College, Durango, Colorado.
Christopher EDENS, University of Pennsylvania Museum of Archaeology, Philadelphia, and the American Institute for Yemeni Studies, Sana'a, Yemen.
David GILL, Department of Classics and Ancient History, University College of Swansea, Wales.
Charles HIGHAM, Department of Anthropology, Otago University, New Zealand.
Tom HIGHAM, Radiocarbon Dating Laboratory, University of Waikato, New Zealand.

John HOFFECKER, Institute of Arctic and Alpine Research, University of Colorado at Boulder.
Simon KANER, Cambridge, England.
Geoffrey G. McCAFFERTY, Department of Anthropology, University of Calgary, Canada.
Jane McINTOSH, Tenbury Wells, England.
Steven SNAPE, School of Archaeology, Classics and Oriental Studies, University of Liverpool, England.
Louise STEEL, Department of Archaeology, University of Edinburgh, Scotland.
Anne THACKERAY, Department of Archaeology, University of Witwatersrand, South Africa.
Karen WISE, Department of Anthropology, Natural History Museum of Los Angeles County, California.

INDEX

EDITOR

DR. PAUL G. BAHN is a freelance writer, translator and broadcaster in archaeology. He obtained his doctorate in archaeology at Cambridge University, England, in 1979, specializing in the prehistory of the Pyrenees. He has lectured all over the world, and has published several hundred papers and articles in journals on both sides of the Atlantic. He is also the author of many books, including *Archaeology: Theories, Methods and Practice* (with Colin Renfrew), *The Cambridge Illustrated History of Prehistoric Art*, and *Journey Through the Ice Age*, and is the editor of, among others, *The Cambridge Illustrated History of Archaeology* and *The Penguin Archaeology Guide*.

CONTRIBUTORS

Dr. Paul BAHN, Hull, England

Dr. Caroline BIRD, Greenmount, Australia

Dr. Peter BOGUCKI, School of Engineering and Applied Science, Princeton University, New Jersey

Dr. Philip DUKE, Department of Anthropology, Fort Lewis College, Durango, Colorado

Dr. Christopher EDENS, University of Pennsylvania Museum of Archaeology, Philadelphia, Pennsylvania, and the American Institute for Yemeni Studies, Sana'a, Yemen

Dr. David GILL, Department of Classics and Ancient History, University College of Swansea, Wales

Professor Charles HIGHAM, Department of Anthropology, Otago University, New Zealand

Dr. Tom HIGHAM, Radiocarbon Dating Laboratory, University of Waikato, New Zealand

Dr. John HOFFECKER, Institute of Arctic and Alpine Research, University of Colorado at Boulder

Simon KANER, Cambridge, England

Dr. Geoffrey G. McCAFFERTY, Department of Anthropology, University of Calgary, Canada

Dr. Jane McINTOSH, Tenbury Wells, England

Dr. Steven SNAPE, School of Archaeology, Classics and Oriental Studies, University of Liverpool, England

Dr. Louise STEEL, Department of Archaeology, University of Edinburgh, Scotland

Dr. Anne THACKERAY, Department of Archaeology, University of Witwatersrand, South Africa

Dr. Karen WISE, Department of Anthropology, Natural History Museum of Los Angeles County, Los Angeles